Lecture Notes in Computer Science 8431

Commenced Publication in 1973
Founding and Former Series Editors:
Gerhard Goos, Juris Hartmanis, and Jan van Leeuwen

Editorial Board

Maritta Heisel   Wouter Joosen
Javier Lopez   Fabio Martinelli (Eds.)

Engineering Secure Future Internet Services and Systems

Current Research

Springer

Volume Editors

Maritta Heisel
Universität Duisburg-Essen, INKO, Software Engineering
47048 Duisburg, Germany
E-mail: maritta.heisel@uni-due.de

Wouter Joosen
KU Leuven, Department of Computer Science
Celestijnenlaan 200A, 3001 Heverlee, Belgium
E-mail: wouter.joosen@cs.kuleuven.be

Javier Lopez
University of Malaga, Computer Science Department
Network, Information and Computer Security (NICS) Lab
29071 Malaga, Spain
E-mail: jlm@lcc.uma.es

Fabio Martinelli
Consiglio Nazionale delle Ricerche (CNR)
Istituto di Informatica e Telematica (IIT)
Via G. Moruzzi 1, 56124 Pisa, Italy
E-mail: fabio.martinelli@iit.cnr.it

ISSN 0302-9743   e-ISSN 1611-3349
ISBN 978-3-319-07451-1   e-ISBN 978-3-319-07452-8
DOI 10.1007/978-3-319-07452-8
Springer Cham Heidelberg New York Dordrecht London

Library of Congress Control Number: 2014939218

LNCS Sublibrary: SL 4 – Security and Cryptology

Typesetting: Camera-ready by author, data conversion by Scientific Publishing Services, Chennai, India

Printed on acid-free paper

Springer is part of Springer Science+Business Media (www.springer.com)

Preface

This volume contains a selection of papers representing state-of-the-art results in the engineering of secure software-based Future Internet services and systems, produced by the NESSoS project researchers (www.nessos-project.eu).

The Network of Excellence NESSoS has been set up in order to create and consolidate a long-lasting research community on engineering secure software-based services and systems. The basis of this community has been created through the inception of European funding. The continuation of the NESSoS activities is currently addressed through the establishment of a new IFIP working group on Secure Engineering (WG11.14) focusing on the topics of the project.

The NESSoS engineering approach of secure software-based services is based on the principle of addressing security concerns from the very beginning in all software development phases, thus contributing to reducing the amount of software vulnerabilities and enabling the systematic treatment of security needs through the engineering process.

NESSoS joint research activities fall into six areas: (1) security requirements for Future Internet services; (2) creating secure service architectures and secure service design; (3) supporting programming environments for secure and composeable services; (4) enabling security assurance; integrating the former results in (5) a risk-aware and cost-aware software development life cycle (SDLC); and (6) the delivery of case studies of Future Internet application scenarios.

The selection of papers of this volume represents examples of NESSoS research, often by means of joint activities of the partners.

In addition to knowledge dissemination, NESSoS contributed to fostering the research on security engineering and to increasing the collaboration among the researchers involved.

NESSoS training and education activities in Europe created a new generation of skilled researchers and practitioners in the area. The project also collaborated with industrial stakeholders to improve the industry best practices and support a rapid growth of software-based service systems in the Future Internet.

March 2014   Maritta Heisel
                                                       Wouter Joosen
                                                       Javier Lopez
                                                       Fabio Martinelli

Table of Contents

A Structured Comparison of Security Standards*

Kristian Beckers[1], Isabelle Côté[3], Stefan Fenz[2],
Denis Hatebur[1,3], and Maritta Heisel[1]

[1] paluno - The Ruhr Institute for Software Technology -
University of Duisburg-Essen, Germany
{firstname.lastname}@paluno.uni-due.de
[2] Vienna University of Technology, Austria
stefan.fenz@tuwien.ac.at
[3] ITESYS
Dortmund, Germany
{i.cote,d.hatebur}@itesys.de

Abstract. A number of different security standards exist and it is difficult to choose the right one for a particular project or to evaluate if the right standard was chosen for a certification. These standards are often long and complex texts, whose reading and understanding takes up a lot of time. We provide a conceptual model for security standards that relies upon existing research and contains concepts and phases of security standards. In addition, we developed a template based upon this model, which can be instantiated for given security standard. These instantiated templates can be compared and help software and security engineers to understand the differences of security standards. In particular, the instantiated templates explain which information and what level of detail a system document according to a certain security standard contains. We applied our method to the well known international security standards ISO 27001 and Common Criteria, and the German IT-Grundschutz standards, as well.

Keywords: structured comparison, security standards, conceptual model, template.

1 Introduction

IT systems become increasingly complex considering the amount of stakeholders and technical parts involved. This complexity makes it hard for customers to trust IT systems. In order to gain their customers' trust, companies have to achieve an acceptable security level. Security standards, e.g. the ISO 27000 series

* This research was partially supported by the EU project Network of Excellence on Engineering Secure Future Internet Software Services and Systems (NESSoS, ICT-2009.1.4 Trustworthy ICT, Grant No. 256980) and the Ministry of Innovation, Science, Research and Technology of the German State of North Rhine-Westphalia and EFRE (Grant No. 300266902 and Grant No. 300267002).

M. Heisel et al. (Eds.): Engineering Secure Future Internet Services, LNCS 8431, pp. 1–34, 2014.
© Springer International Publishing Switzerland 2014

of standards [1] or the Common Criteria (CC) [2], offer a way to achieve this goal. Security standard implementation concerns the development of secure systems, processes, and documents. Implementing security standards is difficult, due to the limited support for system development and documentation provided in the standards.

Security concerns protecting a system against an attacker, who exploits vulnerabilities in the system to harm assets of stakeholders. Security vulnerabilities in software can be treated with countermeasures against threats. However, eliminating all vulnerabilities is difficult, due to monetary and time constraints. Risk management in the context of security concerns the reduction of the probability of a threat and the limitation of its consequences. Thus, the remaining risk can be used as a criteria for countermeasures for vulnerabilities. In addition, the risk of an entire system has to be calculated using risk management. Risk management is a part of security standards, but specific risk management standards exist, e.g. ISO 31000 [3], which consider the topic in more detail. Hence, we investigate risk management as considered in security standards in this work.

We contribute a conceptual model of security standards, based on existing research such as the works of Sunyaev [4] and the experience of the authors. Moreover, we use this model to investigate methodologies for security and risk management in order to understand their similarities and differences. We developed a template that is based on this model. In particular, fields in the template correspond to the concepts in the model. The template can be instantiated for different security standards. Hence, the instantiated templates can be used to compare different security standards by comparing the instantiated fields, e.g., which kind of environment description the different standards demand. The instantiated templates provide a process independent high level overview of the complete security standards, which helps to learn about standards, what to expect from a system documentation according to a specific standard, and select an appropriate standard for certification. We provide tool support for collecting, storing, and comparing the information collected using our template. Our tool support offers the functionality to compare instantiated templates by displaying their attributes next to each other. The results of this comparison can support the selection of a security standard or an evaluation if further standards should be considered. Moreover, the instantiated template can also provide a simple overview of different standards in order to gain an understanding of relevant concepts of a standard with little effort. Moreover, an understanding of the prescribed process of the standards and its documentation demands helps to judge an existing certification of an IT system. Our template provides an overview of the security analysis demanded by the standards and one can decide if this analysis is sufficient enough in order to trust the certification of a system. We applied our method to the international security standards ISO 27001 [1] and Common Criteria [2]. These standards were chosen because of their wide spread application in the industry[1,2,3]. In addition, we added the German IT-Grundschutz standards [5] as an example for a national security standard.

2 A Method for Comparing Security Standards

In the following, we present the steps of our method for CompAring SecuriTy standards (CAST) (see Fig. 1).

1. **Define a Common Terminology.** The Jason institute evaluated the research field of security [6] and concluded that the field is missing a common terminology and a basic set of well defined concepts. We address this concern by defining a common terminology against which the terms of the standards are evaluated. We use the terminology of the ISO 27001 standard and the terms defined in the common body of knowledge (CBK)[4] of the EU project *Network of Excellence on Engineering Secure Future Internet Software Services and Systems (NESSoS)*[5] as a basis.
2. **Analyze Existing Work.** We aim to base our work on existing research and analyze approaches that provide meta-models for security and risk standards. In particular, we focus on the works of Sunyaev [4], who created a security analysis method by identifying common activities in several security standards and the work of Stoneburner et al.[7], who created a model for risk management as part of the NIST SP 800-30 standard. This analysis results in a set of activities, which are often prescribed in security standards.

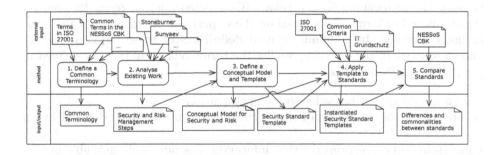

Fig. 1. A Method for CompAring SecuriTy standards (CAST)

---

[1] ISO statistic: http://www.iso.org/iso/iso_survey_executive-summary.pdf
[2] Common Criteria statistic:
http://www.commoncriteriaportal.org/products/stats/
[3] ISO statistics about ISO 27001 certifications:
http://www.iso.org/iso/database_iso_27001_iso_survey.xls
[4] http://www.nessos-cbk.org
[5] http://www.nessos-project.eu/

3. **Define a Conceptual Model and Template.** We use the information from the existing work to create a novel conceptual model, which considers the steps identified by Sunyaev and Stoneburner et al. We propose a novel model based on these related works. Hence, our conceptual model considers the phases of security standards and also considers risk management activities explicitly. In order to apply the conceptual model to security standards, we transform it into a template that can be instantiated. The template contains all phases of security standards considered in the conceptual model, as well as a description on *how* these phases have to be instantiated for a particular standard.
4. **Apply Template to Standards.** In this phase, we instantiate the template for well-known security standards such as Common Criteria [2] , ISO 27001 [1], and the IT Grundschutz standards [5].
5. **Compare Standards.** We compare the standards via comparing the different instantiations of our templates. In addition, we consider which of our common terms are considered by the standards and which are not. These insights shall provide a basis for the evaluation of a particular standard.

3   CAST Step 1: Define a Common Terminology

We propose a common terminology for security standards and define terms based on different sources. The purpose of the common terminology is to provide fixed definitions of important terms with regard to security standards as a baseline to which the terms in the individual standards can be compared. Using this comparison, it can be analyzed, which terms are used in the standards for the terms with the meaning defined below. We selected relevant terms for security standards in the terminology based on the experience of the authors and their industry contacts. In addition, we used definitions of these terms from well-known sources. In the following, we list the terms related to security defined in the ISO 27001 standard [1].

Asset anything that has value to the organization
Availability the property of being accessible and usable upon demand by an authorized entity
Confidentiality the property that information is not made available or disclosed to unauthorized individuals, entities, or processes
Security Control a control shall reduce the risk of an information security incident occurring. Note that we refer to controls also as security control for the remainder of the paper. Note that the ISO 27001 uses just control, but we use security control instead to make it explicit that the control addresses a security concern.

Information Security Incident a single or a series of unwanted or unexpected information security events that have a significant probability of compromising business operations and threatening information security

Integrity the property of safeguarding the accuracy and completeness of assets

We also include the following terms from the NESSoS Common Body of Knowledge (CBK)'s common terminology [8]. These definitions are based on the work of Fabian et al [9].

Stakeholder. A stakeholder is an individual, a group, or an organization that has an interest in the system under construction. A stakeholder view describes the requirements of a particular stakeholder. The stakeholders may express different types of requirements.

Vulnerability. Stakeholders require a security property to hold for a resource, whose violation implies a potential loss to the stakeholder. This violation can be caused by a vulnerability.

Threat. A vulnerability could potentially be exploited by a threat. A realized threat is an attack that actually exploits a vulnerability and is initiated by an attacker.

attacker. An attack actually exploits a vulnerability, and the person initiating the attack is an attacker.

Security Goal. A stakeholder's security goal expresses his or her security concerns towards an asset. Security goals are traditionally classified into integrity, confidentiality, and availability goals.

Security requirements. Security requirements capture security goals in more detail. A security requirement refines one or more security goals. It refers to a particular piece of information or service that explicates the meaning of the asset it concretizes in the context of the system under construction.

We also include the following terms to determine the focus of security standards.

Machine. Jackson [10] defines that the machine is the system or software to be developed. In our context the machine is the thing in the focus of the security analysis process described in security standards.

Environment. The environment includes a description of all relevant entities in the environment of the machine and, in particular, the interfaces to these entities to the machine.

Policy. Security requirements influence formulating security policies, which contain more information than security requirements. "Security policies state what should be protected, but may also indicate how this should be done." [11, p. 5]. "A security policy is a statement of what is, and what is not, allowed" [12, p. 9] "for us, security boils down to enforcing a policy that describes rules for accessing resources" [13, p. 14] and "security policy is a [...] policy that mandates system-specific [...] criteria for security" [14, p. 34].

Security Functions. The machine has descriptions of actual implementable functions that concern the fulfillment of security requirements. The descriptions of these functions are security functions.

4 CAST Step 2: Analyse Existing Work

We base our conceptual model for security standards on the HatSec Method (see Sect. 4.1) and the NIST SP 800-30 standard (see Sect. 4.2),

4.1 The HatSec Method

We base our conceptual model for comparing security standards on the HatSec method, because the author analyzed existing security standards and based his method on the resulting common building blocks of the analyzed standards. Only a few standards in the analysis are specific to the health care domain, but most of them are generic security standards such as ISO 27001 [1]. Moreover, the HatSec method does not create specific building blocks for the medical domain. Hence, the mining of security standard specific building blocks can be re-used for our conceptual model. We rely on the HatSec method as a foundation for our conceptual model, but the difference to our work is that the HatSec method provides a means to conduct a security analysis, while we provide a method to compare the processes, documentation demands, and methodologies in security standards.

The Healthcare Telematics Security (HatSec) method by Sunyaev [4] is a security analysis method developed for the healthcare domain. Sunyaev focuses on security analysis in the investigated standards, even though several of the standards the author investigates concern risk management, as well. However, in these cases the author did not consider the parts in the standards that concern risk in detail. The method consists of seven building blocks, which are derived from the following security and risk management standards: ISO27799 [15] ISO 27001 [1], IT Grundschutz [5], NIST SP 800-30 [7], CRISAM [16], CRAMM [17], ISRAM [18], ISMS JIPDEC for Medical Organisations [19], HB 174-2003 [20], US Department of Health and Human Services - Guideline for Industry, Q9 Quality Risk Management [21]. Note that only the last four standards are specific to the health care domain.

The building blocks of the HatSec method are related to the standard as follows. Each building block of the HatSec method occurs also in these standards. However, not all of the steps in the standards occur in the HatSec method. Fig. 2 shows the seven building blocks of the method. These are further divided into three phases. The *Security Analysis Context and Preparation* phase establishes the context of the security problem. The *Scope Identification* describes the limits of the environment and the system-to-be followed by the *Asset Identification*.

The *Security Analysis Process* covers the actual analysis activities of the method. The *Basic Security Check* reveals countermeasures already in place and the *Threat Identification* shows dangers resulting from possible attacks on the system-to-be. The *Vulnerability Identification* reveals vulnerabilities to security properties that are potentially exploited by threats. The original HatSec method demands an iteration between the Basic Security Check and the Threat Identification. However, we propose to rather iterate between the Vulnerability Identification and the Basic Security Check, because countermeasures are in place to mitigate vulnerabilities and only subsequent threats. These two building blocks shall be executed in iterations, e.g., if a threat is detected, it shall be checked if a countermeasure for the vulnerability is already in place. The *Security Assessment* concludes the Security Analysis Process by determining the level of security required and the risks remaining. In addition, the Security Assessment also initiates the *Security Analysis Product* phase, because the *Security Measures* activity evaluates the results of the Security Assessment in order to determine if the chosen level of security is adequate or if changes have to be made, e.g., adding additional security controls.

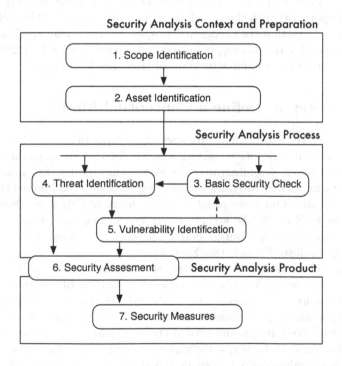

Fig. 2. The HatSec Method by Sunyaev [4]

4.2   NIST SP 800-30 Standard

The entire information security risk management methodology by Stoneburner et al. [7] is subdivided into three main phases: (1) risk assessment, (2) risk mitigation, and (3) evaluation. Risk assessment identifies and evaluates potential risks and their impacts, to recommend preventive and risk-reducing controls. In the risk mitigation phase, the identified risks are prioritized and adequate preventive controls are implemented and maintained. After the control implementation, a continual evaluation phase determines whether the implemented risk-reducing controls decrease the risk to an acceptable level or if further controls are required.

We briefly describe the NIST SP 800-30 risk management methodology, which we use as a basis for adding further building blocks to the HatSec method in order to create a conceptual model to compare security standards and also their approaches towards risk management in more detail. The reasons for having chosen the information security risk management methodology by Stoneburner et al. [7] are: (1) it gives very detailed identification and guidance of what should be considered in the phases of risk assessment, mitigation, and evaluation, (2) the methodology is well-accepted and well-established, (3) it is freely available, and (4) it supports organizations of all sizes. The comparison of the methodology against others shows that the proposed concepts could be easily applied to similar information security risk management methodologies such as ISO 27005 [22] or EBIOS [23] due to the similar structures of these methodologies.

5   CAST Step 3: Define a Conceptual Model

We extended the HatSec Method with several concepts from the NIST SP 800-30 and refined several concepts to ensure a more detailed comparison of security standards. Moreover, we integrated the conceptual model into a sequence of Standard Activities, which are the activities that have to be conducted to establish a security standard. Our conceptual model is shown in Fig. 3, we show example instantiations in Sect. 6. We structure our conceptual model using the three phases *Security Analysis Context and Preparation*, *Security Analysis Process*, and *Security Analysis Product* (see Sect. 4).

We explain the building blocks of the *Security Analysis Context and Preparation* in the following. We split the *scope identification* of the HatSec method into an *environment description* and a *stakeholder description*. The reason is that security is about protection of assets and harm to assets results in a loss to stakeholders. We have to understand the significance of the loss by describing the stakeholder. Moreover, stakeholders can cause threats to assets, and the identification of stakeholders in a scope is a research problem [24,25]. Moreover, we included the building block *Risk Level Description* to include a mechanism to categorize assets already in the beginning of the security analysis. This is done to focus security analysis on assets with a high risk level, as is suggested by NIST SP 800-30 [7] and IT Grundschutz [26].

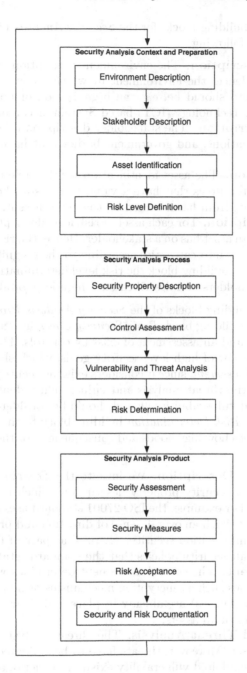

Fig. 3. A Conceptual Framework for Security Standards

We describe our building blocks for the *Security Analysis Context and Preparation* phase in the following.

Environment Description. The environment description states the scope of the standard. Hence, the environment in which the security system shall be integrated into should be, e.g., an organization or an Information and Communication Technology (ICT)-based System or combinations of both.

Stakeholder Description. The stakeholder description describes all relevant persons, organizations, and government bodies that have a relation to the environment.

Asset Identification. The asset identification for the stakeholders collects all information or resources that have a value to the stakeholders. The assets shall be protected from harm caused by the environment.

Risk Level Description. For each asset, a risk level description states the impact the loss of an asset has on a stakeholder. Hence, the risk level description classifies the assets into categories according to their significance for the environment. In this building block the risk level determination is based on the opinion of stakeholders and described on a high level of abstraction.

We explain the building blocks of the *Security Analysis Process* in the following. We divided the building block *Basic Security Check* into a security property definition for assets and an assessment of existing controls. The security properties provide an overview of high level security goals, which should be separated from the *Control Assessment*, since it considers existing security solutions. Moreover, we combined the threat analysis and vulnerability identification, because threats are exploited vulnerabilities [9] and should be considered together in our view. We add also a *Risk Determination* building block to the *Security Analysis Process* that describes how likelihoods and consequences for the resulting threats are assessed.

Security Property Description. We initiate the *Security Analysis Process* with a high level security property description, which determines security goals for assets. For example, the ISO 27001 standard uses high level security objectives to "establish an overall sense of direction and principles for action with regard to information security" [1, p. 4] as part of their ISMS policy, the superset of all security policies that the standard establishment creates.

Control Assessment. The control assessment determines which controls (either technical ones such as encryption mechanisms or non-technical controls such as security policies) are already in place and their ability to ensure a security property of an assets.

Vulnerability and Threat Analysis. The threat analysis assumes vulnerabilities of an asset. Moreover, threats have to be validated by showing that the potentially exploited vulnerability exists. In general, a threat requires a source and an existing vulnerability to become effective. The threat source can either intentionally or accidentally exploit a potential vulnerability. The aim of the threat identification step is to determine potential threats and their corresponding sources such as human threats (e.g. active network attacks, theft, unintentional data alternation, etc.), or environmental threats

Table 1. NIST 800-30 probability definitions [7]

Probability Level	Probability Definition
High	The threat-source is highly motivated and sufficiently capable, and controls to prevent the vulnerability from being exercised are ineffective.
Medium	The threat-source is motivated and capable, but controls are in place that may impede successful exercise of the vulnerability.
Low	The threat-source lacks motivation or capability, or controls are in place to prevent, or at least significantly impede, the vulnerability from being exercised.

(e.g. power failure, water leakage, etc.). On the basis of the threat analysis, the vulnerability analysis shows potential vulnerabilities present in the scope, including the consideration of vulnerabilities in the field of (1) management security (e.g. no assignment of responsibilities, no risk assessment, etc.), (2) operational security (e.g. no external data distribution and labeling, no humidity control, etc.), and (3) technical security (e.g. no cryptography solutions in use, no intrusion detection in place, etc.).

Risk Determination. The risk determination determines useful likelihood and impact scales to conduct risk management for assets. The risk determination considers the output of all previous steps and evaluates these results with regard to risk, considering the likelihood and impact scales. We explain this step further based on the NIST 800-30 standard in the following.

Firstly, a probability determination is concerned with the probability of a threat exploiting a certain vulnerability in the given system. Therefore, the organization has to deal with the following factors: (1) motivation and capability of the attacker, (2) nature of the vulnerability, and (3) existence and effectiveness of the current controls. Stoneburner et al. [7] propose a qualitative probability rating as stated in Table 1.

Secondly, an impact analysis determines the impact on the organization's ability to perform its mission if a threat should successfully exploit a certain vulnerability. The NIST SP 800-30 information security risk management methodology recommends measuring the impact in terms of the loss of integrity, availability, and/or confidentiality. While some impacts can be measured quantitatively in terms of the revenue lost, NIST recommends the measurement of impacts on a qualitative level (e.g. high, medium, and low). The main problem with quantitative measurement methods is that it is very hard to determine if the impact of a certain threat exactly corresponds to a certain amount of money. How can someone determine that a fire would cause a loss of exactly EUR 923.343 and not EUR 923.443? In most cases, people tend to use quantitative methods in a qualitative way, for example assigning monetary ranges (e.g. EUR 0 - EUR 200.000, EUR 200.000 - EUR 400.000, etc.) to the different impact levels.

Thirdly, the organization now knows the components necessary to determine the actual risk: (1) the probability that a given threat source exploits a certain vulnerability, (2) the impact caused if the threat exploited the very vulnerability, and (3) the adequacy of the existing controls for reducing or

Table 2. NIST 800-30 risk scale and necessary actions [7]

Risk Level	Risk Description and Necessary Actions
High	If an observation or finding is evaluated as a high risk, there is a strong need for corrective measures. An existing system may continue to operate, but a corrective action plan must be put in place as soon as possible.
Medium	If an observation is rated as medium risk, corrective actions are needed and a plan must be developed to incorporate these actions within a reasonable period of time.
Low	If an observation is described as low risk, the system's administrator must determine whether corrective actions are still required or decide to accept the risk.

eliminating the risk. By multiplying the threat probability with the magnitude of the impact, the organization is able to determine the risk level and thus to plan the necessary actions as stated in Tab. 2.

Finally, we explain the building blocks of the *Security Analysis Product* phase. We use the *Security Assessment* and *Security Measures* building blocks as described in the HatSec method and we add explicit building blocks for *Risk Acceptance* and *Security and Risk Documentation*. *Risk Acceptance* is an essential step of finishing the security analysis product, and if risks are accepted to soon, the entire security analysis product might not be effective. Hence, we aim to document in the template how the standards address this issue. In addition, the certification process of a security standard is usually based on the documentation of the security analysis product. That is why we want to add a description of the demanded documentation in our conceptual model and template.

Security Assessment. The security assessment evaluates if the existing security controls satisfy the security properties of the assets considering the results of the *Vulnerability and Threat Analysis*, as well as the *Risk Determination*. This step also describes how further security controls have to be selected. For example, the ISO 27001 standard [1] has a mandatory ANNEX A from which controls have to be selected.

Security Measures. The security measures activity specifies a list of new, refined or existing security controls that are required to improve the protection of the assets. This final result of the selection of controls are the *Security Measures*. For example, the ISO 27001 demands a so-called *Statement of Applicability* that reasons about the necessity of the controls in ANNEX A.

Risk Acceptance. The risk acceptance evaluates if the *Security Measures* reduce the risk of attacks on assets to acceptable levels. Often a clear cut criteria has to be defined that is fulfilled or not. For example, the controls prevent threats from attackers with a mediocre skills level and a limited amount of time.

Security and Risk Documentation. The security system description finishes with the security and risk documentation of the security analysis product. The documentation has to usually follow certain guidelines of a standard.

We mapped our conceptual model to a template presented in Tabs. 14, 15, and 16 in the appendix. We have elicited a series of questions for each building block, which shall help to fill in the required information. In addition, we stated which common terms are relevant for each part of the template.

6 CAST Step 4: Instantiate Template with Standards

We instantiate our template with the ISO 27001 standard (Sect. 6.1), IT Grundschutz (Sect. 6.2), and Common Criteria (Sect. 6.3).

6.1 ISO 27001

The ISO 27001 defines the requirements for establishing and maintaining an Information Security Management System (ISMS) [1]. In particular, the standard

Table 3. Instantiation for ISO 27001 of the Security Analysis Context and Preparation Part of the Template for Security Standard Description

Security Analysis Context and Preparation
Environment Description
The machine in this standard is the ISMS and the environment is anything outside the scope of the ISMS. "The standard demands an ISMS scope definition and its boundaries in terms of the characteristics of the business, the organization, its location, assets and technology, and including details of and justification for any exclusions from the scope" [1, p.4,Sect. 4.2.1 a]. The standard mentions the scope explicitly in the following sections. Sect. 4.2.1 d concerns risk identification and the section recommends to consider the scope definition for identifying assets. Section 4.2.3 demands management reviews of the ISMS that also includes to check for possible changes in the scope of the ISMS. Section 4.3 lists the documentation demands of the standard and Sect. 4.3.1 d requires a documentation of the scope of the ISMS. Moreover, the standard demands an explicit to creating an ISMS. In particular, Section 5.1 Management commitment concerns proof the management shall provide for establishing an ISMS objectives, plans, responsibilities and accepting risks. Section 5.2 Resource management concerns the provision of resources for establishing the ISMS and the training of the members of the organization for security awareness and competence.
Stakeholder Description
The stakeholder definition is part of the scope definition. The standard uses the term *Interested Parties* [1, p. vi] instead of stakeholders, who have security "expectations" that are input for the ISMS implementation as well as "security requirements".
Asset Identification
The design goal of the ISO 27001 ISMS is to protect assets with adequate security controls and this is stated already on page 1 of the standard. This is relevant in particular in Section 4 that describes the ISMS and in particular in Sect. 4.2 - Establishing and managing the ISMS states the scope definition. Section 4.2.1 a demands the definition of assets. Section 4.2.1 b concerns the definition of ISMS security policies demands that the policy shall consider assets. Section 4.2.1 d that concerns risk identification uses the scope definition to identify assets, to analyze threats to assets, and to analyze the impacts of losses to these assets. Section 4.2.1 e concerns risk analysis, which also clearly define to analyze assets and to conduct a vulnerability analysis regarding assets in light of the controls currently implemented.
Risk Level Definition
The standard requires a risk level definition in the steps following the scope definition. Section 4.2.1 b states that the ISMS policy has to align with the risk management. Section 4.2.1 c demands a risk assessment that includes criteria for accepting risks and identify the acceptable risk levels.

Table 4. Instantiation for ISO 27001 of the Security Analysis Process Part of the Template for Security Standard Description

Security Analysis Process
Security Property Description
The standard demands the elicitation of high level security goals in the section after the scope definition, this Section 4.2.1 b concerns the definition of ISMS policies of which high level security goals are a part. "The ISMS policy is considered as a superset of the information security policy." [1, p. 4].
Control Assessment
The assessment concerns likelihoods of security failures with regard to threats and vulnerabilities. In addition, impacts to assets should be considered of the controls currently implemented according to ISO 27001 Section 4.2.1 e 2.
Vulnerability and Threat Analysis
The ISO 27001 standard concerns threat analysis in several sections for determining the risks to assets. Section 4.2.1 d demands a threat analysis for assets for the purpose of identifying risks and the vulnerabilities that might be exploited by those threats. Section 4.2.1 e concerns risk analysis and evaluation and demands to determine likelihoods and consequences for threats. Section 4.2.4 d concerns the review process of the ISMS and also demands a threat identification. Section 7.2 that concerns the management review of the ISMS also demands a threat analysis.
Risk Determination
The standard demands a description of a methodology for risk management and it mentions several related activities explicitly. Section 4.2.1 d concerns risk identification and Sect. 4.2.1 e demands risk analysis and evaluation.

describes the process of creating a model of the entire business risks of a given organization and to specify specific requirements for the implementation of security controls. The resulting ISMS provides a customized security level for an organization.

The ISO 27001 standard contains a description of the so-called *ISO 27001 process* [1]. The process contains phases for establishing an ISMS, implementing and operating an ISMS and also monitoring, reviewing, maintaining and improving it.

In the initial phase, the *scope and boundaries* of the ISMS, its *interested parties, environment, assets*, and all the *technology* involved are defined. In this phase, also the ISMS *policies, risk assessments, evaluations*, and *controls* are defined. Controls in the ISO 27001 are measures to *modify risk*.

The ISO 27001 standard demands a set of documents that describe the requirements for the ISMS. Furthermore, the standard demands periodic audits towards the effectiveness of an ISMS. These audits are also conducted using documented ISMS requirements. In addition, the ISO 27001 standard demands that management decisions, providing support for establishing and maintaining an ISMS, are also documented. This support has to be documented via management decisions. This has to be proven as part of a detailed documentation of how each decision was reached and how many resources (e.g., personal, budget, time, etc.) are committed to implement this decision. Moreover, certification of an ISMS according to the ISO 27001 standard is possible, based upon the documentation of the ISMS.

Table 5. Instantiation for ISO 27001 of the Security Analysis Product Part of the Template for Security Standard Description

Security Analysis Product
Security Assessment
Threats to assets have to be analyzed and existing security controls documented. The risk has to be evaluated of these threats according to the criteria set previously, considering the existing security controls. For all unacceptable risks security controls have to be selected to reduce the risk to acceptable level. The control selection is based on security requirements, which are refinements of the high level security goals. This is explained in the following.
Security Measures
The ISO 27001 standard concerns high level ISMS policies during the establishment of the ISMS to guide the focus of security and security policies as controls that define in detail what a specific security controls should achieve. In particular, the Annex A of the ISO 27001 standard describes the normative controls of the standard. This is stated in Section 4.2.1 f concerning risk treatment and Section 4.2.1 g discussing controls for risk treatment.
Risk Acceptance
Criteria for acceptable have to be defined in the beginning of the risk analysis (Section 4.2.1 c) and after. The control selection it has to be shown that the criteria for acceptable risk are fulfilled. The standard also demands management approval for acceptable levels of risk (see Section 4.2.1 h).
Security and Risk Documentation
The ISO 27001 standard demands the following documents: – ISMS policies and objectives – Scope and boundaries of the ISMS – Procedures and controls – The risk assessment methodology – Risk assessment report – Risk treatment plan – Information security procedures – Control and protection of records that can provide evidence of compliance to the requirements of the ISMS – Statement of Applicability describing the control objectives and controls that are relevant and applicable to the organization's ISMS. In addition, the ISO 27001 standard demands the documentation of Management Decisions that provide support for establishing and maintaining an ISMS.

6.2   IT-Grundschutz

The German Bundesamt für Sicherheit in der Informationstechnik (BSI) issued the so-called *BSI series of standards for information security* [26] (see left hand side of Fig. 4). These are based on the ISO 27001 and ISO 27002 standards and refine them with a new methodology. The series of standards consists of BSI-Standard 100-1 that concerns the management issues of the standard such as planning IT processes. The BSI-Standard 100-2 [27] describes the methodology of how to build an ISMS, BSI-Standard 100-3 [5] concerns risk management, and BSI 100-4 [28] considers Business Continuity Management, e.g., data

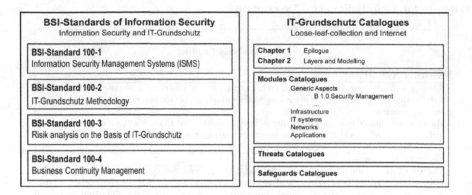

Fig. 4. BSI IT-Grundschutz Overview taken from [26]

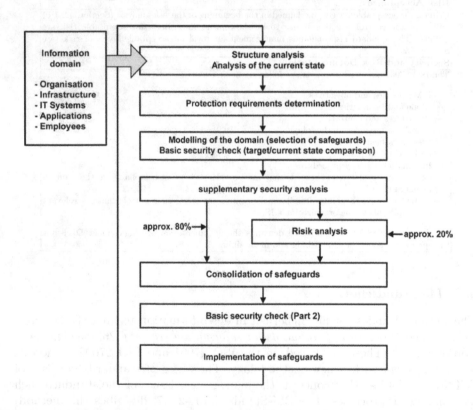

Fig. 5. IT Grundschutz Method taken from [27]

Table 6. Instantiation for BSI 100.2 of the Security Analysis Context and Preparation Part of the Template for Security Standard Description

Security Analysis Context and Preparation
Environment Description
The standard demands a description of the scope and in particular [27, p. 37]: - "Specify which critical business processes, specialised tasks, or parts of an organisation will be included in the scope - Clearly define the limits of the scope - Describe interfaces to external partners"The machine in this standard is an ISMS and the environment are described via interfaces to external partners. The scope definition is accompanied by a structure analysis, which demands a separate documentation of the following parts of the scope: information, application, IT systems, rooms, communication networks.
Stakeholder Description
The employees of the organization that take part in the business processes have to be documented. Moreover, the users of the scope elements such as applications are documented, as well. These are both part of the scope definition. The standard refers to users or employees of the organization instead of stakeholders.
Asset Identification
For each business process in the scope a level of protection has to be determined. The entire processes and in particular the information technology used and information processed it contains are considered as assets.
Risk Level Definition
The standard uses the protection requirements as an indicator for high level risks.

recovery plans. In the following, we focus on BSI 100-2, because it contains the methodology. The BSI standard 100-2 describes how an ISMS can be established and managed. It is compatible to the ISO 27001 standard, meaning that an implementation of the BSI standard 100-2 can be used for an ISO 27001 certification with the German BSI [26, p. 12]. In addition, the standard aims towards reducing the required time for an ISMS implementation. This is achieved by provisioning the IT Grundschutz Catalogues (see right hand side of Fig. 4). This catalog contains a significant collection of IT security threats and controls, and a mapping between them. Note that controls are called *safeguards* in the BSI terminology. The standard offers a method depicted in Fig. 5 that starts with a structural analysis of the organization and the environment. The standard suggests a focus on at least the areas organization, infrastructure, IT-systems, applications, and employees. The next step is to determine the required security level, followed by modeling the security measures, and a basic security check. This security check classifies the assets and executes a risk analysis for the 20 percent of assets with the highest security level. The remaining 80 percent are not considered in a risk

Table 7. Instantiation for BSI 100.2 of the Security Analysis Process Part of the Template for Security Standard Description

Security Analysis Process
Security Property Description
All general security concerns are specified in an information security policy, which describes the general direction of information security in the organization. In addition, for each asset security goals have to be determined in terms of confidentiality, integrity, and availability. The standard calls them protection requirement, which have to be categorized in the levels: normal, high, and very high [27, p. 48]. These categories have the meaning [27, p. 48]: **Normal** "The impact of any loss or damage is limited and calculable." **High** "The impact of any loss or damage may be considerable." **Very High** "The impact of any loss or damage may be of catastrophic proportions which could threaten the very survival of the organisation." Note that the standard also allows to define a different scale, but this is the scale recommended. The protection requirements are refined with damage scenarios [27, p. 48]: "Violations of laws, regulations, or contracts Impairment of the right to informational self-determination Physical injury Impaired ability to perform the tasks at hand Negative internal or external effects Financial consequences" These damage scenarios have to be put in relation to the protection requirement for each organization that establishes the standard. This means it has to be defined for each category what the damage scenario means, e.g., what means normal financial consequences.
Control Assessment
The standard relies on the security controls listed in the IT Grundschutz catalog. These are categorized into [27, p. 48]: **S 1** Infrastructure, **S 2** Organization, **S 3** Personnel, **S 4** Hardware and software, **S 5** Communication, **S 6** Contingency planning. Several of the threats listed in the IT Grundschutz Catalogues have existing mappings to possibly relevant safeguards. These have to be considered as relevant if a threat is selected. The safeguards have to be refined for the scope. The standard refers to safeguards instead of security controls.
Vulnerability and Threat Analysis
The standard demands a model of the scope. The IT Grundschutz catalog provides modules that support this modeling. These modules are categorized in the following domains [27, p. 48]: *General aspects Infrastructure IT systems Networks Application.* The modules contain a mapping to the following threat categories: **T 1** Force majeure, **T 2** Organisational shortcomings, **T 3** Human error, **T 4** Technical failure, **T 5** Deliberate acts. All of the threats in each threat category of the IT Grundschutz catalog have to be analyzed with regard to the scope and the relevant threats have to be documented. The threats have to be refined for the scope of the analysis.
Risk Determination
A risk analysis can be conducted either after the basic security check or the supplementary security check. The management has to make a choice, for which assets a risk analysis has to be conducted. The standard does not prescribe a strict methodology for risk management, but provides rather advice for how to consider threats and safeguards and in which step of the method use to apply the threat analysis. It is not providing a method for e.g. eliciting likelihood or consequences scales.

Table 8. Instantiation for BSI 100.2 of the Security Analysis Product Part of the Template for Security Standard Description

Security Analysis Product
Security Assessment
A security assessment is done using a so-called *basic security check*. The model of the scope and the protection requirements are used to develop a security test plan, which determines the effectiveness of existing security controls. Each test has to describe a target state and after conducting the test it is determined if a control is effective by analyzing the state of the tested scope elements. In a sense the security testing plans are based on security requirements, which refine the protection requirements. This basic security check consists of three different steps. "The first step consists of making the organisational preparations and, in particular, selecting the relevant contact people for the target/actual state comparison. In Step 2, the target state is compared to the actual state by conducting interviews and performing random checks. In the final step, the results of the target/actual state comparison are documented together with the reasoning behind the results. " [27, p. 66].
Security Measures
After considering the threats and safeguards in the IT Grundschutz catalog a supplementary security analysis is conducted. "The supplementary security analysis is to be performed on all target objects in the information domain to which one or more of the following applies: - The target objects have high or very high protection requirements in at least one of the three basic values – confidentiality, integrity, or availability - The target objects could not be adequately depicted (modelled) with the existing modules in the IT-Grundschutz Catalogues - The target objects are used in operating scenarios (e.g. in environments or with applications) that were not foreseen in the scope of IT-Grundschutz. " [27, p. 66].
Risk Acceptance
Accepted risks have to be documented with a reasoning.
Security and Risk Documentation
Each step of the methodology presented in the standard has to be documented.

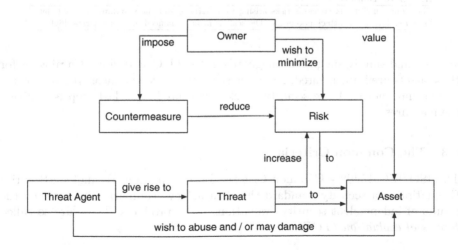

Fig. 6. The Common Criteria Basic Security Model taken from [2]

Table 9. Instantiation for Common Criteria of the Security Analysis Context and Preparation Part of the Template for Security Standard Description

Security Analysis Context and Preparation
Environment Description
The common criteria demands a description of the TOE in its environment. Hence, the TOE is the machine. The environment contains stakeholders, other software components the TOE requires, e.g., a specific operating system. The standard discusses the environment simply as outside the TOE.   "An ST introduction containing three narrative descriptions of the TOE " [2, p. 64, Part 1: Introduction and general model]. The TOE reference provides a description of unique identifications for an ST that describes the TOE such as a version numbers for the revision of the ST. The TOE overview describes the intended functionality of the TOE and security features on a high level of abstraction. The standard describes the TOE and its environment, which is simply referred to as *outside* or *operational environment* of the TOE. Hence, the system consists of the TOE and its *operational environment*.
Stakeholder Description
The Common Criteria focuses on describing a software product and it describes stakeholders just as much as they are required to understand the TOE's functionality or security features. For example, a TOE shall display certain information to a user.   The standard uses the term external entity for all stakeholders that interact with the TOE from the outside. It explicitly states that a user is a external entity. Note that the term external entities also includes IT entities [2, p. 16 and p. 20, Part 1: Introduction and general model].
Asset Identification
"Security is concerned with the protection of assets. " [2, p. 38, Part 1: Introduction and general model]. Stakeholders consider assets valuable (see below), which is highly subjective. Thus, the identification of assets depends upon information from stakeholders, because "almost anything can be an asset " [2, p. 38, Part 1: Introduction and general model]. Hence, assets should have a description and also some information regarding the need for protection. This is aligned with descriptions of existing PPs such as [29]. Furthermore, in PPs the concept of a SecondaryAssets is used [29], whose loss do not cause harm to the ToE Owner directly, but the harm can cause harm to an Asset. This in turn can cause a loss to a ToE Owner.   The standard defines "assets entities that the owner of the TOE presumably places value upon. " [2, p. 16 and p. 20, Part 1: Introduction and general model].
Risk Level Definition
The Common Criteria concerns risks arising from attacks and the standard does not define basic risk levels, but attack potentials. The scale is basic, enhanced-basic, moderate, high.

analysis and simply suggested safeguards in the IT Grundschutz Catalogues for these assets are implemented. After the security check, the measures are consolidated and another basic security check is executed. The last step is realizing the measures.

6.3 The Common Criteria

The ISO/IEC 15408 - Common Criteria for Information Technology Security Evaluation is a security standard that can achieve comparability between the results of independent security evaluations of IT products. These are so-called *targets of evaluation (TOEs)*.

Table 10. Instantiation for Common Criteria of the Security Analysis Process Part of the Template for Security Standard Description

Security Analysis Process
Security Property Description
Security needs of assets are expressed in terms of confidentiality, integrity, and availability or other not specified security goals. "Security-specific impairment commonly includes, but is not limited to: loss of asset confidentiality, loss of asset integrity and loss of asset availability." [2, p. 39]. These terms are not defined in the general term definition section of Part 1, but refined terms are defined in Part 2: security functional components. For example, *FDP_UCT* describes the meaning of user data confidentiality.
Control Assessment
"Subsequently countermeasures are imposed to reduce the risks to assets. These countermeasures may consist of IT countermeasures (such as firewalls and smart cards) and non-IT countermeasures (such as guards and procedures). " [2, p. 39, Part 1: Introduction and general model]. The standard uses the term countermeasure for security control.
Vulnerability and Threat Analysis
The common criteria considers threats from malicious attackers and also from attackers that present unintentional threats such as accidental disconnecting a server from a power supply. "The Common Criteria is applicable to risks arising from human activities (malicious or otherwise) and to risks arising from non-human activities. " [2, p. 16 and p. 20, Part 1: Introduction and general model]. The common criteria suggests further to describe the *attack potential* that "measure of the effort to be expended in attacking a TOE, expressed in terms of an attacker's expertise, resources and motivation. " [2, p. 14, Part 1: Introduction and general model]. The description of attackers leads to threats the attacker present by exploiting vulnerabilities.
Risk Determination
The Common Criteria focuses on identifying vulnerabilities and attackers that might exploit these vulnerabilities. "These threats therefore give rise to risks to the assets, based on the likelihood of a threat being realised and the impact on the assets when that threat is realised. ". [2, p. 39, Part 1: Introduction and general model]. However, the standard does not follow a risk management approach like ISO 31000, but focuses on documenting vulnerabilities and countermeasures of a TOE. An ST shall help to decide if a stakeholder is willing to accept the risk of using a TOE. "Once an ST and a TOE have been evaluated, asset owners can have the assurance (as defined in the ST) that the TOE, together with the operational environment, counters the threats. The evaluation results may be used by the asset owner in deciding whether to accept the risk of exposing the assets to the threats. " [2, p. 58, Part 1: Introduction and general model].

The Common Criteria (CC) is based upon a general security model (see Fig. 6). The model considers TOE owners that value their assets and wish to minimize risk to these assets via imposing countermeasures. These reduce the risk to assets. Threat agents wish to abuse assets and give rise to threats for assets. The threats increase the risk to assets. The concepts of the Common Criteria consider that potential TOE owners infer their security needs for specific types of TOEs, e.g., a specific firewall. The resulting documents are called Security Targets (ST). Protection profiles (PP) state security needs for an entire class of TOEs, e.g., client VPN application. The evaluators check if a TOE

Table 11. Instantiation for Common Criteria of the Security Analysis Product Part of the Template for Security Standard Description (1/2)

Security Analysis Product
Security Assessment
Each of the threats previously identified leads to the formulation of a *security objective*, which is equal to a security requirement in the common terminology. The Common Criteria distinguishes between security objectives, which concern the TOE, and the ones concerning the environment. The latter ones are so-called *security objectives for the environment*. Moreover, the Common Criteria considers organization security policies, which are equal to the policy term. The Common Criteria uses cross-tables that present a mapping of all identified threats to security objectives, security objectives for the environment, assumptions, or organization security policies. Each threat has to mapped to at lease one security objectives, security objectives for the environment, or assumptions.
Security Measures
Security objectives are refined by security functional requirements, which are gap texts that concern specific security functions such as access control functions. Security objectives are on a high abstraction level, while security functional requirements concern concrete implementable security functionalities. All security objectives have to be refined using security functional requirements. A cross-table has to show that all security objectives are refined by at least one security functional requirement.
Risk Acceptance
"Owners of assets may be (held) responsible for those assets and therefore should be able to defend the decision to accept the risks of exposing the assets to the threats. " [2, p. 39, Part 1: Introduction and general model].

meets its ST. Protection profiles (PP) state the security requirements of TOE owners. TOE developers or vendors publish their security claims in security targets (ST). A CC evaluation determines if the ST is compliant to a specific PP. The standard relies upon documents for certification, which state information about security analysis and taken measures.

7   CAST Step 5: Compare Standards

We analyze the instantiated templates (Sect. 6) of the ISO 27001 standard (Sect. 6.1), IT Grundschutz (Sect. 6.2), and Common Criteria (Sect. 6.3) in Sect. 7.1. In addition, we describe the tool support for our method in Sect. 7.2.

7.1   Comparison

We compared the terminology of the security standards ISO 27001, IT Grundschutz, and Common Criteria in Tab. 7.1 with the terminology introduced in Sect. 3. The symbol "∼" means that the term is equal to the definition in our terminology (Sect. 3). A " − " states that the standard does not consider that term explicitly.

Table 12. Instantiation for Common Criteria of the Security Analysis Product Part of the Template for Security Standard Description (2/2)

Security Analysis Product
Security and Risk Documentation
The concepts of the Common Criteria consider that potential ToE owners infer their security needs for specific types of ToE, e.g., a specific database. The resulting documents are called Security Targets (ST). Protection profiles (PP) state security needs for an entire class of ToEs, e.g., client VPN application. The evaluators check if a ToE meets its ST. PPs state the security requirements of ToE owners. ToE developers or vendors publish their security claims in an ST. A CC evaluation determines if the ST is compliant to a specific PP. The standard relies upon documents for certification, which state information about security analysis and taken measures.
The structure of a CC security target starts with an ST *Introduction* that contains the description of the ToE and its environment. The *Conformance Claims* describe to which PPs the ST is compliant. The *Security Problem Definition* refines the external entities, e.g., stakeholders in the environment and lists all assets, assumptions about the environment and the ToE, threats to assets and organizational security policies. The *Security Objectives* have to be described for the ToE and for the operational environment of the ToE. The *Extended Component Definitions* describe extensions to security components described in the CCs part 2. The *Security Requirements* contain two kinds of requirements. The security functional requirements (SFR) are descriptions of security functions specific to the ToE. The security assurance requirements (SAR) describe the measures taken in development of the ToE. These are evaluated against the security functionality specified in the SFR. The Evaluation Assurance Level (EAL) is a numerical rating ranging from 1 to 7, which states the depth of the evaluation. Each EAL corresponds to an SAR package. EAL 1 is the most basic level and EAL 7 the most stringent.
The Common Criteria defines a set of *Security Assurance Components* that have to be considered for a chosen *Evaluation Assurance Level (EAL)*. For these components, developer activities, content of corresponding components, and actions for an evaluator are defined. The Common Criteria defines security assurance components for the following *Assurance classes*:
<ul><li>Protection Profile Evaluation (APE)</li><li>Security Target Evaluation (ASE)</li><li>Development (ADV)</li><li>Life-Cycle support (ALC)</li><li>Tests (ATE)</li><li>Vulnerability Assessment (AVA)</li></ul>
In the Security Target, Security Objectives are defined for the TOE on for the TOE's environment. The Security Objectives are related to Security Functional Requirements. Part of the assurance classes for the development documentation (ADV) is the functional specification (ADV_FSP). In this document, the security functions (SFs) are defined. According to the security architecture (as required in ADV_ARC), the TOE design with details about the subsystems and modules are documented in the TOE design (ADV_TDS). This design document brakes down the security functions (SFs) and relates all subsystems and modules to the security functional requirements (SFRs) they implement. Vulnerabilities are assessed in the corresponding document according to the claimed attack potential (high, medium, low)(AVA_VAN).

Furthermore, we show the results of our comparison in the following by illustrating relevant statements for each of our building blocks of our security standard template instances.

Security Analysis Context and Preparation

Environment description - The ISO 27001 demands a scope definition including assets and justifications. The standard refers explicitly to use the scope in subsequent steps such as risk identification. Moreover, the scope is also referred

Table 13. Term Comparison between Security Standards

terms \standards	ISO 27001	IT Grundschutz	Common Criteria
machine	ISMS	ISMS	TOE
environment	outside the boundaries of the ISMS	interfaces to external partners	operational environment
stakeholder	interested parties	employees and users	TOE owner, users
asset	~	~	~
security control	controls	safeguards	countermeasure
attacker	-	-	threat agent
vulnerability	~	~	~
threat	~ *	~ *	~
policy	ISMS policy, security policy	information security policy	organizational security policy
security goals	security objectives	protection requirements	security needs
security requirements	~	(security test plans)**	security objective
security functions	-	-	security functional requirements

* Note that attackers can be seen as threats.
** Note that the security test plan are not requirements, but are based on refined protection requirements.

to in the documented management commitment. The IT Grundschutz demands also explicitly to document external partners and to document certain parts of the scope separately, such as applications. The Common Criteria focuses on functionalities of the TOE and its environment in the scope description.

Stakeholder description - The ISO 27001 demands stakeholder description as part of the scope description including their security expectations. The IT Grundschutz considers all employees and external staff involved in relevant business processes as stakeholders. The Common Criteria concerns all users of the TOE as stakeholders.

Asset identification - ISO 27001 demands the definition of assets, but does not provide methodological support for it. The IT Grundschutz considers all information technology and information in the business processes as assets. The Common Criteria considers also the concept of a secondary assets. But the standard does not provide a method for identifying them, either.

Risk level determination - The ISO 27001 demands a high level risk definition in alignment with the risk management of the organization. The IT Grundschutz standards use protection requirements as high level risk indicators. The Common Criteria standard does not consider high level risks, but it does define attack potentials.

Security Analysis Process

Risk Determination - The ISO 27001 demands a description of the risk management methodology. The IT Grundschutz proposes a categorization of assets and to conduct a risk analysis only for the assets with significant security concerns. The standard does not demand a specific method for risk management, but it provides advice for considering risk, threats, and security controls. The Common Criteria focuses on documenting vulnerabilities and security controls of the TOE. It does not consider risk management per se, but rather provides the information about threats and countermeasures to stakeholders. Afterwards the stakeholders can use this information to conduct a risk analysis.

Security Property Description - ISO 27001 demands high level security goals as part of the ISMS policy, which defines the focus of security of the ISMS and is described right after the scope. The IT Grundschutz demands to describe protection requirements using confidentiality, integrity, and availability. In addition, the standard demands a categorization into the levels: normal, high, very high. The Common Criteria demands that security concerns are described in terms of confidentiality, integrity, and availability. The standard contains a catalog of refinements of these terms, which have to be used in TOE descriptions.

Control Assessment - The ISO 27001 focuses on likelihoods of threats exploiting existing vulnerabilities and the effect already implemented controls have on these likelihoods. The IT Grundschutz has mappings from threats to security controls and it has to be checked if the recommended security controls are implemented for all identified threats. The Common Criteria documents existing security controls by describing existing security functionalities of the TOE. The gap texts in the security functional requirements of the standard have to be used for these descriptions.

Vulnerability and Threat Analysis - The ISO 27001 concerns threat analysis in order to determine risks for assets. The threat analysis is based on a vulnerability identification. The IT Grundschutz standard relies on a list of threats for the identified scope parts, e.g., applications from the IT Grundschutz Catalogues. The Common Criteria demands to describe threats from malicious and from unintentional attackers. The capabilities of these attackers have to be described in terms of expertise, resources, and motivation.

Security Analysis Product

Security Assessment - The ISO 27001 demands to evaluate the risks to assets considering threats and existing security controls. For all assets with unacceptable risks, additional security controls have to be selected from the normative ANNEX A of the standard. The IT Grundschutz standards begin with a basic security check, which is based on security tests derived from the protection requirements. The tests are used for an effectiveness evaluation of the existing security controls. The Common Criteria relies on cross-tables that map threats to security objectives. All threats have to be addressed by at least one security objective or assumption.

Security Measures - The ISO 27001 demands first high level security policies, which are refined into a set of relevant security controls considering the controls listed in the mandatory ANNEX A of the standard. The IT Grundschutz demands using the mapping from scope elements to threats, and subsequently to security controls in the IT-Grundschutz Catalogues. Only assets that are not considered adequately in the IT-Grundschutz Catalogues demand a separate security analysis. The Common Criteria refines security objectives using a catalog of security functional requirements. A further cross-table has to proof that each security objective is addressed by at least one security functional requirement.

Risk Acceptance - The ISO 27001 demands to define criteria for risk acceptance in the management approval document. The standard demands a reasoning why the selected security controls reduce the risk to acceptable limits for each asset. The IT Grundschutz simply demands a documentation of accepted risks including a reason why these risks are accepted. The Common Criteria demands risk acceptance decisions from asset owners. They have to make an informed decision to accept the risks of the identified threats.

Security and Risk Documentation - The ISO 27001 demands documentation about the scope and security policies, and extensive documentation of the risk management. The IT Grundschutz standards simply demand to document all the steps of the method. The Common Criteria demands an extensive documentation of the security reasoning and the resulting software product, and in particular the security functions of the product.

To sum up, the ISO 27001 concerns a high level process with regard to security. The IT Grundschutz refines the ISO 27001 process and provides further guidances for identifying threats and security controls based on the IT Grundschutz Catalogues. In contrast, the Common Criteria focuses on documenting a software or hardware product including details of its implementation. The reasoning about which security standard is applicable should be based on the concerned application domain. A vendor of a hardware router might want to select the Common Criteria, due to the detailed security analysis of its implementation. A cloud computing provider who offers scalable IT resources and particular business processes concerning these resources might favor ISO 27001. A reason could be that documenting a high level security process allows changes within the cloud implementation, because the process does not consider the implementation in detail. Using the Common Criteria would demand a documentation of its implementation and a re-certification each time the implementation changes.

7.2   CAST Tool Support

We base our tool support on the NESSoS CBK (Sect. 2) that aims to collect knowledge on engineering secure systems. The structure of the *CBK* relates Knowledge Objects (KOs) for specific fields (referred to as Knowledge Areas – KAs). We define the following four types of KOs. *Methods* define a set of activities used to tackle problems in engineering secure software and services in a systematic way. *Techniques* describe an approach that contains only a single activity. *Tools* support a software engineer in achieving a development goal in an (at least partially) automated way. A *Notation* defines symbols, a syntax, and semantics to express relevant artifacts [30]. We included security standards as a fifth type of KO, meaning we implemented the security standard template in its underlying ontology. In addition, the CBK offers the functionality to compare KOs by displaying their attributes next to each other. Hence, we can display two instantiated security standard templates next to each other. This way the comparison of them is supported. Furthermore, a search functionality allows to search the instantiated templates for specific search terms. In the future, we are planning to implement an automatic search for supporting KOs for security standards and a comparison of security standard support methodologies.

7.3 Discussion

Our method provides the means to describe three building blocks of security standards. The first block states how context description and preparation of a security analysis has to be done in a standard. This provides an overview of the level of detail demanded for a security standard compliant system documentation. For example, the IT-Grundschutz standards demand to treat every item in the scope as an asset and conduct a security analysis for it, while the ISO 27001 demands a reasoning about which are the assets in the scope. Hence, the ISO 27001 allows more flexibility in the security analysis.

The security analysis process shows how existing controls, risk, threats and vulnerabilities have to be analyzed. For example, the IT-Grundschutz demands a characterization of the existing controls according to certain categories, while the ISO 27001 simply refers to a statement of how the existing controls reduce the likelihoods of security failures. This is another indication that the ISO 27001 demands a less structured documentation than the IT-Grundschutz standards. In contrast, the Common Criteria controls are clearly separated into IT and non-IT countermeasures. For this reason, the standard can be applied especially for product development.

Finally, the security analysis product shows the overall security assessment and in particular how security measures have to be described, risk acceptance to be determined, and what documentation is required for a certification. As an example, the ISO 27001 demands a specific set of a few documents, while the IT-Grundschutz simply demands to document the entire process.

Our method creates the following main benefits:

- A simple overview of the core activities of security standards.
- Enabling a structured comparison of standard activities by storing the knowledge about standards in defined template fields.
- Providing indication of the focus, level of detail, and effort for providing or even reading a system documentation according to a specific standard.

We could identify the following points for improvement of our work:

- The approach could be extended to compare also support tools for standard compliant system documentation and analysis.
- Our templates can be analyzed for re-using artifacts and results of the certification of one standard for another. This could lead to a possible optimal sequence of certifications of different standards with regard to resources spent in terms of time and money.
- The overview is provided on an abstract level and the engineers still have to read the standards to compare these on a more granular level. Our method could be extended to support a more detailed analysis of the standard documents.

8   Related Work

To the best of our knowledge, no structured method exists to compare security standards using a conceptual model, template and a common terminology.

The U.S. Department of Energy compared the ISO/IEC 17799, NIST PC-SRF, ISA-TR99.00.01-2004 and ISA-TR99.00.02-2004 security standards [31]. The authors compare terms and notions of the standards, but they do not rely on a conceptual model or template.

Siponen and Willison [32] analyzed to which kinds of organizations the standards and guidelines BS7799, BS ISO/IEC17799: 2000, GASPP/GAISP, and the SSE-CMM are helpful. They do not compare notions, concepts or terminology.

Sommestad et al. [33] compare standards for Cyber security of Supervisory Control And Data Acquisition (SCADA). SCADA systems are crucial for critical infrastructures, e.g., electrical power system. Sommestad et al. compare a number of SCADA standards and the ISO 27002 standard. The authors compare the sets of threats and countermeasures stated in the standards. Sommestad et al. divide the standards into those that focus on technical countermeasures and those that focus on organizational countermeasures and analyze their commonalities and differences. This research can complement our own by refining our building block that concerns countermeasures using their results.

Phillips et al. [34] analyze security standards for the RFID market: ISO/IEC 15693, ISO/IEC 10536, ISO/IEC 11784-11785, ISO/IEC 18000-3, ISO/IEC 18000-2. The authors list the availability, integrity, and confidentiality demands of these standards. Their aim is to provide a complete set of security goals for the RFID market and not to compare the standards.

Kuligowski [35] compares the FISMA security standards and the ISO 27001 standard by comparing terminology and mapping their activities. The work does not provide a common terminology or conceptual model that could be applied to further standards.

NIST [36] compares the standards FIPS 140-1 AND FIPS 140-2 regarding their specification of cryptographic modules. The authors also compare terminologies and description of cryptographic functionalities. This work does not aim at creating a terminology or conceptual model for security standards.

Arora [38] compares the ISO 27001 and the COBIT standard using a template that contains the fields: focus, paradigm, scope, structure, organizational model, and certification. The author does not provide a conceptual model or terminology comparison. Moreover, the template is lacking a detailed focus on security and risk management activities.

The government of Hong Kong released a report about security standards [37]. The report provides summaries of the standards ISO 27001, ISO 27002, COBIT, ITIL, etc. and also legal norms such as SOX and HIPAA. The report is not comparing the standards, but just aims at providing easily readable introductions into these standards. Hence, the report does not provide terminology comparisons, conceptual models, or templates.

9   Conclusion and Future Work

We contributed a conceptual model of security standards based on existing research such as the HatSec method and the NIST SP 800-30 standard. Furthermore, we derived a template from the conceptual model that can be instantiated for different security standards. We applied this idea to several security standards and compared the resulting template instances.

Our approach offers the following main benefits:

- A structured method for comparing security standards.
- A common terminology and a conceptual model of security standards.
- A template that supports the structured collection of knowledge by using common security standard activities, e.g., asset identification
- A set of instantiated security standard templates for the standards ISO 27001, IT Grundschutz, and Common Criteria. The templates provide an overview of the most relevant standard activities.
- Improving the understanding of commonalities and differences of security standards by analyzing the difference in the common standard activities, e.g., how do ISO 27001 and Common Criteria identify assets?
- Supporting security engineers in the decision which certification scheme to pursue and what kind of information to expect from a security standard documentation.
- Providing tool support for the comparison of security standards.

In the future, we will compare further standards and include also the comparison of risk management standards such as ISO 31000. In addition, we will extend the common terminology and also add a change template specifically designed to compare different versions of a standard.

References

1. International Organization for Standardization (ISO), International Electrotechnical Commission (IEC): Information technology - Security techniques - Information security management systems - Requirements (2005)
2. ISO/IEC: Common Criteria for Information Technology Security Evaluation. ISO/IEC 15408, International Organization for Standardization (ISO) and International Electrotechnical Commission, IEC (2012)
3. ISO/IEC: Risk management Principles and guidelines. ISO/IEC 31000, International Organization for Standardization (ISO) and International Electrotechnical Commission, IEC (2009)
4. Sunyaev, A.: Health-Care Telematics in Germany - Design and Application of a Security Analysis Method. Gabler (2011)
5. Bundesamt für Sicherheit in der Informationstechnik (BSI): Standard 100-3 Risk Analysis based on IT-Grundschutz, Version 2.5 (2008)
6. JASON: Science of Cyber-Security. Technical report, The MITRE Corporation, JSR-10-102 (2010)

7. Stoneburner, G., Goguen, A., Feringa, A.: Risk management guide for information technology systems. NIST Special Publication 800-30, National Institute of Standards and Technology (NIST), Gaithersburg, MD 20899-8930 (July 2002)
8. Beckers, K., Eicker, S., Faßbender, S., Heisel, M., Schmidt, H., Schwittek, W.: Ontology-based identification of research gaps and immature research areas. In: Quirchmayr, G., Basl, J., You, I., Xu, L., Weippl, E. (eds.) CD-ARES 2012. LNCS, vol. 7465, pp. 1–16. Springer, Heidelberg (2012)
9. Fabian, B., Gürses, S., Heisel, M., Santen, T., Schmidt, H.: A comparison of security requirements engineering methods. Requirements Engineering – Special Issue on Security Requirements Engineering 15(1), 7–40 (2010)
10. Jackson, M.: Problem Frames. Analyzing and structuring software development problems. Addison-Wesley (2001)
11. Gollmann, D.: Computer Security, 2nd edn. John Wiley & Sons (2005)
12. Bishop, M.: Computer Security: Art and science, 1st edn. Pearson (2003)
13. Viega, J., McGraw, G.: Building secure software: How to avoid security problems the right way, 1st edn. Addison-Wesley (2001)
14. Firesmith, D.: Common concepts underlying safety, security, and survivability engineering. Technical report sei-2003-tn-033, Carnegie Melon University (2003)
15. ISO/FDIS: ISO/IEC 27799:2007(E), Health Informatics - Information Security Management in health using ISO/IEC 27002 (November 2007)
16. Stallinger, M.: CRISAM - Coporate Risk Application Method - Summary V2.0 (2004)
17. Farquhar, B.: One approach to risk assessment. Computers and Security 10(10), 21–23 (1991)
18. Karabacak, B., Sogukpinar, I.: Isram: Information security risk analysis method. Computers & Security 24(2), 147–159 (2005)
19. Japan Information Processing Development Corporation and The Medical Information System Development Center: ISMS User's Guide for Medical Organizations (2004)
20. Standards Australia International; Standards New Zealand: Guidelines for managing risk in healthcare sector: Australian/ New Zealand handbook, Standards Australian International (2001)
21. Food and Drug Administration: Guideline for Industry, Q9 Quality Risk Management (2006); In US Department of Health and Human Services
22. ISO/IEC: ISO/IEC 27005: 2007, Information technology - Security techniques - Information security risk management (November 2007)
23. DCSSI: Expression des Besoins et Identification des Objectifs de Scurit (EBIOS) - Section 2 - Approach. General Secretariat of National Defence Central Information Systems Security Division (DCSSI) (February 2004)
24. Sharp, H., Finkelstein, A., Galal, G.: Stakeholder identification in the requirements engineering process. In: DEXA Workshop, pp. 387–391 (1999)
25. Pouloudi, A.: Aspects of the stakeholder concept and their implications for information systems development. In: HICSS (1999)
26. Bundesamt für Sicherheit in der Informationstechnik (BSI): Standard 100-1 Information Security Management Systems (ISMS), Version 1.5 (2008)
27. BSI: IT-Grundschutz-Vorgehensweise. BSI standard 100-2, Bundesamt für Sicherheit in der Informationstechnik (BSI) (2008)
28. BSI: BSI Standard 100-4 Business Continuity Management, Version 1.0. BSI standard 100-4, Bundesamt für Sicherheit in der Informationstechnik (BSI) (2009)

29. BSI: Protection Profile for the Gateway of a Smart Metering System (Gateway PP). Version 01.01.01 (final draft), Bundesamt für Sicherheit in der Informationstechnik (BSI) - Federal Office for Information Security Germany, Bonn, Germany (2011), `https://www.bsi.bund.de/SharedDocs/Downloads/DE/BSI/SmartMeter/PP-SmartMeter.pdf?__blob=publicationFile`
30. Schwittek, W., Schmidt, H., Eicker, S., Heisel, M.: Towards a Common Body of Knowledge for Engineering Secure Software and Services. In: Proceedings of the International Conference on Knowledge Management and Information Sharing (KMIS), pp. 369–374. SciTePress - Science and Technology Publications (2011)
31. U.S. Department of Energy: A comparison of cross-sector cyber security standards. Technical report, Idaho National Laboratory (2005)
32. Siponen, M., Willison, R.: Information security management standards: Problems and solutions. Inf. Manage 46(5), 267–270 (2009)
33. Sommestad, T., Ericsson, G., Nordlander, J.: Scada system cyber security: A comparison of standards. In: 2010 IEEE Power and Energy Society General Meeting, pp. 1–8 (July 2010)
34. Phillips, T., Karygiannis, T., Kuhn, R.: Security standards for the rfid market. IEEE Security Privacy 3(6), 85–89 (2005)
35. Kuligowski, C.: Comparison of IT Security Standards. Technical report (2009), `http://www.federalcybersecurity.org/CourseFiles/WhitePapers/ISOvNIST.pdf`
36. NIST: A Comparison of the Security Requirements For Cryptographic Modules In FIPS 140-1 and FIPS 140-2. Nist special publication 800-29, National Institute of Standards and Technology (NIST), Gaithersburg, United States (2001) `http://csrc.nist.gov/publications/nistpubs/800-29/sp800-29.pdf`
37. HKSAR: An Overview of Information Security Standards. Technical report, The Government of the Hong Kong Special Administrative Region (HKSAR), Hong Kong, China (2008), `http://www.infosec.gov.hk/english/technical/files/overview.pdf`
38. Arora, V.: Comparing different information security standards: COBIT vs. ISO 27001. Technical report, Carnegie Mellon University, Qatar, United States (2010), `http://qatar.cmu.edu/media/assets/CPUCIS2010-1.pdf`

Appendix

A   Template for Security Standards

Table 14. Security Analysis Context and Preparation Part of the Template for Security Standard Description

Security Analysis Context and Preparation
Environment Description
  – Which essential parts of the environment have to be described? – How do relations between these parts have to be described? – What is the required abstraction level of the description?   **Relevant common terms:** *machine, environment*
Stakeholder Description
  – How are stakeholders defined? – Which relation to the machine is required to be a stakeholder? – Are there restrictions on stakeholders, e.g., do they have to be humans?   **Relevant common terms:** *stakeholder*
Asset Identification
  – How are assets identified? – Which relation does a stakeholder have to an asset? – Are assets categorized?   **Relevant common terms:** *asset*
Risk Level Definition
  – What kinds of risk levels are defined? – What is the required abstraction for these risk levels? – How do the risk levels relate to assets and stakeholders?

Table 15. Security Analysis Process Part of the Template for Security Standard Description

Security Analysis Process
Security Property Description
  – Do specific security goals have to be considered for assets, e.g., confidentiality? – Which further security properties are used and how are they defined? – What kind of methodology is required to elicit security goals?   **Relevant common terms:** security goal, availability, confidentiality, integrity
Control Assessment
  – How are existing security controls identified? – Is it mandatory to described the threats that existing controls mitigates? – Is it required to describe which assets an existing control protects?   **Relevant common terms:** security control
Vulnerability and Threat Analysis
  – What kind of attacker model does the standard consider? – Which activities does the standard demand for threat and vulnerability analysis? – When is the threat and vulnerability analysis complete?   **Relevant common terms:** attacker, vulnerability, threat
Risk Determination
  – How is risk defined e.g. as a product of likelihoods and consequences? – Is a process for risk management defined? – Is a qualitative or quantitative risk determination required?

Table 16. Security Analysis Product Part of the Template for Security Standard Description

Security Analysis Product
Security Assessment
<ul><li>How are controls selected?</li><li>Does a categorization exist for controls, e.g., types of threats the controls protect against?</li><li>Do relations between controls have to be considered, e.g., one control has a working access control as a precondition?</li></ul>**Relevant common terms:** security requirements, policies
Security Measures
<ul><li>What criteria are used to determine that a control is relevant to mitigate a particular threat?</li><li>Is there a demand to describe the improved protection these controls provide?</li><li>How is the reasoning done that the selected controls are sufficient and no further controls are required?</li></ul>**Relevant common terms:** security functions, policies
Risk Acceptance
<ul><li>How are acceptable risk levels defined?</li><li>Which kind of assessment determines that a security control reduces the risk to an acceptable risk?</li><li>What kind of review is required to ensure that the risk is acceptable?</li></ul>
Security and Risk Documentation
<ul><li>What methods are used to document the results e.g. templates, check lists?</li><li>What kind of documents are required for certification?</li><li>Can documents from other certifications be re-used?</li></ul>

Empirical Assessment of Security Requirements and Architecture: Lessons Learned

Riccardo Scandariato[2], Federica Paci[1], Le Minh Sang Tran[1],
Katsiaryna Labunets[1], Koen Yskout[2], Fabio Massacci[1], and Wouter Joosen[2]

[1] Università degli Studi di Trento, I-38100 Trento, Italy
[2] iMinds-DistriNet, KU Leuven, 3001 Leuven, Belgium

Abstract. Over the past three years, our groups at the University of
Leuven and the University of Trento have been conducting a number of
experimental studies. In particular, two common themes can be easily
identified within our work. First, we have investigated the value of several threat modeling and risk assessment techniques. The second theme
relates to the problem of preserving security over time, i.e., security
evolution. Although the empirical results obtained in our studies are
interesting on their own, the main goal of this chapter is to share our experience. The objective is to provide useful, hands-on insight on this type
of research work so that the work of other researchers in the community
would be facilitated. The contribution of this chapter is the discussion
of the challenges we faced during our experimental work. Contextually,
we also outline those solutions that worked out in our studies and could
be reused in the field by other studies.

Keywords: security, empirical research, requirements, software
architecture.

1 Introduction

Over the past three years, our groups at the University of Leuven and the University of Trento have been conducting a number of experimental studies. Given
the expertise of the two research groups, our work has focused on the early
phases of the software development life-cycle. In particular, the group in Trento
specializes in security requirements while the group in Leuven focuses on security in the architectural design. It is well-known that requirements and software
architecture have a close relationship and it is sometimes difficult to draw a
crisp separating line between these two development phases [1,2]. Therefore, our
empirical work is highly complementary and there are a number of touch points
between our respective studies.

In particular, two common themes can be easily identified within our work.
First, we both have investigated the value of several *threat modeling* and risk assessment techniques. Most of the textbooks on software security identify threat
modeling as one of the most important activities to identify security issues early

M. Heisel et al. (Eds.): Engineering Secure Future Internet Services, LNCS 8431, pp. 35–64, 2014.
© Springer International Publishing Switzerland 2014

Table 1. Empirical studies reported in this chapter

	Descriptive studies	Controlled experiments
Threat modeling	STRIDE [7]	CORAS vs. SREP [8]
Evolution	Requirements evolution in Si* [9]	Change Patterns [10]

on [3,4]. Moreover, those textbooks suggest to continue performing threat modeling at later stages, e.g., whenever the software system is refined. Several techniques for threat modeling have become well-known over the years and have been used in case studies. However, no rigorous, empirically-founded assessment has been performed prior to our own work. Overall, we have considered three techniques: Microsoft's STRIDE [3], CORAS [5], and SREP [6].

The second common theme relates to the problem of preserving security over time, i.e., *security evolution*. Many modern software systems are characterized by a long life and are subject to changes over time. On one hand, new functionality is often added to satisfy the changing nature of users' requirements and, consequently, the security mechanisms need to be updated. On the other hand, the assumptions initially made on the system's deployment environment also change (e.g., a new security threat emerges) and the security mechanisms need to adapt. Our research teams have assessed how well different requirements and design techniques provide support for evolving the security of a system over time. In particular, we have studied the Si^* security requirements evolution approach and the Change Patterns secure design technique.

As summarized in Table 1, this chapter reports on four empirical studies: two for each of the above mentioned themes. In the table we underscore a fundamental distinction in the type of studies. Controlled experiments are a well-known technique to compare two approaches. Typically, a number of participants (or subjects) are randomly divided in two 'treatment groups'. The two groups are assigned the same task, like, for instance, identify security requirements or design a software architecture. However, each group carries out the task by means of a different approach, which is often referred to as the 'treatment' in medical terminology. The results of the two groups are compared according to quantitative and qualitative criteria in order to understand which treatment performs better. An experiment is executed under controlled conditions so that, with high confidence, the differences in the outcomes are due to the treatments.

In a descriptive study, instead, there is only one treatment. That is, a single approach is tested under controlled conditions with the collaboration of the participants, which are assigned to a single group. The goal is to understand how the approach performs on average. While a typical research question in a controlled experiment could be "which approach is completed in shorter time?", in a descriptive study the question would be "how fast is the approach?".

Although the empirical results obtained in our studies are interesting on their own, the main goal of this chapter is to share our experience. The objective is to provide useful, hands-on insight on this type of research work so that the work of other researchers in the community would be facilitated. The *contribution* of this chapter is the discussion of the challenges we faced during our experimental work. Contextually, we also outline those solutions that worked out in our studies and could be reused in the field by other studies.

The rest of the chapter is organized as follows. Section 2 discusses the related work in the area of empirical studies applied to the early phases of the secure software development life-cycle. Sections 3 and 4 summarize the four studies that have been mentioned earlier. Sections 5 and 6 discuss the challenges and opportunities in this research area. Finally, Section 7 gives the concluding remarks.

2 Related Work

In this section we review the literature related to the empirical evaluation of threat modeling and security risk assessment methods and of approaches to requirements evolution.

2.1 Empirical Studies on Threats Modeling and Security Requirements

Organizations look to standards bodies for guidance on security best practices. In this respect there are many standards, practices, and methods available for security risk assessment and threat modeling, which differ in terms of focus and process. Therefore, there is the need of conducting experimental comparisons of existing methods and standards for security risk assessment and threat modeling to understand which are their main strengths and weaknesses and to guide their application by security professionals.

Despite the need of practical evidence of effectiveness of threat modeling and security risk assessment methods, little research has been devoted to understand whether existing methods are successful in practice.

Massacci et al. [11] reported the results of eRISE (engineering RIsk and SEcurity Requirements) challenge, an empirical study conducted in 2011 with 36 practitioners and 13 master students. The aim of the study was to compare the effectiveness of four academic methods for elicitation and analysis of threats and security requirements and to study their strengths and limitations. The participants were divided into groups composed by students and practitioners and were asked to identify the security requirements of a health care collaborative network using one of the methods under evaluation. The aim of eRISE challenge is similar to the one of the experiments reported in this chapter: assessing methods' effectiveness. However, in eRISE effectiveness is assessed using a qualitative approach through questionnaires, post-it notes and focus group interviews with the participants.

Threat modeling has been put to the test of empirical validation. Opdahl and Sindre compared misuse cases to attack trees, which represent a well-known technique based on brainstorming by security experts [12]. Their study involved 63 students and shows that attack trees might lead to a higher number of identified threats. However, the study did not evaluate the correctness of the identified threats. The participants did not show any preference with regard to the two techniques.

Diallo et al. assessed common criteria, misuse cases and attack trees by means of a comparative evaluation [13]. In a case study, the authors applied the three techniques andperformed an evaluation with respect to the ease of learning of each technique, the usability and the correctness of the results. Despite the limitations of this type of study (case study performed by the authors), the paper provides useful insights. For instance, the common criteria appears to be hard to learn and use, while attack tree misuse cases are easier.

Hogganvik et al. studied the role played by graphical models in the field of risk modeling [14–16]. The goal of these user studies was to optimize the representation in the diagrams that are used in CORAS (a risk analysis technique). The authors showed that the CORAS graphical notation provides advantages over UML.

No evaluation of the Microsoft STRIDE threat modeling technique has been performed so far. Dhillon has criticized STRIDE openly and compared it to an alternative, derivative technique that has been developed in-house [17]. Citing 30 industrial projects, the author reports that this technique is more time-efficient. However, the comparison is only anecdotal.

2.2 Empirical Studies on Requirements Evolution

There is little research that uses an empirical basis to understand the impact of requirements evolution, why and when it happens and to assess the effectiveness of methods to manage requirements change.

Villela et al. [18] present a quasi-experiment in the field of Ambient Assisted Living to study the adequacy and feasibility of PLEvo-Scoping method [19]. That method is based on a software evolution model to help requirements engineers and product managers identify the unstable features of an embedded system and their potential needed adaptations. It allows to identify and prioritize likely future adaptation needs and to select solutions to deal with them. Their quasi-experiment follows the Goal-Question-Metric template [20] and involves three kinds of roles: method expert, stakeholder, and domain expert. The quasi-experiment took place in the form of two two-day workshops where two groups consisting of three domain experts applied PLEvo-Scoping. The first part of each workshop was dedicated to the presentation of the application domain, and the quasi-experiments task. Both quantitative and qualitative measures were used to evaluate the adequacy and the feasibility of the method. However, due to the small number of subjects, the authors were not able to perform any statistical tests.

McGee and Greer [21] conducted a case study [22] to assess if a changed taxonomy proposed by the authors helps to understand the consequences of requirements change, why and when it happens. The study was conducted during the execution of a software development project in the government sector and involved 15 software developers and analysts. Data on requirements changes were collected during the different phases of the software development life cycle.

The quality of changes was assessed by a researcher and a project manager. The authors defined quantitative metrics to answer their research questions like the number of changes and the cost of changes and used hypothesis testing to evaluate the hypotheses related to their research questions.

Another study on requirements evolution by Herrmann et al. [23] is one of the pioneers in specifying the delta requirements without having to describe a complete system in details. Delta requirements refer to changes in requirements identified when comparing the as-is system with the system-to-be. Herrmann et al. investigate the applicability of TORE, a requirements engineering approach to identify delta requirements for an engineering tool. The study measures improvements in the as-is-analysis, the to-be-analysis, and the prioritization of requirements.

Maiden et al. [24–26], have presented several case studies in the Air Traffic Management (ATM) domain to validate RESCUE, a scenario-driven requirements engineering process. In the studies, the authors ran several creativity workshops with ATM experts with different expertise to study how RESCUE helps to discover stakeholder and system requirements. The workshops were organized in three main phases: a *training* phase about RESCUE, a *brainstorming* phase, and then an *application* phase where the experts applied RESCUE to discover requirements for different ATM tools. During the workshops, color-coded idea cards, post-it notes, A3 papers have been used to collect the results. The authors claimed that, although not all the workshop sessions were a success, the overall process definitely was – as it helped to set up a common understanding and facilitated the interaction among people involved.

3 Experiments on Threat and Risk Modeling

Threat modeling is recognized as one of the most important activities in software security. A threat modeling technique guides the security analyst to the discovery of the actions that a malicious agent (insider or outsider) might perform in order to misuse a software system. Threats are often referred to as anti-requirements and are an important driver for the definition of the security requirements of a system. Threat modeling can be used to analyze the soundness of software architectures and to spot flaws early on.

Several techniques to perform threat modeling have emerged. However, few empirical studies have been carried out to quantify the cost and effectiveness of these techniques. In the following sections we summarize the results from two studies. The first characterizes Microsoft's STRIDE, a technique that is commonly used in the industry. The second study compares two types of risk-based methods, namely visual and textual methods.

3.1 Assessing the STRIDE Approach[1]

Microsoft's STRIDE is a popular threat modeling technique commonly used to discover the security weaknesses of a software system. The interested reader can

---

[1] This sub-section contains excerpts from [7].

find a detailed description of STRIDE in the book of Howard and Lipner [3]. This section presents a descriptive study evaluating STRIDE by means of quantitative observations that have been performed in controlled, laboratory conditions in the context of a university course. The study involved 41 students (organized in 10 teams) in their last year of the master in computer science. Contrary to controlled experiments, in a descriptive study a phenomenon is characterized and no attempt is made to analyze the effects of variables on the phenomenon itself. This type of study was instrumental in order to understand a technique and eventually formulate research hypotheses to be further investigated by means of comparative experiments. Incisively, Grimes and Schulz portray descriptive studies as "the first scientific toe in the water in new areas of inquiry" [27].

The participants of the study were asked to perform the threat analysis of a medium-sized distributed system. The main goal of the study was to evaluate STRIDE by providing an answer to the following research questions:

RQ1: Productivity. *How many valid threats per hour are produced?*
RQ2: Correctness. *Is the number of incorrect threats small?*
RQ3: Completeness. *Is the number of overlooked threats small?*

Design of the Study. In the study, the participants analyzed a Digital Publishing System (DPS), which is a medium-scale distributed system developed in the context of an industry-oriented research project carried out in partnership with major news publishers in European countries. The main stakeholder of the system is a news publisher (like a company publishing newspapers) transitioning to Internet-based distribution channels. The main purpose of the system is (i) to support the journalists and the editors during the creation and the updating of a digital edition and (ii) to provide subscribed consumers on-line access to the editions, e.g., via e-paper terminals.

The participants were given a description of the above system (including the use cases and the architectural model in UML) and were requested to perform the STRIDE analysis of the DPS according to the four steps of STRIDE:

Step 1 Model the system by means of a DFD, which includes elements like external entities, processes, data flows and data stores.
Step 2 Map the DFD elements into the six threat categories of STRIDE (spoofing, tampering, repudiation, information disclosure, denial of service, elevation of privilege).
Step 3 Elicit the threats by means of the threat catalogs provided in [3].
Step 4 Document the elicited threats.

Prior to the study, the participants had been familiarized with the STRIDE technique by means of a series of three lectures. The study was conducted during a laboratory session of 4 hours. The assigned task was of a rather realistic size and certainly not a "toy example". Therefore, the students were expected to get started during the four laboratory hours and then complete the assignment (and compile the report) as homework. As the teams also worked outside the

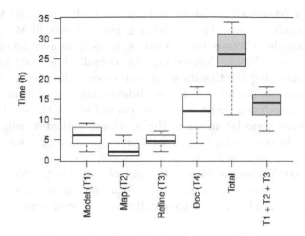

Fig. 1. Boxplot of time per STRIDE step

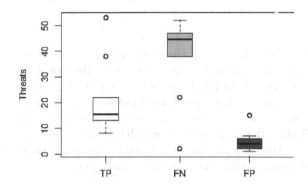

Fig. 2. True positives, false negatives and false positives by threat category

supervised laboratory hours, we asked them to track the time they spent on the project. The reports turned in by the teams were assessed by two security experts, which counted the number of correctly identified threats (true positives), the number of mistakenly reported threats (false positives), and the number of missing threats (false negatives). The experts compared their results, and in case of mismatches, they discussed until a consensus was reached. This happened in a very small number of cases (less than 4 % of the 260 threats reviewed).

Results. Fig. 1 reports the boxplot of the time spent by the participants in each of the four steps of the STRIDE methodology (see the white boxes). The gray boxes refer to the aggregate time. Fig. 2 reports the boxplot of the true positives (TP), false negative (FN) and false positives (FP) produced by the participants during the study.

The first research question refers to the *productivity* of the participants. We measured productivity as the ratio $\frac{TP}{TIME}$. Considering only the time spent in identifying (and not documenting) the threats, an average *productivity* of 1.8

threats per hour (standard deviation of 1.5) was to be expected for a system similar to the analyzed one. The confidence interval was [0.94, 3.25] threats per hour (one-sample Wilcoxon test). That is, it took an average of 33 minutes to identify a correct threat. Considering the overall time (i.e., including the time spent documenting the threats as misuse cases), the average productivity dropped to 0.9 threats per hour with a confidence interval of [0.48, 1.33].

The second research question refers to the *correctness* of the produced results. We measured correctness by means of the precision indicator, which is defined as $P = \frac{TP}{TP+FP}$. In our study, the average precision was 81% with a standard deviation of 11%.

The third research question refers to the *completeness* of the produced results. We measured completeness by means of the recall indicator, which is defined as $R = \frac{TP}{TP+FN}$. In our study, the average recall was 36% with a standard deviation of 25%.

In summary, the participants did not make too many mistakes (precision is quite high), but the number of overlooked threats was worrying (recall is quite low).

Threats to Validity. Concerning the conclusion validity, the time each team spent on the task was reported by the participants themselves. To prevent this threat, we kept reminding the participants to track the time they were spending on the assignment. Concerning the external validity, the main issue threatening the generalization of the results concerns the use of master students instead of professionals. Finally, the results might be influenced by the experimental object used in this study. For instance the results might not apply to other application domains or to systems of different size and complexity.

3.2   Empirical Comparison of Two Types of Risk-Based Methods[2]

This section reports a controlled experiment conducted with 28 master students to compare two classes of risk-based methods, visual methods (CORAS [5]) and textual methods (SREP [6]). CORAS is a visual method which consists of three tightly integrated parts, namely, a method for risk analysis, a language for risk modeling, and a tool to support the risk analysis process. The risk analysis in CORAS is a structured and systematic process which uses diagrams (see Fig. 3a) to document the result of the execution of each step. The Security Requirements Engineering Process (SREP) is an asset-based and risk-driven method for the establishment of security requirements in the development of secure Information Systems. The result of the execution of each step of the process is represented using tables or natural language (see Fig. 3b). For additional details about CORAS and SREP we refer the reader to [5, Chap. 3] and [6]. Note that, in the rest of the section, we denote with "security requirements" both the concepts "treatments" in CORAS and "security requirements" in SREP because they have the same

---

[2] This sub-section contains excerpts from [8].

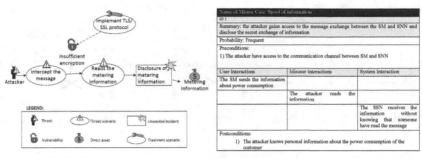

(a) CORAS - Threat Diagram   **(b)** SREP - Threat Specification using misuse cases

Fig. 3. Examples of Visual (CORAS) and Textual (SREP) Methods' Artifacts

semantics: they are both defined as a means to reduce the risk level associated with a threat.

The goal of the experiment was to evaluate the *effectiveness* of visual and textual methods, and the participants' *perception* of the methods. Hence, the dependent variables were the *effectiveness* of the methods measured as the number of threats and security requirements and the participants' *perceived ease of use*, *perceived usefulness* and *intention to use* of the two methods. The independent variable was the *method*. The experiment involved 28 participants: 16 students of the master in Computer Science and 12 students of the EIT ICT LAB master in Security and Privacy. They were divided into 16 groups using a randomized block design. Each group applied the two methods to identify threats and security requirements for different facets of a Smart Grid application scenario (ranging from security management to database security). The experiment was complemented with participants' interviews to gain insights on *why* the methods are effective or they are not.

We wanted to investigate the following research questions:

RQ1 *Is the effectiveness of the methods significantly different between the two types of methods?*

RQ2 *Does the effectiveness of the methods vary with the assigned tasks?*

RQ3 *Is the participants' preference of the method significantly different between the two types of methods?*

RQ4 *Is the participants' perceived ease of use of the method significantly different between the two types of methods?*

RQ5 *Is the participants' perceived usefulness of the method significantly different between the two types of methods?*

RQ6 *Is the participants' intention to use the method significantly different between the two types of methods?*

Design of the Study. Participants of the experiments were recruited among master students enrolled in the Security Engineering course at the University

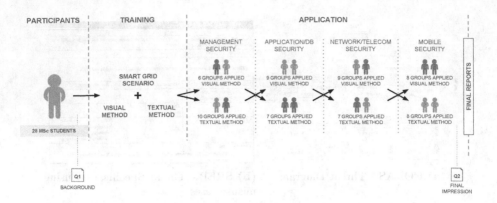

Fig. 4. Experimental Procedure

of Trento. The participants had no previous knowledge of the methods under evaluation. A within-subject design where all participants apply both methods was chosen to ensure a sufficient number of observations to produce significant conclusions. In order to avoid learning effects, the participants had to identify threats and mitigations for different types of security facets of a Smart Grid application scenario. The Smart Grid is an electricity network that can integrate in a cost-efficient manner the behavior and actions of all users connected to it like generators, and consumers. They use information and communication technologies to optimize the transmission and distribution of electricity from suppliers to consumers.

The experiment was performed during the Security Engineering course held at the University of Trento from September 2012 to January 2013. The participants were divided into 16 groups so that each group applied the visual method (CORAS) to exactly two facets and the textual method (SREP) to the remaining two facets. For each facet, the method to be applied by the groups was randomly

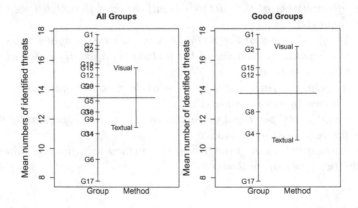

Fig. 5. Means of identified threats in all groups (left) and good groups (right)

Table 2. Post Task Questionnaire

QN	Type	Left statement	1 2 3 4 5	Right statement
Q1	PEOU	I found X hard to use	○ ○ ○ ○ ○	I found X easy to use
Q2	PU	X made the security analysis easier than an ad hoc approach	○ ○ ○ ○ ○	X made the security analysis harder than an ad hoc approach
Q3	PEOU	X was difficult to master	○ ○ ○ ○ ○	X was easy to master
Q4	ITU	If I need to identify threats and security requirements in a future project course, I would not use X	○ ○ ○ ○ ○	If I need to identify threats and security requirements in a future project course I would use X
Q5	PU	I would have found threats and security requirements more quickly using common sense	○ ○ ○ ○ ○	X made me find threats and security requirements more quickly than using common sense
Q6	ITU	If I need to identify threats and security requirements in a future project at work, I would avoid X if possible	○ ○ ○ ○ ○	If I need to identify threats and security requirements in a future project at work, I would use X if possible
Q7	PEOU	I was often confused about how to apply X to the problem	○ ○ ○ ○ ○	I was never confused about how to apply X to the problem
Q8	PU	X made the search for threats and security requirements less systematic	○ ○ ○ ○ ○	X made the search for threats and security requirements more systematic
Q9	ITU	If a company Im employed by in the future discusses what technique to introduce for early security analysis argue and someone suggests X, I would against that	○ ○ ○ ○ ○	If a company Im employed by in the future discusses what technique to introduce for early security analysis and someone suggests X, I would support that
Q10	PEOU	X will be easy to remember (in case I must use it again in the future)	○ ○ ○ ○ ○	X will be hard to remember (in case I must use it again in the future)
Q11	PU	X made me less productive in finding threats and security requirements	○ ○ ○ ○ ○	X made me more productive in finding threats and security requirements
Q12	ITU	If working as a freelance consultant for a customer who needs help finding security threats and security requirements to his software, I would not use X in discussions with that customer	○ ○ ○ ○ ○	If working as a freelance consultant for a customer who needs help finding security threats and security requirements to his software, I would like to use X in discussions with that customer
Q13	Control	X process is well detailed	○ ○ ○ ○ ○	X process is not well detailed
Q14	Control	A catalog of threats would have made the identification of threats easier with X	○ ○ ○ ○ ○	A catalog of threats would have made the identification of threats harder with X
Q15	Control	A catalog of security requirements would have made the identification of security requirements easier with X	○ ○ ○ ○ ○	A catalog of security requirements would have made the identification of security requirements harder with X
Q16	Control	X helped me in brainstorming on the threats for the tasks	○ ○ ○ ○ ○	X did not help me in brainstorming on the threats for the tasks
Q17	Control	X helped me in brainstorming on the security requirements for the tasks	○ ○ ○ ○ ○	X did not help me from brainstorming on the security requirements for the tasks
Q18*	Tool	CORAS tool is hard to use	○ ○ ○ ○ ○	CORAS tool is easy to use

* - This question is asked only in the questionnaire about CORAS

determined. The facets differed in the security tasks for which the groups had to identify threats and security requirements. The security facets included Security Management (Mgmnt), Application/Database Security (App/DB), Network/Telecommunication Security (Net/Teleco), and Mobile Security (Mobile). For example, in the App/DB facet, groups had to identify application and database security threats like cross-site scripting or aggregation attacks and propose mitigations. Fig. 4 illustrates the experimental procedure.

The post-task questionnaire was adapted from the questionnaire reported in [12] which was inspired to the Technology Acceptance Model (TAM) [28]. The questionnaire is reported in Table 2.

Results. In this subsection we present the main findings regarding each of the research questions and possible explanations for the findings.

Methods' effectiveness To assess the effectiveness of visual and textual methods, the final reports delivered by the groups were coded by the researchers to count the number of threats and security requirements. An expert on security of the Smart Grid was asked to assess the quality of the threats and security requirements. The level of quality was evaluated on a four item scale: *Unclear* (1), *Generic* (2), *Specific* (3) and *Valuable* (4).

Based on this scale, the groups who got an assessment *Valuable* or *Specific* were classified as *good groups* because they produced threats and security requirements of good quality. On the contrary, the groups who were assessed *Generic* or *Unclear* were considered as not so good (bad) groups.

Fig. 5 and Fig. 6 show the means of identified threats and security requirements in all groups and good groups.

The results of report analysis showed that visual method was more effective in identifying threats than textual method and this was statistically significant for all groups (ANOVA test returned $F = 18.49$, *p-value* $= 1.03 \cdot 10^{-4}$) and good groups ($F = 26.10$, *p-value* $= 1.59 \cdot 10^{-4}$). This result was also confirmed when we considered the *number of threats* identified with visual and textual methods across the task assigned to the groups (ANOVA test returned a p-value $2.78 \cdot 10^{-3}$ ($F = 9.95$)). Since the difference in the number of threats identified by the two methods was statistically significant, we could positively answer $RQ1$ and $RQ2$ in part related to threat identification. Instead, with respect to *a*

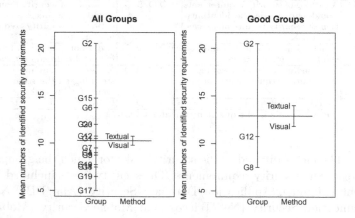

Fig. 6. Means of identified security requirements in all groups (left) and good groups (right)

number of security requirements, textual method was slightly more effective than the visual one in identifying security requirements, but the difference was not statistically significant across all groups ($F = 1.18$, *p-value* $= 0.28$) and tasks ($F = 10.66$, *p-value* $= 1.79 \cdot 10^{-3}$). The research questions $RQ1$ and $RQ2$ with respect to the security requirements identification could be answered negatively.

Methods' perception To test participants' responses on post-task questionnaire we used the exact Wilcoxon signed-ranks test with Wilcoxon method for handling ties [29]. We set the significance level α to 0.05. The results of the analysis showed that participants' *overall preference* is higher for visual method than for textual one. Among all the groups the difference had 10% significance level, while for the participants who were part of groups who produced good quality threats and security requirements, the difference in the overall preference was statistically significant. The conclusion was that the null hypothesis H_3 of no difference in the overall preference of the two methods was not upheld. Similarly, for all participants, there was no statistically significant difference in *perceived ease of use* and *usefulness*, while for "good" participants the difference had a 10% significance level. For this reason, the research questions $RQ4$ and $RQ5$ remained open. With respect to *intention to use*, "good" participants intended to use more visual than textual method and the difference in participants' perception was statistically significant. The research question $RQ6$ could be answered positively, i.e., there was a difference in the participants' intention to use of the methods.

Qualitative Explanation The different number of threats and security requirements identified with visual and textual methods could be likely explained by the differences between the two methods indicated by the participants during the interviews. Diagrams in visual method helped brainstorming on the threats because they gave an overview of the possible threats (who initiates the threats), the threat scenarios (possible attacks) and the assets, while the identification of threats in textual method was not facilitated by the use of tables because it was difficult to keep the link between assets and threats. As suggested by the answers to question $Q14$ in the post-task questionnaire, the identification of threats in textual method could be made easier if a catalog of common threats was available. In addition, during the interviews some of the participants indicated that a visual representation of threats was better than a tabular one.

Textual method was slightly more effective in eliciting security requirements than visual approach because the order of steps in the textual method process guides the analyst in the identification of security requirements, while the same it seemed not to hold for the visual method's process.

Threats to Validity. The main threats to the validity of our studies were related to *bias in subjects' training* and to *bias in methods' effectiveness*. Differences in the methods' performance may occur if a method was presented in a better way than the other. In our experiment we limited this threat by giving the same structure and the same duration to the tutorials on textual and visual methods. To avoid bias in the evaluation of effectiveness of the two methods, the coding of the participants' reports was conducted by the authors of the paper independently. In addition, the quality of the threats and security requirements identified by each group was assessed by an expert external to the experiment.

4 Experiments on Software Evolution

Supporting evolution in a principled way is becoming of uttermost importance for larger and larger classes of software systems. Modern software systems are continuously updated in their functionality and seamlessly re-deployed. For instance, mobile applications and cloud-based applications provide a good example of this type of continuous development. Obviously, evolution and adaptation pose a challenge to the soundness of the security posture of a changed software. Therefore, some software engineering techniques have emerged to deal with the impact of change on security. We evaluated two of these approaches.

4.1 Assessing Requirements Evolution [3]

In this section we present the results of an empirical evaluation, which aimed to assess the *effectiveness* of a requirements engineering approach [30, 31] in modeling requirements evolution and whether the effectiveness depends on the analyst's level of knowledge of the approach and of the application domain.

Requirements Evolution in Si^* Modeling Language. Here we sketch an approach to deal with requirements evolution and its uncertainty [30, 31]. In this approach, evolution was captured by two kinds of *evolution rules*: *observable rules* and *controllable rules*. The former captures different possibilities that a requirements model before evolution happens − *before model* − could evolve into other models after evolution happens − *after models* − with different levels of uncertainty − *evolution probabilities*. The latter captures different design alternatives of both *before* models and *after* models.

Example 1 (Before Model). Figure 7 presents an excerpt of the goal model [4] − a requirements model in Si^* language − for the Sector Team who are in charge of managing the arrival sequence of aircrafts at the airport. Their top goal is to have the arrival sequence managed (goal g_1). For this goal, they want to have the arrival sequence optimally generated (goal g_2), and to deliver this sequence to aircrafts (goal g_3). In order to achieve g_3, they have to prepare the advisories for aircrafts by themselves (goal g_4), and deliver these advisories to aircrafts (goal g_5).

---

[3] This sub-section contains excerpts from [9].
[4] Note that this model is kept simple for illustrative purposes.

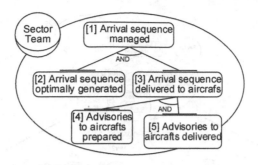

Fig. 7. An excerpt of the goal model for the Sector Team

Example 2 (Evolution Rules). We now illustrate how the Sector Team's goal model in Figure 7 can evolve due to the introduction of a new tool, namely Arrival Manager (AMAN). We focus on goal g_3: *"Arrival sequence delivered to aircrafts"*. We call *Before* the sub-model rooted at g_3. Figure 8 represents one observable rule and one controllable rule. The observable rule consists of three *evolution branches* (i.e., evolution possibilities): each branch corresponds to the arrow that links the before model *Before* to one of the after models *After1*, *After2* and *Before*. In the first evolution possibility, g_4 is delegated to AMAN. This dependency is presented by the line labeled with **De** connecting goal g_4 to the actor AMAN. The actor AMAN satisfies g_4 by either g_9: *"Basic advisory generator"*, or by g_{10}: *"Detail advisory generator"*. The probability that this possibility becomes true is 0.35. In the second evolution possibility, *Before* might evolve into *After2* where a new goal g_{11}: *"Detail advisories to aircrafts prepared"* replaces g_4. The g_{11} is also delegated to AMAN, and it is fulfilled by g_{10}: *"Detail advisory generator"*. The probability that this possibility occurs is 0.4. The third evolution possibility is that the model *Before* does not change with probability 0.25.

The controllable rule is represented by the OR-decomposition of g_4 into goals g_9 and g_{10} in *After1*. This rule has only two branches corresponding to the branches of the OR-decomposition.

Research Questions and Hypotheses. Following the Goal-Question-Metric template [20], the goal of our studies was to assess if the method proposed in [30, 31] is effective in capturing potential requirements changes and whether *effectiveness* is influenced by knowledge of the domain or the method itself. Given the goal of our research, we wanted to answer the following research questions:

RQ_1 *Is the approach effective in modeling requirements evolution?*
RQ_2 *How is the effectiveness of the approach impacted by domain knowledge and method knowledge?*

We borrowed the definition of *effectiveness* from the Method Evaluation Model proposed by Moody [32] where the effectiveness of a method was defined as how well it achieves its objectives. We used the following variables that correspond

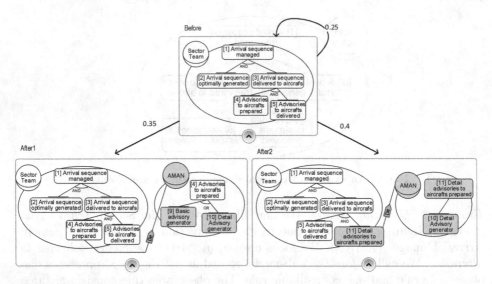

The rectangles with label on top are the containers of *before* and *after* models. The label is the name of the contained model. Each container has a chevron at the bottom to collapse/expand its content. The arrows labeled with probability connecting two containers indicate that the source model evolves into the target model.

Fig. 8. The graphical representation of the observable rule for goal g_3

to the main characteristics of evolution rules, which represent the main outcome of the method's application:

- *size of baseline.* It is the number of unique model elements and interconnections in the before model of an observable rule.
- *size of change.* It is the number of unique model elements and interconnections across all after models that are not in the before model or disappeared from the before model of an observable rule.
- *number of evolution rules.*
- *number of branches for evolution rules.*

To investigate the second research question RQ_2, we used as control variables the method knowledge and the domain knowledge of subjects participating in our studies. We also defined the following set of null hypotheses $H_{n.m.0}$: n denotes the research question to which the hypothesis is related, m denotes the progressive hypothesis number, and 0 denotes that it is a null hypothesis.

$H_{2.1.0}$ *There is no difference in the size of baseline identified by researchers, practitioners and master students.*

$H_{2.2.0}$ *There is no difference in the size of changes identified by researchers, practitioners and master students.*

$H_{2.3.0}$ *There is no difference in the number of evolution rules identified by researchers, practitioners and master students.*

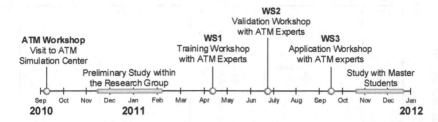

Fig. 9. Chronology of the family of empirical studies

$H_{2.4.0}$ *There is no difference in the number of branches for evolution rules identified by researchers, practitioners and master students.*

Experiment Design. Figure 9 summarizes how our empirical studies developed along a two-year horizon. We conducted three empirical studies with participants having different levels of knowledge of the modeling approach and of the application domain. First, we ran a preliminary study where the participants were the same researchers who proposed the approach: the researchers had a good knowledge of the approach but were domain ignorant. Second, we conducted a study with domain experts (also referred to as ATM experts, or practitioners) who were novice to the approach, but had a very good knowledge of the ATM domain. Third, we conducted a study with master students who were method and domain ignorant (i.e., they had no prior knowledge of the approach and of the ATM domain).

Study 1: Preliminary Study within the Research Group. Three researchers participated in the study. The researchers first gained the domain knowledge in the ATM workshop (Sep 2010, Figure 9). The researchers then identified evolution and produced Si^* models (both *before* and *after* models) for three scenarios related to the ATM domain.

Study 2: Workshops with ATM experts. The study was organized into three separated workshops: WS1, WS2 and WS3, see Figure 9. The workshops involved both researchers and ATM experts. The training workshop (WS1) trained the ATM experts about the modeling approach. The validation workshop (WS2) focused on the evaluation of the quality of the models and the evolution rules drawn by the researchers. The application workshop (WS3) asked ATM experts to apply the approach by drawing an original model and one possibility of the evolution model. Due to the limited time availability of the participants, the application phase did not terminate with the third workshop, but continued remotely over a three-month period going from September to November 2011.

Study 3: Study with Master Students. Eleven students enrolled in the Master in Computer Science at the University of Trento participated in the study. Students were trained about the approach for evolving requirements (by giving lectures), and were introduced to the ATM scenarios (by giving documents). Students were

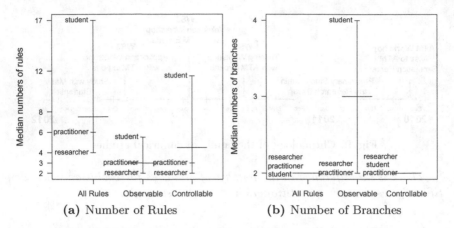

(a) Number of Rules   (b) Number of Branches

Fig. 10. Number of Rules and Branches for Participants Type

diveded into four groups. Each group worked on different scenarios, which are
related to the ATM domain, to identify and model evolution.

Data Analysis and Results. We collected the artifacts produced by researchers, practitioners and students. Researchers, practitioners and students
were able to produce requirements models of medium size and identify new
requirements associated with evolution scenarios. The quality of models by researchers and students were assessed by an ATM expert in terms of requirements
and identified evolution. All produced models were qualified with good quality;
the identified evolution rules are qualified as specific to the scenarios. Since the
number and the quality of the requirements model and evolution rules identified
by the participants were reasonably good, we can conclude that the proposed
framework is effective in modeling requirements evolution.

We compared the difference in the number of evolution rules and number of
branches for evolution rules across the different type of participants.
Figure 10a shows the median of the number of evolution rules by participants,
and Figure 10b reports the median of the number of branches. Students produced significantly more evolution rules than researchers and practitioners, who
produced around the same number of rules. The same holds if we consider the
number of controllable rules, but not the number of observable rules.

We then compared the size of baseline and size of changes identified by researchers, practitioners and students. Figure 11a shows that researchers sketched
requirement models of lower size but considered changes of small, medium and big
size. Similarly, practitioners produced a single big requirement model and changes
of similar complexity of researchers. Students produced two different kinds of artifacts: some group of students produced small models and small changes; other
groups identified one big model and changes of increasing complexity like practitioners. However, Figure 11b shows that there was no difference in the size of
changes identified by researchers, practitioners, and students. We checked with

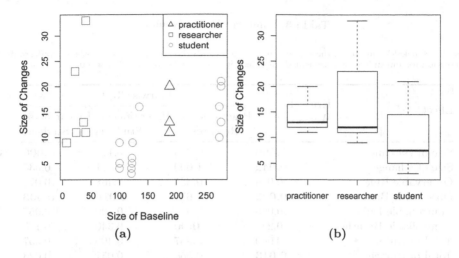

Fig. 11. Size of Baseline and Size of Changes for Type of Participants

Kruskal-Wallis test if these results were statistically significant. The results are summarized in the second column of Table 3. These results were confirmed by the pairwise comparison that we ran with Wilcoxon rank-sum test as shown in the last three columns of Table 3. In these tables, bold values indicate significant difference among the participants.

With respect to the hypotheses, we could conclude that the hypothesis $H_{2.1.0}$ was rejected because there was a significant difference in the size of baseline ($p-value \approx 0$ for Kruskal-Wallis test, and $p-value \approx 0$ for the pair researchers–students). The hypothesis $H_{2.2.0}$ was inconclusive because a significant difference in the size of change was shown in the Kruskal-Wallis test ($p-value = 0.04$) but not in the pairwise test (all $p-value(s) > 0.017$). The hypothesis $H_{2.3.0}$ was accepted because there was no significant difference in the observable rule, controllable rule, and total of rules. The last hypothesis $H_{2.4.0}$ was rejected for the observable branches because the Kruskal-Wallis test gave the $p-value = 0.002$, and the pairwise test gave the $p-value = 0.016$ (practitioners–researchers) and $p-value = 0.003$ (researchers–students), but non conclusive for controllable branches and total of branches.

Threats to Validity. A main threat is *low statistical power*. The size of our sample was too small to have a power of 0.80. Therefore, it would be necessary to run the experiment again with more subjects for each user's cohorts - researchers, practitioners and students. Another relevant threat was represented by a communication gap between the research team and the domain experts. The research team and domain experts might use the same terms with different meanings and this could lead to misunderstandings; therefore, wrong or unrelated feedback might be provided. To mitigate this threat we included a *"mediator"* who occasionally reformulated questions of the research team for the domain experts and reformulated domain experts' feedback to the researchers.

Table 3. Summary of test results

For the Kruskal-Wallis tests, the significant level $\alpha = 0.05$. For the pairwise tests, the Bonferroni-correction for multiple comparisons, the modified significant level α' is $0.05/3 = 0.017$.

Effect	Kruskal-Wallis test	Pairwise-Test		
		Practitioners–Researchers	Practitioners–Students	Researchers–Students
Size of Baseline	**0.000**	0.025	0.171	**0.000**
Size of Change	**0.042**	1.000	0.111	0.035
Observable Rule	0.098	0.637	0.468	0.074
Observable Branches	**0.002**	0.637	**0.016**	**0.003**
Controllable Rule	0.060	0.637	0.400	0.057
Controllable Branches	0.246	**0.00**	0.340	0.175
Total of Rules	0.060	0.637	0.400	0.057
Total of Branches	**0.013**	0.556	0.051	0.023

4.2   Assessing Co-Evolution[5]

Change has a multi-level impact, where change in the requirements analysis reaches down to the run-time configuration of systems. As illustrated by Mens et al. [33], achieving co-evolution between different types of software artifacts is a challenging task that is still open to seminal research. Intuitively, some artifacts expose a tighter relationship vis-a-vis change. That is, they co-evolve in ways that go beyond a generic, imprecise ripple effect. In particular, the interdependency of requirements and software architecture is known in the literature [1]: changing one will likely affect the other. Change Patterns are an approach to deal with the co-evolution of requirements and architecture in a precise and practical way.

Change Patterns. In general, a change pattern is a reusable source of knowledge concerning the co-evolution of two related artifacts. The changes in a given artifact (e.g., the requirements) are characterized via a change scenario. In order to cope with this change, a change pattern provides guidance about how to transform the second artifact (e.g., the architecture). The guidance provides a principled way of executing a model transformation that fulfills certain constraints, e.g., the minimization of the architectural impact.

A generic kind of change at the requirements level is captured by means of a *change scenario*, which consists of a pair of requirements templates that describe, in a generic way, the situations before and after the anticipated change. To interpret a scenario in the context of a concrete system, a binding needs to be defined in order to link a requirements template to that system's requirements model.

The pattern provides a collection of *architecture-level solutions* that enable the system to respond to the change, while minimizing the effort required to

---

[5] This sub-section contains excerpts from [10].

evolve the architecture. Additionally, the principled solutions suggested by a change pattern aim at reducing the impact (in terms of disruptive change) of the evolution. This is important when the system that evolves has already been deployed, and recalling the system to carry on major changes to the architecture is prohibitive.

Example. Consider a crisis management system (CMS). When an eyewitness of a traffic accident calls the crisis management center, an operator answers the call. Based on the information provided by the caller, the operator locates the position of the accident and enters it into the system. An available coordinator is assigned to the accident and handles the situation by starting a sequence of missions, like transporting the injured to the hospital, redirecting traffic, and towing the vehicle.

In this system, a possible change scenario could be that the stakeholders want to have the possibility to switch their custom geocoding application (to translate the location information provided by the witnesses to GPS coordinates) to a more powerful geocoding system, which will likely be offered by an external party in the future. The (simplistic) scenario is represented in the top part of Fig. 12 by means of the Si^* notation, which has been introduced previously. The solution (in the lower part of the figure) suggests to prepare the architecture by adding an adaptation layer (proxy), so that the switch-over to the external service has less impact.

Experiment and Hypotheses. To validate the efficiency of the change patterns approach, a controlled experiment was devised. For the experiment, the master students of a course on software architecture at KU Leuven were enrolled. In summary, we divided a total of 12 participants into two equally sized groups. The participants were given the two evolution scenarios described in Table 4. For each scenario, the first group (treatment group) had to prepare the architecture of the CMS system (described above) for the upcoming evolution, using the change patterns. Then, they had to evolve the architecture according to the change patterns approach, so that the changed requirements in the scenario were fully supported. The second group (control group) carried out the same assignment consisting of the same scenarios, but used common software engineering knowledge instead of the change patterns.

The goal was to understand whether the change patterns approach gives an overall competitive edge and if the effort in the evolution phase is reduced. Therefore, the following two *null hypotheses* were formulated:

H_0' The combined effort of preparing (T1) and evolving (T2) the architecture is the same in the control group and the treatment group.
H_0'' The effort to evolve (T2) the architecture is the same in the control group and the treatment group.

Each participant attended two lab sessions in total. In Lab 1, the participants were given the Si^* model for the system. The assignment was asking the

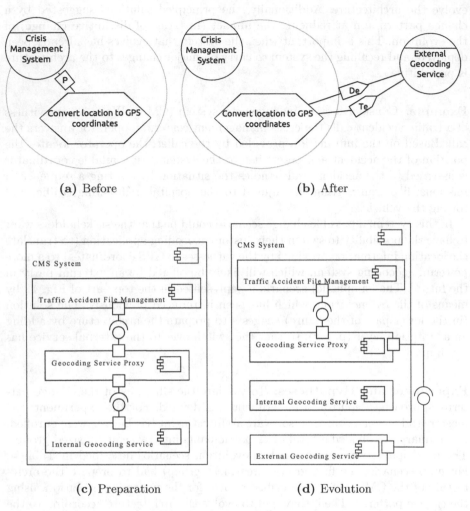

(a) Before

(b) After

(c) Preparation

(d) Evolution

Fig. 12. A change scenario

participant to prepare the architecture according to the tasks in Table 4. They performed the tasks sequentially. The order of the tasks for each participant, however, was randomized. The students had to complete the assignment using both lab hours and homework, while preparing a lab report on their actions and rationale.

In Lab 2, the participants were asked to execute the evolution phase for the change scenarios. The participants had to reuse the architecture they prepared in Lab 1. They performed the tasks sequentially but the order of the tasks for each participant was randomized. Again, the students had to complete the assignment using both lab hours and home work. They turned in a lab report before the exam period started.

Table 4. Change scenarios

Scenario	Description
A	Over time, some service providers (e.g., the towing services) may no longer perform their assigned missions correctly. To avoid liability problems, the architecture should be designed such that these liability issues can be resolved if they occur.
B	The police shares its availability information with the crisis management center, without restrictions. The representatives of the police have the fear that this sensitive information might be abused. In the future some stronger guarantee should be put in place.

The tasks entailed the modification of UML and Si^* models. To this aim, a tailored tool was provided to the participants. The tool integrated with Eclipse (Helios release) the Si^* tool [34] and the Topcased UML editor [35]. The tool was instrumented to keep track of the modification to the models executed by the participants and the time they spent on each task. The tool had a "pause" button that the participant could press when taking a break. Further, the participants were asked to work exclusively via the tool. For instance, the use of pen and paper for drafting was discouraged. The rationale for this request was to make the measure more accurate.

The study was semi-supervised. The students were fully supervised during lab hours and, for instance, the instructors were taking care that the tool was used at all times and that the pause button was pressed during breaks. However, the students had to complete the assignments during homework. They used the tool at home as well, but we had to trust that they were following the above instructions.

Results. The analysis of the data revealed that there are some outliers. Because of the already limited sample size, however, these points were retained. However, since outliers were present, it was more meaningful to report the median value rather than the mean, as it was less biased by extreme values. Due to the limited sample size, the non-parametric two-tailed Mann-Whitney-Wilcoxon was used as location test. Table 5 gives the median values for $T2$ and $T1 + T2$.

Table 5. Descriptive and test statistics

Median effort in minutes	$T2$		$T1 + T2$	
	Scenario A	Scenario B	Scenario A	Scenario B
Control group	49.26	41.80	68.10	89.97
Treatment group	21.22	42.42	53.47	61.86
p-value	0.240	0.699	0.485	0.589

In summary, the treatment group performed better than the control group in terms of overall effort (H'_0). For the treatment group using change patterns, the median of $T1 + T2$ was 21% smaller for scenario A and 31% smaller for scenario B. For H''_0, the effort spent in the evolution phase $(T2)$ in the experiment was about the same (for scenario B) or 57% lower (scenario A).

The results of the 2-tailed Mann-Whitney-Wilcoxon test are shown in the second-last row of Table 5. Statistical significance $(p < 0.05)$ was never achieved. Hence, the null hypotheses could not be rejected.

Threats to Validity. The subjects were not familiar with all the technologies that were used in the experiment (in particular, the Si^* notation). This may have negatively influenced their performance.

The main issue threatening the generalization of the results concerns the use of master students instead of professionals. However, it is generally advised to test new theories starting with students via exploratory studies [36,37]. Further, Runeson observes that the differences can be small between graduate students (our case) and professionals [38].

The tasks are also of a small size with respect to real-world design endeavors. Larger tasks require more time for the experiment execution, and loosen the control on the experiment itself.

5 Challenges and Lessons Learned

Our studies highlighted a number of aspects that should be considered when designing an empirical study because, as they may introduce threats to the validity.

Students as Subjects? In our studies, we used students as subjects rather than practitioners, which was known as a major threat to external validity. We mitigated this threat by using master students enrolled in a course on software security or in a software engineering course with a strong focus on security. Further, the topic of the empirical study was well integrated with the syllabus of the hosting course. This allowed us to rely on students with the required expertise in security and to ensure that they had the same level of knowledge on the subject.

Which Applications? In a typical study set up, we asked the participants to apply an approach on a given application (the so-called object). Hence, another important aspect referred to the selection of the scenario to be analyzed by the participants during the study. Indeed, a lack of understanding of the application scenario may introduce bias in the effectiveness of the studied methodologies. In our studies, we chose realistic scenarios like ATM, a content management system, or a smart metering infrastructure. However, it was difficult to determine which was the right amount of information to be provided to the participants so that they could gain a good understanding of the application scenario.

Some subjects complained that they had not enough information to understand the application domain, others complained that there was too much information. A possible solution that we adopted in our studies was to have a domain expert who introduced the participants to the application scenario and is available (physically or remotely) during the study to provide any additional information missing in the scenario description. An alternative solution if a domain expert could not be involved was to select an application scenario that was very familiar to the students, like a banking system or a hospital system. When the study was embedded in a course, it was also useful to let the students get gradually acquainted with the application scenario during the course and prior to the study itself. In any case, the scenario description should cover at least the following aspects: humans involved and their roles with respect to the system, physical equipment, services and functionalities provided by the system, information and computational assets, communication channels, and operational scenarios (possibly with model diagrams). In order to make the results of the studies more comparable (or repeatable), it could be useful to develop the documentation of reference application scenarios and to make it publicly available.

What Is More Secure? Another aspect to consider is how to evaluate the effectiveness of the methodologies under evaluation. A methodology is effective based on the quality of the results that it produces. If we consider just the number of results (e.g., number of threats identified) but not the quality, threats to conclusion validity may arise. In our studies, we followed two approaches to evaluate the quality of methodologies' outcomes. They both require the involvement of security experts. In the first approach, we asked the security experts to produce a reference solution for the task that is given to the participants. This solution was used as a yardstick to objectively assess the correctness and completeness of results of the participants. We successfully applied this approach in the descriptive study of Section 3.1. Of course, the quality of the reference solution must be flawless. To this aim, we employed multiple experts, where each expert prepared a reference solution independently, compared the results to those of other experts and, finally, came to an agreement on what the final solution should have looked like. The second approach requires a panel of security experts that directly evaluate the results the subjects have produced. In order to even out the discrepancies of opinions that might emerge among the experts, we resorted to either majority voting or consensus after discussion. In any case, it is important to keep track of the number of diverging assessments and to report them, if possible. For instance, in case of voting, it is useful to compute the inter-rater agreement statistic (Cohen's kappa).

What Is the Ideal Length of a Study? Most experiments in the literature have a duration of about two hours. Clearly, a study that can be executed in the turn of one lab session has some advantages. First, the whole study can be closely supervised in order to avoid that the participants share information. Further, it can be easier to measure the outcome (e.g., time) in a precise and reliable way. However, if the duration of the experiment is too short for the subjects to understand the application scenario and to apply the methodologies under evaluation, there may be bias in the evaluation. Subjects may produce bad results not because a methodology is not effective but rather because the time for training was not sufficient. To avoid this threat, it is important to schedule enough time dedicated to the training of the participants and to 'warm them up', e.g., by letting them apply the methodologies under evaluation on a simple example (before the actual study begins). Further, if the time for the execution of the study is short, it is impossible to use a realistically-sized application scenario. Hence, the methodologies under evaluation are applied to toy applications and the results might not generalize to real-world scenarios.

How to Collect the Measurements? In a quantitative study, the accuracy of the measurements is key. However, if the task assigned to the participants is large, it is necessary to 'spread' the study over a longer period of time and multiple lab sessions. In this case, the experimenters must rely on the diligence of the participants when these are working at home on their task (and, for instance, they must keep track the effort they spent on the task). In general, it is acceptable to rely on self-reported measures for some of the parameters. However, the experimenters need to provide some level of tool support, which facilitates the tracking of the necessary parameters on the side of the participants. For instance, in our experiments we routinely resorted to simple and seamless time-sheeting tools whenever we asked the participants to track their own effort. If the number of participants is large and the study spans a longer time (than a single lab), it is beneficial to invest in the development of more advanced, ad-hoc tools for the measurement of the participant activity. In one case, for instance, we modified the tool that the participants were supposed to use in order to apply the methodology. This way, the measurements were very accurate and completely un-intrusive from the participant's perspective.

How to Overcome Language Gaps? Another interesting lesson concerns the language gap among participants. The level of engagement of the subjects depends on two main factors: the means to provide feedback, and the language in which such feedback needs to be provided. Some of our studies included participants of different nationalities (e.g., from Italy, France and some African countries) who sometimes had difficulties to understand the tasks they had to undertake during the experiment. Also, they faced difficulties in providing feedback to the experimenters about their perception of the methodologies under evaluation. A possible solution is that the subjects can discuss in their mother tongue language and then provide summary feedback in English, but this hampers the immediacy of the feedback, and "minority opinions" might not be reported (we noticed this phenomenon during our studies). The alternative solution is to have a mediator who occasionally reformulates questions of the research team for the subjects and reformulates subjects' feedback to the researchers.

6   A Roadmap for Future Research

Given the limited reach of existing results in the area of empirical secure software engineering, there is a lot of room for novel research. In this section, we outline some interesting research themes that lend themselves to an empirical approach. It is not our intention to be complete or exhaustive. Rather, we try to focus on the most promising research questions that have the potential, if answered, to contribute to the foundational knowledge of secure software engineering.

How to Deal with Lack of Information about Requirements Evolution? Requirements evolution is inevitable due to changes in the working environment, business agreement, or growing user demands; however, it is not possible to predict all the possible changes in advance, especially for complex systems. This issue was pointed out and agreed by the ATM experts during our focus group interviews in the studies presented in Section 4.1. Eliciting the evolution of requirements, hence, is problematic and should be an iterative process with the essential work amount. Although there exist empirical studies on this issue such as the work by Herrmann et al. [23] and Maiden et al. [24–26], it would be promising to run empirical studies on different subjects of users (such as experts in a specific domain, or requirement analysts and more) to understand to which level of abstraction and completeness that requirements evolution could be produced.

How are Security Concerns Conceptualized? In the introduction, we mentioned the concept of 'twin peaks': requirements and architecture are closely related and their refinement intertwines and goes hand-in-hand [1]. This phenomenon is assumed to have a general applicability, including the software quality of security [2]. However, this phenomenon belongs to the field of intuitions (or axioms). It is believed to hold in the reality and practice of requirements engineering and architectural design. No one, however, has studied how this phenomenon unfolds in the software development process and how it influences the activities of requirements engineers and software architects. Characterizing this phenomenon with some degree of precision would improve our knowledge on how security requirements are conceptualized and how security solutions take shape accordingly. Possibly, this research question can be tackled best via a descriptive study, like the one presented in Section 3.1.

How to Represent Security? Concerning security in software architectures, several proposals have emerged to represent security concepts in design models. A selection of these methods is presented by van den Berghe et al. [39]. However, none of these proposals has gone through the lens of empirical validation. Hence, there is a significant amount of work to be done in order to understand which approaches are more effective (i.e., produce more secure designs), are more usable by practitioners and are easier to learn. These research questions lend themselves to an investigation based on controlled experiments comparing two or more techniques.

When to Build Security in? In the process of designing a software architecture, several software qualities like performance, maintainability and security compete for the 'attention' of the architect. Often, trade-offs need to be made between these qualities and priorities need to be set, e.g., when conflicting requirements emerge or when time and budget are limited. It is key to understand when it is the right time to start tackling the security concerns in the above mentioned design process. Too soon could be problematic, as the key software assets needing protection have not emerged in the design yet. Too late could be cumbersome, as too many design constraints due to other qualities might be already in place. Finding the soft spot is a non-trivial task that is often a matter of trial and error. This research question could be addressed with a combination of case studies and controlled experiments.

7   Conclusion

In this chapter, we have summarized our most relevant experience in the field of empirical secure software engineering. Through the description of four studies, we have provided basic guidelines on how to structure either a descriptive study or a controlled experiment in the domain of security requirements and secure software architecture. We have also collected the most significant challenges that experimenters are likely to face, should they venture in this difficult yet rewarding research area. In this respect, the chapter also outlines several interesting directions for future work. They represent an engaging opportunity for, say, a newly started PhD scholar. We hope that this chapter has been inspirational for some of the readers, as the secure software engineering community has the utter necessity of providing more quantitatively-rooted evidence that the methodologies it has produced are indeed advancing the state of the practice for the many security engineers out there.

Acknowledgement. This research is partially funded by the Research Fund KU Leuven, and by the EU FP7 project NESSoS. With the financial support from the Prevention of and Fight against Crime Programme of the European Union (B-CCENTRE).

References

1. Nuseibeh, B.: Weaving together requirements and architectures. IEEE Computer 34, 115–119 (2001)
2. Heyman, T., Yskout, K., Scandariato, R., Schmidt, H., Yu, Y.: The security twin peaks. In: Erlingsson, Ú., Wieringa, R., Zannone, N. (eds.) ESSoS 2011. LNCS, vol. 6542, pp. 167–180. Springer, Heidelberg (2011)
3. Howard, M., Lipner, S.: The Security Development Lifecycle. Microsoft Press (2006)
4. McGraw, G.: Software Security: Building Security. Addison-Wesley (2006)

5. Lund, M.S., Solhaug, B., Stølen, K.: Model-Driven Risk Analysis: The CORAS Approach. Springer (2011)
6. Mellado, D., Fernández-Medina, E., Piattini, M.: Applying a security requirements engineering process. In: Gollmann, D., Meier, J., Sabelfeld, A. (eds.) ESORICS 2006. LNCS, vol. 4189, pp. 192–206. Springer, Heidelberg (2006)
7. Scandariato, R., Wuyts, K., Joosen, W.: A descriptive study of Microsoft's threat modeling technique. Requirements Engineering (2014)
8. Labunets, K., Massacci, F., Paci, F., Tran, L.M.: An experimental comparison of two risk-based security methods. In: Proceedings of the 7th International Symposium on Empirical Software Engineering and Measurement (ESEM), pp. 163–172 (2013)
9. Massacci, F., Paci, F., Tran, L.M.S., Tedeschi, A.: Assessing a requirements evolution approach: Empirical studies in the air traffic management domain. Journal of Systems and Software (2013)
10. Yskout, K., Scandariato, R., Joosen, W.: Change patterns: Co-evolving requirements and architecture. Software and Systems Modeling (2012)
11. Massacci, F., Paci, F.: How to select a security requirements method? a comparative study with students and practitioners. In: Jøsang, A., Carlsson, B. (eds.) NordSec 2012. LNCS, vol. 7617, pp. 89–104. Springer, Heidelberg (2012)
12. Opdahl, A.L., Sindre, G.: Experimental comparison of attack trees and misuse cases for security threat identification. Information and Software Technology 51, 916–932 (2009)
13. Diallo, M.H., Romero-Mariona, J., Sim, S.E., Alspaugh, T., Richardson, D.J.: A comparative evaluation of three approaches to specifying security requirements. In: Proceeding of the 12th International Working Conference on Requirements Engineering: Foundation for Software Quality, REFSQ (2006)
14. Hogganvik, I., Stølen, K.: On the comprehension of security risk scenarios. In: Proceedings of the 13th International Workshop on Program Comprehension (IWPC), pp. 115–124. IEEE (2005)
15. Hogganvik, I., Stølen, K.: A graphical approach to risk identification motivated by empirical investigations. In: Wang, J., Whittle, J., Harel, D., Reggio, G. (eds.) MoDELS 2006. LNCS, vol. 4199, pp. 574–588. Springer, Heidelberg (2006)
16. Hogganvik, I., Lund, M., Stølen, K.: Reducing the effort to comprehend risk models: Textlabels are often preferred over graphical means. Risk Analysis 51, 916–932 (2009)
17. Dhillon, D.: Developer-driven threat modeling: Lessons learned in the trenches. IEEE Security & Privacy 9, 41–47 (2011)
18. Villela, K., Dörr, J., John, I.: Evaluation of a method for proactively managing the evolving scope of a software product line. In: Wieringa, R., Persson, A. (eds.) REFSQ 2010. LNCS, vol. 6182, pp. 113–127. Springer, Heidelberg (2010)
19. Villela, K., Dörr, J., Gross, A.: Proactively managing the evolution of embedded system requirements. In: Proceeding of the 16th IEEE International Requirements Engineering Conference (RE), pp. 13–22. IEEE Computer Society (2008)
20. Basili, V., Rombach, H.: The TAME project: Towards improvement-oriented software environments. IEEE Transactions on Software Engineering 14, 758–773 (1988)
21. McGee, S., Greer, D.: Software requirements change taxonomy: Evaluation by case study. In: Proceeding of the 19th IEEE International Requirements Engineering Conference (RE), pp. 25–34 (2011)
22. Runeson, P., Host, M.: Guidelines for conducting and reporting case study research in software engineering. Empirical Software Engineering 14, 131–164 (2009)

23. Herrmann, A., Wallnöfer, A., Paech, B.: Specifying changes only — a case study on delta requirements. In: Glinz, M., Heymans, P. (eds.) REFSQ 2009 Amsterdam. LNCS, vol. 5512, pp. 45–58. Springer, Heidelberg (2009)
24. Ncube, C., Lockerbie, J., Maiden, N.: Automatically generating requirements from i* models: Experiences with a complex airport operations system. In: Sawyer, P., Paech, B., Heymans, P. (eds.) REFSQ 2007. LNCS, vol. 4542, pp. 33–47. Springer, Heidelberg (2007)
25. Maiden, N., Robertson, S.: Integrating creativity into requirements processes: Experiences with an air traffic management system. In: Proceeding of the 13th IEEE International Requirements Engineering Conference (RE), pp. 105–116 (2005)
26. Maiden, N.A.M., Jones, S.V., Manning, S., Greenwood, J., Renou, L.: Model-driven requirements engineering: Synchronising models in an air traffic management case study. In: Persson, A., Stirna, J. (eds.) CAiSE 2004. LNCS, vol. 3084, pp. 368–383. Springer, Heidelberg (2004)
27. Grimes, D., Schulz, K.: Descriptive studies: what they can and cannot do. The Lancet 359, 145–149 (2002)
28. Davis, F.D.: Perceived usefulness, perceived ease of use, and user acceptance of information technology. MIS Quarterly, 319–340 (1989)
29. Conover, W.J.: On methods of handling ties in the wilcoxon signed-rank test. Journal of the American Statistical Association 68, 985–988 (1973)
30. Tran, L.M.S., Massacci, F.: Dealing with known unknowns: Towards a game-theoretic foundation for software requirement evolution. In: Mouratidis, H., Rolland, C. (eds.) CAiSE 2011. LNCS, vol. 6741, pp. 62–76. Springer, Heidelberg (2011)
31. Tran, L.M.S.: Managing the Uncertainty of the Evolution of Requirements Model. PhD thesis, University of Trento (2014)
32. Moody, D.L.: The method evaluation model: A theoretical model for validating information systems design methods. In: Proceeding of the European Conference on Information Systems (ECIS), pp. 1327–1336 (2003)
33. Mens, T., Wermelinger, M., Ducasse, S., Demeyer, S., Hirschfeld, R., Jazayeri, M.: Challenges in software evolution. In: Proceeding of the 8th International Workshop on Principles of Software Evolution, pp. 13–22 (2005)
34. Si* Tool website: http://sesa.dit.unitn.it/sistar_tool
35. Topcased UML editor: http://www.topcased.org/
36. Tichy, W.: Hints for reviewing empirical work in software engineering. Empirical Software Engineering 5, 309–312 (2000)
37. Carver, J., Jaccheri, L., Morasca, S.: A checklist for integrating student empirical studies with research and teaching goals. Empirical Software Engineering 15, 35–59 (2010)
38. Runeson, P.: Using students as experiment subjects - an analysis on graduate and freshmen student data. In: Proceeding of the International Conference on Empirical Assessment in Software Engineering (EASE), pp. 95–102 (2003)
39. van den Berghe, A., Scandariato, R., Joosen, W.: Towards a systematic literature review on secure software design. In: Doctoral Symposium of the International Symposium on Engineering Secure Software and Systems, ESSoS-DS (2013)

STS-Tool: Security Requirements Engineering
for Socio-Technical Systems

Elda Paja[1], Fabiano Dalpiaz[2], and Paolo Giorgini[1]

[1] University of Trento, Italy
{elda.paja,paolo.giorgini}@unitn.it
[2] Utrecht University, The Netherlands
f.dalpiaz@uu.nl

Abstract. We present the latest version of STS-Tool, the modelling and analysis support tool for STS-ml, an actor- and goal-oriented security requirements modelling language for socio-technical systems. We show how the STS-Tool supports requirements analysts and security designers in (i) modelling socio-technical systems as a set of interacting actors, who have security needs over their interactions, and (ii) deriving security requirements for the system-to-be. The tool integrates a set of automated reasoning techniques that allow checking if a given STS-ml model is well-formed, verifying whether there are any conflicts among security requirements, and calculating the threat trace of events threatening actors' assets. We first illustrate the modelling and reasoning activities supported by STS-ml, to then guide the design of a secure socio-technical system from the eGovernment domain through a series of exercises.

1 Introduction

Socio-technical systems are an interplay of social actors (human and organizations) and technical subsystems, which interact with one another to reach their objectives [2]. Each participant acts, guided by its objectives, according to its business policies, and the socio-technical system comes into existence when the participants interact to get things done. In e-commerce, buyers and sellers interact with one another (social actor - social actor interaction) making use of the web application (social actor - technical actor interaction), which relies on secure channels (technical actor - technical actor interaction) to ensure the transactions among the buyer and the seller are secure. The diversity and autonomy of participants makes the design of a secure socio-technical system a challenging task, for which the study of technical aspects alone is not enough, instead social aspects need to be investigated too.

STS-ml [3,7] (Socio-Technical Security modelling language), is an actor (to represent the various stakeholders) and goal-oriented (capturing their main objectives) security requirements modelling language based upon these principles. It allows tackling security issues already in the early phases of socio-technical system design. STS-ml is based on the idea of relating security requirements to *interaction*. The language allows stakeholders to express *security needs* over their interactions to constrain the way interaction is to take place. For example, if a buyer sends its personal data to a seller, the buyer may require the data not to be disclosed to third parties, only the seller should

M. Heisel et al. (Eds.): Engineering Secure Future Internet Services, LNCS 8431, pp. 65–96, 2014.
© Springer International Publishing Switzerland 2014

have access to them. STS-ml specifies security requirements in terms of *social commitments* [8], promises with contractual validity made by an actor to another. One actor commits (responsible) to another (requester) that, while delivering some service, it will comply with the required security needs. In the example above, a security requirement is that the seller commits not to disclose buyer's personal data to other parties.

Differently from other goal-oriented approaches to security requirements engineering [4,5,6], STS-ml offers a more expressive ontology. It supports expressing fine-grained and contradictory authorisations over information, which allow to effectively represent real-world information security requirements [1,9].

We show how STS-Tool, the case tool for STS-ml, supports requirements analyst and security engineers in designing secure socio-technical systems. The tool is the result of an iterative development process, following several evaluation activities, in the scope of the FP7 European Project Aniketos [1]. It has been used in modelling and reasoning over models of a large size from different domains, such as eGovernment, Telecommunications, and Air Traffic Management Control. We first introduce STS-ml in Sect. 2 as the baseline for using STS-Tool, briefly presenting its modelling features (Sect. 2.1) and then providing the users with a modelling process to design socio-technical systems with STS-ml and STS-Tool (Sect. 2.2). Sect. 3 describes the main features of STS-Tool, while Sect. 4 demonstrates the use of the tool in modelling a scenario from eGovernment, guiding the user step by step through a series of exercises that follow the phases of the modelling method. Finally, Sect. 5 concludes with a discussion of related work and future directions.

2   Baseline: STS-ml

STS-ml is an actor- and goal-oriented security requirements engineering modelling language. It includes high-level organisational concepts such as actor, goal, delegation, etc.

STS-ml is a diagrammatical language, i.e., graphical concepts and relations are used to create the models. A particular feature of STS-ml is that it allows modelling socio-technical systems by focusing on different perspectives (views) at a time. This feature is known as: *multiview modelling*. Below, we introduce STS-ml constructs and show how they are used to model socio-technical systems. Additionally, we present an iterative process to model socio-technical system with STS-ml, as well as to analyze the models built, to then derive security requirements for the system to be.

2.1   Multiview Modelling with STS-ml

STS-ml modelling consists of three complementary views, *social*, *information*, and *authorisation* view. The three views together form the overall model for the system-at-hand (STS-ml model). To facilitate the description of STS-ml, we will use a small running example.

Example 1 (Travel Planning). A tourist wants to organise a trip using a Travel Agency Service (*TAS*). *TAS* allows end users to read about various destinations, book flights and

---

[1] http://www.aniketos.eu

hotels, hire a car, etc., and uses the *Amadeus flight service* to book flight tickets. To book hotels, the *Tourist* has chosen to directly contact the *Hotel* himself, without interacting with *TAS*.

The *social view* (Fig. 1a) represents actors as intentional and social entities. Actors are intentional as they aim to attain their objectives (*goals*), and they are social, for they interact with others to fulfill their objectives (by *delegating goals*) and obtain information (by *exchanging documents*). STS-ml supports two types of actors: *agents*—concrete participants, and *roles*—abstract actors, used when the actual participant is unknown. In our example, we represent the *TAS* as a role, and the *Amadeus Service* as an agent, as it refers to a specific flight service. Actors may *possess* documents, they may *use*, *modify*, or *produce* documents while achieving their goals. For instance, *Tourist* wants to achieve the goal *Trip planned*, for which it needs to both have *Tickets booked* and *Hotel booked*. To book the hotel it needs document *ID Doc copy*.

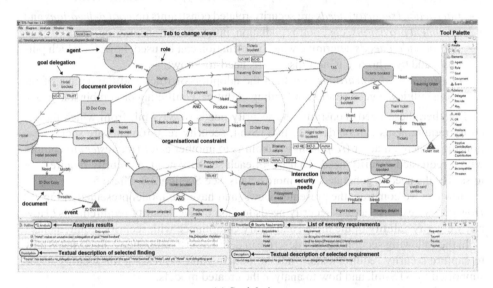

(a) Social view

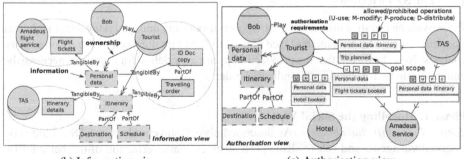

(b) Information view   (c) Authorisation view

Fig. 1. Multi-view modelling for the travel planning scenario

The *information view* (Fig. 1b) shows how information and documents are interconnected to identify which information actors manipulate, when they *use, modify, produce*, or *distribute* documents to achieve their goals in the social view. Additionally, it gives a structured representation of actors' information and documents. Information can be represented by one or more documents (through Tangible By), and on the other hand one or more information entities can be part of some document. For instance, information *Personal data* is represented by both *ID Doc copy* and *Flight tickets* documents.

The *authorisation view* (Fig. 1c) shows the authorisations actors grant to others over information, specifying which operations they are allowed (prohibited) to do, for which goals (scope), and whether authorisation can be further transferred or not. For instance, *Tourist* authorises *TAS* to use (U selected) information *Personal data* and *Itinerary* in the scope of the goal *Tickets booked* granting a transferrable authorisation (authorisation's arrow line is continuous).

Through its three views, STS-ml supports different types of security needs:

- *Interaction (security) needs* are security-related constraints on *goal delegations* and *document provisions*, e.g., non-repudiation, integrity of transmission, etc.;
- *Authorisation needs* determine which information can be used, how, for which purpose, and by whom, e.g. non-disclosure, need-to-know;
- *Organisational constraints* constrain the adoption of roles and the uptake of responsibilities, e.g. separation or binding of duties, conflicting or combinable goals.

Together, these needs constitute the security needs of STS-ml, from which the security requirements can be derived. In STS-ml, security requirements are social relationships where an actor (*responsible*) commits to another actor (*requester*) to comply with a requested security need. That is, for each security need, a security requirement to satifsy the need is generated. For more details, see Section 2.2, Phase 5.

How can we construct the presented views, and have the model presented in Fig. 1? How can we express actors' security needs to then derive security requirements? How can we verify validity of the model and verify compliance with security requirements?

In the following section we will describe in detail how to built the various views, how to capture security requirements, while introducing and expressing the security needs supported by STS-ml, and how to analyze the created models.

2.2   The STS Method

We provide an iterative process, which supports modelling and analysing socio-technical systems, namely the STS method (see Fig. 2), to facilitate the work of the requirements analysts. Note, however, that the provided steps are a guideline for them, not necessarily mandatory to be followed in the indicated order.

Phase 1. Modelling the Social View
Step 1.1. Identify stakeholders. As described above, stakeholders in STS-ml are represented via agents and roles [2]. Role is an abstract characterization of the behavior of an active entity within some context. Most participants are unknown at design time,

---

[2] We use the general term *actor* whenever relationships are applicable to both agents and roles.

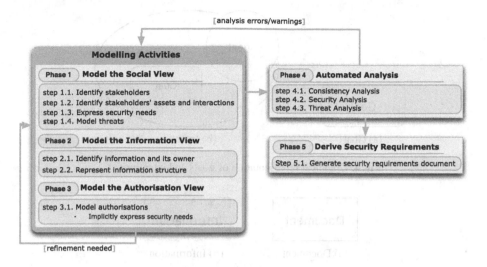

Fig. 2. The STS method

e.g., Tourist, Travel Agency Service (TAS), Hotel, etc. Agents play (adopt) roles at run-time, and they can change the roles they play, e.g., Bob, John, CheapTravels Inc. Some agents are known already at design time when we build STS-ml models, e.g., Amadeus Service. Fig. 3 shows how roles and agents are represented graphically in STS-ml. See the identified roles and agents for the tourist example in Fig. 1.

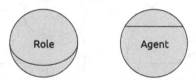

Fig. 3. Graphical representation of roles and agents

Step 1.2. Identify assets and interactions. When talking about security, stakeholders of a system wish to protect their important assets. Stakeholders in the socio-technical system participate in order to achieve their desired objectives—modelled in STS-ml through the concept of *goal*. A goal is a *state of affairs that an actor intends to achieve*, e.g., trip planned, flight tickets booked. They are used to capture motivations and responsibilities of actors. Thus, we consider goals as assets for an actor, and refer to them as *intentional assets*. In addition, their owned *information* entities are another important asset for stakeholders. We refer to them as *informational assets*. The graphical representation of goals and actors' intention to fulfil them is shown in Fig. 4.

Information as is, cannot be exchanged among actors, nor can it be manipulated by them. We use the concept of *documents*—representing information—to allow stakeholders to make use of and exchange information. Information and documents are graphically represented as shown in Fig. 5.

In Fig. 1, *Amadeus Service* has the goal *Flight tickets booked*, for which it is responsible. Goals can be refined into subgoals through *and/or-decompositions*:

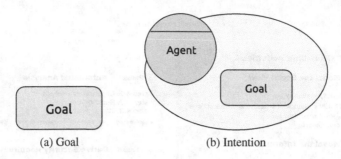

(a) Goal   (b) Intention

Fig. 4. Graphical representation of goals and intentions

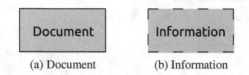

(a) Document   (b) Information

Fig. 5. Graphical representation of informational assets

and-decomposition (Fig. 6a) represents the process of achieving a goal, while or-decomposition (Fig. 6b) represents alternative ways for achieving a goal. In Fig. 1a, *TAS* or-decomposes goal *Tickets booked* into goals *Flight ticket booked* and *Train ticket booked*.

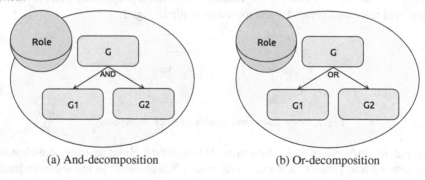

(a) And-decomposition   (b) Or-decomposition

Fig. 6. Graphical representation of goal and/or decompositions

The goal model of an actor ties together goals and documents, in various ways: an actor *possesses* a set of documents; an actor *needs* one or more documents to fulfil a goal; an actor *produces* documents while fulfilling a goal; an actor *modifies* a document while fulfilling a goal, see Fig. 7. The relation *possesses* indicates that actors have a specific document, i.e., they can furnish or provide it to other roles. Graphically, this is represented by including a document in the actor's scope, see Fig. 8a. Note that this is different from ownership (Fig. 8b), an actor might have a document without necessarily being the owner of the information it contains. For instance, *TAS* possesses document *Traveling order*, but it is not the owner of information *Personal data*, the *Tourist* is, see Fig. 1a and 1b.

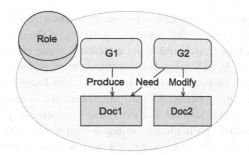

Fig. 7. Graphical representation of goal-document relationships

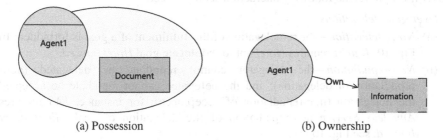

(a) Possession   (b) Ownership

Fig. 8. Graphical representation of document possession and information ownership

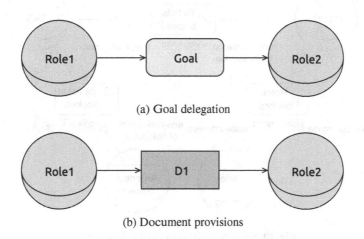

(a) Goal delegation

(b) Document provisions

Fig. 9. Graphical representation of goal delegation and document provision

Within the same step, we need to identify interactions among actors as well. *Goal delegations* capture the transfer of responsibility for the fulfillment of the goal from one actor to another, i.e., a delegator actor delegates the fulfillment of a goal (delegatum) to another actor (delegatee), see Fig. 9a. Note that in STS-ml, only leaf goals can be delegated, in Figure 1a *Tourist* delegates to *TAS* the fulfillment of *Tickets booked*. *Document provision*, on the other hand, specifies the exchange of information between actors, a sender actor provides a document to a receiver actor, see Fig. 9b. Providing the document refers strictly to the actual supply or delivery of the document. Information as is (e.g. ideas) cannot be transferred if not explicitly made concrete by a document (e.g. a paper, an e-mail). In STS-ml, a document can be provided only by an actor that possesses it, see in Fig. 1a how *Tourist* provides document *Traveling order* to *TAS*.

Step 1.3. Express security needs. STS-ml allows actors to express security needs over their interactions, in this step we analyze these interactions (goal delegations and document provisions) actors participate in to elicit their needs with regard to security. To specify security needs over goal delegations and document provisions, these relationships are annotated via security needs the interacting parties (being them agents or roles) want each other to comply with.

STS-ml supports the following interaction security needs:

1. *Over goal delegations:*
   (a) *No-redelegation*—the re-delegation of the fulfilment of a goal is forbidden; In Fig. 10, *Tourist* requires *Hotel* not to redelegate goal *Hotel booked*.
   (b) *Non-repudiation*—the delegator cannot repudiate he delegated (non-repudiation of delegation); and the delegatee cannot repudiate he accepted the delegation (non-repudiation of acceptance); for instance, *TAS* requires *Amadeus Service* non-repudiation of the delegation of goal *Flight ticket booked*, see Fig. 10.

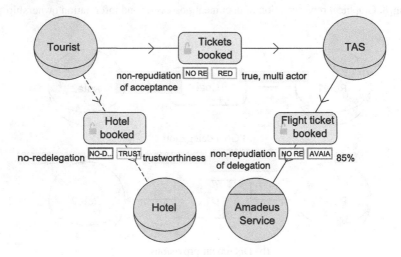

Fig. 10. Security needs over goal delegations

   (c) *Redundancy*—the delegatee has to employ alternative ways of achieving a goal; We consider two types of redundancy: *True* and *Fallback*. *True redundancy*: at least two or more different strategies are considered to fulfil the goal, and they are executed simultaneously to ensure goal fulfillment. *Fallback redundancy*: a primary strategy is selected to fulfill the goal, and at the same time a number of other strategies is considered and maintained as backup to fulfill the goal. None of the backup strategies is used as long as the first strategy successfully fulfils the goal. Within these two categories of redundancy, two sub-cases exist: (i) only one actor employs different strategies to ensure redundancy: single actor redundancy; and (ii) multiple actors employ different strategies to ensure redundancy: multi actor redundancy. In total, we can distinguish four types of redundancy, which are all mutually exclusive, so we can consider them as four different security needs, namely, (i) fallback redundancy single, (ii) fallback redundancy multi, (iii) true redundancy single, and (iv) true redundancy multi. In Fig. 10, *Tourist* requires *TAS* true redundancy multi for goal *Tickets booked*.

(d) *Trustworthiness*—the delegation of the goal will take place only if the delegatee is trustworthy; for instance, the delegation of goal *Hotel booked* from *Tourist* to *Hotel* will take place only to trustworthy hotels, see Fig. 10.

(e) *Availability*—the delegatee should ensure a minim availability level for the delegated goal; for instance, *TAS* requires *Amadeus Service* 85% availability for goal *Flight ticket booked*, see Fig. 10.

2. *Over document provisions:*

(a) *Integrity of transmission*—the sender should ensure that the document shall not be altered while providing it;

(b) *Confidentiality of transmission*—the sender should ensure the confidentiality of transmission for the provided document;

(c) *Availability*—the sender should ensure a minimal availability level (in percentage) for the provided document. In Fig. 11, *TAS* should ensure integrity and confidentiality of transmission, as well as an availability level of 98% when providing the document *Itinerary details* to *Amadeus flight service*.

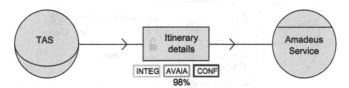

Fig. 11. Security needs over document provisions

3. *From organisational constraints* [3]:

(a) *Separation of duties* (SoD)—defines incompatible roles and incompatible goals, so we define two types: role-based SoD—two roles are incompatible, i.e., cannot be played by the same agent, and goal-based SoD—two goals shall be achieved by different actors; for instance, the goals *eticket generated* and *credit card verified* are defined as incompatible (unequals sign, see Fig. 12).

(b) *Combination of duties* (CoD)—defines combinable roles and combinable goals, so we distinguish between role-based CoD—two roles are combinable, i.e., shall be played by the same agent; and goal-based CoD—two goals shall be achieved by the same actor. Note that these security needs from organisational constraints are translated to a set of relationships, *incompatible* (represented as a circle with the unequal sign within) and *combines* (represented as a circle

---

[3] Organisational constraints are imposed either by the rules and regulations of the organisation, or by law.

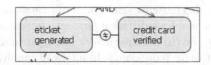

Fig. 12. Security needs from organisational constraints

with the equals sign within) respectively. This is related to the fact that they are not directly expressed over a social relationship, but constrain the uptake of responsibilities of stakeholders. Both relationships are symmetric, therefore there are no arrows pointing to the concepts they relate.

Step 1.4. Modelling threats. In STS-ml we represent events threatening stakeholders' assets. STS-ml proposes the concept *event* and the relationship *threaten* relating the event to the asset it threatens. As introduced earlier, we consider two types of assets, *intentional assets* and *informational assets* respectively. However, in the social view stakeholders exchange and manipulate information via documents, so in this step we model the events that threaten actors' *goals* and *documents* respectively, see Fig. 13. For instance, the event *ID Doc Copy lost* threatens document *ID Doc Copy*, see Fig. 1. Broadly, an event threatening a goal means that the goal cannot be reached, while an event threatening a document means that the document becomes unavailable.

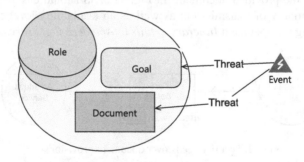

Fig. 13. Graphical representation of events threatening actors' assets in STS-ml

Phase 1. Summary. Each of the above steps is repeated until all stakeholders have been modelled, all their assets and interactions have been represented, their desired security needs have been expressed, and events threatening actors' assets have been modelled. The result of this iterative modelling process supported by **Phase 1** is Fig. 1a.

Phase 2. Modelling the Information View

To protect information, it is important to first identify information, its representation (documents), and to know who information owners are, for they are the ones concerned with what happens to their information.

Step 2.1. Identify information and its owner. Documents represent information, so when modelling the information view we first identify which are the informational entities represented by each document in the social view. For each identified information, we identify who are the owners of this information. For instance, *Tourist* is the owner of his *Personal data*, see Fig. 1b. Note that there can be multiple owners for the same information, to represent shared ownership.

Step 2.2. Represent information structure. Information view gives a structured representation of actors' information and documents, and the way they are interconnected. Information can be represented by one or more documents (through the Tangible By relationship), see Fig. 14a. On the other hand, one or more information pieces can be made tangible by the same document. In Fig. 1b, information *Personal data* is made tangible by document *Eticket* and document *ID Doc Copy*.

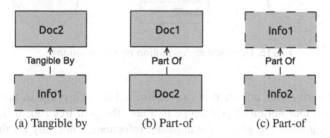

(a) Tangible by   (b) Part-of   (c) Part-of

Fig. 14. Graphical representation of part-of and tangible by

Another feature of the information view is to support composite information (documents). We enable that by means of the part Of relations (see Fig. 14b and 14c), which can be applied between information (documents). For instance, this allows representing that information *Destination* and *Schedule* are part of the information *Itinerary*, while document *ID Doc Copy* is part of document *Traveling Order* (see Fig. 1b).

Phase 2. Summary. These steps are repeated till all important information entities are represented, their owners are identified and they are connected to their corresponding documents or parts of information. The result of the iterative modelling process supported by **Phase 2** is Fig. 1b.

Phase 3. Modelling the Authorisation View

An adequate representation of authorisations is necessary to determine if information is exchanged and used in compliance with confidentiality restrictions. Information owners are the unique actors that can legitimately transfer rights to other actors. However, when they transfer full rights to another actor, the latter becomes entitled to transfer the same rights the owner can grant.

Step 3.1. Model authorisations. Authorisations support the transfer of rights between two actors. An actor can grant (receive) an arbitrary number of authorisations about information, specifying:

– *Operations*: refer to actions that an actor can perform on the information. STS-ml supports four basic operations: *use* (U), *modify* (M), *produce* (P), and *distribute* (D). The four supported operations are directly linked to the way information is manipulated within an actor's model in the social view. Usage goes in parallel with the need relation; modification relates to the modify relation, production is reflected by the produce relation, and distribution relates to the document provision relation

between actors. Graphically the allowed operation is highlighted in yellow (see Fig. 15). In Fig. 1c, *Tourist* authorises *TAS* on usage (U is selected).
– *Information*: the transferred rights are granted over at least one information entity. In Fig. 15, authority to *use* and *modify* information *Info1* and *Info2* is granted to *Role2*. In our running example, the authorisation from *Tourist* to *TAS* is granted over information *Personal data* and *Itinerary*, see Fig. 1c.

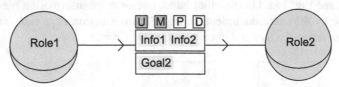

Fig. 15. Graphical representation of authorisations

– *Scope*: authority over information can be limited to their usage in the scope of a certain goal. Our notion of goal scope includes the goal tree rooted by that goal. As a result, authority is given to manipulate information not only for the specified goal, but for its sub-goals as well. For instance, the *Tourist* permits the *TAS* to use his *Personal data* only to book the tickets (i.e., for goal *Tickets booked*), see Fig. 1c.
– *Transferability*: this dimensions allows to specify whether the actor receiving the authorisation can further re-authorise actors, that is, the authorisee not only is granted the permission to perform operations, but also that of further propagating rights over the specified information to other actors. Note that reauthorisation should be compatible with the authority scope the delegator has. Non-transferrability is represented through a dashed authorisation line to show that the authorisation chain should end with the authorisee. For instance, the authorisation from *Tourist* to *TAS* is transferrable, while that from *TAS* to *Amadeus Service* is not, see Fig. 1c.

Implicitly express security needs. Security needs over authorisations are expressed by allowing only certain operations and limiting the scope:

– limiting the scope expresses a security need on *Need-to-know*—requires information is used, modified, produced only for the specified scope; for instance, *Tourist* expresses a need-to-know security need to *Hotel*, which can use *Personal data* only in the scope of *Hotel booked*, see Fig. 16.
– not allowing usage expresses a security need on *Non-usage*— requires the information is not used in an unauthorised way; it implies that the authorisee should not make use of (need) any documents making tangible the specified information. There are no cases of non-usage from our running example.
– not allowing modification expresses a security need on *Non-modification*—requires the information is not modified in an unauthorised way; it implies that the authorisee should not modify any documents making tangible this information. In Fig. 16, *Hotel* cannot modify documents representing *Personal data*.
– not allowing production expresses a security need on *Non-production*—requires the information is not produced in an unauthorised way; it implies that no new

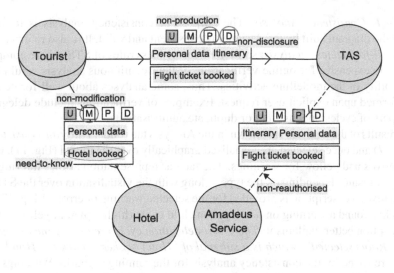

Fig. 16. Security needs over authorisations

document, representing the given information, is produced. In Fig. 16, *TAS* cannot produce documents that represent *Personal data* or *Itinerary*.

- not allowing distribution expresses a security need on *Non-disclosure*—requires the information is not disclosed in an unauthorised way; it implies that no document, representing the given information, is transmitted to other actors. In Fig. 16, *TAS* cannot distribute documents representing *Personal data* or *Itinerary*.
- not allowing transferrability expresses a security need on *Not-reauthorise*—requires the authorisation is not transferrable, i.e., the authorisee does not further transfer rights either for operations not granted to him (implicitly) or when the transferability of the authorisation is set to false (explicitly). This means that any non-usage, non-modification, non-production or non-disclosure security need implies a not-reauthorise security need for the operations that are not allowed. In Fig. 16, *Amadeus Service* cannot further authorise other actors, for the authorisation coming from *TAS* is non-transferable.

Phase 3. Summary. The steps are repeated until all authorisation relationships have been drawn and authorisation needs have been expressed. The result of the iterative modelling process supported by **Phase 3** is Fig. 1c.

Phase 4. Automated Analysis

After the security requirements engineer has performed the modelling activities, the STS method allows him to perform automated analysis over the created STS-ml model. The analyses are supported by the case tool of STS-ml, namely STS-Tool. Details on the tool will follow in Section 3. Currently three types of analysis are supported:

- Consistency Analysis (*step 4.1.*)
- Security Analysis (*step 4.2.*)
- Threat Analysis (*step 4.3.*)

Step 4.1. Consistency Analysis. The purpose of consistency analysis is to verify whether the diagram built by the designer is consistent and valid. It is also referred to as *Offline well-formedness analysis*: some well-formedness rules of STS-ml are computationally too expensive for online verification, or their continuous analysis would limit the flexibility of the modelling activities. Thus, some analyses about well-formedness are performed upon explicit user request. Examples of verifications include delegation cycles, part-of cycles, inconsistent or duplicate authorisations, etc.

The results of the analysis are shown in the Analysis tab (under *Diagram consistency*, see Fig. 17) and once selected are visualised graphically over the model (Fig. 17), using red for errors and yellow for warnings. The tabular representation allows filtering and ordering of results depending on the type. Along with the visualisation over the STS-ml model, a textual description is provided for the selected warning or error. In Fig. 17, this analysis has found a warning on a delegation child cycle (highlighted in yellow color), the description better explains it: *There is a delegation cycle created by the delegation of goal "Room selected", which is a subgoal of "Hotel booked", back to "Hotel"*. No errors were found by the consistency analysis for the running scenario. Warnings may be disregarded by the designer, while errors must be solved.

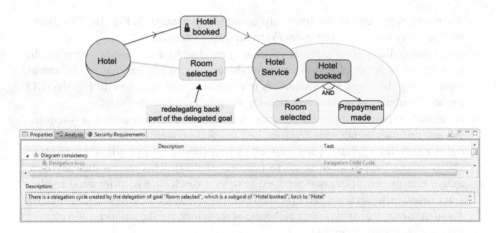

Fig. 17. Results of the consistency analysis

Step 4.2. Security Analysis. For each elicited security need, a security requirement is generated in STS-ml, see **Phase 5.** for more detail. Security analysis is concerned with verifying: (i) if the security requirements specification is consistent—no requirements are potentially conflicting; (ii) if the STS-ml model allows the satisfaction of the specified security requirements. This analysis is implemented in disjunctive Datalog and consists of comparing the possible actor behaviors that the model describes against the behavior mandated by the security requirements. The results are again shown in the Analysis tab visualised on the STS-ml model itself (in red color) when selected, see Fig. 18, which shows a violation of no-redelegation by *Hotel* for goal *Hotel booked*. A textual description provides details on the selected error. In this case, the description states that this is an error because: *"Tourist" has expressed a no-redelegation security*

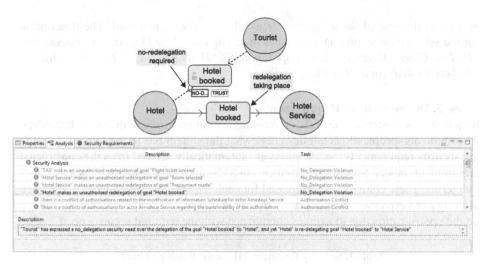

Fig. 18. Results of the security analysis

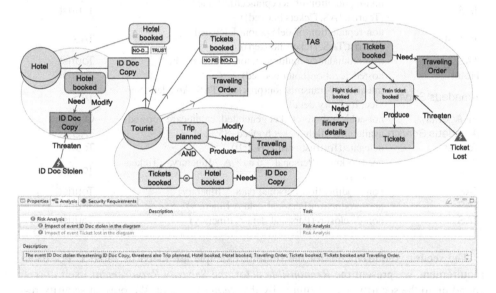

Fig. 19. Results of the threat analysis: threat trace from the event ID Doc Stolen

need over the delegation of the goal "Hotel booked" to "Hotel", and yet "Hotel" is re-delegating goal "Hotel booked" to "Hotel Service".

Step 4.3. Threat Analysis. This analysis calculates the propagation of threatening events over actors' assets. It answers the question: *How does the specification of events threatening actors' assets affect their other assets?'* The results are shown in the Analysis tab, see Fig. 19, which shows the threat trace (highlighted in red color), i.e., the threat propagation for the event *ID Doc Stolen* threatening document *ID Doc Copy* (given this is the one selected). Threatened document affects the goals that need and modify it, as well as the goal of the delegator, should this be a delegated goal. The description for the selected threat propagation states that: *The event "ID Doc Stolen" threatening "ID Doc Copy", threatens also "Trip planned", "Hotel booked", "Traveling Order", "Tickets booked", and "Traveling Order".*

Phase 5. Derive Security Requirements

Requirements models are useful for communication purposes with the stakeholders. Requirements specifications tell designers what the system has to implement. In STS-ml, security requirements specifications are automatically derived from the constructed requirements model. Security requirements in STS-ml constrain interactions in contractual terms. These contracts are expressed for each required security need, i.e., for each security need expressed from one actor to the other, a security requirement is generated on the opposite direction to express compliance with the required security need.

Table 1. Security Requirements for the running example

Responsible	Security Requirement	Requester
TAS	non-repudiation-of-acceptance(delegated (Tourist,TAS,Tickets booked))	Tourist
Tourist	non-repudiation-of-delegation(delegated (Tourist,TAS,Tickets booked))	TAS
TAS	true-redundancy-multiple-actor(Tickets booked)	Tourist
Hotel	no-redelegation(hotel booked)	Tourist
Amadeus Service	integrity-of-transmission(provided(TAS, Amadeus Service, Itinerary details)	TAS
All Agents	not-achieve-both(eticket generated, credit card verified)	Org
Amadeus Service	availability(flight ticket booked, 85%)	TAS
Tourist	delegatedTo(trustworthy(Hotel))	Tourist
TAS	need-to-know(Personal data ∧ Itinerary, Tickets booked)	Tourist
TAS	non-modification(Personal data ∧ Itinerary)	Tourist
TAS	non-production(Personal data ∧ Itinerary)	Tourist
TAS	non-disclosure(Personal data ∧ Itinerary)	Tourist

The security requirements for the running example are listed in Table 1. For each requirement, we present the *Responsible* actor, the *Security Requirement* itself corresponding to the security need required by the *Requester* actor. We present security requirements showing the responsible actor first, in order to present who are the actors in charge for bringing about or complying with these security requirements. Note that organisational constraints are applicable to "All agents" since they are derived by the organisational rules and regulations, which we denote as *Org*.

Step 5.1. Generate security requirements document. As an output of the fifth phase the method supports the creation of a security requirements document, which contains the list of security requirements derived from the created STS-ml model, as well as information describing the views (information that is customisable by the designers by selecting which concepts or relations they want more information about), and the details of the findings of the automated analyses.

3 STS-Tool: The Case Tool for STS-ml

The STS-Tool is the modelling and analysis support tool for STS-ml. It is an Eclipse Rich Client Platform application written in Java, it is distributed as a compressed archive for multiple platforms (Win 32/64, Mac OS X, Linux). The current version of STS-Tool (v1.3.2) is ready for public use, it is freely available for download from *www.sts-tool.eu*. The website includes extensive documentation including manuals, video tutorials, and lectures. STS-Tool has the following features:

- *Diagrammatic*: the tool enables the creation (drawing) of diagrams. Apart from typical create/modify/save/load operations, the tool also supports:
  - *different views* on a diagram, specifically: *social view, information view*, and *authorisation view*. STS-Tool ensures inter-view consistency to facilitate the modelling process.
  - ensuring diagram validity (online): the models are checked for syntactic/ well-formedness validity while being drawn. Examples include enforcing the drawing of relationships over the allowed elements and not others.
  - exporting diagrams to different file formats, such as png, jpg, pdf, svg, etc.
- *Automatic derivation of security requirements*: security requirements are derived from an STS-ml model as relationships between a *requester* (expressing a security need) and a *responsible* actor (in charge of bringing about the security need) for the satisfaction of a *security need*.
- *Automated analysis*: STS-Tool integrates the three automated analyses described in Section 2—consistency, security, and threat analysis. The results of the analyses are enumerated in tabular form below the diagram, and visualised on the diagram itself when selected (see Fig. 1).
- *Generating requirements documents*: the modelling process terminates with the generation of a *security requirements document*: the requirements analyst can customise this document by for instance including only a subset of the actors, concepts or relations, views, etc. The diagrams are described in detail both in textual and tabular form. See [4] for an example.

4 Modelling and Reasoning with STS-Tool

We demonstrate the features of STS-Tool by modelling a scenario from a case study on e-Government following the steps of the STS method and using the constructs of the STS-ml language. The demonstration is organised in terms of modelling and analysis exercises to guide the users in building and analysing STS-ml models, and deriving security requirements for the system-to-be.

4.1 Illustrating Scenario: Lot Searching

The Department of Urban Planning (DoUP) wants to build an application which integrates the existing back-office system with the available commercial services to facilitate the interaction of involved parties when searching for a lot. The *Lot Owner* wants

---

[4] http://www.sts-tool.eu/Documentation.php

to sell the lot, he defines the lot location and may rely on a Real Estate Agency (*REA*) to sell the lot. *REA* then creates the lot record with all the lot details, and has the responsibility to publish the lot record together with additional legal information arising from the current Legal Framework. *Ministry of Law* publishes the accompanying law on building terms for the lot. The *Interested Party* is searching for a lot and: (i) accesses the DoUP application to invoke services offered by the various REAs; (ii) defines a trustworthiness requirement to allow only trusted REAs to contact him; (iii) sets a criteria to search and select a *Solicitor* and a *Civil Engineer* (CE) to asses the conditions of the lot; (iv) assigns solicitor and CE to act on his behalf so that the lot information is available for evaluation; and (v) populates the lot selection for the chosen CE and Solicitor. *Aggregated REA* defines the list of trusted sources to be used to search candidate lots, it collects candidate lots from trusted sources, and ranks them to visualize to the user. *The Chambers* provide the list of creditable professionals (CE and Solicitors).

4.2   Modelling Activities

We present here the steps the designer will follow in order to perform the modelling steps, depicted in see Fig. 2, Section 2.2, while illustrating them building the models for the Lot searching scenario. This activity, apart from guiding the designer through the modelling phases, shows how the tool facilitates and supports the modelling process.

Phase 1. Modelling the Social View
We start the tool (Fig. 20) to begin with the modelling activities, for which we can use the concepts and relations from the Palette.

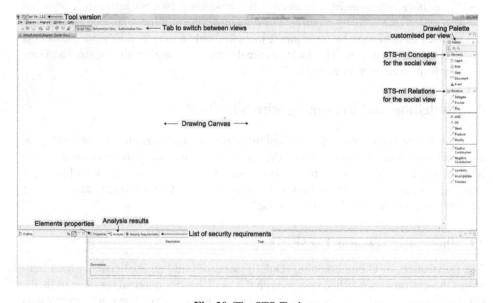

Fig. 20. The STS-Tool

Exercise 1. Identify Stakeholders. Which are the stakeholders we can identify from the Lot Searching scenario? How can they be represented in terms of roles and agents? Explain why. Draw identified roles and agents using STS-Tool. Use properties to better describe them.

Solution: This corresponds to *step 1.1* of STS method. Make sure you are on the Social View, selecting it as shown in Fig. 21.

Fig. 21. STS-Tool screenshot: selecting the social view

The identified roles and agents are:

– *Roles*: Lot owner, REA, Map Service Provider, Interested Party, Solicitor, CE Chambers, and Solicitor Chambers
– *Agents*: DoUP Application, Aggregated REA, and Ministry of Law

The reason for this is that *roles* refer to general actors that are instantiated at run time, while *agents* refer to concrete entities already known at design time. So we do not know who Lot owner or Interested Party is going to be, but there is only one Aggregated REA and one Ministry of Law in this scenario, so we know them already at design time.

We draw the identified roles and agents as shown in Fig. 22, and use the properties tab to better describe these roles and agents. In this case, we provide a description for the role *Lot owner*. This feature is helpful because the tool sets a limit of 25 characters on concept names, allowing longer descriptions to be inserted in the properties tab.

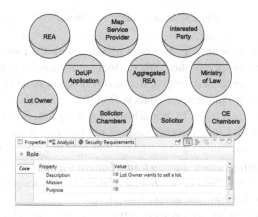

Fig. 22. Stakeholders for the Lot searching scenario

Exercise 2. Building actor models. For each modelled actor (role and agent) identify its assets. What are the goals they have and how they are achieved? What are the documents actors have and manipulate (use, modify, produce)?

Solution: This corresponds to the first part of *step 1.2* of STS method, identifying actors' assets. We start with role Lot Owner, whose actor model is shown in Fig. 23. The Lot Owner wants to sell a lot, therefore his main goal is to have lot sold. He could sell the lot either privately or through an agency. In the Lot searching scenario, the lot owner interacts with a real estate agency (REA), hence we can further refine how this is achieved. To sell the lot through an agency: a lot record should be created, lot information needs to be provided, the lot location needs to be defined and finally the lot price needs to be approved. This is represented through the and-decomposition of goal *lot sold via agency* into the above enumerated goals. In order to create the lot record, the owners personal data are needed (goal *lot record created* needs document *owner personal info*). In order to provide lot info, details about the lot are needed (goal *lot info provided* needs document *lot info*). The tool helps the designer by allowing this relation to be drawn only starting from the goal to the document, not vice-versa.

The same modelling is performed for the other identified actors, we will provide more details for some of them in the following.

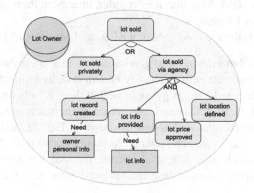

Fig. 23. Actor models: Lot owner

When first created, roles and agents come together with their rationale (open compartment), so that we can specify the goals or documents (assets) they have. The rationales can be hidden or expanded, to give the designer the possibility to focus on some role or agent at a time. We place actor goals within their rationale. STS-Tool facilitates a correct modelling of goal trees, by not allowing goal cycles. Several checks are performed live by the tool for this purpose, such as not permitting the designer to draw a decomposition link from a subgoal to a higher level goal in a goal tree.

Exercise 3. Identifying actors' interactions. For each actor identify: (i) the goals for which he needs to rely on others (goal delegations); (ii) the documents which he needs to get from (provide to) others (document provisions).

Solution: This corresponds to the second part of *step 1.2* of STS method, identifying actors' interactions. We start with Lot Owner's interactions. To have the lot record published Lot Owner delegates goal *lot record created* to REA, see Fig. 24.

Note that, when drawing a delegation, the tool makes sure that the actor does have a goal it wants to pursue, before allowing the designer to draw the goal delegation relationship starting from the given actor. It is worth emphasising that STS-ml allows only

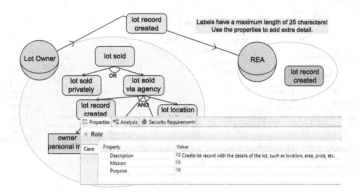

Fig. 24. Actor interactions: lot owner

the delegation of leaf goals, delegation of upper level goals is forbidden, and STS-Tool support this. If a leaf goal is delegated and the designer decides to further decompose this goal within the delegator, the tool will prompt him with a message and not allow the further decomposition. Once the goal delegation relationship is drawn, the delegated goal is automatically created within the compartment of the delegatee. This goal is represented in a darker color than the original goal, in order to clearly distinguish for each actor its own goals from the goals delegated to it. Additionally, the tool does not allow the goal to be deleted from the delegatee's compartment unless the delegation is deleted. Importantly, delegation cycles are not permitted by the tool.

STS-ml models are built iteratively, so now we will iteratively build actors' models. For this, the designer should think of: *How can the delegatee achieve the delegated goal?* Answering this question allows one to find out more details on the interacting actors: goal and/or-decompositions, document, goal-document relationships, document provisions and re-delegations if applicable. We continue the solution of *Exercise 2* by building the actor model for REA, see Fig. 25.

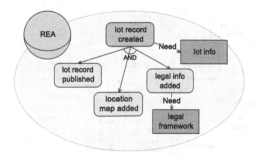

Fig. 25. Actor models: REA

Exercise 4. Expressing security needs. Analyze goal delegations and identify any applicable security needs.

Solution: This solution follows *step 1.3.* of the STS method. We have represented two actors so far and the interactions among them, so at this step we consider security needs applicable to this interaction, analysing the drawn goal delegations and document

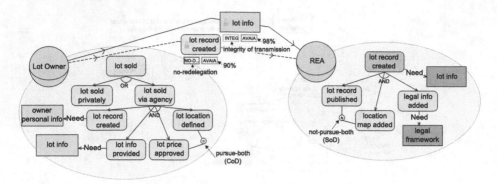

Fig. 26. Expressing security needs: REA

provisions. We focus on the identified goal delegation, and consider which of the supported security needs (Non-repudiation, Redundancy, No-redelegation, Trustworthiness, Availability) applies to it.

In Fig. 26 *Lot Owner* requires the *Real Estate Agency* no-redelegation of the goal *lot record created*, and an availability level of 85% for the same goal. To specify this using the tool, the designer needs to right-click on the delegated goal, to have a drop down list of security needs and select the desired ones. Graphically security needs can be specified by right-clicking on the goal or document and selecting the desired security needs from a given list. The selection of at least one security need, shows a padlock on the goal or document (see Fig. 26). The selected security need can be shown explicitly by clicking on the padlock, which shows small boxes below the delegated goal or provided document; each box has a different colour and different label (see Fig. 26).

Iteratively building actor models. What about other actors? This is another iteration of *step 1.2.* in identifying actors' assets. We consider now the Interested Party and build its actor model as shown in Fig. 27.

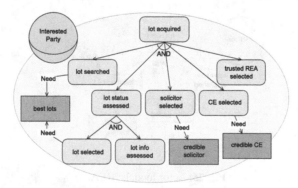

Fig. 27. Actor models: Interested Party

Iteratively identifying actors' interactions. Identify goal delegations and document provisions (iteration of *step 1.2.*) the *Interested Party* relies upon. In addition to goal delegations, we need to consider document provisions. The *Interested Party* needs *best lots* to perform a search over lots and find the best one, the document is provided by *DoUP Application*, see Fig. 28.

Iteratively expressing security needs. Considering *Interested Party* and his interactions, we determine which are the applicable security needs (iteration of *step 1.3.*). See Fig. 28 for the details of the actor model for *Interested Party*, its interactions, and the security needs expressed over them. For instance, *Interested Party* expresses a trustworthiness security need over the delegation of goal *trusted REA selected* to *DoUP Application*. Additionally, a combination of duties is specified between the goals *solicitor selected* and *CE selected*, among others.

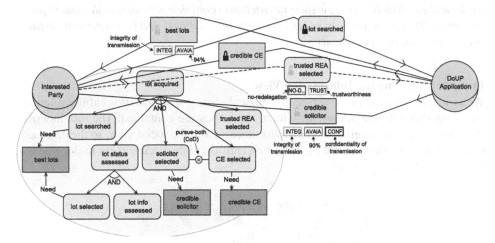

Fig. 28. Actor model and expressing security needs for Interested Party

Exercise 5. Modelling threats. *Which actors' goals and documents are threatened? Represent threats over goals and over documents. Use properties to describe the threats.*

Solution: This corresponds to *step 1.4.* of the STS method. Fig. 29 represents the events identified to threaten actors' assets. For instance, event *file stolen* threatens document *credible CE* of *CE Chambers*.

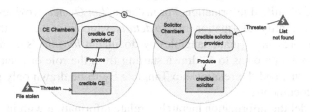

Fig. 29. Modelling threats

Phase 1. Summary. As it can be inferred by the above exercises (1–4), modelling an STS-ml model is an iterative process, *step 1.2.* and *step 1.3.* are repeated till all actor models are built and all security needs are captured. Termination criteria is defined by answering these questions: *Are there any remaining actors? Who are they? Have we* *captured all their interactions? What about security needs?* If there are still actors to be represented, then answer: *How can they achieve their goals by themselves? What documents do they manipulate? What operations do they need to perform over these documents? Do they posses the said documents? Do they need to rely on other actors for some goals? Are there any events threatening their assets?*

Exercise 6. Completing the Social View. *Complete the modelling of the social view for the Land searching scenario. As identified in the beginning of this phase, the remaining actors are: DoUP application, Aggregated REA, Ministry of Law, The Chambers (Solicitors' Chambers and CE Chambers), and Solicitor. For the remaining actors: (i) draw their models, (ii) draw their interactions (goal delegations and document provisions), (iii) express security needs over their interactions, and (iv) represent threats over their goals and documents.*

Phase 2. Modelling the Information View

We switch to *Information View* (see Fig. 30) and *represent information* entities relating them together with the *documents* within which they are contained. The tool inherits the roles and agents together with their documents from the social view, so the designer is left with the modelling of the information entities, to then relate them to documents via TangibleBy relationships.

Fig. 30. STS-Tool screenshot: switching to the information view

Exercise 7. Identify information and owners *What is the informational content of the documents represented in the social view? Who are the owners of this information? What is the structure of information? Is there a structure of documents?*

Solution: This corresponds to *steps 2.1* and *2.2* of the STS method. We first need to identify information entities and relate them with documents. We determine who is the owner of the identified information. For instance, *Lot Owner* provides information about the lot, we identify information *lot info details*, which is owned by the *Lot Owner* himself and is represented (made tangible) by document *lot info* (see Fig. 31). STS-Tool allows the relation owns to be drawn starting from the role or agent towards the information it owns, and the relationship Tangible By to be drawn only starting from information to documents.

Then, we model the information hierarchy (relate information with information). In Fig. 31, information *lot geo location* is part of information *lot info details*. Finally, we model the document hierarchy (relate documents with documents). Documents *trusted REA* and *best lots* are part of document *trusted sources*, see Fig. 31.

The tool helps the designer in building this structure by allowing the Part Of relations to be drawn only between information or documents respectively. Additionally, cycles of Part Of are not allowed by the tool.

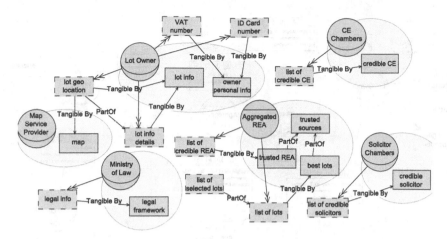

Fig. 31. Part of information view for the Land searching scenario

Iteratively building the Information View. Similarly to the previous identified information, the designer considers for each document what is its informational content. An information could be made tangible by more documents, as well as the same document can make tangible more information pieces. The designer continues modelling until all the relevant information entities have been represented.

Phase 2. Summary. Steps 2.1. and 2.2. are repeated till all information entities have been modelled, their owners have been identified, they have been related to their corresponding documents and information or document structure is determined.

Exercise 8. Completing the Information View. Complete the modelling of the information view for the Land searching scenario.

Phase 2. Modelling the Authorisation View
We switch to the authorisation view. Starting from information owners, we draw the authorisations they grant to other actors.

Fig. 32. STS-Tool screenshot: switching to the authorisation view

Exercise 9. Modelling transfer of authorisations. Are there any authorisations granted from the information owners? Is authority to transfer authorisations granted? Which are the information for which authorisation is granted? Are there any limitations of authority?

Solution: This corresponds to *step 3.1.* of the STS method. Starting from information owners or authorised parties, we identify authorisation relationships between actors. Fig. 33 depicts the authorisations granted by information owners. For instance, the *Lot Owner* authorises *REA* to use, produce, and distribute information *lot info*

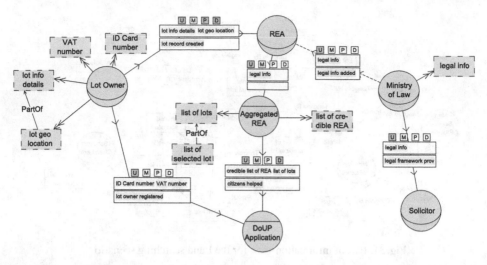

Fig. 33. Authorisation view: authorisations from information owners

details and *lot geo location* in the scope of goal *lot record created*, granting a transferable authorisation.

Fig. 33 shows the authorisations granted by authorised parties. For instance, the *Solicitor* authorises the *DoUP Application* to use and distribute the information *legal info* for goal *citizens helped* granting a transferable authorisation.

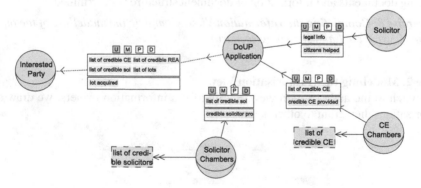

Fig. 34. Authorisation view: authorisations from authorised parties

Implicitly express security needs. Security needs over authorisations are captured implicitly. For instance, from the authorisation relationship from the *Lot Owner* to the *Real Estate Agency* we can derive that a security need for non-modification of information *lot info details* and *lot geo location* is expressed, as well as a need-to-know security need of using and producing this information for goal *lot record created*.

Iteratively building the Authorisation View. For all the represented actors, consider whether there are permissions being granted to them or whether they grant any permissions to the interacting actors.

Phase 3. Summary. Step 3.1 is repeated till all authorisation relationships have been drawn. Termination criteria is established depending on whether all authorisations have been captured and all the correct authorisation security needs have been expressed.

Exercise 10. Completing the Authorisation View. *Complete the modelling of the authorisation view for the Land searching scenario.*

Modelling Activities Summary. The modelling process (Phases 1—3) is iterative. The views can be further refined, depending on the level of detail that is needed. The changes in one view have effects on other views. As described above, the different roles or agents are maintained throughout the views, so the addition or deletion of some role or agent would affect the other views. However, even in these cases, the tool provides support by checking that a role or agent is deleted only when it does not have any inter-actions with other roles (agents). Termination criteria is established by answering these questions: Did I capture all important interconnections? Did I express all the security needs? For a more comprehensive model, use properties to better describe its elements.

4.3   Running Automated Analysis

After constructing the STS-ml model for the Lot searching scenario, we can run the automated analyses to verify its consistency, the satisfaction (possible violation) of se-curity needs, and the threat propagation over actors' assets.

Phase 4. Automated Analysis

Exercise 11. Consistency Analysis. *Is the STS-ml model for the Lot searching scenario well-formed?*

Fig. 35. Executing consistency analysis

Solution: This corresponds to *step 4.1.* of the STS method. The consistency analysis can be executed in the tool by using the Consistency Analysis tab, see Fig. 35. The consistency analysis for the lot searching scenario did not find any warnings or errors.

Exercise 12. Security Analysis. *Is it possible in the model that a security requirement is violated? Identify violations.*

Solution: This corresponds to *step 4.2.* of the STS method. The security analysis can be executed in the tool by using the Security Analysis tab, see Fig. 36. Whenever the designer runs the security analysis the tool automatically call the consistency analysis, in order to ensure that the constructed model is well-formed. Only when the consistency analysis finds no errors, the tool continues with the execution of the security analysis.

The results of the analysis are shown in the Analysis tab, and once selected are visualised graphically over the model (Fig. 37).

In our example, the security analysis found several violations of the specified security needs (errors), such as for instance the violation of non-production by the Map Service

Fig. 36. Executing security analysis

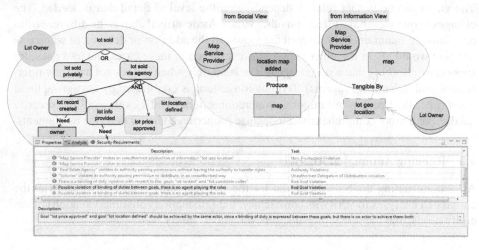

Fig. 37. Executing security analysis: visualisation of results

Provider. As it can be seen by the diagram in Fig. 33 and 34 showing authorisation relations, there is no authorisation relationship towards *Map Service Provider*, but *Map Service Provider* can produce *lot geo location* since there is a produce relationship from its goal *location map added* towards document *map* representing (making tangible) information *lot geo location*, information that is owned by *Lot Owner*.

Similarly, there is a possible violation of a combination (binding) of duties between the goals *lot price approved* and *lot location defined* of *Lot Owner*, as there appears to be no single actor achieving both these goals, see Fig. 37 showing this warning.

Fig. 38. Executing threat analysis

Exercise 13. Threat Analysis. What are the effects of the events threatening actors' assets? Identify the threat propagation.

Solution: This corresponds to *step 4.3.* of the STS method. Go to the Threat Analysis tab, Fig. 39. The results of the threat analysis are shown in the Analysis tab, and once selected are visualised graphically over the model (Fig. 39), which shows the impact of the event *List not found* threatening goal *credible solicitor provided*.

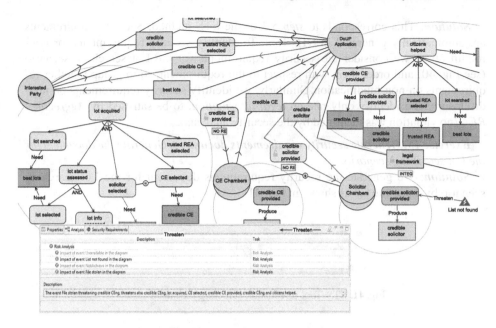

Fig. 39. Executing threat analysis

4.4 Deriving Security Requirements

Requirements specifications define what the system has to implement.

Phase 5. Derive Security Requirements

In STS-ml, security requirements specifications are automatically derived from requirements models.

Responsible	Requirement	Requester
Aggregated REA	non-modification({legal info})	Real Estate Agency
Aggregated REA	non-production({legal info})	Real Estate Agency
Aggregated REA	non-disclosure({legal info})	Real Estate Agency
Aggregated REA	non-repudiation-of-acceptance(delegated(DoUP Application,Aggregated REA,tru	DoUP Application
Aggregated REA	non-repudiation-of-acceptance(delegated(DoUP Application,Aggregated REA,lot	DoUP Application
Aggregated REA	integrity(provided(DoUP Application,Aggregated REA,trusted REA))	DoUP Application
CE Chambers	non-repudiation-of-acceptance(delegated(DoUP Application,CE Chambers,credit	DoUP Application
DoUP Application	need-to-know({ID Card number,VAT number},{lot owner registered})	Low Owner
DoUP Application	non-modification({ID Card number,VAT number})	Low Owner
DoUP Application	non-production({ID Card number,VAT number})	Low Owner
DoUP Application	non-disclosure({ID Card number,VAT number})	Low Owner
DoUP Application	need-to-know({legal info},{citizens helped})	Solicitor
DoUP Application	non-modification({legal info})	Solicitor
DoUP Application	non-production({legal info})	Solicitor
DoUP Application	need-to-know({list of credible CE},{credible CE provided})	CE Chambers

Description:
DoUP Application requires CE Chambers non-repudiation of the delegation of goal credible CE provided, by accepting this delegation.

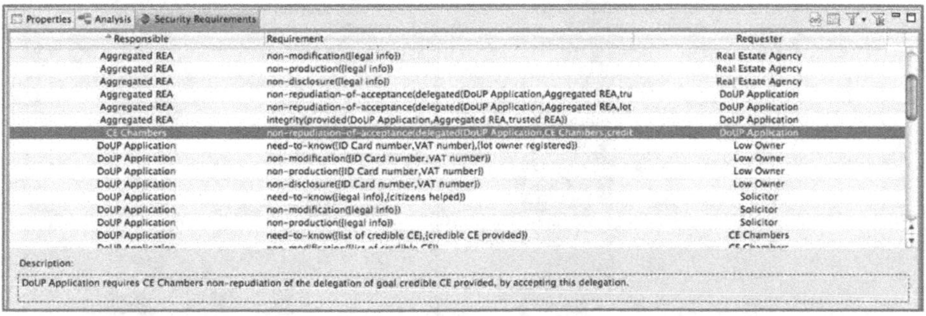

Fig. 40. Security requirements for the Lot searching scenario

Exercise 14. Generate security requirements document. *What are the security requirements for non-modification in the Lot searching scenario? What about security requirements for non-disclosure of legal information?*

Solution: This corresponds to *step 5.1* of the STS method. Security requirements are automatically generated in STS-Tool. To identify security requirements for non-modification, we consider the security requirements for the Lot searching scenario (see Fig. 40) and order them with respect to the requirement, so to group together requirements on non-modification. Similarly, we identify security requirements on non-disclosure, and identify only one on *legal information*, to be satisfied by *Aggregated REA* (no violation was identified by the security analysis).

Exercise 15. Generate security requirements document. *Generate the document for the Lot searching scenario.*

Solution: We generate the security requirements document for the Lot searching scenario by using the tab as shown in Fig. 41.

Fig. 41. STS-Tool screenshot: selecting the social view

This opens up a sequence of dialogue windows to determine the title and author for the document (Fig. 42a), and deciding what to include, which views, elements within the views, or analysis results (see Fig. 42b).

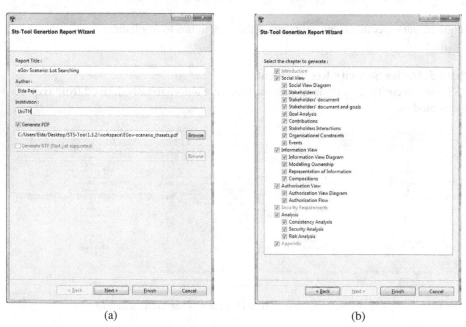

(a)   (b)

Fig. 42. Customising the security requirements document

5 Conclusions

Many security requirements engineering frameworks and methods are available in the literature. Secure Tropos [6] models security concerns throughout the whole development process. It expresses security requirements as *security constraints*, considers potential threats and attacks, and provides methodological steps to validate these requirements and overcome vulnerabilities.

Liu et al. [5] extend $i*$ to deal with security and privacy requirements. Their methodology defines security and privacy-specific analysis mechanisms to identify potential attackers, derive threats and vulnerabilities, thereby suggesting countermeasures. Their solution falls short when considering security issues through the later phases of the development process [6].

SI* [4] is a security requirements engineering framework that builds on $i*$ [10] by adding security-related concepts, including delegation and trust of execution or permission. SI* uses automated reasoning to check security properties of a model, reasoning on the interplay between execution and permission of trust and delegation relationships. Our framework supports a more expressive ontology (featuring sophisticated authorisations) to represent information security requirements, and clearly decouples business policies (the goals of an individual actor) from security requirements.

We have presented how STS-Tool—the case tool for STS-ml—allows an effective security requirements engineering process, following the steps of the STS method. STS-Tool supports modelling and reasoning activities, while aiding the requirements analyst and the security engineer at each step.

We have demonstrated how modelling and reasoning activities can be performed with the help of a case study from eGovernment. STS-ml supports a rich set of security requirements that are derived from security needs expressed over actors' interactions.

Our future work includes improving the usability of STS-Tool for a better user experience, as well as extending its reasoning capabilities for more sophisticated reasoning.

Acknowledgments. The research leading to these results has received funding from the European Union Seventh Framework Programme (FP7/2007-2013) under grant no 257930 (Aniketos) and 256980 (NESSoS).

References

1. Bertino, E., Jajodia, S., Samarati, P.: A flexible authorization mechanism for relational data management systems. ACM Transactions on Information Systems 17(2), 101–140 (1999)
2. Dalpiaz, F., Giorgini, P., Mylopoulos, J.: Adaptive Socio-Technical Systems: A Requirements-driven Approach. Requirements Engineering 18(1), 1–24 (2013)
3. Dalpiaz, F., Paja, E., Giorgini, P.: Security requirements engineering via commitments. In: Proceedings of STAST 2011, pp. 1–8 (2011)
4. Giorgini, P., Massacci, F., Mylopoulos, J., Zannone, N.: Modeling security requirements through ownership, permission and delegation. In: Proc. of RE 2005, pp. 167–176 (2005)
5. Liu, L., Yu, E., Mylopoulos, J.: Security and privacy requirements analysis within a social setting. In: Proc. of RE 2003, pp. 151–161 (2003)
6. Mouratidis, H., Giorgini, P.: Secure Tropos: A security-oriented extension of the tropos methodology. IJSEKE 17(2), 285–309 (2007)

7. Paja, E., Dalpiaz, F., Giorgini, P.: Managing security requirements conflicts in socio-technical systems. In: Ng, W., Storey, V.C., Trujillo, J.C. (eds.) ER 2013. LNCS, vol. 8217, pp. 270–283. Springer, Heidelberg (2013)
8. Singh, M.P.: An ontology for commitments in multiagent systems: Toward a unification of normative concepts. Artificial Intelligence and Law 7(1), 97–113 (1999)
9. Whitman, M.E., Mattord, H.J.: Principles of Information Security, 4th edn. Course Technology Press (2011)
10. Yu, E.: Modelling strategic relationships for process reengineering. PhD thesis, University of Toronto, Canada (1996)

Model-Driven Development of a Secure eHealth Application

Miguel A. García de Dios[1], Carolina Dania[1], David Basin[2], and Manuel Clavel[1]

[1] IMDEA Software Institute, Madrid, Spain
{miguelangel.garcia,carolina.dania,manuel.clavel}@imdea.org
[2] ETH Zürich, Switzerland
basin@inf.ethz.ch

Abstract. We report on our use of ActionGUI to develop a secure eHealth application based on the NESSoS eHealth case study. ActionGUI is a novel model-driven methodology with an associated tool for developing secure data-management applications with three distinguishing features. First, it enables a model-based separation of concerns, where behavior and security are modeled individually and subsequently combined. Second, it supports model-based quality assurance checks, where the properties proven about the models transfer to the generated applications. Finally, for data-management applications, the ActionGUI tool automatically generates complete, ready-to-deploy, security-aware, web applications. We explain these features in the context of the eHealth application.

1 Introduction

In [3] we proposed a novel methodology, called ActionGUI, for the model-driven development of secure data-management applications. This methodology enables a model-based separation of concerns, where an application's behavior and security are modeled individually and subsequently combined. Moreover, it supports model-based quality assurance checks, where relevant properties may be proven about the combined models. These properties then transfer to the automatically generated data-management applications.

We report here on our use of ActionGUI to develop a secure data-management application. This application is based on a case study proposed within NESSoS, the European Network of Excellence on Engineering Secure Future Internet Software Services and Systems [12]. The eHealth case study consists of a web-based system for electronic health record management (EHRM). Electronic health records (EHR) store information created by, or on behalf of, a health professional in the context of the care of a patient.

Electronic health records are highly sensitive and therefore their access must be controlled. Part of the challenge in this case study was to model the access control policy and build an application that enforces it at runtime. The policy consists of various authorization rules along the lines of: *The access control criteria for an EHR depends, among others, on the type of EHR. For instance,*

M. Heisel et al. (Eds.): Engineering Secure Future Internet Services, LNCS 8431, pp. 97–118, 2014.
© Springer International Publishing Switzerland 2014

a highly sensitive record might be only available to the patient's treating doctor (and perhaps a few others, in rare situations). Such rules necessitate fine-grained access control, where access control decisions depend not only on the user's credentials but also on the satisfaction of constraints on the state of the persistence layer, i.e. on the values of stored data items.

We show how ActionGUI's modeling languages can be used to specify the application's data model (e.g., hospital staff, health records), security policy (e.g., rules like the above) and behavior. Moreover, by illustrative examples, we highlight various features of the ActionGUI methodology and associated tool. Overall, the eHealth case study is interesting as an example of developing a secure data-management application and it provides a proof-of-concept for the application of the ActionGUI methodology to an industry-relevant problem.

Organization. In Section 2 we provide background on the ActionGUI methodology and tool. In Section 3 we give an account of our modeling and generation of the EHRM application with ActionGUI. In Section 4 we describe a proof method for checking that the behavior of the modeled data-management application respects the invariants of the application's underlying data model, and we apply it to our EHRM models. Finally, in Section 5, we draw conclusions.

2   ActionGUI

ActionGUI [3] is a methodology for the model-driven development of secure data-management applications. It consists of languages for modeling multi-tier systems, and a toolkit for generating these systems. Within this methodology, a secure data-management application is modeled using three interrelated models:

1. A *data model* defines the application's data domain in terms of its classes, attributes, associations, and methods.
2. A *security model* defines the application's security policy in terms of authorized access to the actions on the resources provided by the data model.
3. A graphical user interface, or *GUI model*, defines the application's graphical interface and application logic. Note, in particular, that this model formalizes both *UI structure* and *behavior*.

The heart of this methodology, illustrated in Figure 1, is a model-transformation function that automatically lifts the policy that is specified in the security model to the GUI model. The idea is simple but powerful. The security model specifies under what conditions actions on data are authorized. The control information in the GUI model specifies which actions are executed in response to which events. Lifting essentially consists of prefixing each data action in the GUI model with the authorization check specified in the security model. The resulting GUI model is security aware. It specifies UI structure, information flow with persistent storage, and all authorization checks.

The ActionGUI methodology is implemented within a toolkit, also called ActionGUI [1], which performs the aforementioned many-models-to-model transformation. From the resulting security-aware GUI model, ActionGUI generates

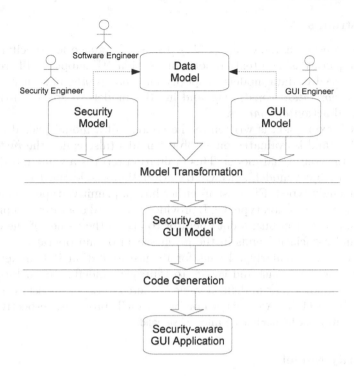

Fig. 1. Model-driven development of security-aware GUIs

a deployable application along with all support for access control. In particular, when the security-aware GUI model contains only calls to execute CRUD actions, i.e., those actions that create, read, update, and delete data, then ActionGUI will generate the complete implementation automatically.

In the remaining part of this section we briefly introduce the languages that are used within the ActionGUI methodology to model the applications' data, security, and GUI models, including their constraints, as well as the tools supporting the ActionGUI methodology. In the next section we will use the NESSoS EHRM application scenario to illustrate these modeling languages as well as the model-based separation of concerns supported by the ActionGUI methodology.

2.1 Data Models

Data models provide a data-oriented view of a system. They typically specify how data is structured, the format of data items, and their logical organization, i.e., how data items are grouped and related. ActionGUI employs Component-UML [4] for data modeling. ComponentUML provides a subset of UML class models where *entities* (classes) can be related by *associations* and may have *attributes* and *methods*.

2.2   Constraints

The Object Constraint Language (OCL) [13] is a language for specifying constraints and queries using a textual notation. ActionGUI supports different uses of OCL: it is used in data models to specify *data invariants*, in security models to specify *authorization constraints*, and in GUI models to specify if-then-else *conditions* and action *arguments*.

Every OCL expression is written in the context of a model (called the *contextual model*), and is evaluated on an object model (also called the *instance* or *scenario*) of the contextual model. This evaluation returns a value but does not alter the given object model, since OCL's evaluation is side-effect free.

OCL is strongly typed. Expressions either have a primitive type, a class type, a tuple type, or a collection type. OCL provides: standard operators on primitive data, tuples, and collections; a dot-operator to access the values of the objects' attributes and association-ends in the given scenario; and operators to iterate over collections. Particularly relevant for its use in ActionGUI models, OCL includes two constants, null and invalid, to represent undefinedness. Intuitively, null represents unknown or undefined values, whereas invalid represents error and exceptions. To check if a value is null or invalid, OCL provides, respectively, the Boolean operators ocIlsUndefined() and ocIlsInvalid().

2.3   Security Models

SecureUML [4] extends Role-Based Access Control (RBAC) [9] with *authorization constraints*. These constraints are used to specify policies that depend on properties of the system state. SecureUML supports the modeling of *roles* and their hierarchies, *permissions*, *actions*, *resources*, and *authorization constraints*.

In ActionGUI, we use an extension of SecureUML for specifying security policies over data models. In this extension:

- The protected *resources* are the entities, along with their attributes, methods, and association-ends.
- The controlled *actions* are: to create and delete entities; to read and update attributes; to read, create, and delete association-ends; and to execute methods.
- The authorization constraints are specified using OCL.

The contextual model of the authorization constraints is the underlying data model. Additionally, authorization constraints may contain the variables self, caller, value, and target, which are interpreted as follows:

- self refers to the root resource upon which the action will be performed if permission is granted. The root resource of an attribute, a method, or an association-end is the entity to which it belongs.
- caller refers to the user that will perform the action if the permission is granted.
- value refers to the value that will be used to update an attribute if the permission is granted.

– target refers to the object that will be added to (or removed from) the (root) resource at an association-end if the permission is granted.

2.4 GUI Models

GUI models provide a human-interface oriented view of a system. A GUI consists of widgets, which are visual elements that display information and trigger events that execute actions. In ActionGUI, we use GUIML [3] for modeling both

– the GUI's *structure*, i.e, the elements (*widgets*) that comprise it,
– and the GUI's *behavior*, i.e., how its elements will react (*actions*) in response to user interactions with them (*events*).

Behavioral modeling is a key feature of GUIML and uses OCL to specify both the conditions and the arguments for the different actions; the contextual model of these conditions and arguments is again the underlying data model. This enables both the security model and the GUI model to "speak" the same language, namely OCL in the context of the common, underlying data model. This allows us to define rigorously the transformation function that lifts the security policy to the GUI level.

We next briefly describe the main elements of GUIML, namely, *widgets* (with their associated *variables*), *events*, and *actions*.

Widgets. A GUI model consists of widgets of different kinds. Examples include windows (pages, when referring to web applications), combo-boxes (selectable lists), tables, date fields, boolean fields (check boxes), buttons, text fields, and labels.

Variables. Widgets may own *variables*, which store values for later use. Each widget declaration may contain variable declarations, listing the variables owned by the widget. There are variables that are, by default, owned by every widget of a given type. In particular, the variables caller and role are predefined in every window. They store, respectively, the application's user and the user's role.[1] The variable text is predefined in every label, button, and text field. This variable stores the string displayed on the screen within the label, button, and text field. The variable rows is predefined in every combo-box and table. This variable stores the collection of items that can be selected from the combo-box or table. The variable row is also predefined in every combo-box and table where, for each row, it stores the item that corresponds to this row. Finally, the variable selected is also predefined in every combo box or table where it stores the item(s) selected in the combo box or table.

---

[1] Currently, it is a task for the GUI modeler to guarantee that the variables caller and role always store an *authenticated* user and a valid role. This can be done, for example, by modeling a login window, where the users will need to enter a valid nickname and password before accessing the application.

Events. Widgets may trigger events, which execute actions either on data or on other widgets. The actions executed when an event is triggered are specified using *statements*. A statement is either an action, a conditional statement, an iteration, a try-catch, or a sequence of statements. The conditions in conditional statements are specified using OCL expressions, whose context is the underlying data model. Additionally, they can refer to the widget variables. Note that each sequence of statements associated to an event is executed as a single *transaction*: either all statements in the sequence successfully execute in the given order, or none of them are executed at all.

Actions. Events trigger actions that can be executed either on objects belonging to the persistence tier or on objects belonging to the presentation tier. The former are called *data actions* and the latter are called *GUI actions*. Data actions are precisely those controlled in the security model, namely: to create and delete entities; to read and update attributes; to read, create, and delete association-ends; and to execute methods. GUI actions include those for setting the value of a widget variable, opening a window (**open**), moving back to the previous window (**back**), and forcing a rollback of the current transaction (**fail**). Note that some actions may take arguments. The values of these arguments are specified using OCL expressions, whose context is the underlying data model, and they can also refer to the widget variables.

2.5   Security-Aware GUI Models

The heart of ActionGUI is a model-transformation function *Sec* that, given a GUIML model G and a SecureUML model S, automatically generates a new GUIML model $\mathrm{Sec}(G, S)$. The generated model is identical to G except that it is *security aware* with respect to S. The transformation function *Sec* works by wrapping around every data action *act* in G an if-then-else statement with the following arguments:

- a condition that reflects the constraints associated to the permissions specified in S, for each of the different roles, to execute the action *act*;
- a **then** branch that contains the action *act*; and
- an **else** branch that contains the action **fail**.

Thus, the semantics of an if-then-else statement ensures that *act* will only be executed if the constraints associated to the corresponding permissions are satisfied. Moreover, if these constraints are not satisfied, then the action **fail** will be executed, forcing a rollback in the current transaction.

2.6   Tool Support

Security-aware GUI models are platform independent and can be mapped to implementations employing different technologies. This includes desktop applications, web applications, and mobile applications. The ActionGUI Toolkit [1], automatically generates web-based data-management applications from security-aware GUIML models.

The ActionGUI Toolkit features model editors for constructing and manipulating ComponentUML, SecureUML, and GUIML models. Crucially, the ActionGUI Toolkit implements our model transformation to generate security-aware GUIML models. Moreover, it includes a code generator that, given a security-aware GUIML model, produces a web application based on the following three-tier architecture:

1. Presentation tier (also known as front-end): Users access web applications through standard web browsers, which render the content (HTML and JavaScript) dynamically provided by the application server.
2. Application tier: The toolkit generates Java Web Applications, implemented using the Vaadin framework. The applications run in a servlet container (such as Tomcat or GlassFish), process client requests and generate content, which is sent back to the client for rendering.
3. Persistence tier (also known as data tier or back-end): The generated application manages information stored in a database.

3   The EHRM ActionGUI Application

The NESSoS EHRM application scenario defines different system use cases along with the associated access control policy. The use cases include: register new patients in a hospital and assign them to clinicians, such as nurses or doctors; retrieve patient information; register new nurses and doctors in a hospital and assign them to a ward; change nurses or doctors from one ward to another; and reassign patients to doctors. Due to space limitations, we will not describe how we model all of these use cases. We focus instead on a representative use case as a running example: reassigning patients to doctors. We will use this example to illustrate ActionGUI's modeling languages as well as the model-based separation of concerns supported by the ActionGUI methodology.

3.1   The EHRM's Data Model

The full data model for the EHRM application contains 18 entities, 40 attributes, and 48 association-ends. We discuss below just the entities, attributes, and association-ends that are required for our running example.

Figure 2 presents this data model, formalized using ActionGUI's textual syntax. In this syntax, entities are declared with the keyword **entity** followed by the entity's name, and its attributes and association-ends, which are enclosed within brackets. Attributes and association-ends are declared together with their types. Moreover, since associations are binary, each association-end is declared together with its opposite association-end, designated by the keyword **oppositeTo**.

As this example shows, ActionGUI data models specify how the application's data is structured, independently of how it will be visualized or accessed.

Professional. This entity represents the EHRM's users. The role assigned to each user is specified by its role attribute. The roles considered are DIRECTOR, ADMINISTRATOR, DOCTOR, NURSE, and SYSTEM. The medical centers where a user works are linked to the user through the association-end worksIn. If a user is a doctor, then it is linked to the corresponding doctor information through the association-end asDoctor. Similarly, if a user is an administrative staff, then it is linked to staff information through the association-end asAdministrative.

MedicalCenter. This entity represents medical centers. The departments belonging to a medical center are linked to the medical center through the association-end departments. The professionals working for a medical center are linked to the medical center through the association-end employees.

Doctor. This entity represents doctor information. Doctor information is linked to the corresponding professional through the association-end doctorProfessional. The departments where a doctor works are linked to the doctor's information through the association-end doctorDepartments. The patients treated by a doctor are linked to the doctor's information through the association-end doctorPatients.

Administrative. This entity represents administrative staff information. Administrative staff information is linked to the corresponding professional through the association-end administrativeProfessional.

Department. This entity represents departments. The medical center to which a department belongs is linked to the department through the association-end belongsTo. The doctors working in a department are linked to the department through the association-end doctors. The patients treated in a department are linked to the department through the association-end patients.

Patient. This entity represents patients. The doctor treating a patient is linked to the patient through the association-end doctor. The department where a patient is treated is linked to the patient through the association-end department.

3.2 The EHRM Data Model's Invariants

The full EHRM application data model is constrained by 66 data invariants, formalized using OCL. The following three invariants are representative.

1. *Each patient is treated by a doctor.*
   Patient.allInstances()→forAll(p|not(p.doctor.oclIsUndefined()))
2. *Each patient is treated in a department.*
   Patient.allInstances()→forAll(p|not(p.department.oclIsUndefined()))
3. *Each patient is treated by a doctor who works for a set of departments, including the department where the patient is treated.*
   Patient.allInstances()→forAll(p| p.doctor.doctorDepartments→includes(p.department))

```
entity Professional {
  Role role
  Set(MedicalCenter) worksIn oppositeTo employees
  Doctor asDoctor oppositeTo doctorProfessional
  Administrative asAdministrative oppositeTo administrativeProfessional  }
entity MedicalCenter {
  Set(Department) departments oppositeTo belongsTo
  Set(Professional) employees oppositeTo worksIn  }
entity Doctor {
  Professional doctorProfessional oppositeTo asDoctor
  Set(Department) doctorDepartments oppositeTo doctors
  Set(Patient) doctorPatients oppositeTo doctor  }
entity Administrative {
  Professional administrativeProfessional oppositeTo asAdministrative  }
entity Department {
  MedicalCenter belongsTo oppositeTo departments
  Set(Doctor) doctors oppositeTo doctorDepartments
  Set(Patient) patients oppositeTo department  }
entity Patient {
  Doctor doctor oppositeTo doctorPatients
  Department department oppositeTo patients  }
enum Role { DIRECTOR ADMINISTRATOR DOCTOR NURSE SYSTEM }
```

Fig. 2. The eHRMApp's data model (partial)

These invariants make precise the intended meaning of the associations between the entities Patient, Doctor, and Department. The first two invariants state that the doctor and the department associated to a patient cannot be undefined, i.e., *null*. The third invariant states that a doctor who treats a patient must work in the department where the patient is treated, although the doctor may also work in other departments.

3.3   The EHRM's Security Model

Electronic health records are by their nature highly sensitive and the NESSoS case study informally defines the policy that regulates their access. As expected, the authorization to carry out certain actions is not only role-based, but also context-based. In other words, the EHRM access control policy is *fine grained*.

The full EHRM application's security model contains 5 roles and 573 permissions, where each permission authorizes users in a role to execute an action upon the satisfaction of an authorization constraint formalized in OCL. In Figure 3 we present examples of two permissions, modeled using ActionGUI's textual syntax. In this syntax, the roles that users can take are declared with the keyword **role** followed by the role's name, and its permissions, which are enclosed within brackets. Permissions are introduced by naming the root resources to which they grant access. Each permission consists of a list of actions through which the corresponding root resource can be accessed. Actions on attributes, methods, or association-ends are declared along with their names. For example, **update(***attr***)** denotes the update action on the attribute *attr*. The keyword **constrainedBy** is used to declare that the permission to execute an action is constrained by the given condition (enclosed in square brackets).

The first permission authorizes a user (*caller*) with the role ADMINISTRATOR to reassign a patient to a department (*value*) provided that the user works in a set of medical centers that includes the one to which the department belongs where the patient will be reassigned. The second permission authorizes a user (*caller*) with the role ADMINISTRATOR to reassign a patient (*self*) to a doctor (*value*) provided two conditions are satisfied: (i) among the medical centers where the user works, there is at least one where the doctor to which the patient will be reassigned also works; and (ii) the user works in medical centers that includes the center to which the department belongs where the patient is currently being treated. Note that no other role has permissions associated to the actions of reassigning a patient to a department or to a doctor.

As this example illustrates, ActionGUI security models are formulated in terms of the application's data. This formalization is independent of how the data is visualized or accessed through the application's graphical user interface.

```
1  role ADMINISTRATOR {
2    Patient{
3      update (department) constrainedBy [caller.worksIn→includes(value.belongsTo)] }
4    Patient{
5      update (doctor) constrainedBy
6        [caller.worksIn→exists(m | value.doctorProfessional.worksIn→includes(m))
7          and caller.worksIn→includes(self.department.belongsTo)] }
```

Fig. 3. Examples of the EHRM security model's permissions

3.4   The EHRM's GUI Model

The full EHRM application's GUI model contains 8 windows for the following use cases: login to the application; access a medical center's information; register a new patient; review a patient's information; reassign a patient to a doctor and department; access options reserved for the medical center's director; introduce a professional into the system; and reassign a professional to a department.[2]

We discuss below the window relevant for our running example: the window movePatientWI for reassigning a patient to a doctor and a department. Figures 4 and 5 present our model of this window, in ActionGUI's textual syntax. Figure 6 contains a screenshot of the actual window generated from this model.

---

[2] Here are some other concrete figures about the size of the GUI model: i) Widgets: 19 buttons; 73 labels; 19 text fields; 5 boolean fields; 1 date field; 1 combo box; and 9 tables; ii) Statements: 34 if-then-else statements; iii) Data actions: 11 create actions; 41 update actions; 5 add link actions; and 2 remove link actions; iv) GUI actions: 157 set actions; and 7 open actions; v) OCL expressions: 361 expressions (77 non-literals).

In ActionGUI's textual syntax, a widget is declared with a keyword like **Window**, **Button**, and **TextField**, according to its type, followed by the widget's name, and the declaration of the variables it owns, the events it triggers, and the widgets it contains, all enclosed in brackets. A variable declaration consists of the variable's type followed by its name, possibly followed by the variable's initial assignment (if any) and by the statement that will be executed every time the variable's value changes (if any), the latter enclosed in brackets. Events are declared by indicating their types followed by the sequence of statements that they execute, enclosed in brackets. The syntax for declaring the different data and GUI actions should be clear from the example below.

The window movePatientWI assumes that both a medical center and a patient have previously been selected. This information is stored, respectively, in the variables medicalCenter and patient (lines 2-3). The window movePatientWI contains the following widgets:

- A label patientLa that displays the name and surname of the selected patient (lines 5–7).
- A label departmentLa that displays the name of the department where the selected patient is treated (lines 8–9).
- A label doctorLa that displays the name and surname of the doctor who treats the selected patient (lines 10–13).
- A label departmentsLa that displays a message inviting the user to select a department (lines 14–15).
- A label doctorsLa that displays a message inviting the user to select a doctor (lines 16–17).
- A table departmentsTa that displays information about the departments that belong to the selected medical center (line 22); in particular, the name of each of these departments is shown (line 31-34). Also, when the user selects a department from this list, it refreshes the list of doctors displayed in the table doctorsTa (see below) with the doctors who work for the selected department (lines 19–21).
- A table doctorsTA that is initially empty (line 24). As previously explained, upon selection of a department in the table departmentsTa, it displays information about the doctors who work for the selected department (lines 19–21); in particular, the name and surname of each of these doctors are shown (lines 35-41).
- A button moveBu that, when clicked upon, if there is a department selected in the table departmentsTa (line 44), and there is also a doctor selected in the table doctorsTa (line 45), then:
  - it reassigns the selected department to the selected patient (line 46);
  - it reassigns the selected doctor to the selected patient (line 47);
  - it notifies the user that the reassignment succeeded (lines 48).
  Otherwise, it notifies the user that either a doctor (line 50) or a department (line 52) must first be selected.
- A button backBU that, when the user clicks on it, it returns to the previous window (line 55).

As this example illustrates, ActionGUI GUI models depend on how the application's data is structured — after all, they describe how users interact with this data — but not on the application's security policy. Of course, in terms of the final application's *usability*, there is a dependency: a GUI can end up being unusable precisely because of the application's security policy.

3.5   The EHRM's Security-Aware GUI Model

As explained in Section 2.5, the heart of ActionGUI is a model-transformation function that, essentially, prefixes each data action in the GUI model with the authorization check specified in the security model. The full EHRM application's GUI model contains 59 data actions, and therefore the automatically generated EHRM application's security-aware GUI model contains the same number of authorization checks.

To illustrate our model-transformation function, we show in Figure 7 the part of the security-aware GUI model for the button moveBu's event **onClick** that is relevant for our running example. The action of reassigning the selected patient to the department selected in the table departmentsTa (line 46 in Figure 5) is now wrapped by an if-then-else statement (lines 46.1-46.5 in Figure 7) whose condition reflects the permission for executing this action given by line 3 in Figure 3. Similarly, the action of reassigning the selected patient to the doctor selected in the table doctorsTa (line 47 in Figure 5) is wrapped by an if-then-else statement (lines 47.1-47.7 in Figure 7) whose condition reflects the permission for executing this action given by lines 5–7 in Figure 3.

3.6   Generating the EHRM Application

The ActionGUI Toolkit automatically generates the complete EHRM application in under 10 seconds. The generated .war file includes the Vaadin library as well as other external libraries. The Vaadin library is responsible of 70% of the size of the generated file and only 10% of this file corresponds to the code that ActionGUI automatically generates to interpret the application's model. The size of the .war file containing the complete application is roughly 15 MB.

4   Analyzing the EHRM ActionGUI Application

Model-Driven Architecture supports the development of complex software systems by generating software from models. Of course, the quality of the generated code depends on the quality of the source models. If the models do not properly specify the system's intended behavior, one should not expect the generated system to do so either. *Quod natura non dat, Salmantica non praestat.*[3] Experience shows that even when using powerful, high-level modeling languages, it is easy to make logical errors and omissions. It is critical not only that the modeling

---

[3] Less elegantly said, *garbage in, garbage out.*

```
1  Window movePatientWi {
2    MedicalCenter medicalCenter
3    Patient patient
4    String text := ['Move a patient']

5  Label patientLa {
6    String text := ['Patient: '.concat($movePatientWi.patient$.contact.name)
7                    .concat(' ').concat($movePatientWi.patient$.contact.surname)] }
8  Label departmentLa {
9    String text := ['Department: '.concat($movePatientWi.patient$.department.name)] }

10 Label doctorLa {
11   String text := ['Doctor: '.concat($movePatientWi.patient$.doctor.
12                   doctorProfessional.name).concat(' ').
13                   concat($movePatientWi.patient$.doctor.doctorProfessional.surname)] }

14 Label departmentsLa {
15   String text := ['Select the new department:'] }

16 Label doctorsLa {
17   String text := ['Select the new doctor:'] }

18 Table departmentsTa {
19   Department selected {
20     if [not $selected$.oclIsUndefined()] {
21       movePatientWi.doctorsTa.rows := [$selected$.doctors] } }
22   Set(Department) rows := [$movePatientWi.medicalCenter$.departments] }

23 Table doctorsTa {
24   Set(Doctor) rows := [Doctor.allInstances()→select(false)]
25   Doctor selected }

26 Button moveBu {
27   String text := ['Move the patient'] }

28 Button backBu {
29   String text := ['Back']
30 }
```

Fig. 4. A window for reassigning a selected patient (part I)

```
31    Table movePatientWi.departmentsTa {
32      columns{
33            ['Department'] : Label department {
34                                String text := [$departmentsTa.row$.name] } } }

35    Table movePatientWi.doctorsTa {
36    columns {
37      ['Doctor'] : Label doctor {
38                  String text :=
39                    [$doctorsTa.row$.doctorProfessional.name
40                      .concat(' ')
41                      .concat($doctorsTa.row$.doctorProfessional.surname)]}}}

42    Button movePatientWi.moveBu {
43      event onClick {
44          if [not $departmentsTa.selected$.oclIsUndefined()] {
45            if[not $doctorsTa.selected$.oclIsUndefined()] {
46            [$movePatientWi.patient$.department] := [$departmentsTa.selected$]
47            [$movePatientWi.patient$.doctor] := [$doctorsTa.selected$]
48            notification(['Success'],['The patient has been reassigned.'],[0]) }
49            else {
50            notification(['Error'],['Please, select first a doctor.'],[0]) } }
51          else {
52            notification(['Error'],['Please, select first a department.'],[0]) } } } }

53    Button movePatientWi.backBu {
54      event onClick {
55            back } }
```

Fig. 5. A window for reassigning a selected patient (part II)

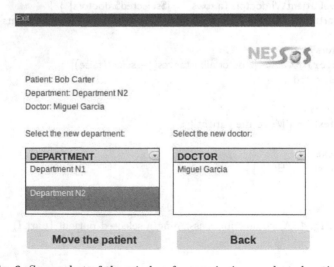

Fig. 6. Screenshot of the window for reassigning a selected patient

```
46.1   if [[$movePatientWi.role$ = ADMINISTRATOR
46.2        and $movePatientWi.caller$.worksIn
46.3           →includes($departmentsTa.selected$.belongsTo)] {
46.4     [$movePatientWi.patient$.department] := [$departmentsTa.selected$] }
46.5     else { fail }


47.1   if [[$movePatientWi.role$ = ADMINISTRATOR
47.2        and $movePatientWi.caller$.worksIn→exists( m |
47.3             $doctorsTa.selected$.doctorProfessional.worksIn→includes(m))
47.4       and $movePatientWi.caller$.worksIn
47.5           →includes($movePatientWi.patient$.department.belongsTo))]  {
47.6     [$movePatientWi.patient$.doctor] := [$doctorsTa.selected$] }
47.7     else { fail }
```

Fig. 7. The security-aware actions for reassigning a selected patient

language has a well-defined semantic, so one can know what one is doing, but also that there is tool support for analyzing the modeled systems' properties.

In this section we explain how we can reason about an important property of ActionGUI models, called *data invariant preservation*. We use the EHRM application for illustration.

4.1   Data Invariant Preservation

We first introduce some terminology. Recall that the actions triggered by an event may be specified using if-then-else statements. At execution time, the exact sequence of actions taken is determined by how the different conditions of each if-then-else statements are evaluated in the system's state at the time of evaluation. Note that this state includes both the state of the persistence layer and the state of the GUI, in particular, its widget variables. Since each action may update the system's state, a sequence of actions gives rise to a sequence of states, which we call an *execution path*.

ActionGUI's data model may include *data invariants*. We have given several examples of these in Section 3.2. These are properties that are *required* to be satisfied in every (reachable) system state. Invariance of a property must be *proven* and the standard way to do this is to show that the property is inductive, that is, it is satisfied in the system's initial state and, whenever it is satisfied in a state, it is satisfied in all possible successor states. Below we shall focus on the inductive step: proving invariant preservation.

Formally, let Φ be a collection of data invariants. An event *preserves a data invariant* $\phi \in \Phi$ if and only if for every execution path triggered by the event, if every data invariant $\psi \in \Phi$ is satisfied at the initial state of the execution path, then ϕ is also satisfied at the final state. Here we leverage ActionGUI's transaction semantics and that transactions are implemented in a way that ensures their atomicity: The intermediate states of an execution path may be considered to be internal and may therefore (temporarily) violate ψ. An event is Φ-*data invariant preserving* when it preserves all data invariants in Φ.

Our proof procedure, illustrated below, is based on the fact that each event defines an *action tree*. The nodes in this tree are the actions triggered by the event and branching corresponds to the if-then-else conditions governing the execution of these actions. As expected, every successful transaction corresponds to executing a sequence of actions given by one of the branches of the action tree, from the root to a leaf. Note that, to simplify our exposition we omit both iteration statements and event-triggering actions; including these would lead to action graphs rather than trees.

1	*Each patient is treated by a doctor.*
	Patient.allInstances()→forAll(p|not(p.doctor.oclIsUndefined()))
2	*Each patient is treated in a department.*
	Patient.allInstances()→forAll(p|not(p.department.oclIsUndefined()))
3	*Each patient is treated by a doctor who works for a set of departments that includes the department where the patient is treated.*
	Patient.allInstances()→forAll(p|
	p.doctor.doctorDepartments→includes(p.department))

Fig. 8. Examples of the EHRM data model's invariants

Reassigning Doctors and Departments to Patients. We show in Figure 9 the action tree defined by the the button moveBu's event **onClick**. For ease of later reference, we assign labels for the actions and the if-then-else conditions. Note that:

– Branch 1 corresponds to the case when a department and a doctor are both selected when the button moveBU is clicked-on. In this situation, the patient will be first assigned to the selected department, and then to the selected doctor; finally, a message confirming these actions will be displayed.
– Branch 2 corresponds to the case when a department is not selected when the button moveBU is clicked-on. In this situation, a message stating that a department must be first selected will be displayed.
– Branch 3 corresponds to the case when a department is selected, but a doctor is not, when the button moveBU is clicked-on. In this situation, a message stating that a doctor must first be selected will be displayed.

Next, we use this action tree to reason about whether the button moveBu's event **onClick** preserves the data invariants 1–3.

Branch 1: Data invariants 1 and 2. Recall that these data invariants state that every patient is assigned to exactly one doctor and one department. Observe that

Actions

assign_dept	= [$movePatientWi.patient$.department] := [$departmentsTa.selected$]
assign_doctor	= [$movePatientWi.patient$.doctor] := [$doctorsTa.selected$]
notify_reassign	= notification(['Success'],['The patient is reassigned.'],[0])
error_select_doctor	= notification(['Error'],['Select first a doctor.'],[0])
error_select_dept	= notification(['Error'],['Select first a department.'],[0])

If-then-else conditions

a_dept_is_selected	= not $departmentsTa.selected$.oclIsUndefined()
a_doctor_is_selected	= not $doctorsTA.selected$.oclIsUndefined()

Branch 1

a_dept_is_selected = true ∧ a_doctor_is_selected = true	
nodes	actions
1	*assign_dept*
2	*assign_doctor*
3	*notify_reassignment*

Branch 2

a_dept_is_selected = false	
nodes	actions
1	*error_select_dept*

Branch 3

a_dept_is_selected = true ∧ a_doctor_is_selected = false	
nodes	actions
1	*error_select_doctor*

Fig. 9. Action tree for the button moveBU's **onClick**

the initial state in every successful transaction in this branch will satisfy the conditions *a_dept_is_selected* and *a_doctor_is_selected*. Therefore the arguments of the actions *assign_dept* and *assign_doctor* will necessarily not be null when these actions are called. Thus, the conditions *a_dept_is_selected* and *a_doctor_is_selected*, together with the postconditions of the actions *assign_dept* and *assign_doctor*, guarantee that every successful transaction in this branch preserves the data invariants 1 and 2.

Branch 1: Data invariant 3. Recall that this data invariant states that every patient is assigned to a department where its doctor works. Interestingly, there is no guarantee that every successful transaction in this branch preserves the data invariant 3. This is because the doctors shown in the table doctorsTa are those belonging to the selected department at the time of this selection (line 19–21 in Figure 4); however, there is no guarantee that, by the time the user clicks on the button moveBu, this relationship still holds for the selected doctor.

To guarantee that data invariant 3 is preserved by every successful transactions in this branch, we can simply enclose the sequence of actions *assing_dept*, *assig_dept*, and *notify_reassignment* (lines 46-54 in Figure 5) within an (additional) if-then-else with the following condition:

$departmentsTa.selected$.doctors→includes($doctorsTa.selected$).

Branch 2 and 3. Since these branches do not contain any data actions, every successful transaction in these branches will trivially preserve all the data model's invariants.

We conclude this section by summarizing in Figure 10(a) our analysis of data invariant preservation for the button moveBu's event **onClick**. For the sake of illustration, we also consider in Figures 10(b) and 10(c) data invariant preservation for two modified versions of the button moveBu's event **onClick**. In the first case, we have removed the innermost if-then-else, i.e., the one whose condition checks that a doctor has been selected. In the second case, we have removed the outermost if-then-else, i.e., the one whose condition checks that a department has been selected. As expected, if we remove the innermost if-then-else, there is no guarantee that data invariant 1, i.e., that every patient is assigned to exactly one doctor, will be preserved. Similarly, if we remove the outermost if-then-else, there is no guarantee that data invariant 2, i.e., that every patient is assigned to exactly one department, will be preserved.

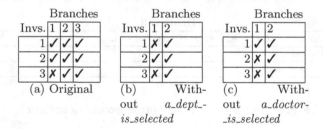

	Branches		
Invs.	1	2	3
1	✓	✓	✓
2	✓	✓	✓
3	✗	✓	✓

(a) Original

	Branches	
Invs.	1	2
1	✗	✓
2	✓	✓
3	✗	✓

(b) Without a_dept_is_selected

	Branches	
Invs.	1	2
1	✓	✓
2	✗	✓
3	✗	✓

(c) Without a_doctor_is_selected

Fig. 10. Checking data invariants preservation for different versions of the button moveBu's **onClick**

4.2 Checking Data Invariant Preservation

We now describe how we check whether modeled events preserve data invariants.

Fix a data model D and a GUI model G. Let Φ be D's declared invariants. Let ev be an event in G and let B be a branch of ev's action tree containing n actions. To check that every instance of B preserves the invariants in Φ, we proceed as follows:

1. We define a ComponentUML data model D_n that represents all sequences of n states. Recall that a state is any instance of the data model D along with any assignment to the widget variables in G.
2. For $1 \leq i < n$, we formalize an OCL expression, in the context of D_n, that the i-th action's postconditions are satisfied in the $(i+1)$-th state. We denote by $Posts(B)$ the resulting set of OCL expressions.

3. For $1 \leq i \leq n$, we formalize an OCL expression, in the context of D_n, that the *guard* of the i-th action is satisfied in the i-th state. We denote by $Guards(B)$ the resulting set of OCL expressions.
4. For each invariant $\phi \in \Phi$, we formalize an OCL expression, in the context of D_n, that ϕ is satisfied in the first state (initial state). We denote by $\Phi(1)$ the resulting set of OCL expressions.
5. For each invariant $\phi \in \Phi$, we formalize an OCL expression $\psi(n)$, in the context of D_n, stating that ψ is satisfied in the n-th (final) state.
6. We prove that there is no instance of D_n that satisfies

$$\Phi(1) \cup Posts(B) \cup Guards(B) \cup \{\neg\psi(n)\}.$$

This formula expresses that there is no sequence of n states where the first state satisfies all the invariants, each state satisfies the postcondition of the action leading to it, each state satisfies the condition that guards the action leading to the next state, and the final state does not satisfy ψ.

We have built a tool that implements the above steps. For every data model D with invariants Φ, GUI model G, and event ev in G, our tool automatically generates the set of branches Π corresponding to ev. Then, for each branch $B \in \Pi$ and invariant $\psi \in \Phi$, it generates the data model D_n and the sets of OCL expressions $\Phi(1)$, $Posts(B)$, $Guards(B)$, and $\{\neg\psi(n)\}$, where n is B's length. Finally, our tool uses the mapping OCL2FOL$^+$ [8] to generate the first-order proof-score corresponding to step 6 above, both in SMT-LIB syntax [2] and DFG syntax [14].

4.3   Analyzing the EHRM Application

We report here on preliminary experiments where we used our tool to check data invariant preservation for the EHRM application. The application's full GUI model only contains 8 events whose associated statements include data actions, and therefore must be checked. Moreover, the action trees defined by these events contain 49 branches in total, but only 8 of these branches include data actions. Therefore, since the full EHRM application's data model contains 66 invariants, we must perform a total of 528 checks (8 branches × 66 invariants) to prove data invariant preservation for this application.

We ran these checks on a laptop computer, with a 2.66GHz Intel Core 2 Duo processor and 4Gb 1067MHz. memory, using SPASS [15] as the back-end theorem-prover. Here we summarize the results. First, for branches containing up to 3 data actions (50% of the non-trivial checks fall into this category, including our running example) checking takes less than 10 milliseconds to return "proof found" when the invariants are preserved. Second, when checking branches containing 8-10 actions and 8-10 conditions (45% of the non-trivial checks), we also obtain "proof found" in less than 30 seconds when the invariants are preserved, except for some complex invariants where checking takes up to 3 minutes. Third, for a branch containing 30 actions and 6 conditions, checking also takes less than 40 seconds to return "proof found" when the invariants are preserved, except again for some complex invariants where it takes up to 5 minutes.

Finally, note that all these results depend on the interaction between (i) the way we formalize sequences of n states, OCL invariants, actions' guards, and actions' post-conditions, and (ii) the heuristics implemented in the verification back-end we use, here SPASS. We are currently analyzing this interaction in depth to better understand the scope and limitations of our tool. For example, we already know that SPASS seems not able to return "completion found" (we timed out after four days) when, for the sake of experiment, we remove some conditions from the branches, thereby violating some of the invariants.

5   Conclusions

This chapter complements the article [3], where we present the ActionGUI methodology and tool in detail. [3] also contains an extensive comparison with related work and provides summary statistics from five different developments. The eHealth application was one of the smallest examples considered there and other examples are roughly an order of magnitude larger, e.g., with hundreds of windows, buttons, labels, and if-then-else-statements and thousands of OCL statements. In contrast, in this paper, we present one case study in detail. We also describe model-based property checking, which was not addressed in [3].

Among the methodologies and tools reviewed in [3], UWE [7,6,11] and ZOOM [10] are the most closely related to our work. As a modeling tool, UWE provides the modeler with a higher-level of abstraction than ActionGUI. In particular, the actions executed by the widgets' events are described in UWE using natural language. Thus, unless the models are appropriately refined, as discussed in [11], UWE does not support code-generation. In contrast, UWE provides specific diagrams for modeling GUI *presentations* and *navigations*, which facilitate the task of GUI modeling. [6] extends UWE to use SecureUML for modeling security policies. However, this work does not use model-transformation to lift automatically the security policy to the GUI level. Instead the UWE modeler is responsible for adding all the appropriate authorization checks to the GUI model. Like ActionGUI, ZOOM allows GUI modelers to specify widgets, their events, and their actions. Moreover, using an extension of Z [16], one can specify the conditions of the actions and their arguments, similar to how this is done in ActionGUI using OCL. In contrast to ActionGUI, ZOOM does not provide a language for modeling security and security aspects are not explicitly considered in this approach. Moreover, ZOOM does not support code-generation. It only provides interpreters for model animation.

In the following we draw some conclusions based on our experience with the eHealth application and developing other applications with ActionGUI. First, ActionGUI's security modeling language is well suited for modeling access control policies that combine both *declarative* and *programmatic* aspects. Declarative access control policies depend on static information, namely the assignments of users and permissions to roles. Programmatic access control depends on dynamic information, namely the satisfaction of authorization constraints in the current system state. Programmatic access control is formalized using authorization constraints and, as Section 3.3 illustrates, this allows us to model directly the kinds of authorization rules considered in the eHealth case study.

Second, ActionGUI's graphical user interface modeling language is well suited for modeling *dynamic web pages*. These are pages, displayed at the client, that are generated at the time of access by a user or that change as a result of user interaction. As Section 3.4 illustrates, an important aspect of our methodology is that developers can model this behavior independent of the access control policy. The policy is later lifted from the security model to this behavioral model, as described in Section 3.5.

Third, as explained in Section 3.6, the ActionGUI code generator can automatically generate ready-to-deploy, security-aware, data-management web applications. By data-management, we mean that most of the behavior described in the GUI model is built from CRUD actions (which create, read, update and delete data). When all behavior can be described this way, then the entire application can be generated from the models, including a complete, configured security infrastructure and back-end database support.

Finally, our case study illustrates how users can specify properties of ActionGUI models, such as invariant preservation. Moreover, as described in Section 4, our approach to checking these properties based on translation to first-order logic is practical, see also [5]. This is a form of model-checking and, as in other domains, it has an important role to play in building and certifying security-critical systems. Designers and system certifiers can reason about systems at the model level using automated tool support. Moreover, with our approach, they can afterwards generate model-conform, and therefore property conform, systems simply by pressing a button. Our experience with ActionGUI shows that this is not merely a vision for the future, but it is realizable today, at least for small and medium-scale data-management applications.

Acknowledgements. This work is partially supported by the EU FP7-ICT Project "NESSoS: Network of Excellence on Engineering Secure Future Internet Software Services and Systems" (256980) and by the Spanish Ministry of Economy and Competitiveness Project "StrongSoft" (TIN2012-39391-C04-04).

References

1. ActionGUI. The ActionGUI project (2013), http://www.actiongui.org
2. Barrett, C., Stump, A., Tinelli, C.: The SMT-LIB Standard: Version 2.0. In: Gupta, A., Kroening, D. (eds.) Proceedings of the 8th International Workshop on Satisfiability Modulo Theories, Edinburgh, UK (2010)
3. Basin, D., Clavel, M., Egea, M., de Dios, M.A.G., Dania, C.: A model-driven methodology for developing secure data-management applications. IEEE Transactions on Software Engineering (to appear, 2014)
4. Basin, D., Doser, J., Lodderstedt, T.: Model driven security: From UML models to access control infrastructures. ACM Transactions on Software Engineering and Methodology 15(1), 39–91 (2006)

5. Basin, D.A., Clavel, M., Egea, M.: A decade of model-driven security. In: Proceedings of the 16th ACM Symposium on Access Control Models and Technologies (SACMAT 2011), Innsbruck, Austria, vol. 1998443, pp. 1–10 (2011)
6. Busch, M.: Integration of security aspects in web engineering. Master's thesis, Institut für Informatik, Ludwig-Maximilians-Universität, München, Germany (2011)
7. Busch, M., Koch, N.: MagicUWE - a case tool plugin for modeling web applications. In: Gaedke, M., Grossniklaus, M., Díaz, O. (eds.) ICWE 2009. LNCS, vol. 5648, pp. 505–508. Springer, Heidelberg (2009)
8. Dania, C., Clavel, M.: OCL2FOL+: Coping with Undefinedness. In: Cabot, J., Gogolla, M., Ráth, I., Willink, E.D. (eds.) OCL@MoDELS. CEUR Workshop Proceedings, vol. 1092, pp. 53–62. CEUR-WS.org (2013)
9. Ferraiolo, D.F., Sandhu, R.S., Gavrila, S., Kuhn, D.R., Chandramouli, R.: Proposed NIST standard for role-based access control. ACM Transactions on Information and System Security 4(3), 224–274 (2001)
10. Jia, X., Steele, A., Qin, L., Liu, H., Jones, C.: Executable visual software modeling—the ZOOM approach. Software Quality Control 15, 27–51 (2007)
11. Kroiss, C., Koch, N., Knapp, A.: UWE4JSF: A model-driven generation approach for web applications. In: Gaedke, M., Grossniklaus, M., Díaz, O. (eds.) ICWE 2009. LNCS, vol. 5648, pp. 493–496. Springer, Heidelberg (2009)
12. NESSoS. The European Network of Excellence on Engineering Secure Future internet Software Services and Systems (2010), http://www.nessos-project.eu
13. Object Management Group. Object constraint language specification version 2.3.1. Technical report, OMG (2012), http://www.omg.org/spec/OCL/2.3.1
14. Weidenbach, C.: SPASS input syntax version 1.5 (1999)
15. Weidenbach, C., Dimova, D., Fietzke, A., Kumar, R., Suda, M., Wischnewski, P.: SPASS version 3.5. In: Schmidt, R.A. (ed.) CADE-22. LNCS, vol. 5663, pp. 140–145. Springer, Heidelberg (2009)
16. Woodcock, J., Davies, J.: Using Z: specification, refinement, and proof. Prentice-Hall, Inc., Upper Saddle River (1996)

Modeling Security Features of Web Applications*

Marianne Busch[1], Nora Koch[1], and Santiago Suppan[2]

[1] Institute for Informatics, Ludwig-Maximilians-Universität München
Oettingenstraße 67, 80538 München, Germany
{busch,kochn}@pst.ifi.lmu.de
[2] Siemens AG, Germany
Otto-Hahn-Ring 6, 81739 München, Germany
santiago.suppan.ext@siemens.com

Abstract. Securing web applications is a difficult task not only, because it is hard to implement bulletproof techniques, but also because web developers struggle to get an overview of how to avoid security flaws in a concrete application. This is aggravated by the fact that the description of a web application's security concept is often scattered over lengthy requirements documents, if documented at all. In this chapter, we extend the graphical, UML-based Web Engineering (UWE) language to model security concepts within web applications, thus providing the aforementioned overview. Our approach is applied to a case study of an Energy Management System that provides a web interface for monitoring energy consumption and for configuring appliances. Additionally, we give an overview of how our approach contributes to the development of secure web applications along the software development life cycle.

Keywords: UML-based web engineering, secure web engineering, web applications, UML, security, Energy Management System, Smart Home.

1 Introduction

The rising cybercrime and the growing awareness of data privacy due to global surveillance disclosures imply an urgent need to secure web applications. Besides confidential connections and authentication, both data access control and navigational access control are the most relevant security features in this field. However, adding such security features to already implemented web applications is an error-prone task.

Therefore, the goal is to include security features in early stages of the development process of web applications, i.e., at requirements specification and design modeling level. Secure web engineering approaches as ActionGUI [1] and the UML-based Web Engineering (UWE) [2] have been developed, trying to abstract from as many implementational details as possible.

---

* This work has been supported by the EU-NoE project NESSoS, GA 256980.

M. Heisel et al. (Eds.): Engineering Secure Future Internet Services, LNCS 8431, pp. 119–139, 2014.
© Springer International Publishing Switzerland 2014

The way that seems right for most modeling methods, raises questions when dealing with design decisions related to more web-security specific concerns: How should Cross-Site-Request-Forgery (CSRF) [3] be prevented, in order to avoid end users to execute unintentionally malicious actions for an attacker, on a web application in which they are currently authenticated? What should happen in case the web application is under attack, e.g., under denial-of-service attack, making the machine or network resource unavailable to its intended users?

So far, those questions tend to be answered in lengthy specification documents or they are just documented by the code itself. However, a straightforward understanding of the way how web security is managed for a certain web application is crucial.

Our approach aims at addressing the answer to these questions at design level, extending the set of modeling elements provided by the UWE language in order to be able to express protection-specific security concerns. The challenge is to find means for recording security-related design decisions for the web, while maintaining the necessary abstraction a modeling language needs. Therefore, we extend UWE's UML profile to support modeling solutions that should be deployed to shield a web application and its users against attacks. Such is the aim of providing language elements to model features like *CSRF prevention* and *injection prevention* or special behavior for the case that an application is *under attack*.

In this chapter, we not only introduce the latest UWE extension along with a case study about the web interface of an Energy Management System (EMS), but also give an overview of how UWE's security features, which have been developed within the EU project NESSoS [4], support the phases of the software development life cycle (SDLC). This begins with the requirement and design phase, where UWE enables security engineers to get an overview of the application, but also serves as a notation for documentation. Aside from that, UWE models can be used as input for tools that generate artifacts for the implementation. For the testing phase, two approaches are available, (1) for testing that a user can only navigate the web application using a predefined path and (2) a toolchain for testing access control policies generated from UWE models. For the latter, the interested reader is referred to chapter [5].

The remainder of this chapter is structured as follows: In Sect. 2 we introduce the EMS case study, which is our running example. Section 3 gives an overview of security features that play a major role in the web and which are required for our case study, before the UWE approach is introduced in Sect. 4. In Sect. 5 we describe our UWE extensions for protection-specific security concerns, by applying them to the case study. Section 6 positions UWE in the SDLC. Finally, we present related work in Sect. 7 and conclude in Sect. 8.

2   Case Study: Energy Management System

This section describes the Energy Management System (EMS) case study and in particular the web application of the EMS that controls Smart Homes, which are households with interconnected appliances. We start by introducing Smart Home components, continue by presenting actors and conclude by explaining concrete functionality, before we go in the next section into more security-related details.

2.1 Components of Smart Homes

Figure 1 visualizes the entities in a Smart Home. Generally, the EMS is an interface for the Smart Grid customer that visualizes consumption data. Concrete instantiations can be realized by means of mature web application technology, which provides several ways of advanced functionality, as for energy trading or for regulating the current drain. Ideally, most appliances, as e.g., ovens, dishwashers, washing machines or lamps are so-called Smart Appliances (SAs), which means they contain a small embedded-system, that receives control commands from the EMS and that informs the EMS about the current status. Additionally, SAs can be controlled by pushing a button or by using an integrated touch screen.

For a household, exactly one EMS and one Smart Meter are installed locally, in a place where they are protected from physical tampering. The Smart Meter is responsible for monitoring the amount of energy that is sold or bought. As the EMS is connected to the web, remote access to its web application allows users to interact with the EMS and to monitor energy consumption from outside their homes.

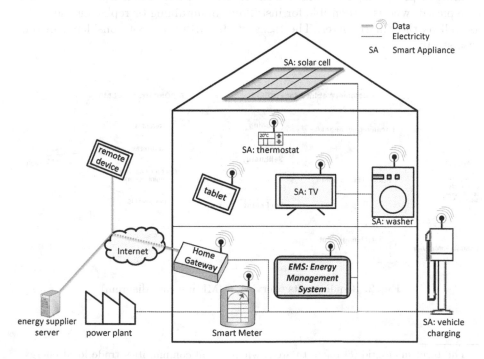

Fig. 1. Entities in the Smart Home (adapted from [6])

A possibility to control energy consumption more globally is Demand Side Management. It envisions to adapt the consumption level according to messages sent by energy providers. For example, in situations when lots of energy is needed in an area, the energy provider notifies all Energy Management Systems. Consequently, the EMS can send command messages to SAs in order to turn them off. The concrete behavior when receiving a Demand Side Management message can be controlled by user defined policies in the EMS.

2.2   Actors

According to [7], the *pro*sumer (producer / consumer) is the end customer, who is consuming energy as well as producing energy, e.g., by using photovoltaic or wind energy as decentralized energy resources. Prosumers are also able to store energy, for instance in the batteries of the electric vehicle and to resell the energy later to the so called microgrid[1] when the prices are higher. We also refer to the prosumer simply as "(private) user" or "customer".

Figure 2 depicts a UML use case diagram, which gives an overview of the actors in our case study and the main functionalities of the EMS. On the left, the private user is shown. Users can create and configure other users, e.g., under-aged family members can be allowed to sign into the EMS web application and to see their energy consumption, but they should not be able to trigger electricity vending or purchasing functions. On the right, the Meter Point Operator (MPO) is depicted, who is responsible for installing, maintaining or replacing the EMS as well as the Smart Meter. The tasks of the MPO are not considered in our case study.

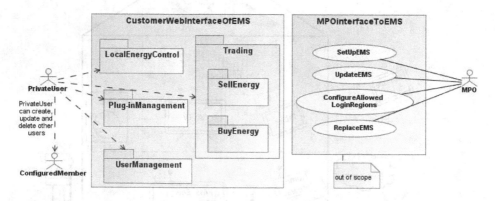

Fig. 2. Requirements overview (UML use case diagram)

---

[1] The term microgrid [8] refers to areas where small communities trade local energy, in addition to the energy supply provided by professional energy suppliers.

2.3   Functionality

The main functionality of the EMS is shown in Fig. 2: a user can buy or sell energy, control local energy consumption by configuring SAs, install plugins to automate tasks or manage other users. These use cases are described in more detail in the following:

Local Energy Control. As more and more Smart Appliances will be added to the home network, their heterogeneous functionality has to be made available to the customer. The EMS web application can present, in a uniform way, a coherent view to the user in the form of a portal, presenting information that the EMS has collected from diverse sources (appliances or external servers). SAs, even new ones that were non-existent when the web application was programmed and deployed, offer their services through a standard interface to the EMS (cf. lower half of Fig. 3, use case InteractWithSA, depicted in bold font because it might be used relatively often). Hereby, auto-configuration (in the sense of plug-and-play support) is important, as many customers may not become acquainted with the full potential of the EMS. This case applies particularly to senior citizens.

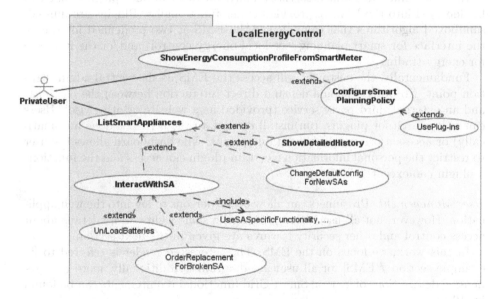

Fig. 3. Requirements of local energy control (UML use case diagram)

Easy access to real-time information supports the users, e.g., to pay attention to their energy consumption, as depicted at the top of Fig. 3. Additionally, automatic peak load management provides smart planning for reducing energy consumption. This Smart Planning feature (cf. Configure Smart Planning Policy) can be enriched by plugins, which have to be installed separately. Plugins might also be allowed to access the local usage history from SAs. This way they can base their plan on previous user's behavior. For example, hydronic heating might be reduced automatically at times where usually no great quantity of hot water is needed.

Energy Trading. Selling and buying energy is a critical task, if the user wants the system to perform a trade automatically. Consequently, policies have to ensure that the system acts in the interest of the prosumer. The recommendation / trade system can also be enriched by plugins, offering so called value added services. A value added service, such as a price comparing third party service (e.g., when and who is offering the best conditions for green energy?) functions as follows: The third party provides a plugin which obtains current market prices from the third party's server. The plugin compares prices and consumption data locally. The result of the comparison can either be a visual notification in the EMS or a process is started to renegotiate Energy Supplier contracts, if the prosumer has defined a policy that allows the process to negotiate automatically. In the latter case, a notification is sent to the user after the (un-)successful provider change.

Plugin Management. As mentioned before, a key functionality is the interplay of the EMS and value added services. Third parties can offer plugins that can be deployed into the EMS to provide further functionality. Plugins are limited, sandboxed algorithms that can enhance the EMS at two predefined interfaces: the interface for smart planning (see local energy control) and/or the interface for energy trading.

Fundamentally, the customer will access the EMS as the central administration point. No process should demand direct interaction between the customer and an external third party service (provided as a website or otherwise). Users can only search for plugins, (un)install or update them (if not done automatically) or access a privacy dashboard for plugins. The dashboard allows the user to restrict the personal information a certain plugin can access and the functions a plugin can execute.

User Management. Prosumers can allow other persons to log into the web application. However, not all users have to have the same rights. More details about access control and other security features are given in the next section.

In this work, we focus on the EMS. The interested reader is referred to [9, example section / EMS] for all use case diagrams. Additionally, more comprehensive descriptions of general Smart Grid functional requirements can be found in [10,11].

3   Secure Web Applications

This section introduces common security features, including those which are special for web applications. Security features, detailed in the following, are: authentication, panic mode, reauthentication, secure connections, authorization, user zone concept, cross-site-request-forgery prevention, under attack mode and SQL-injection prevention.

Implementing coherent *authentication* is a challenge, as users must be able to log-in to their EMS internally, from their home, and externally, using a mobile device, or a public terminal. A two-factor authentication should be employed to access sensitive information of the EMS. Two-factor authentication requires a knowledge factor ("something only the user knows") and either a possession factor ("something only the user has") or an inherence factor ("something only the user is") from the user for the authentication to succeed. For example, a password has to be entered together with a code that the user's smart phone generates.

A feature rarely implemented in current web applications, is the *panic mode*. When the panic mode is activated, the user interface will be displayed with reasonable information generated by the EMS that does not reflect the users real information. This is especially needed for coercion situations, where criminals might physically force users to reveal information of themselves or to conclude long-term contracts with certain parties. The panic mode also protects threatened users by pretending to malfunction or to execute functions successfully without any real impact. Therefore, users have to authenticate themselves with predefined credentials which differ from the usual ones: using the same username in combination with a panic mode password loads the alternative user interface.

Besides the first authentication, prosumers can be forced to *reauthenticate* themselves. This is often the case after a certain time of inactivity (often referred to as "automatic logout" in online banking applications), but it is also common for critical areas. For example, web shops often allow to store cookies to keep the user authenticated while browsing their offers. However, if the last authentication is older than a certain amount of time, the users have to reauthenticate themselves before being able to make a purchase. Regarding the EMS plugin installation functions, the last authentication of a prosumer should not be older than 10 minutes, a typical time threshold also used in online banking. The timeout avoids a takeover of a session by another person who has access to the prosumers browser.

All kinds of authentication are useless, if the login process can be eavesdropped. *Secure connections*, as e.g., HTTP Strict Transport Security (HSTS) connections can be used to ensure the confidentiality, integrity and freshness of all user's request as well as of all response of the EMS. As encrypting a connection is a time consuming task, it is an important design decision which parts of an application should be secured. In the case of Energy Management, security weights more than speed, even if Demand Side Management and energy trading are very time demanding [12]. Compromises in speed can have impact on economic aspects, but compromises in security could mean a total blackout of the power supply, producing high economic damages.

Apart from secure session management after authentication, a well implemented *authorization (access control)* concept is needed to satisfy customer needs. There are several roles to be considered, as family members might be involved in the customization of the Smart Home.

Many web applications require a *user zone concept*. If users are accessing the EMS from the home area, they are permitted to access all prosumer managing functions (depending on their roles). But if they are requesting access externally, stricter policies have to be enforced, depending on the requester's location, i.e. the IP address of the requester's device. To configure this policy, users inform their MPO that they are on holiday and that a certain location is the source of legitimate requests.

A telling example is an attack from a foreign country. An attacker that is mimicking a user will, by policy enforcement, be denied to alter the Smart Appliances' behavior, if he is accessing the EMS remotely from a very far place. This feature will not hold up against versatile attackers, as several proxies or even computers that have been compromised by an attacker, could be available in the desired geo-location. Still, this mechanism represents a filter against unambitious attackers. There are several other mature attacks on web based technologies that also could have an impact on the EMS, mostly related to so-called "common web application vulnerabilities" [13]. As the EMS is remotely accessible by means of a web client, there is room for session riding attacks. Depending on the user's browsing application, *cross-site-request-forgery* (abbreviated "CSRF") might be used by a malicious attacker to trigger actions without the user's consent. For example, an attacker could trick users into interacting with the web server of a Smart Appliance by letting them call an address like:

`http://EMSremoteIP.com/SmartApplianceName/SmartApplianceFunction`

This request cannot be called by an unauthorized person due to the policy enforcement inside the EMS, but it can be triggered by means of CSRF.

The *under attack mode* is a dynamic protection against attempts of compromising the EMS functionality, as the EMS reacts accordingly and reduces the attackers possibilities. An example is the reduced functionality when under denial of service attack. The EMS will try to reduce the number of allowed connections and/or deny any connection from IPs that have exceeded a certain number of requests in a certain time frame. Additionally, CAPTCHA-challenges could be displayed to verify that the requester is a person and not merely a program.

Another feature is *the protection of the EMS database*. The EMS database should only accept statements that have been generated by the EMS itself. In order to avoid SQL-injection attacks within generated statements, parameterized queries should be used.

As announced in the introduction, some security features can be handled at an abstract level, as e.g., authorization, whereas others are to be thought of at the end of the design phase, as SQL-injection prevention. Note that we do not claim to cover all possible web security features, although we try to cover the most common ones.

4   Overview of UML-Based Web Engineering (UWE)

This section introduces the modeling language UML-based Web Engineering (UWE) [9,2], which we use to model secure web applications.

One of the cornerstones of the UWE language is the "separation of concerns" principle using separate models for the different views of a web application, such as the navigation and the presentation view. However, we can observe that security features are cross-cutting concerns which cannot be separated completely. The views and corresponding UWE models are:

Requirements View defines (security) requirements of a project.

Content View contains the data structure used by the application.

Access Control View is given by a *UWE Role Model* and a *Basic Rights Model*. The former describes the hierarchy of user groups to be used for authorization and access control issues. It is usually part of a *User Model*, which specifies basic structures, as e.g., that a user can take on certain roles simultaneously. The latter defines the access control policies. It constrains elements from the *Content Model* and from the *Role Model*.

Presentation View sketches the web application's user interface.

Process View details the flow of actions to be executed.

Navigation View defines the navigation flow of the application and navigational access control policies. The former shows which possibilities of navigation exist in a certain context. The latter specifies which roles are allowed to navigate to a specific state and the action taken in case access cannot be granted. In a web application such actions can be, e.g., to logout the user and to redirect to the login form or just to display an error message. Furthermore, secure connections between server and browser are modeled, too.

The following table maps UWE views to security features that they can express. We introduce concrete modeling elements for this security features in the next section.

View	Security Features
Content	SQL-injection prevention, cross-site-request-forgery prevention
Navigation	authentication, reauthentication, secure connections, under attack mode
Access Control	authorization, under attack mode, user zone concept
Process	user zone concept, panic mode

For each view, an appropriate type of UML diagram is selected, e.g., a state machine for the navigation model. The UWE approach defines a UML profile that consists of a set of stereotypes, tag definitions, constraints and patterns for modeling secure web applications. The profile can be downloaded from the UWE website [9].

Stereotypes can be applied to UML model elements (e.g. classes, states, dependencies) and values can be assigned to tags. UML tags are always associated to a stereotype and stereotypes can inherit tags from other stereotypes. In the UWE profile, patterns are provided for modeling widely used elements, as e.g., different types of authentication mechanisms.

5   Designing Secure Web Applications with UWE

This section shows how to model security features with the most recently introduced UWE profile elements. The main advantages of these specific modeling elements for the modeler are on the one hand to promote the inclusion of security aspects from the early phases of the development. On the other hand it enables documentation and, due to brevity, a quick understanding of security features that are or should be employed. The elements are introduced using our EMS case study.

5.1   Content View

When modeling larger web systems, such as the EMS web application, it is useful to divide the system into manageably small components. The main characteristic of components is encapsulation, which means that components can only share information using predefined interfaces. Encapsulation is advantageous, because each component can be implemented and tested individually. Regarding modeling, components contribute to a clear structure, as the division of tasks within an application becomes apparent. Consequently, it is easy to define appropriate security properties for each part of a web application.

In the case of our EMS, a component EMScore is created, which contains components that are built into the EMS system by default, as depicted in the class diagram shown in Fig. 4. Smart Appliances (SAs) can communicate with the EMS using the SA interface, shown on the lower left. According to the description in the previous section, plugins are also external components that can enhance the smart planning or the trader / recommender. Some plugins might provide both functionalities (as e.g., PluginA does).

The EMScore contains four internal components that correspond to the main areas we identified in the requirements phase (cf. Fig. 2): local energy control, user management, energy trade system and plugin management. As can be seen in Fig. 4, the user manager is used by all components, because the system does not allow access without having granted permission first. The interface PluginList publishes the list of installed plugins within the system so that the user can advise the internal components to exchange the planing or trading plugin.

As far as security is concerned, the UWE profile redefines the UML stereotype «component» with the following tags:

csrfPrevention models how cross-site-request-forgery (CSRF) should be repelled. The modeler can choose from the options presented at the OWASP CSRF Cheat Sheet[2]. For the EMS example the most common "Synchronizer Token Pattern" is used, which includes a randomly generated challenge token to all server requests in a web page. An attacker cannot hope to guess a valid token when sending the user a prepared URL.

---

[2] OWASP CSRF Prevention Cheat Sheet. https://www.owasp.org/index.php/Cross-Site_Request_Forgery_(CSRF)_Prevention_Cheat_Sheet

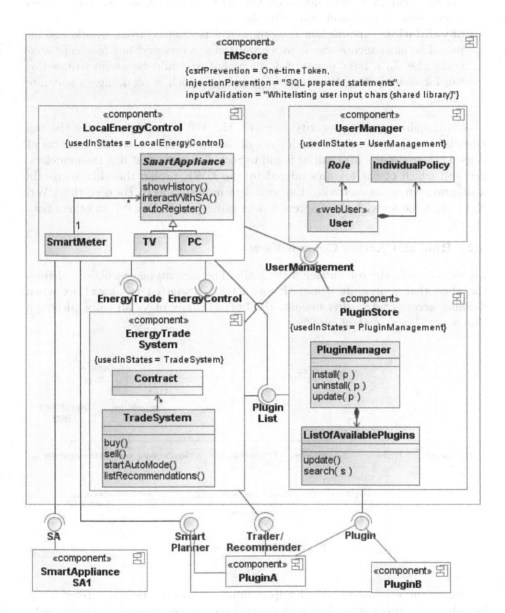

Fig. 4. UWE: Content model

injectionPrevention records how SQL injections (and others injection attacks) are prevented. In most programming languages, SQL prepared statements shield from SQL injection, but other solutions, as e.g., server-sided stored procedures could also be used.

inputValidation explains how the component is shielded from unvalidated input. The most secure way is to whitelist characters and not to accept anything else. In a later phase of development, it could be useful to use this tag for documenting the concrete technique which is used, e.g., a software library.

Additionally to these security features, the UWE profile provides the tag {usedInStates} to denote in which state of the application a certain component is used. More about states can be found in Sect. 5.3. Note that it is the modelers' decision which of the features offered by the UWE profile they like to use in a diagram. In some scenarios, the modelers may decide to connect the UWE Navigation model with the Content model using {usedInStates}, in others not.

5.2   Role and Access Control View

Figure 5 depicts the role model of the EMS. The stereotype «webUser» defines the class that represents a user. It can later be referred to as `caller` when defining access control. Per default, the `DefaultUser` plays all roles, although this is not shown in the figure.

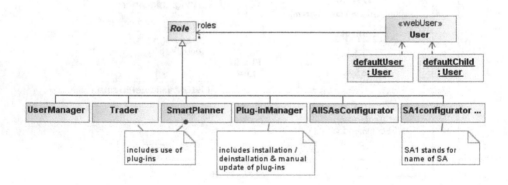

Fig. 5. UWE: Role model

Defining access control for web applications, has already been described in [2]. For our EMS application, Fig. 6 shows an excerpt. For example, someone with the role `UserManager` is allowed to «delete» users, as long as the «authorizationConstraint», which has to be specified in OCL [14], is fulfilled. The constraint defines that the user instance (referred to as `self`) is not equal to the `caller` (referring to the «webUser» who executes this deletion). If the constraint would not be given, users might delete their own accounts accidentally.

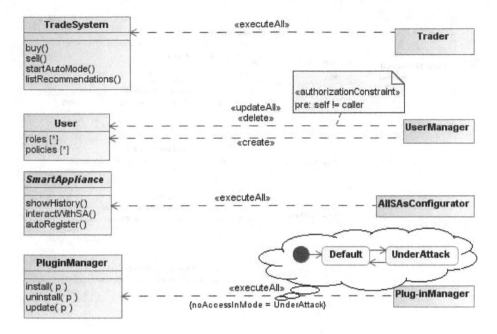

Fig. 6. UWE: Basic Rights model excerpt

Regarding our security requirements, the UWE Basic Rights model has to be extended to enable the specification of different modes. Therefore, the tag {noAccessInMode} is added. It allows to choose from a set of states in which the application should not be available. Please note that these states do not refer to navigational states, but general states of an application. When modeling with a CASE tool as MagicDraw [15], the UWE profile with its typed tags makes sure that the value for the tag can only be chosen from all available state elements.

As depicted at the bottom of Fig. 6, the EMS only allows to install plugins when it is not under attack.

5.3   Navigation and Process View

User navigation is one of the most distinguished web features. Since 2011, UML state charts are used in UWE to express the navigation possibilities a user has within a certain state of the web application [2]. By default, all states in the UWE navigation model are thought to be stereotyped «navigationalNode». The {isHome} tag refers to the entry point of a web application (cf. Fig. 7).

The stereotype «integratedMenu» is defined to be a shortcut for showing menus entries for all menus of Submachine States, in case the user is allowed to access them. Submachine states contain a state machine by themselves, so that more details can be shown in another diagram. Note that transitions that start at the border of a state, leave the state and enter again when triggered. Navigational access control can be specified using a rolesExpression as "caller.roles.includes(PluginManager)".

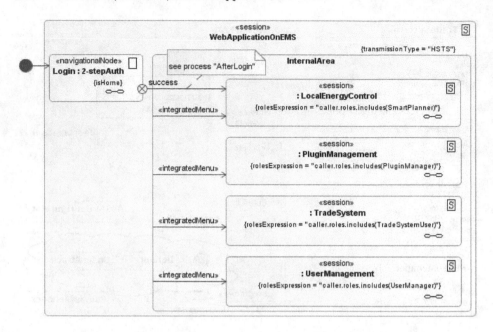

Fig. 7. UWE: Navigation model overview

As shown on the left in Fig. 7, a UWE pattern is used for the specification of 2-step authentication. The UWE profile includes such kind of patterns to reduce the amount of modeling effort. In case a pattern should be adapted, it can easily be copied from the profile to the model.

Additionally, we decided to include more implementation specific details in the navigation model, which are relevant in the late design phase. Thus, HTTP Strict Transport Security (HSTS) is specified as web security policy mechanism to ensure secure HTTPS connections for the whole web application, indicated by the «session»-related tag {transmissionType=HSTS}.

If needed, activity diagrams can be added to detail the process that is executed behind the scenes. For example, Fig. 8 depicts what happens internally after the login was completed successfully. For our EMS, this gives a hint to implement the panic mode as well as the restricted access, when accessing the EMS from a distant region.

Exemplarily, the submachine state diagram of the plugin management is shown in Fig. 9. The stereotype «search» denotes that a search is done when using the `searchPlugins` transition, as searching is a typical process in applications. The stereotype «collection» refers to a list of elements with the given {itemType} tag from the Content model. For transitions, an underscore can be used to denote an element of this type. In our example, the underscore is an abbreviation for `p : Plugin`.

The UWE profile provides a new tag called {reauth} for the stereotype «session» to specify critical areas. In those areas, as e.g., for plugin management, users have to reauthenticate themselves, except when the previous login is not

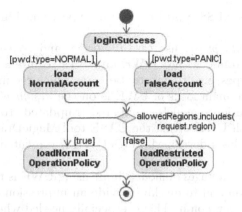

Fig. 8. UWE: Process after successful login

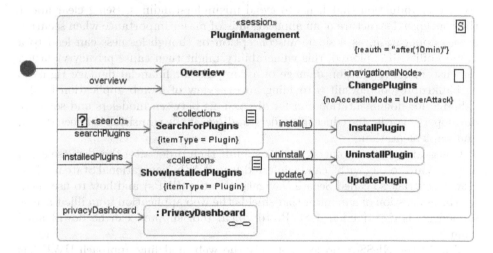

Fig. 9. UWE: Navigation model for plugin management

older than the given amount of time. In addition, the tag {noAccessInMode} is specified for the stereotype «navigationalNode». In our example, this prevents navigating to the interface for (un)installing or updating plugins in the **UnderAttack** mode.

All diagrams of our EMS case study can be found on the UWE web page [9, example section / EMS]; the original model can be downloaded as MagicDraw project or XMI file.

6   UWE in the Software Development Life Cycle

We consider an iterative Service Development Life Cycle (SDLC), consisting of at least the phases: requirements, design, implementation, testing and deployment [16]. In the following, we show how security-related UWE extensions developed during the NESSoS project [4] can be positioned in this development process.

In the *requirements phase*, use case diagrams and coarse-grained activity diagrams record customer wishes. UWE enhances requirements models using web-specific stereotypes, e.g., to denote use cases which require server-side processing. However, the main focus of UWE is on the *design phase*, in which the rest of the above-mentioned models are created or updated. To ease the design of web applications with UWE within the CASE tool MagicDraw [15], the plugin MagicUWE [17] has been developed. MagicUWE is presented in more detail in chapter [5].

One of the main advantages of models built using UWE is to get an overview of the web application and to quickly provide an impression of what is important in the different views on it. This is especially needed when new developers join an existing project, because clean documentation serves as a basis for a concise introduction that helps to avoid misunderstandings. Being clear about the conceptual structure of an application is of major importance when securing a web application, as a single misconception or thoughtlessness can lead to a vulnerability. If exploited, this vulnerability might then cause privacy violation for customers, reputation damage of a company or financial damage right up to bankruptcy or lawsuit. Providing an overview of a web application is also valuable for documentation and for discussions between modelers and software developers in order to reduce misunderstandings at the transition between design and implementation.

Constraints as "customers can only submit their order after they have selected a credit card to pay with" can be inferred from UWE Navigational State models. How to extract so called Secure Navigation Paths (SNPs) and how to use them for the generation of a monitor that shields the web application from illicit access sequences, is described in [18]. Prototypical tool support can be downloaded from [9].

Within the NESSoS project not only the web modeling approach UWE has been improved, but also ActionGUI has been developed further, which strives to implementing the whole application logic from models (cf. Sect. 7). Due to ActionGUI's different focus, it has been interesting to consider a model-to-model transformation from UWE to ActionGUI, as described in [19].

In the *implementation phase* code is written, based on the models. Tool support is preferable, but as can be expected, code generation is only possible where detailed information is given in the models. Therefore, modelers have to balance the need for abstraction against the need for detailed information. Consequently, UWE does not aim to generate complete web applications, as it turned out to overload models and the maintenance for a code generator like UWE2JSF [20] became unreasonable high, in order to keep up with the rapid development of web features.

Nonetheless, it has proven to be helpful to transform some parts of the UWE models to code or other implementation-related artifacts. An example is the specification of role based access control (RBAC) rules. The model to text transformation language XPand [21] is used to transform UWE Basic Right models to XACML [22] and to code snippets. For the latter, a prototypic transformation of the data structure, roles and RBAC rules to Apache Wicket with Apache Shiro and Hibernate has been implemented [23].

Exporting XACML policies, which can include RBAC policies from the Basic Rights model as well as from the navigational states model, is implemented in a tool called UWE2XACML. In [24], Busch et al. explain how XACML can be transformed to FACPL [25], a formal policy language with the advantage of fully specified semantics. The transformation comprises several tools, which are integrated in the Service Development Environment (SDE) [26,16]. The SDE is a tool workbench, which allows to build tool chains of tools that are integrated, i.e. that provide a wrapper for the SDE.

As far as the *testing phase* of the SDLC is concerned, UWE's Basic Rights model can be the starting point for generating test cases by using a tool chain, as described in chapter [5]. The advantage is that policies are modeled at a high level of abstraction so they are easy to understand and to maintain, whereas policies written in XACML tend to become lengthy and error-prone so that thorough testing is mandatory.

In addition to enforcing Secure Navigation Paths by monitors (as introduced above), the modeled paths can also be used for automatic testing to check that a web application correctly prohibits attempts to break out of the predefined navigation structure [18].

7   Related Work

This section introduces related work for the Energy Management System (EMS) case study and approaches for secure web engineering.

Energy Management Systems. The EMS is a component of a Smart Grid. Unfortunately, literature [11,27,28] does not offer a coherent view of the components of a Smart Grid. For our case study, we rely on the components as described in [6,29].

In [11], the Energy Management System is described as a *consumption display unit*, which is regarded as an optional device that helps advanced metering infrastructure (AMI) objectives, i.e., Demand Side Management events. For sustainable energy supply, Demand Side Management has to considered as a key technology. Furthermore, the Energy Management System supports the user in interacting with the Smart Home, which is another key to the successful acceptance of the Smart Grid. This requires to manifest the EMS as a crucial part of the Smart Grid.

The Energy@Home Project[3] illustrates Smart Meter and Home Energy Management implementations. The overall description matches with our case study, but it does not give any insight on security or privacy.

---

[3] Energy@Home. http://www.enel.com/en-GB/innovation/smart_grids/
smart_homes/smart_info/

The OpenNode Project [27] emphasizes research on electrical distribution grid operation. The prosumer endpoint is mentioned, but it does left out any details on the required end point functionality. From a holistic point of view, the OpenNode architecture is complementary with our view of Smart Homes and the proposed EMS functionality depicted in this chapter.

The British Department of Energy and Climate Change give in their technical reports in [28] detailed functional requirements on the Smart Home including technical and functional descriptions of the Energy Management System ("In Home Display") in the report. The report's functional requirements are equivalent to the functionality from our case study. Security requirements on the other hand are referenced, but clearly not in the report's scope.

Secure Web Application Modeling. According to a survey, "86% of all websites had at least one serious vulnerability in 2012", which means that an "attacker could take control over all, or some part of the website, compromise user accounts on the system" or "access sensitive data" [30]. One way to counter this trend is to use security-aware modeling approaches for web applications. Existing approaches are briefly introduced in the following, adapted from [31].

ACTIONGUI [1] is an approach for generating complete, but simplified, data-centric web applications from models. It provides an OCL specification of all functionalities, so that navigation is only modeled implicitly by OCL constraints. In general, ActionGUI abstracts less from an implementation than UWE does.

UMLSEC [32] is an extension of UML with emphasis on secure protocols. It is defined in form of a UML profile including stereotypes for concepts like authenticity, freshness, secrecy and integrity, role-based access control, guarded access, fair exchange, and secure information flow. In particular, the use of constraints gives criteria to evaluate the security aspects of a system design, by referring to a formal semantics of a simplified fragment of UML. UMLsec models, compared to UWE models, are extremely detailed and therefore quickly become very complex. Tool support is only partly adopted from UML1.4 to UML2. However, the new tools[4] have not been updated for almost two years.

SECUREUML [33] is a UML-based modeling language for secure systems. It provides modeling elements for role-based access control and the specification of authorization constraints. A SecureUML dialect has to be defined in order to connect a system design modeling language as, e.g., ComponentUML to the SecureUML metamodel, which is needed for the specification of all possible actions on the predefined resources. In our approach, we specify role-based execution rights to methods in a basic rights model using dependencies instead of the SecureUML association classes, which avoids the use of method names with an access related return type. However, UWE's basic rights models can easily be transformed into a SecureUML representation.

A similar approach is UACML [34] which also comes with a UML-based meta-metamodel for access control, which can be specialized into various meta-models for, e.g., role-based access control (RBAC) or mandatory access control (MAC).

---

[4] UMLsec tools. http://carisma.umlsec.de

Conversely to UWE, the resulting diagrams of SecureUML and UACML are overloaded, as SecureUML uses association classes instead of dependencies and UACML does not introduce a separate model to specify user-role hierarchies.

Other approaches address modeling of security aspects of service-oriented architectures (SOAs), such as the SECTET framework [35], UML4SOA [36], and SecureSOA [37]. The first one proposes the use of sequence diagrams for the representation of a set of security patterns, in UML4SOA security features are modeled as non-functional properties using class diagrams, and the latter relies on FMC block diagrams and BPMN notation.

8   Conclusion and Future Work

In summary, it can be stated that our approach for engineering secure web applications using UWE contributes to the task of securing web applications. Consequently, a long-term impact should be the reduction of security flaws and of necessary security patches. As it is not easy to measure the long-term impact of UWE, we at least can tell that UWE helps to get clear about which security features are important for certain functions of concrete web applications. In particular, UWE addresses security features starting in the early phases of development.

For future work, we plan to include more web-specific security features and to validate our approach by modeling further case studies. Additionally, we extend our approach to cover model validation. Therefore, we are working on a textual version of UWE, called TextualUWE, which is based on a domain specific language. Our aim is to use functional Scala on TextualUWE to check for inconsistencies in the models, as unreachable navigational states or contradictory access control rules. Besides, it would also be interesting to investigate on transferring UWE's security concepts to other web modeling languages that have not yet incorporated security features.

References

1. Basin, D., Clavel, M., Egea, M., Schläpfer, M.: Automatic Generation of Smart, Security-Aware GUI Models. In: Massacci, F., Wallach, D., Zannone, N. (eds.) ESSoS 2010. LNCS, vol. 5965, pp. 201–217. Springer, Heidelberg (2010)
2. Busch, M., Knapp, A., Koch, N.: Modeling Secure Navigation in Web Information Systems. In: Grabis, J., Kirikova, M. (eds.) BIR 2011. LNBIP, vol. 90, pp. 239–253. Springer, Heidelberg (2011)
3. Barth, A., Jackson, C., Mitchell, J.C.: Robust defenses for cross-site request forgery. In: Proceedings of the 15th ACM Conference on Computer and Communications Security, CCS 2008, pp. 75–88. ACM, New York (2008)
4. NESSoS: Network of Excellence on Engineering Secure Future Internet Software Services and Systems (2014), http://nessos-project.eu/
5. Bertolino, A., Busch, M., Daoudagh, S., Lonetti, F., Marchetti, E.: A Toolchain for Designing and Testing Access Control Policies. In: Heisel, M., Joosen, W., Lopez, J., Martinelli, F. (eds.) Engineering Secure Future Internet Services and Systems. LNCS, vol. 8431, pp. 266–286. Springer, Heidelberg (2014)

6. Cuellar, J., Suppan, S.: A smart metering scenario (2013),
   https://securitylab.disi.unitn.it/lib/exe/fetch.php?media=research_
   activities:erise:erise_2013:erise2013-smartmeteering-description.pdf
7. Cuellar, J.: NESSoS deliverable D11.4 – Pilot applications, evaluating NESSoS
   solutions (to appear, 2014)
8. Guerrero, J.M.: Microgrids: Integration of distributed energy resources into
   the smart-grid. In: IEEE International Symposium on Industrial Electronics,
   pp. 4281–4414 (2010)
9. LMU. Web Engineering Group.: UWE Website (2014),
   http://uwe.pst.ifi.lmu.de/
10. Cubo, J., Cuellar, J., Fries, S., Martín, J.A., Moyano, F., Fernández, G., Gago,
    M.C.F., Pasic, A., Román, R., Dieguez, R.T., Vinagre, I.: Selection and documen-
    tation of the two major applicationcase studies. NESSoS deliverable D11.2 (2011)
11. Gómez, A., Tellechea, M., Rodríguez, C.: D1.1 Requirements of AMI. Technical
    report, OPEN meter project (2009)
12. Bennett, C., Wicker, S.: Decreased time delay and security enhancement recom-
    mendations for ami smart meter networks. In: Innovative Smart Grid Technologies
    (ISGT), pp. 1–6 (2010)
13. OWASP Foundation: OWASP Top 10 – 2013 (2013),
    http://owasptop10.googlecode.com/files/OWASPTop10-2013.pdf
14. OMG.: OCL 2.0 (2011), http://www.omg.org/spec/OCL/2.0/
15. No Magic Inc.: Magicdraw (2014), http://www.magicdraw.com/
16. Busch, M., Koch, N.: NESSoS Deliverable D2.3 – Second Release of the SDE for
    Security-Related Tools (2012)
17. Busch, M., Koch, N.: MagicUWE — A CASE Tool Plugin for Modeling Web
    Applications. In: Gaedke, M., Grossniklaus, M., Díaz, O. (eds.) ICWE 2009. LNCS,
    vol. 5648, pp. 505–508. Springer, Heidelberg (2009)
18. Busch, M., Ochoa, M., Schwienbacher, R.: Modeling, Enforcing and Testing Se-
    cure Navigation Paths for Web Applications. Technical Report 1301, Ludwig-
    Maximilians-Universität München (2013)
19. Busch, M., García de Dios, M.A.: ActionUWE: Transformation of UWE to
    ActionGUI Models. Technical report, Ludwig-Maximilians-Universität München,
    Number 1203 (2012)
20. Kroiss, C., Koch, N., Knapp, A.: UWE4JSF - A Model-Driven Generation Ap-
    proach for Web Applications. In: Gaedke, M., Grossniklaus, M., Díaz, O. (eds.)
    ICWE 2009. LNCS, vol. 5648, pp. 493–496. Springer, Heidelberg (2009)
21. Eclipse: XPand (2013), http://wiki.eclipse.org/Xpand
22. OASIS: eXtensible Access Control Markup Language (XACML) Version 2.0 (2005),
    http://docs.oasis-open.org/xacml/2.0/
    access_control-xacml-2.0-core-spec-os.pdf
23. Wolf, K.: Sicherheitsbezogene Model-to-Code Transformation für Webanwendun-
    gen (German), Bachelor Thesis (2012)
24. Busch, M., Koch, N., Masi, M., Pugliese, R., Tiezzi, F.: Towards model-driven de-
    velopment of access control policies for web applications. In: Model-Driven Security
    Workshop in Conjunction with MoDELS 2012. ACM Digital Library (2012)
25. Masi, M., Pugliese, R., Tiezzi, F.: Formalisation and Implementation of the
    XACML Access Control Mechanism. In: Barthe, G., Livshits, B., Scandariato,
    R. (eds.) ESSoS 2012. LNCS, vol. 7159, pp. 60–74. Springer, Heidelberg (2012)
26. SDE: Service Development Environment (2014),
    http://www.nessos-project.eu/sde

27. Soriano, R., Alberto, M., Collazo, J., Gonzales, I., Kupzo, F., Moreno, L., Lugmaier, A., Lorenzo, J.: OpenNode. Open Architecture for Secondary Nodes of the Electricity SmartGrid. In: 21st International Conference on Electricity Distribution (2011)
28. Department of Energy and Climate Change: Smart Metering Implementation Programme, Response to Prospectus Consultation, Overview Document. Technical report, Office of Gas and Electricity Markets (2011)
29. Beckers, K., Fabender, S., Heisel, M., Suppan, S.: A threat analysis methodology for smart home scenarios. In: SmartGridSec 2014. LNCS. Springer (2014)
30. Grossman, J.: Website security statistics report. Technical report, WhiteHat Security (2013), https://www.whitehatsec.com/resource/stats.html
31. Busch, M.: Secure Web Engineering supported by an Evaluation Framework. In: Modelsward 2014. Scitepress (2014)
32. Jürjens, J.: Secure Systems Development with UML. Springer (2004), Tools and further information: http://www.umlsec.de/
33. Lodderstedt, T., Basin, D., Doser, J.: SecureUML: A UML-Based Modeling Language for Model-Driven Security. In: Jézéquel, J.-M., Hussmann, H., Cook, S. (eds.) UML 2002. LNCS, vol. 2460, pp. 426–441. Springer, Heidelberg (2002)
34. Slimani, N., Khambhammettu, H., Adi, K., Logrippo, L.: UACML: Unified Access Control Modeling Language. In: NTMS 2011, pp. 1–8 (2011)
35. Hafner, M., Breu, R.: Security Engineering for Service-Oriented Architectures. Springer (2008)
36. Gilmore, S., Gönczy, L., Koch, N., Mayer, P., Tribastone, M., Varró, D.: Nonfunctional Properties in the Model-Driven Development of Service-Oriented Systems. J. Softw. Syst. Model. 10(3), 287–311 (2011)
37. Menzel, M., Meinel, C.: A Security Meta-model for Service-Oriented Architectures. In: Proc. 2009 IEEE Int. Conf. Services Computing (SCC 2009), pp. 251–259. IEEE (2009)

On the Synthesis of Secure Services Composition*

Jose A. Martín[1], Fabio Martinelli[2], Ilaria Matteucci[2], Ernesto Pimentel[1],
and Mathieu Turuani[3]

[1] E.T.S. Ingeniería Informática, Universidad de Málaga,
Campus de Teatinos, 29071 Málaga, Spain
{jamartin,ernesto}@lcc.uma.es
[2] Istituto di Informatica e Telematica - C.N.R., Pisa, Italy
name.surname@iit.cnr.it
[3] INRIA
Mathieu.Turuani@inria.fr

Abstract. Web service composition is one of the main research challenges of the last decades. Several frameworks have been developed to compose services in order to meet requirements and constraints imposed by a service consumer. Hereafter, we survey research work on evaluation and automatic synthesis of service composition with a particular eye to security aspects.

Furthermore, we describe our logical approach based on the *partial model checking* technique and *open system analysis* for the *synthesis* of secure service orchestrators that are also able to exploit some cryptographic primitives. We also show two implementations able to automatically generate an orchestrator process that composes several services in such a way to guarantee both functional and security requirements.

Keywords: Synthesis of Functional and Secure Processes, Secure Service Composition, Partial Model Checking, Process Algebras, Quantitative Security.

1 Overview

Services are software components developed to be re-usable, which expose their definition and which are accessible by third parties. Web services are the most promising class of services. They offer various functionalities to their consumers that range over data storage, information retrieval, social interaction and more. Web Services export their description and are accessible through standard network technologies, *e.g.*, SOAP, WSDL, UDDI, WS-BPEL, WS-Transaction, *etc.*.

Service Oriented Computing (SOC) investigates on new approach for building software applications by composing and configuring existing services. Web Service composition combines existing services, available on the web, to provide

---

* The research leading to these results has received funding from the European Union Seventh Framework Programme (FP7/2007-2013) under grants no 256980 (NESSoS).

M. Heisel et al. (Eds.): Engineering Secure Future Internet Services, LNCS 8431, pp. 140–159, 2014.

added-value services featuring higher level functionalities. Every functionality of a service network depends on how the services compose each other. Service composition can be done in two ways: as a *choreography* or through an *orchestration*. Choreography identifies the end-to-end composition between two services by mainly considering cooperation rules, *e.g.*, the sequence of the exchanged messages and their content. Orchestration deals with the composition of multiple services in terms of the business process they generate.

In this chapter we survey about the existing literature on service composition approaches and security aspects in the synthesis procedure. In particular, we discuss separately research work about i) logical approaches for service composition, ii) security aspects in service composition, and iii) other synthesis approaches. We then describe our framework based on partial model checking [1] and the open system paradigm for the synthesis of secure service compositions with also the possibility of introducing cryptographic primitives in the orchestrator process. The framework we propose is both for verification and synthesis of secure service composition using a secure and functional orchestrator.

The chapter is structured as follows: next section describes service composition approaches, other synthesis approaches that already exist in literature, and the specification and verification of web service orchestrators in timed setting. Section 4 presents our approach for the synthesis of secure service composition. We also describe two possible implementation solutions for the automatic generation of such orchestrators. Section 5 drafts the conclusion of the chapter.

2 Security Aspects of Service Composition

A service and its clients, or two (or more) services, interact with one another through specific interfaces defining the syntax and semantics of the exchanged messages (and their parameters). Papazoglou [46] defines some key roles for Service Oriented Computing, among them, the service consumer and the service provider are the two most important ones. The two entities share knowledge only about the service interface, *i.e.*, the protocols that they use to communicate. Existing protocols can guarantee security properties, *e.g.*, authenticity and secrecy, on these communications. However, messages can carry complex data or even executable instructions, which makes the computation distributed over the involved systems. Needless to say, the problem of providing security guarantees is one of the most studied in the last decades. Indeed, the pervasiveness of web services increases the necessity for consumers to access and use them in a *secure* way. A service composition is secure if it satisfies a certain *security property*. A *security property* is a statement that specifies acceptable executions of the system. The research on several aspects of service composition has made a great step further. In particular, several frameworks have been developed to compose services in order to satisfy security and functional requirements and constraints imposed by a service consumer. The composition of services presents a lot of challenges in terms of security. For instance, services may not be able to directly communicate with one another because they use different communication (cryptographic) protocols. It is also possible that different services provide the same functionality but in a different way and one could fit better than another with the customer's functional and security requirements. Furthermore, the distributive nature of web services makes the development of some machinery to guarantee security very important. Consumers should require strong guarantees that their security policies are satisfied. Unfortunately, Service Oriented Computing is adverse to most techniques of control and analysis which, usually, require the direct access to either execution or implementation.

3 Automated Synthesis Mechanisms

In this section we discuss on some literature about synthesis mechanisms. During the last decades, a lot of research work has been done in order to define different strategies for synthesizing service composition. Some of them have addressed also security issues. For the best of our knowledge, hereafter, we recall works that deal with both functional and security aspects. Several works deal with a possible modeling of orchestrators by process algebras, see *e.g.*, [11,12,20,26,56], by automata [52], or by an Architecture Description Language (ADL) [50,45].

In [13,15] the authors have developed a static approach to deal with the composition of web services by the usage of *plans*. Only some of these take into account also security aspects in the service composition procedure. In particular they use a distributed, enriched λ-calculus for describing networks of services. Both, services and their clients, can protect themselves, by imposing security constraints on each other's behavior. Then, service interaction results in a *call-by-property* mechanism [14], that matches the client requests with services.

The planning approach is followed also by Pistore *et al.* [48,49] in order to generate an orchestrator. As a matter of fact, the authors have proposed a novel planning framework for the automated composition of Web Services in which they generate automatically a concrete process that interacts asynchronously with the published services. Basically they compose all services and then, after building all possible plans, they extract the plan that satisfies the user's request.

Also Zavattaro *et. al* [18], deals with the problem of composition on services. They have studied choreography more than orchestration. They have introduced a formal model for representing choreography. Their model is based on a *declarative part* and on a *conversational* one. The declarative part of their choreography formal model is based on the concept of *role* that represents the behavior that a participant has to exhibit in order to fulfill the activity defined by the choreography. Each role can store variables and exhibit operations.

In [19] the authors have formalized the concept of orchestrator as a process, associated to an identifier, that is able to exchange information, represented by variables, with other processes. This model takes inspiration form the abstract non-executable fragment of BPEL and abstracts away from variables values focusing on data-flow. Orchestrators are executed on different locations, thus they can be composed by using only the parallel operator ($\|$). Processes can be composed in parallel, sequence and alternative composition. Communication mechanisms model Web Services *One-Way* and *Request-Response* operations.

Enabling the specification of dynamic Web service-oriented architectures is a key challenge for an Architecture Description Language (ADL). In [50,45] the authors address three research challenges: i) support the description of dynamic service-oriented architectures from structural and behavioral viewpoints; ii) support the description of service-oriented architectures where business processes are modeled in visual notations such as BPMN [43]; and iii) support the description of service-oriented architectures enabling to rigorously reason about and verify their qualities, in particular related to conformance and correctness.

In [22], the automatic composition of services under security policies is investigated. Work in [22] uses the AVISPA tool [58,2] and acts in two stages: first, it derives a protocol to allow composition of some services; then, some desired security properties are implemented. The latter step uses the functionality of AVISPA and, for the former step, the desired composition is turned into a security property, so that AVISPA itself can be used to derive an "attacker" which actually is the orchestrator. The AVANTSSAR Platform [21,3] extends the AVISPA tool. It is an integrated toolset for the formal specification and automated validation of trust and security of service-oriented architectures and other applications in the Internet of Services. The authors extend this research line in [7,9] by presenting a novel approach to automated distributed orchestration of Web Services tied with security policies with a particular eye to trust and security relations. The construction of an orchestration complying with the policies is based on the resolution of deducibility constraint systems and has been implemented for the non-distributed case as part of the AVANTSSAR Validation Platform. More details are given in Section 4.5

The research line on the synthesis of secure controller programs [37] has been extended with the introduction of cryptographic primitives in [23,24]. These two works try to simplify the approach in [33] for the synthesis of deadlock-free orchestrators that are compliant with security adaptation contracts [34]. Compared to [33], this new approach loses the ability to specify fine-grained constrains in the desired orchestration but, on the other hand, there is no need to design an adaptation contract. We discuss these works later on in Section 4.

In [31], Li et al. present an approach for securing distributed adaptation. A plan is synthesized and executed, allowing the different parties to apply a set of data transformations in a distributed fashion. In particular, the authors synthesize "security boxes"that wrap services, providing them with the appropriate cryptographic capabilities. Security boxes are pre-designed, but interchangeable at run time. In our case the orchestrator is synthesized at run time and is able to cryptographically arrange secure service composition.

In [30] the authors introduce COWS, *calculus for orchestration of Web services*, as a new foundational language for service oriented computing. In order to facilitate the use of model-checking techniques to business analysts, the authors of [5] created a model-checking plugin for SAP NetWeaver Business Process Management. This plugin support the verification of secrecy properties with a push of a button and the subsequent visualization of possible attack traces. However, since this plugin is intended as a design tool, the designer is left with the task to solve possible flaws in the business process.

A bunch of works deals with web services in timed settings. In particular, some of those deal with modeling a timed BPEL with formal methods.

In [38] the authors proposed possible mapping of BPEL operators into process algebra operators. Furthermore, a possible orchestrator operator has been proposed in such a way to deal also with time. In [28] the authors propose the *Web Service Timed Transition System* model, which adopts the formalism of timed automata for capturing the specific aspects of the web service domain. In this formalism, the fact that the operation takes a certain amount of time is represented by time increment in the state, followed by the immediate execution of the operation. Intuitively, WSTTS is a finite-state machine equipped with a set of clock variables. The values of these clock variables increase with the elapsing of time. Thus a Web Service composition is represented as a network of several such automata, where all clocks progress synchronously. The semantic of WSTTS is defined as a labeled transition system, where either the time passes or a transition from one state to another immediately takes place. In [16,17] the authors have discussed the augmentation of business protocols with specifications of temporal abstractions, focusing in particular on problems related to compatibility and replaceability analysis. In [25] the authors, firstly, have defined a timed automata semantics for the *Orc* language, introduced in order to support a structured way of orchestrating distributed Web services. *Orc* is intuitive because it offers concise constructors to manage concurrent communication, time-outs, priorities, failure of sites or communication and so forth. The semantics of *Orc* is also precisely defined. Timed automata semantics is semantically equivalent to the original operational semantics of *Orc*.

4   Synthesize a Secure and Functional Service Composition

There are some papers proposing compositional approaches to synthesize processes able to compose or coordinate components in such a way to ensure security, depending on some runtime behavior of a possible attacker, *e.g.*, [37,27,55,4,6,29,47,51,53,54].

Our works starts from the necessity to make systems secure regardless the behavior of possible intruders, *i.e.*, we suppose that the system we consider works in parallel with unknown components, that represent a possible malicious agent, and we have developed mechanisms to guarantee the system is secure whatever the behavior of the possible malicious agent is. A lot of work has been done in order to study and analyze systems to guarantee that they satisfy certain security properties. In this chapter we present how the logical approach based on the open system paradigm for the security analysis, in particular for the specification and verification (see [36]). This research stream has been extended to the synthesis of secure controller programs [37] and with the introduction of cryptographic primitives in [23,24].

The approach can be also used to guarantee security in service composition. We aim to automatically synthesize an orchestrator process able to coordinate the communication among several services in a secure and functionally correct way.

Example 1. (cfr. [24]) Consider a user willing to receive a certificate of residence by the city hall. In order to provide such document, the city hall has to retrieve information by other two services, the healthcare office and the driving license office, in order to have all the information that is required in order to produce a certificate. As expected in the service-oriented approach, this can be achieved by the orchestration of different services. The exchanged data circulating among different services are encrypted in such a way the privacy issues are guaranteed. Hence, both the healthcare office and the driving license office receive the identification number of the user (Id) and send back the identification number of the health card (Id_healthcare) and the identification number of the driving license (Id_driving), respectively. As soon as the city hall receives the required information, it sends a residency certificate in which the health card and the driving license are both associated to the address of the user. The user receives the certificate encrypted with her public key. This guarantees that only the user can open it. Once the user opens the certificate, she sends back a success message. This message is encrypted with the private key of the user that, in this way, proves her identity.

There are some communication issues in this apparently simple procedure. For example, the user might be unable to manage both operations because she does not know which information is needed for releasing the certificate. One needs to synthesize a new service, *orchestrator*, whose aim is to make the system functional, *i.e.*, fully satisfying its goal (request and successfully obtain the certificate of residence). The correct execution of the whole procedure is guaranteed by the reception of the certificate by the user that sends back a success message.

4.1   The Synthesis Problem

We refer to a formal definition of the synthesis problem given by Merlin and Bochman in [41]. The synthesis problem occurs when one deals with a system in which some components are completely or partially unspecified, *e.g.*, a partially implemented software or a Web service relying on components designed and developed separately. Let us consider a partially specified system, we wonder if there exists an implementation that can be plugged into the system, replacing the missing one, such that the whole system satisfies the properties it needs to.

Hence the problem that must be solved is the following one:

$$\exists Y \quad S(Y) \models \phi$$

where ϕ is a logic formula representing the property to be satisfied, S is a model of the partially specified system, and Y is the plugged element.

The synthesis problem for *secure systems* is slightly different. Indeed, due to the unpredictable behavior of the possible attacker, this can be seen as an unspecified component of the system under investigation, *i.e.*, as a *black-box*. Hence, we model as an *open system* following the approach proposed in [35,32,36]. A system is *open* if it has some unspecified components. We want to make sure that the system with this unspecified component works properly, *e.g.*, fulfills a certain property. Thus, the intuitive idea underlying the verification of an open system is the following:

An open system satisfies a property if and only if, whatever component is substituted to the unspecified one, the whole system satisfies this property.

Whatever the unspecified term is, it is appealing that the resulting system works properly, *e.g.*, satisfies a consumer's requirement. According to these premises, the system must be secure regardless of their real behaviors, which is exactly a *verification* problem of open systems. According to [36], the problem that we want to study can be formalized as follows:

$$\text{For every component } X \quad S\|X \models \varphi \tag{1}$$

where X stands for the possible attacker, S is the system under examination, consisting of several services composed in parallel through the $\|$ parallel-composition operator, φ is a logic formula expressing the customer requirement. It roughly states that the property φ holds for the system S, regardless of the component (*i.e.*, intruder, malicious user, hostile environment, *etc.*) which may possibly interact with it.

4.2   Crypto-CCS and Partial Model Checking in a Nutshell

The preservation of secrecy properties is one of the main aspects that has to be considered in secure service composition. This is because service composition happens through communication among services [8].

Given the sensitive nature of a communication protocol, one can imagine the presence of a hostile adversary trying to interfere with the normal execution of the protocol in order to achieve some advantage. To this aim, hereafter, we assume the Dolev-Yao threat model which has been widely accepted as threat model for cryptographic protocols. This threat model assumes that:

- All communications are visible by the attacker, *i.e.*, an attacker can receive any message transmitted through the network.
- The attacker can alter, forge, replay or drop any message.
- The attacker can reroute messages to another principal.
- The attacker can be a principal or an outsider. This means that an attacker can be a legitimate user of the network and thus in particular he is able to initiate communication with any other principal or to act as a receiver to any principal.

Crypto-CCS is a variant of CCS [42], endowed with cryptographic primitives. A model defined in Crypto-CCS consists of a set of sequential agents able to communicate by exchanging messages (*e.g.*, data manipulated by the agents).

$$A \doteq 0 \mid c!m.A \mid c?x.A \mid [m_1 \cdots m_n \vdash_r x]A; A_1$$

Table 1. Operational semantics of Crypto-CCS. Symmetric rules are omitted

$$(!)\frac{}{(c!m.A)_\phi \xrightarrow{c!m} (A)_\phi} \quad (?)\frac{m:T \in Tmsgs(T)}{(c?x:T.A)_\phi \xrightarrow{c?m} (A[m/x])_{\phi \cup \{m:T\}}} \quad (\tau)\frac{}{(\tau.A)_\phi \xrightarrow{\tau} (A)_\phi}$$

$$(+)\frac{(A_1)_\phi \xrightarrow{\alpha} (A_1')_{\phi'}}{(A_1 + A_2)_\phi \xrightarrow{\alpha} (A_1')_{\phi'}} \quad (\backslash L)\frac{S \xrightarrow{\alpha} S' \ ch(\alpha) \notin L}{S \backslash L \xrightarrow{\alpha} S' \backslash L}$$

$$([]_1)\frac{m = m' \quad (A_1)_\phi \xrightarrow{\alpha} (A_1')_{\phi'}}{([m = m']A_1; A_2)_\phi \xrightarrow{\alpha} (A_1')_{\phi'}} \quad ([]_2)\frac{m \neq m' \quad (A_2)_\phi \xrightarrow{\alpha} (A_2')_{\phi'}}{([m = m']A_1; A_2)_\phi \xrightarrow{\alpha} (A_2')_{\phi'}}$$

$$(\mathcal{D}_1)\frac{\langle\langle m_i : T_i\rangle\rangle_{i \in I} \vdash_{IS} m : T \quad (A_1[m/x])_{\phi \cup \{m:T\}} \xrightarrow{\alpha} (A_1')_{\phi'}}{([\langle\langle m_i\rangle\rangle_{i \in I} \vdash_{IS} x:T]A_1; A_2)_\phi \xrightarrow{\alpha} (A_1')_{\phi'}}$$

$$(\mathcal{D}_2)\frac{\nexists(m:T)\langle\langle m_i : T_i\rangle\rangle_{i \in I} \vdash_{IS} m : T \quad (A_2)_\phi \xrightarrow{\alpha} (A_2')_{\phi'}}{([\langle\langle m_i\rangle\rangle_{i \in I} \vdash_{IS} x:T]A_1; A_2)_\phi \xrightarrow{\alpha} (A_2')_{\phi'}}$$

$$(\|_1)\frac{S \xrightarrow{\alpha} S'}{S\|S_1 \xrightarrow{\alpha} S'\|S_1} \quad (\|_2)\frac{S \xrightarrow{c?m} S' \quad S_1 \xrightarrow{c!m} S_1'}{S\|S_1 \xrightarrow{\tau} S'\|S_1'}$$

where $m_1, \ldots, m_n, m$ are closed messages or variables, x is a variable and c is an element of the set Ch of channels. Informally, the Crypto-CCS semantics used in the remained of this text is: 0 denotes a process that does nothing; $c!m.A$ denotes a message m sent over channel c and then behave as A; $c?x.A$ denotes a message m received over channel c which replaces the variable x and then behave as A; $[m_1 \cdots m_n \vdash_r x]A; A_1$ denotes an *inference* test that a process may use to check whether message m is derivable from premises $m_1, \ldots, m_n$; the continuations in positive and negative cases are A (where m replaces x), or A_1, respectively. Deduction is the message-manipulating construct of the language, responsible for its expressive power. In particular, it allows to model asymmetric encryption. Let y be a key belonging to an asymmetric pair of keys. We denote by y^{-1} the corresponding complementary key. If y is used for encryption, then y^{-1} is used for decryption, and vice versa. Given a set of messages ϕ, then message $m \in \mathcal{D}(\phi)$, the set of deduced messages, if and only if m can be deduced from the rules modeling public key cryptography.

The control part of the language consists of *compound systems*:

$$S \doteq S_1 \parallel S_2 \mid S \backslash L \mid A_\phi$$

Informally, $S_1 \parallel S_2$ denotes the parallel composition of S_1 and S_2, i.e., $S_1 \parallel S_2$ performs an action if either S_1 or S_2 does. A synchronization (or *internal*) action, denoted by τ, is observed whenever S_1 and S_2 can perform two complementary send and receive actions over the same channel; $S \backslash L$ prevents actions whose channels belong to the set L, except for synchronization. A_ϕ is a single sequential agent whose knowledge is described by ϕ. The formal semantics of the Crypto-CCS agents are summarized in Table 1.

Figure 1 reports the Crypto-CCS description of the services introduced in Example 1.

$U(k_u, k_u^{-1}) \doteq$ $sso!id.$ *send user identifier,*
    $sso?Enc\_Cert.$ *receive encrypted certificate,*
    $[Enc\_Cert \quad k_u^{-1} \vdash_{dec} Cert]$ *decrypt with k_u^{-1},*
    $sso!E(success, k_u^{-1}).0$
        send encrypted success message and stop

$CH(k_{sso}) \doteq$
    $co?Healthcare\_ID.$ *receive a healthcare identifier,*
    $co?Driving\_ID.$ *receive a driving license identifier,*
    $[resid_{cert} \quad k_{sso} \vdash_{enc} E(resid_{cert}, k_{sso})]$
        encrypt certificate with k_{sso},
    $co!E(resid_{cert}, k_{sso}).0$ *send encrypted certificate and stop*

$DL(-) \doteq$
    $c\_do?ID.$ *receive an identifier,*
    $c\_do!driving\_id.0$ *send a driving license identifier and stop*

$HC(-) \doteq$
    $c\_ho?ID.$ *receive an identifier,*
    $c\_ho!healthcare\_id.0$ *send a healthcare identifier and stop*

Fig. 1. Crypto-CCS description fo service in Example 1 [24]

Partial model checking is a technique that relies upon compositional methods to provide properties of concurrent systems [1].

The intuitive idea underlying the partial model checking is the following: let φ be a formula expressing a certain consumer's requirement (see [36,23] for some logical languages), then proving that $E\|F$ satisfies φ is equivalent to prove that F satisfies a modified specification $\varphi = \varphi_{//E}$, where $//_E$ is the partial evaluation function for the parallel composition operator. Hence, the behavior of a component has been partially evaluated and the requirements are changed in order to respect this evaluation.

We give the following main result:

Lemma 1 ([1]). *Given a process $E\|F$ and an equational specification φ we have:*

$$E\|F \models \varphi \quad \text{iff} \quad F \models \varphi_{//E}$$

A lemma similar to the previous one holds for each process algebra operator.

Using partial model checking, we aim to reduce such a verification problem as in Formula (1) to a validity checking problem as follows:

$$\forall X \quad S\|X \models \varphi \quad \text{iff} \quad X \models \varphi_{//s} \tag{2}$$

In this way we have found the sufficient and necessary condition on X, expressed by a logical formula $\varphi_{//s}$, so the whole system $S\|X$ satisfies φ.

Several results exist about the decidability of such problems for temporal logic and, for the more interesting properties, like several *safety properties* ("nothing bad happens"), the validity problem of the formula obtained after the partial evaluation may be solved in linear time in the dimension of the formula itself. Another advantage of the partial model checking technique is that it is not necessary to find the most general intruder and prove its attack capabilities.

4.3   Synthesis of Functional and Secure Orchestrators

Mathematical methods in program semantics and security very often need to be validated through implementation and technology transfer. Traditionally, this task has been hindered by the gap between abstract results and applications. The advent of software engineering brought to light the so-called semi-formal languages and methods, such as Unified Modeling Language (UML) [44] or Business Process Model and Notation (BPMN) [43]. These formalisms provide clean syntax to support abstraction in software and system design, and in the development phase. Semi-formal methods are nowadays part of the standard background of software engineers, and may be used to bridge the mentioned gap, providing a clean path from theoretical results to implementation.

Our approach for the synthesis of secure system consists in using partial model checking [36] and the extension of the PaMoChSA tool [39] for BPMN orchestrator processes [23,24]. Indeed, we extend the line of research based on partial model checking, logic languages and satisfiability, in order to synthesize an orchestrator process able to i) combine several services and provide a unified interface that satisfies a consumer's request and ii) guarantee that the composite service is secure. Hereafter, from a functional perspective, we concentrate on successful service completion, and from a security perspective, we concentrate on the *secrecy* property.

The workflow we adopt is described in Figure 2.

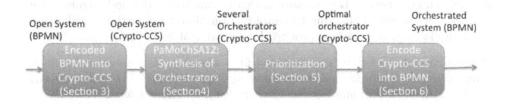

Fig. 2. The workflow of the proposed approach

Indeed, let us assume that each service in the composition is not able to communicate with the others for accomplishing the consumer's requirements, *i.e.*, the set of channels over which S_i is able to communicate does not intersect the set of channels over which S_j is able to communicate, for each pair S_i and S_j in S. We may wonder if there exists an orchestrator O that, by communicating with the services in S and assuming any unspecified component X, guarantees that the overall system satisfies the required security property. This scenario can be specified using BPMN as a set of *white box*, representing the services S_j, and a *black box*, representing the orchestrator. According to [24], the BPMN description of services can be encoded into Crypto-CCS processes. Hence, the synthesis problem is specified as follow:

$$\exists O \quad \forall X \quad S\|O\|X \models \varphi$$

The synthesized orchestrator process is consider functional and secure. Let m_F be a message that denotes the end of a service execution, ϕ_O be the knowledge of the orchestrator, and ϕ_X be the knowledge of the attacker. An orchestrator is functional and secure if it is able to:

- **Functional:** combine several services in such a way that m_F falls into the orchestrator's knowledge ϕ_O. This implies that all services have successfully terminated their execution. We consider the formula φ_T for this property.
- **Secure:** guarantee that the composite service is secure by checking that the secret message m does not belong to ϕ_X. We consider the formula φ_{sec} for this property.

Let us consider the process $(S\|O_{\phi_O}\|X_{\phi_X})$. No matter what the behavior of X is, we require that this process satisfies both functional and security requirements. It is worth noting that in this case there are two components whose behavior is unknown: the orchestrator O and the intruder X.

One issue is to *decide* if there exists an orchestrator O such that, for all the possible behaviors of X, after the computation of maximal length $\gamma(max)$, m_F is in the knowledge of O and m is not in the knowledge of X.

$$\exists O_{\phi_O} \forall X_{\phi_X} (S\|O_{\phi_O}\|X_{\phi_X}) \models \varphi_T \wedge \varphi_{sec} \tag{3}$$

An important aspect is how to automatically *synthesize* the orchestrator. We can use partial model checking to simplify Equation 3 by partially evaluating the formula $\varphi_T \wedge \varphi_{sec}$ with respect to the behavior of S.

Proposition 1. *Let S be a system and O_{ϕ_O} and X_{ϕ_X} two sequential agents, where ϕ_O and ϕ_X are finite sets representing the knowledge of O and X. If m_i, $i = 1, \ldots, n$, are secret messages and m_F is the final one, we have:*

$$(S\|O_{\phi_O}\|X_{\phi_X}) \models \varphi_T \wedge \varphi_{sec}$$
$$\text{iff}$$
$$O_{\phi_O}\|X_{\phi_X} \models (\varphi_T \wedge \varphi_{sec})_{//ns,S}$$

This result identifies the necessary and sufficient conditions that the orchestrator, interacting with every possible X, must satisfy in order to guarantee that the final message m_F is delivered correctly without any disclosure of information to X.

However, the presence of the universal quantifier on X makes the formula $\varphi_T = \forall \gamma(max) : m_F \in K_{O,\gamma(max)}^{\phi_O}$ not satisfiable, since X can always interfere with the normal execution of S getting the overall system stuck, so that the final message m_F is not delivered.

However, still keeping the intuition behind Equation 3, we can weaken the property to the conjunction of the following properties:

A1. When there is not an intruder, the orchestrator always drives the services to correct termination.

A2. When there is an intruder, no matter what actions it takes, it is not able to learn the secret m.

Now we need to determine whether it is possible to determine an orchestrator O satisfying this weaker assumption. Decidability comes from the following proposition.

Proposition 2. *Given a system S, and two finite sets ϕ_O and ϕ_X, it is decidable if $\exists O_{\phi_O}$ s.t. $\forall X_{\phi_X}$*

$$
\begin{array}{lll}
A1 & (S\|O_{\phi_O}) \setminus L & \models \varphi_T \\
A2 & (S\|O_{\phi_O}\|X_{\phi_X}) \setminus L & \models \varphi_{sec}
\end{array}
$$

In A1, we are assuming that the attacker X is the empty process, with an empty initial knowledge ϕ_X.

According to Proposition 1, we can apply the partial model checking techniques to A1 and A2 obtaining:

$$
\begin{array}{ll}
A1' & O_{\phi_O} & \models (\varphi_T)//_{ns,S} \\
A2' & (O_{\phi_O}\|X_\phi) \models (\varphi_{sec})//_{ns,S}
\end{array}
$$

Hence, since the formulas in A1 and A2 are finite, the application of the partial model checking, in conjunction with the usage of some satisfiability procedure allows us to synthesize an orchestrator, whenever it exists.

4.4 PaMoChSA 2012: Tool Description

The tool PaMoChSA2012 [23] is an extension of the Partial Model Checker Security Analyser (PaMoChSA), see [39].

PaMoChSA: The Partial Model Checking Security Analyser. The development of the theory has lead to the implementation of a partial model checker namely the Partial Model Checking Security Analyser [40], for short, PaMoChSA, through which it is possible to analyse distributed systems. As usual, only systems with finite computations will be investigated. This is possible since:

1. the operational language used to specify protocols does not allow recursion;
2. the messages are of a fixed structure;
3. a finite number of parties and sessions running the protocol are considered;

4. even if the attacker is allowed to generate fresh messages, their structure is subject to the same constraints mentioned above.

It is worth noting that, though maintaining the analysis over a finite number of parties and sessions, the absence of attacks over a particular system running the protocol does not guarantee that there are no attacks on larger systems running the same protocol.

The PaMoChSA tool needs the following set of inputs: i) the protocol specification; ii) the security property to be checked; iii) the initial knowledge of the intruder. When developing the theory, the operational language Crypto-CCS has been used for specifying the protocols. The PaMoChSA tool takes as input the protocol description, the secret, *i.e.*, the message that may not to be disclosed to a possible intruder, and the initial knowledge of the possible intruder. The tool gives as output the possible attacks if any, or states the absence of attacks.

PaMoChSA2012: The Synthesizer. The PaMoChSA tool has been extended in order to be able to automatically synthesize a functional and secure orchestrator starting from the description of services. The tool can be downloaded at http://www.iit.cnr.it/staff/vincenzo.ciancia/tools.html.

We provide a security-aware execution semantics to BPMN, incorporating secure communication facilities, by means of Crypto-CCS. We define BPMN processes that exchange cryptographic messages. More precisely, we use existing BPMN facilities to include asymmetric cryptography in the modeling language. In this way, existing tools may be used to design cryptography-aware systems. We provide a proof-of-concept implementation, in the form of two XQuery [59] transformations. The first one translates a BPMN process into Crypto-CCS, whose syntax is represented using a custom XML format. The second transformation turns an XML representation of a sequential Crypto-CCS process back into a BPMN process. The translation is made to interoperate with the PaMoChSA2012 tool, performing synthesis of (sequential) Crypto-CCS orchestrators [23].

The algorithm implements the two formulas of Proposition 2. It can be more intuitively explained as path-finding in a state graph. In principle, the behavior of an orchestrator is a tree. However, since the system and the orchestrator are assumed to be deterministic, such a tree has an equivalent description in terms of all its paths. The input of PaMoChSA2012 is the same as PaMoChSA plus the initial knowledge of an orchestrator.

A practical way to account for possible attacks is to build the state graph in such a way that additional transitions are present, simulating eavesdropping and manipulation of messages by the intruder. Thus, whenever a service can receive a message from the orchestrator, then it evolves and it can also be instantiated with all messages of the same type that can be deduced from the knowledge of the intruder K_X. Likewise, whenever the service can send a message to the orchestrator, the knowledge K'_O of the orchestrator can also be augmented with all the messages of the same type that can be deduced from K_X. This machinery implements the ability of X to interfere with communications between the orchestrator and the system.

Finally, the knowledge of the intruder is always augmented with the messages that are exchanged between the orchestrator and the system, unless the used channel is in H. The rationale is that the intruder can eavesdrop such communications in order to acquire new information.

The result is a tool that accepts a BPMN collaboration diagram, containing a black-box process representing the orchestrator as input. The black-box in the original collaboration diagram is filled with the synthesized process that orchestrates the BPMN processes, driving all components to successful termination. The orchestrator is secure, in the sense that it uses asymmetric cryptography to forbid an attacker to learn a user-specified secret message.

The PaMoChSA 2012 specification of Example 1 is the following:

```
<GOAL>
success : Success
</GOAL>


<ORCH_KNOWLEDGE>
k_lo : EKey; k_u : EKey; k_ho : EKey; k_co : EKey ; k_sso : DKey
</ORCH_KNOWLEDGE>


<FORMULA>
residency_certificate : Residency_certificate
</FORMULA>


<KNOWLEDGE>
k_lo : EKey; k_ho : EKey; k_co : EKey ; k_sso : EKey
</KNOWLEDGE>


<HIDE_CHANNELS>
no_channels
</HIDE_CHANNELS>


<SPEC>
Parallel

(* User *)
Send(sso,id : Id).
Recv(sso,ENC_CERT : Enc(Residency_certificate * EKey)).
If Deduce (CERT = Decrypt(ENC_CERT, k_u : DKey)) Then
  Send(sso,Encrypt(success : Success,k_u : DKey)). 0
End Deduce
And

(* City hall *)
```

```
Recv(co,ID_HEALTHCARE : Id_healthcare).
Recv(co,ID_DRIVING_LICENSE : Id_driving_licence).
Send(co,Encrypt(residency_certificate :
          Residency_certificate, k_sso : EKey)). 0
```

And

(* Driving license office *)

```
Recv(c_do,ID : Id).
Send(c_do,id_driving_license : Id_driving_license). 0
```

And

(*Healthcare office*)

```
Recv(c_ho,ID : Id).
Send(c_ho,id_healthcare : Id_healthcare). 0
```

```
End Parallel
</SPEC>
```

As output, the tool returns the following orchestrator:

```
 Orchestrator:
Recv(sso,id : Id).
Send(c_do,id : Id).
Send(c_ho,id : Id).
Recv(c_do,id_driving_license : Id_driving_license).
Recv c_ho,id_healthcare : Id_healthcare).
Send(co,id_driving_license : Id_driving_license).
Send(co,id_healthcare : Id_healthcare).
Recv(co,Enc[k_sso](residency_certificate) :
      Enc(Residency_certificate*Ekey)).
Send(sso,Enc[k_u](residency_certificate) :
      Enc(Residency_certificate*Ekey)).
Recv(sso,Enck[k_u](success) : Enc(Success*Dkey)).0
```

 is secure.

Thus, the orchestrator is functional because it receives the success message from the user and it is secure because its way of acting does not let a potential intruder learn the secret message residency_certificate. The tool also explores the knowledge of the attacker in an exhaustive way and this guarantees that the attacker cannot obtain the secret.

4.5 Avantssar's Orchestrator: Tool Description

The AVANTSSAR Orchestrator [22] is a tool for automatic orchestration of Web Services with respect to their security policies. It is built over Cl-Atse [57], a tool for solving web services and cryptographic protocols insecurity in presence of a Dolev-Yao intruder, which it uses as a black-box to generate traces in presence of an active adversary. Systems are investigated with respect to a bounded number of legal transitions, *i.e.*, the number of actions done by honest agents is bounded, while those done by the intruder are not. Note that the name of the tool (AVANTSSAR's Orchestrator) should not be mistaken for the name of the agent O_{ϕ_O} (called orchestrator) that it must produce to show a secure orchestration.

AVANTSSAR's Orchestrator: The Synthesis Method. The orchestration approach of this tool follows the ideas of [7,9] and relies on the analogy with a state reachability problem in the analysis domain. Exploiting this idea, the tool converts the input problem into an insecurity problem where the adversary plays the role of the orchestrator O_{ϕ_O}, and where a successful completion of the orchestration (prop. φ_T) is converted into a successful attack by the adversary. This approach has the advantage to provide secure orchestrations for the framework, the specification languages, and the tools already defined and created for the AVANTSSAR's platform, but it requires to analyse the new system $S \| O_{\phi_O}$ it produces with respect to the security policies φ_{sec} using any or all of the three security analysers from the AVANTSSAR's platform (including Cl-Atse itself already used to produce the orchestrator), to make sure that:

$$\forall X_{\phi_X} (S \| O_{\phi_O} \| X_{\phi_X}) \models \varphi_{sec} \tag{4}$$

Thus it is a two-pass method, while the PaMoChSA2012 generates the orchestrator in one step. However, in practice usually only very few iterations are needed to produce a secure orchestration, if any exists. This is primarily due to an extension of Cl-Atse which permits it to generate attacks satisfying negative deductibility conditions for the intruder. This allows the AVANTSSAR's Orchestrator to produce an orchestrator O_{ϕ_O} that already partially validates the security policies φ_{sec} before the final verification, thus eliminating most useless iterations. Moreover, the iteration process guaranties to eliminate not only wrong individual orchestrations from the system, but whole families of them at once, thus reducing useless iterations even more.

The Input Problem. It is described in the ASLan language [10], extended with some keywords in order to distinguish agents like, *e.g.*, the client, some service, etc. The client is a special agent, since the tool must automatically generate an orchestrator O_{ϕ_O} able to satisfy each client's requests. The available services and the client are specified in the form of transition systems in the ASLan language, but the orchestrator is defined only by its initial knowledge. Another type of input is allowed: instead of specifying a client, one may partially define an orchestrator by providing only the part related to the communication with the putative client. The iteration process can be either automatic or manual, thus accepting a job identifier to continue solving a previously defined problem.

Output. In the case where a specification of the client is given, an ASLan specification of the orchestrator O_{ϕ_O} that securely satisfies the client's requests is produced. In the case where a partial specification of the orchestrator is given, a specification of the putative client is generated. Moreover, a new orchestrator service is issued, which extends the one given in the input with the necessary interactions with the available services. The tool can be downloaded or directly queried online from the CASSIS website (`http://cassis.loria.fr/`). It is part of the AVANTSSAR Platform, and has been integrated in the NESSoS' SDE.

5   Conclusion

In the last decades, the research on several aspects of service composition has been improved by a lot of research activities. In particular, several frameworks have been developed in order to compose services that can satisfy requirements and constraints imposed by a user. In this chapter, we have collected and discussed several research works outlining different approaches and techniques that have been proposed to tackle specific security aspects in service composition.

We also present our framework based on partial model checking for guaranteeing security in web service composition. In particular, we exploit cryptographic protocols analysis for checking that the communication among different services happens in a secure way. Furthermore, we extend the same framework for synthesizing an orchestrator process able to manage the communication among services by using also cryptographic primitives.

We also present two different tools for the automatic synthesis of orchestrators: the PaMoChSA2012 tool and the AVANTSSAR platform. Both tools solve the same problem by using different mechanisms: PaMoChSA2012 using partial model checking is able to generate an orchestrator in one step while AVANTSSAR generates orchestrators in a 2-steps procedure.

References

1. Andersen, H.R.: Partial model checking. In: LICS, p. 398. IEEE (1995)
2. Armando, A., et al.: The avispa tool for the automated validation of internet security protocols and applications. In: Etessami, K., Rajamani, S.K. (eds.) CAV 2005. LNCS, vol. 3576, pp. 281–285. Springer, Heidelberg (2005)
3. Armando, A., et al.: The AVANTSSAR platform for the automated validation of trust and security of service-oriented architectures. In: Flanagan, C., König, B. (eds.) TACAS 2012. LNCS, vol. 7214, pp. 267–282. Springer, Heidelberg (2012)
4. Arnold, A., Vincent, A., Walukiewicz, I.: Games for synthesis of controllers with partial observation. Theoretical Computer Science 303(1), 7–34 (2003)
5. Arsac, W., Compagna, L., Pellegrino, G., Ponta, S.E.: Security validation of business processes via model-checking. In: Erlingsson, Ú., Wieringa, R., Zannone, N. (eds.) ESSoS 2011. LNCS, vol. 6542, pp. 29–42. Springer, Heidelberg (2011)

6. Asarin, E., Maler, O., Pnueli, A.: Symbolic Controller Synthesis for Discrete and Timed Systems. In: Antsaklis, P.J., Kohn, W., Nerode, A., Sastry, S.S. (eds.) HS 1994. LNCS, vol. 999, pp. 1–20. Springer, Heidelberg (1995)
7. Avanesov, T., Chevalier, Y., Anis Mekki, M., Rusinowitch, M., Turuani, M.: Distributed Orchestration of Web Services under Security Constraints. In: Garcia-Alfaro, J., Navarro-Arribas, G., Cuppens-Boulahia, N., de Capitani di Vimercati, S. (eds.) DPM 2011 and SETOP 2011. LNCS, vol. 7122, pp. 235–252. Springer, Heidelberg (2012)
8. Avanesov, T., et al.: Intruder deducibility constraints with negation. Decidability and application to secured service compositions. CoRR, abs/1207.4871 (2012)
9. Avanesov, T., Chevalier, Y., Rusinowitch, M., Turuani, M.: Towards the Orchestration of Secured Services under Non-disclosure Policies. In: Kotenko, I., Skormin, V. (eds.) MMM-ACNS 2012. LNCS, vol. 7531, pp. 130–145. Springer, Heidelberg (2012)
10. AVANTSSAR. Deliverable 2.3 (update): ASLan++ specification and tutorial (2011), http://www.avantssar.eu
11. Baldoni, M., Baroglio, C., Martelli, A., Patti, V.: Reasoning about interaction protocols for web service composition. Electr. Notes Theor. Comput. Sci. 105, 21–36 (2004)
12. Bao, L., Zhang, W., Zhang, X.: Describing and Verifying Web Service Using CCS. pdcat, 421–426 (2006)
13. Bartoletti, M., Degano, P., Ferrari, G.L.: Plans for Service Composition. In: Workshop on Issues in the Theory of Security (WITS) (2006)
14. Bartoletti, M., Degano, P., Ferrari, G.-L.: Security issues in service composition. In: Gorrieri, R., Wehrheim, H. (eds.) FMOODS 2006. LNCS, vol. 4037, pp. 1–16. Springer, Heidelberg (2006)
15. Bartoletti, M., Degano, P., Ferrari, G.L.: Types and Effects for Secure Service Orchestration. In: Proc. 19th Computer Security Foundations Workshop (CSFW) (2006)
16. Benatallah, B., Casati, F., Ponge, J., Toumani, F.: Compatibility and replaceability analysis for timed web service protocols. In: BDA (2005)
17. Benatallah, B., Casati, F., Ponge, J., Toumani, F.: On Temporal Abstractions of Web Service Protocols. In: CAiSE Short Paper Proceedings (2005)
18. Bravetti, M., Zavattaro, G.: Service oriented computing from a process algebraic perspective. The Journal of Logic and Algebraic Programming 70(1), 3–14 (2007)
19. Busi, N., Gorrieri, R., Guidi, C., Lucchi, R., Zavattaro, G.: Choreography and orchestration: A synergic approach for system design. In: Benatallah, B., Casati, F., Traverso, P. (eds.) ICSOC 2005. LNCS, vol. 3826, pp. 228–240. Springer, Heidelberg (2005)
20. Cámara, J., Canal, C., Cubo, J., Vallecillo, A.: Formalizing WSBPEL Business Processes Using Process Algebra. ENTCS 154(1), 159–173 (2006)
21. Carbone, R., Minea, M., Mödersheim, S.A., Ponta, S.E., Turuani, M., Viganò, L.: Towards Formal Validation of Trust and Security in the Internet of Services. In: Domingue, J., et al. (eds.) Future Internet Assembly. LNCS, vol. 6656, pp. 193–207. Springer, Heidelberg (2011)
22. Chevalier, Y., Mekki, M.A., Rusinowitch, M.: Automatic Composition of Services with Security Policies. In: SERVICES 2008 - Part I, pp. 529–537. IEEE (2008)
23. Ciancia, V., Martin, J.A., Martinelli, F., Matteucci, I., Petrocchi, M., Pimentel, E.: A tool for the synthesis of cryptographic orchestrators. In: ACM (ed.) Model Driven Security Workshop, MDSEC (2012)

24. Ciancia, V., Martinelli, F., Matteucci, I., Petrocchi, M., Martn, J.A., Pimentel, E.: Automated synthesis and ranking of secure BPMN orchestrators (2013) (to apper)
25. Dong, J.S., Liu, Y., Sun, J., Zhang, X.: Verification of Computation Orchestration Via Timed Automata. In: Liu, Z., Kleinberg, R.D. (eds.) ICFEM 2006. LNCS, vol. 4260, pp. 226–245. Springer, Heidelberg (2006)
26. Ferrara, A.: Web services: A process algebra approach. In: ICSOC, pp. 242–251 (2004)
27. Havelund, K., Roşu, G.: Synthesizing monitors for safety properties. In: Katoen, J.-P., Stevens, P. (eds.) TACAS 2002. LNCS, vol. 2280, pp. 342–356. Springer, Heidelberg (2002)
28. Kazhamiakin, R., Pandya, P., Pistore, M.: Timed modelling and analysis in web service compositions. In: ARES 2006: Proceedings of the First International Conference on Availability, Reliability and Security, ARES 2006, pp. 840–846. IEEE Computer Society, Washington, DC (2006)
29. Kupferman, O., Madhusudan, P., Thiagarajan, P.S., Vardi, M.Y.: Open systems in reactive environments: Control and synthesis. In: Palamidessi, C. (ed.) CONCUR 2000. LNCS, vol. 1877, pp. 92–107. Springer, Heidelberg (2000)
30. Lapadula, A., Pugliese, R., Tiezzi, F.: A calculus for orchestration of web services. In: De Nicola, R. (ed.) ESOP 2007. LNCS, vol. 4421, pp. 33–47. Springer, Heidelberg (2007)
31. Li, J., Yarvis, M., Reiher, P.: Securing Distributed Adaptation. Computer Networks 38(3) (2002)
32. Marchignoli, D., Martinelli, F.: Automatic verification of cryptographic protocols through compositional analysis techniques. In: Cleaveland, W.R. (ed.) TACAS 1999. LNCS, vol. 1579, pp. 148–162. Springer, Heidelberg (1999)
33. Martín, J.A., Martinelli, F., Pimentel, E.: Synthesis of secure adaptors. J. Log. Algebr. Program. 81(2), 99–126 (2012)
34. Martín, J.A., Pimentel, E.: Contracts for security adaptation. J. Log. Algebr. Program. 80(3-5), 154–179 (2011)
35. Martinelli, F.: Languages for description and analysis of authentication protocols. In: Proceedings of 6th Italian Conference on Theoretical Computer Science, pp. 304–315 (1998)
36. Martinelli, F.: Analysis of security protocols as open systems. Theoretical Computer Science 290(1), 1057–1106 (2003)
37. Martinelli, F., Matteucci, I.: A framework for automatic generation of security controller. In: STVR (2010)
38. Martinelli, F., Matteucci, I.: Synthesis of web services orchestrators in a timed setting. In: Dumas, M., Heckel, R. (eds.) WS-FM 2007. LNCS, vol. 4937, pp. 124–138. Springer, Heidelberg (2008)
39. Martinelli, F., Petrocchi, M., Vaccarelli, A.: Automated Analysis of Some Security Mechanisms of SCEP. In: Chan, A.H., Gligor, V. (eds.) ISC 2002. LNCS, vol. 2433, pp. 414–427. Springer, Heidelberg (2002)
40. Martinelli, F., Petrocchi, M., Vaccarelli, A.: Formal analysis of some secure procedures for certificate delivery. STVR 16(1), 33–59 (2006)
41. Merlin, P., Bochmann, G.V.: On the Construction of Submodule Specification and Communication Protocols. ACM Transactions on Programming Languages and Systems 5, 1–25 (1983)
42. Milner, R.: Communication and Concurrency. Prentice-Hall, Inc., Upper Saddle River (1989)
43. OMG. Business Process Model and Notation (BPMN)

44. OMG. Introduction To OMG's Unified Modeling Language
45. Oquendo, F.: p-ADL for WS-Composition: A Service-Oriented Architecture Description Language for the Formal Development of Dynamic Web Service Compositions. In: SBCARS, pp. 52–66 (2008)
46. Papazoglou, M.P.: Web Services - Principles and Technology. Prentice-Hall, Inc. (2008)
47. Pinchinat, S., Riedweg, S.: A Decidable Class of Problems for Control under Partial Observation, vol. 95, pp. 454–460 (2005)
48. Pistore, M., Roberti, P., Traverso, P.: Process-Level Composition of Executable Web Services: "On-the-fly" Versus "Once-for-all" Composition. In: Gómez-Pérez, A., Euzenat, J. (eds.) ESWC 2005. LNCS, vol. 3532, pp. 62–77. Springer, Heidelberg (2005)
49. Pistore, M., Traverso, P., Bertoli, P.: Automated Composition of Web Services by Planning in Asynchronous Domains. In: ICAPS, pp. 2–11 (2005)
50. Qayyum, Z., Oquendo, F.: .NET Extensions to the p-architecture Description Languages. In: SEKE, pp. 244–249 (2008)
51. Raclet, J., Pinchinat, S.: The control of non-deterministic systems: A logical approach. In: Proc. 16th IFAC Word Congress, Prague, Czech Republic (2005)
52. Reisig, W.: Modeling- and analysis techniques for web services and business processes. In: Steffen, M., Zavattaro, G. (eds.) FMOODS 2005. LNCS, vol. 3535, pp. 243–258. Springer, Heidelberg (2005)
53. Riedweg, S., Pinchinat, S.: Quantified Mu-Calculus for Control Synthesis. In: Rovan, B., Vojtáš, P. (eds.) MFCS 2003. LNCS, vol. 2747, pp. 642–651. Springer, Heidelberg (2003)
54. Riedweg, S., Pinchinat, S.: You Can Always Compute Maximally Permissive Controllers Under Partial Observation When They Exist. In: Proc. 2005 American Control Conference, Portland, Oregon (2005)
55. Rosu, G., Havelund, K.: Synthesizing Dynamic Programming Algorithms from Linear Temporal Logic Formulae. Technical report (2001)
56. Salaun, G., Bordeaux, L., Schaerf, M.: Describing and Reasoning on Web Services using Process Algebra. In: Proceedings of the IEEE International Conference on Web Services (ICWS 2004), p. 43. IEEE Computer Society, Washington, DC (2004)
57. Turuani, M.: The CL-Atse Protocol Analyser. In: Pfenning, F. (ed.) RTA 2006. LNCS, vol. 4098, pp. 277–286. Springer, Heidelberg (2006)
58. Viganò, L.: Automated Security Protocol Analysis with the AVISPA Tool. ENTCS 155, 69–86 (2006)
59. W3C. Xquery 3.0: An xml query language

Privacy and Access Control in Federated Social Networks

Animesh Pathak[1], George Rosca[1], Valerie Issarny[1],
Maarten Decat[2], and Bert Lagaisse[2]

[1] Inria Paris-Rocquencourt, France
firstname.lastname@inria.fr
[2] iMinds-DistriNet, KU Leuven, 3001 Leuven, Belgium
firstname.lastname@cs.kuleuven.be

Abstract. Online social networks (OSNs) are increasingly turning mobile and further calling for decentralized social data management. This trend is only going to increase in the near future, based on the increased activity, both by established players like Facebook and new players in the domain such as Google, Instagram, and Pinterest. The increasing adoption of social networks in the workplace has further led to the development of corporate social networks such as those provided by Yammer, which was recently acquired by Microsoft. As individuals from different companies will need to interact as part of joint teams in these federated social networks, questions of privacy and access control arise. This chapter identifies the challenges concerning the above aspects, surveys the state of the art, and identifies directions of future research.

Keywords: social networks, access control, privacy, federation.

1 Introduction

As recent trends show, online social networks (OSNs) are increasingly turning mobile and further calling for decentralized social data management. This trend is only going to increase in the near future, based on the increased activity, both by established players like Facebook and new players in the domain such as Google, Instagram, and Pinterest. Modern smart phones can thus be regarded as *social sensors*, collecting data not only passively using, e.g., Bluetooth neighborhoods, but actively in the form of, e.g., "check-in"s by users to locations. The resulting (mobile) social ecosystems are thus an emergent area of interest.

The recent years have seen three major trends in the world of online social networks: *i)* users have begun to care more about the privacy of their data stored by large OSNs such as Facebook, and have won the right (at least in the EU [1]) to remove it completely from the OSN if they want to; *ii)* OSNs are making their presence felt beyond casual, personal interactions to corporate, professional ones as well, starting with LinkedIn, and most recently with the purchase by Microsoft of Yammer, the enterprise social networking startup [2], and the launch of Google Plus for enterprise customers [3]; and *iii)* users are increasingly using the capabilities of their (multiple) mobile devices to enrich their

M. Heisel et al. (Eds.): Engineering Secure Future Internet Services, LNCS 8431, pp. 160–179, 2014.

social interactions, ranging from posting cellphone-camera photos on Instagram to "checking-in" to a GPS location using foursquare.

In view of the above, we envision that in the near future, the use of ICT to enrich our social interactions will grow (including both personal and professional interactions [4]), both in terms of size and complexity. However current OSNs act mostly like data silos, storing and analyzing their users' data, while locking in those very users to their servers, with non-existent support for federation; this is reminiscent of the early days of email, where one could only email those who had accounts on the same Unix machine. The knee-jerk reaction to this has been to explore completely decentralized social networks [5], which give the user complete control over and responsibility of their social data, while resorting to peer-to-peer communication protocols to navigate their social networks. Unfortunately, there are few techniques available to reconcile with the fact that the same user might have multiple devices, or that it is extremely resource-consuming to perform complex analysis of social graphs on small mobile devices.

Our view lies somewhere in the middle of the two extremes, taking inspiration from the manner in which users currently use email. While their inboxes contain an immense amount of extremely personal data, most users are happy to entrust it to corporate or personal email providers (or store and manage it individually on their personal email servers) all the while being able to communicate with users on any other email server. The notion of **Federated Social Networks** (FSNs) —already gaining some traction [6]— envisions a similar ecosystem where users are free to choose OSN providers which will provide storage and management of their social information, while allowing customers using different OSN providers to interact socially. Such a federation can be beneficial in three major ways, among others: *i)* it allows users to enjoy properties such as reliability, availability, and computational power of the hosting infrastructure of their choice, while not being locked down in terms of whom they can communicate with; *ii)* much like spam filtering services provided by modern email providers, that are tuned by feedback from their users, FSN users can benefit from the behavior of others sharing the same OSN provider[1]; and *iii)* this fits perfectly with enterprise needs, where ad-hoc teams can be formed across corporate OSN providers of two organizations to work on a joint project.

1.1   Illustrative Example and Challenges

As an example of the circumstances discussed above, let us consider two organizations, companies A and B, which already use social networking platforms internally, but want to allow some of their employees to collaborate together as part of a joint team in order to achieve some goal (Working group B in Figure 1). This will involve exchanging messages, publishing shared contents, documents, but also participating in events, etc. Additionally, Company A uses a third party solution for behavior analysis of their employees based on their socializing logs

---

[1] This also gives an incentive to commercial OSN providers to provide value-added services.

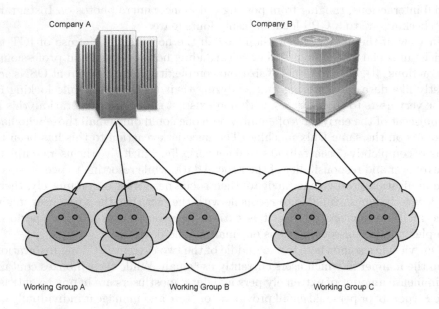

Fig. 1. An Example for Federation Among Enterprise Social Networks

(e.g., for suggesting team constitutions to managers for future projects). Alice from company A and Bob from company B are assigned to this working group, and add each-other to their contacts. Later, Alice shares a private document with her contacts. From a trust and privacy perspective, the following questions may arise:

- Can the system warn of leaks caused by interaction of certain type? Remembering that Alice shared the document with her contacts, from which Bob is part of, should he be able to see it? How can the system either warn or prevent such an incident?
- If Bob adds comments to the private document which Alice shared, are those comments subject to the same access control policy? Can we pre-determine that the social networking platform of company B will restrict access to these comments only to those members of company B who received Alice's initial post?
- Can company B be assured that their employees interaction within the common project will not be analyzed by A's third party solution?
- Is sharing information outside the company a decision held by the user itself or network administrator?

Clearly, for addressing questions such as those posed above, expressive, flexible, yet easy-to-specify privacy and access control policies are needed so that users can feel safe as more and more of their (social) life is made available online, thanks in large part to mobile clients for OSNs. As we have discovered in the course of our recent work, most current policy and trust frameworks are unable to adequately address the complexity of social networks, resorting to simple role-based access control. The need of the hour is a privacy and access control framework founded on the clear data and interaction models discussed earlier. Such a framework will also allow OSN providers to adequately evaluate whether or not a certain data of a user should be shared with another OSN provider (e.g., replies to a Facebook wall post have the privacy settings of the original post, while replies to a status message on Twitter have those of the user posting the reply, thus rendering them incompatible). Equally important is the availability of such techniques in mature, ready-to-deploy software platforms.

This chapter presents the reader with a set of requirements (Section 2, followed by a survey of the state of the art in social networking solutions, with a special focus on their ability to support rich privacy and access control policies in federated settings (Section 3). Through this extensive analysis we offer a broad vision on existing social networking platforms, protocols involved but also their privacy and access policies. By doing so, we identify the main components of a federated social platform together with presenting the current trends in standards and security paradigms underlying actual open source solutions which offers their implementation. Section 4 provides recommendations on constructing such systems. We then conclude in Section 5 with directions for future research.

2   Social Networking Platform Requirements

Before presenting the survey of social networking platforms, proposed in literature as well as available on the market, we introduce the criteria which form the basis of our assessment:

- **Person to Person links**: We will distinguish between symmetric and asymmetric 'friend' relationships among resources of type 'Person' (users). Needless to say, in order to semantically describe social ties between people we address a more realistic approach of being able to model both symmetric friendship like those seen in traditional OSNs like Facebook (where one is "friends" with all their friends) but also asymmetric links (e.g.'follow', 'knows', etc.).
- **Ease of Application Development on the Platform**: We highlight, if needed, the programming language, license, the API offered, native mobile support and the object model. The object model here refers to what kind of social resources and the connections between these the system utilizes (e.g. groups, events, etc.) with an emphasis on the ease of use but also the ability to extend this model when it comes to creating applications on top of the platform.
- **Federation Support**: Allowing the interaction between various decentralized systems raises the need to establish or make use of existing open protocols on which all these systems must comply in regards to information exchange. These protocols must provide identity, data interoperability and real-time communication.

– **Privacy and Access-control Policies**: Between individuals or communities access policies must be defined. Towards this direction a decentralized system must support a comprehensive set of mechanism which enable fine-grain control over the users who will have access to the data generated within such systems.

3 Existing Platforms

We now describe, based on the criteria identified previously, existing platforms together (summarized in Table 1). Broadly, we categorize social networking platforms as follows:

3.1 Siloed

Siloed social networks are the most common type found in commercial social networks open to the public. In the systems below, all the users share the same social networking service provider, and can not usually interact with users of another provider.

Facebook. Currently one of the leading commercial online social networking platforms, Facebook [7] offers a high level of API maturity allowing a large variety of application to be built on top of it, both online but also mobile specific. It offers a predefined data model which does not allow class extensions, offering the ability only for resource of type 'content' to be customized based on one's needs as depicted from their Open Graph API ('custom stories'). Between users the notion of friendship is symmetric while it allows support for asymmetric 'follow' links acting as a subscription which aggregates data on the main activity feed ('timeline'). It provides native application support for mobile environments so that applications build on top of the Facebook platform can benefit from the Single Sign On feature for authentication while also enabling traditional OAuth [8] through thin clients as well. It has a full-fledged mature API client and search capabilities but it does not allow federation since users of this platform are limited to interact with other users under the same centralized authority.

Privacy and Access Control. Since Facebook does not support federation no Server-to-Server rules are supported; it provides a robust access control mechanism for both the user and his data but also policies for third party applications build on top of the Facebook platform which might use sensitive user information. In regards to sharing data it offers a role-based policy mechanism (e.g. share with custom list), while in terms of data re-sharing it preserves the originator's policy. Note that in Facebook, tagging people in pictures will extend the visibility of those causing a leak of information, though when a private content is shared tagged comments will not have the same effect.

Twitter. Twitter's [9] online social networking platform is considered to be a device-agnostic real-time message-routing infrastructure which relies on the well known Redis [10] framework. Its object model is rather limited, it does not have events or groups but the friend relationship is asymmetrical ('follower' or 'followee'), while for authentication it offers OAuth support. The challenges which Twitter as a platform addresses are real-time syndication of content among connected users. It offers the ability to build applications on top of their platform providing only thin web clients for mobile and desktop environments.

Privacy and Access Control. In Twitter social networking platform the user can control by whom is he followed and each individual post's visibility which can be either public or visible by the ones who are following the user. However when a 'tweet' is private that can not be re-tweeted which means that re-sharing of the data is, in some ways, protected according to the originator's policies.

Mosco. Though Mosco [11] as a social platform is intended to be for portable devices ('middleware for mobile social computing') its architecture (see Figure 2) is mixed between cloud (Google's App Engine) and mobile implementation, having a rather limited basic model (stored in databases) with the ability to extend. The entities model is depicted in Figure 3 which better shows the connection between them and also which entities can be extended: `AbstractPrivacyData` for enriching the privacy policy access control manager and `AbstractData` for new object types with no ability however to define new connection between the resources available. The `AbstractData` extensions can be then accessed via SQL-like queries.

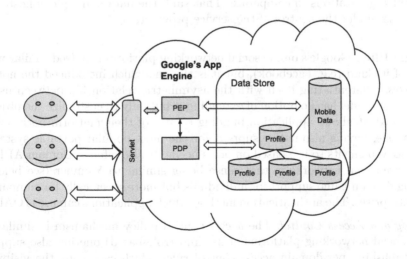

Fig. 2. Mosco Architecture Overview

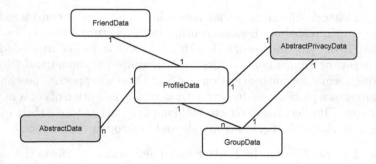

Fig. 3. UML diagram representing main entities in the data model present in Mosco platform. The shaded entities are to be extended when implementing a new application.

Privacy and Access Control. The complex and flexible access control policy manager of Mosco is an extension of the popular XACML [12] with a set of predefined policies suitable for social computing. As an example it allows users to create context-specific policy rules like sharing the current location with people in the immediate proximity or patient records when some threshold is reached. In order to define new privacy rules application developers must extend `AbstractPrivacyData`.

3.2   Social Networking as a Service

These platforms employ the Software as a Service (SaaS) paradigm, thus enabling organizations to define their own networks or domains, enabling individuals from different organizations to co-operate. That said, the data and logic is hosted in most cases under the control of the service provider.

Google Plus. Google's online social networking platform is indeed similar with other of its kind (e.g. Facebook), but it is the one which introduced the notion of *circles*, differentiating itself with the asymmetric relationship between users. The object model has no option of extending it but only to customize the objects maintained. It allows application building on top of their platform both online and mobile, having also native support for the most popular portable systems, but also web clients to use based on one's needs. It also offers a Domain API for enterprise social networks in that sense being similar to Yammer (see below), offering domain name support for individuals but more specifically for companies and enterprises. The authentication method which applications can use is OAuth.

Privacy and Access Control. The access control policy mechanism is similar to other social networking platforms of its kind (role-based) offering also support for establishing per-domain access control rules which can scope the visibility of content within a domain. Google Plus mixes between traditional OSNs and Enterprise Social Networks (ESNs) by offering the ability for network administrators to specify domain specific policies as well as domain-wide delegation of authority. In that direction the scope of posts within a domain can be limited to be only visible inside the organization. In terms of data re-sharing outside the organization it is believed that the decision to allow data outside the domain should reside with the user rather than administrators. When a private content is being shared a simple comment with a tagged person will extend the content's visibility making the comments but also the original post available for the one who has been tagged.

Ning. Ning [13] is an online social networking platform which allows people or organization to create their own customized micro-blogging network which will primarily be hosted on a subdomain of Ning. In terms of social resources it has a limited model containing user profiles, groups, pictures, messages, contents without the ability to extend or define new resource types. It implements OpenSocial [14] protocol which allows the creation of applications which are able to interact with the platform. It allows applications to be build for mobile using Javascript and HTML5, so no real native support is available. Since it is a commercial software it enables easy creation of networks inside Ning without needing any programming experience (drag and drop) allowing users from different networks (or subnetworks) to interact as if they were in the same network.

Privacy and Access Control. From a privacy perspective, Ning offers its users fine-grain access control, providing granular content moderation allowing anyone, just friends or members of the same network to view information. Also, in the same manner, users are able to choose who can comment on their content or even moderate which comments can appear attached to their content or information.

Yammer. Yammer [15] is the leading software in enterprise social networking platforms. It offers an Open Graph API with an actor-action-object structure (as described in Figure 4) which is extensible and allows the description of any kind of fact, offering the ability to describe new object types under different namespaces. It offers virtual storage for companies and easy deployment and installation with further interaction between users on different companies further maintaining their privacy policies (NDA). From a UI perspective Yammer maintained the same pattern as Facebook which they have identified as being the 'DNA for socializing' so that user adoption will be much easier. Cross-domain collaboration can be achieved allowing companies to establish communities with their customer in a secure manner thus providing federation among deployments of Yammer.

Privacy and Access Control. It offers support for SAML [16] 1.1/2.0-based Single Sign On mechanism supporting also OAuth both for desktop and mobile environments. It provides TLS encrypted e-mail transport, session management and built-in logical firewalls for the data centers. What is different from Google Plus Domain API is the fact that the user starts in a private network and they can collaborate with other corporate networks if invited.

```
{
    "activity":{
        "actor":{
            "name":"Sidd Singh",
            "email":"sidd@xyz.com"
        },
        "action":"create",
        "object": {
            "url":"https://www.sched.do",
            "title":"Lunch Meeting"
        },
        "message":"Hey, let s get sushi!",
        "users":[{
            "name":"Adarsh Pandit",
            "email":"adarsh@xyz.com"
        }]
    }
}
```

Fig. 4. Example actor action object JSON code structure in Yammer

3.3 Federated Social Networks

Federated social networks are networking services that allow interactions between users across distinct social networking service providers. However, their architecture is not completely distributed since the users in each network still depend on servers whom they must trust regarding the processing of sensitive data.

Status.net. One of the most powerful microblogging social networking platform, Status.net [17] (formerly Laconica) is a ready-to-deploy decentralized solution, written in PHP, which can be accessed via multiple standard protocols including e-mail, sms, XMPP. Formerly it has been supporting identi.ca [18] and pump.io [19], but since late December 2012, the latter decided to change its infrastructure to NodeJS from performance reasons, while maintaining the same concept of microblogging making use of ActivityStrea.ms. It also implements OStatus which allows notifications of status updates between distributed social platforms including Friendica. For discovery it offers an implementation of WebFinger [20] protocol. Its data model contains groups, asymmetric relationships between people, being extensible through ActivityStrea.ms. It also provides 1 - 1 messaging support. It also offers support for updates through XMPP, cross posting to Twitter, Facebook integration. It also implements the Salmon protocol which allows the unification of conversation through content from different servers to happen. There is no native support for mobile environment but it has an Open Source client for both Desktop and Mobile based on the Appcelerator [21] platform.

Privacy and Access Control. It implements OpenID [22] for identity, but offers support for Apache Authentication which allows any kind of such mechanisms to be integrated. The access control policies are limited to role-based policies as well as domain specific policies.

Friendica. Friendica is a decentralized open source social networking platform which provides fully distributed protocols for secure communication such as DFRN [23] or Zot [24], the two complementing each other. It supports LDAP [25] for authentication having a limited data model which can only be extended by the support of server side plugins. As an example of the latter it offers plugins for displaying locations on the map or connectors for popular social networks such as Twitter or Google Plus. It does not offer native mobile support but since their API is similar to Status.net, the latter's mobile clients can be used along with existing Friendica's available clients. Since it was intended for small networks, in order to solve the scalability problem they have introduced Red [26] which is addressed for companies and organizations in which case it dramatically reduces the abilities in cross-service federation.

Privacy and Access Control. In terms of security, Friendica offers both server-to-server but also one-to-one advanced message encryption, while all the items (messages, posts, etc.) are controlled by a fine grained access control mechanisms. Groups can also have specific policies which are applicable to all the members contained, profile visibility can as well be controlled by the individuals, together with its data which can easily be backed-up on home computers.

Diaspora. The open source decentralized social networking platform Diaspora [27] addresses the privacy concerns related to centralized social networks allowing users or developers to deploy their own server solution thus interacting with other users from other deployment. It offers social aggregation facilities by importing data from Twitter, Tumblr and Facebook. Written on Ruby on Rails under AGPLv3 license, Diaspora has a fixed social data model without the ability to extend it. Regarding mobile integration there is no native support but there are a couple of web clients which can be used, without allowing applications to be developed on top of the middleware. In terms of federation, Diaspora facilitates this by providing an implementation of Salmon [28] protocol and for discovery it provides support for the WebFinger open protocol.

Privacy and Access Control. Diaspora offers a fine grained aspect-oriented access policy mechanism. This provides the ability to control posts' visibility to either public or limited, which is the traditional role-based but named 'aspects' in this case. It has some already built-in 'aspects' such as friends, family or co-workers but other lists can be constructed as well.

OneSocialWeb. OneSocialWeb [29] is an interesting social networking platform licensed under Apache 2.0, having a communication layer relying on XMPP which allows federation to be achieved much easier. Though the code base is not maintained anymore, it allows an already to deploy solution on the server side with the possibility to use existing clients for mobile devices. It implements ActivityStrea.ms protocol as for data modeling and an activity based policy mechanism which ensures flexibility in terms of storage, offering an implementation of OpenID for authentication.

Privacy and Access Control. Like in any other social networking platform One-SocialWeb offers the ability to control the access for individual posts, profile items or even relationships. It is interesting to note that their mechanism is fine grained in the sense that you can define the subject or 'accessor' of the information which can be either a contact, a group, people from a certain domain, everyone or a specific individual. Also, the action performed on the data can be customized which can be read, write, delete, update or append. Some real examples would include: a post visible to everyone but only friends can add comments or a public photo album which only family can edit.

Buddycloud. buddycloud [30] is a decentralized open source social platform, licensed under Apache 2.0. Working in collaboration with W3C, Mozilla Foundation and XSF [31], they offer multiple open standards such as ActivityStrea.ms, ATOM syndication format and XEP [32] which is an extension of XMPP protocol offering useful functionalities such as discovery. They offer an easy to install federated server side code base, written in node.js (offer a version in java as well) and as for mobile support an Android client is provided which relies on Backbone (JavaScript library). It offers messaging support including a couple of other useful social engines such as recommendation, real-time search, resource discovery and push notification. The data model is rather limited (e.g. it does not contain events or groups) having an asymmetric relation between users, but it does give you the ability to extend the basic model in some ways by making use of ActivityStre.ms. Users will authenticate via traditional basic HTTP method with the option for using a secure connection. A summarization of the platform architecture is depicted in Figure 5.

Privacy and Access Control. Users can share almost anything through media channels having the ability to limit posts visibility through a rather simple access control mechanism which allow black/white listing. Also, it provides a 'butler' which enables users to securely share their location with friends. It provides support for SSL/TLS communication for both client - server and server - server communication so that user's privacy will be preserved.

ELGG. ELGG [33] is one of the most popular PHP open source social networking software platforms which is easy to deploy and configure, providing a large variety of components for individuals and companies having an already stable community with lots of already-made plugins for different purposes. Its architecture is decentralized in the sense that multiple federated ELGG server

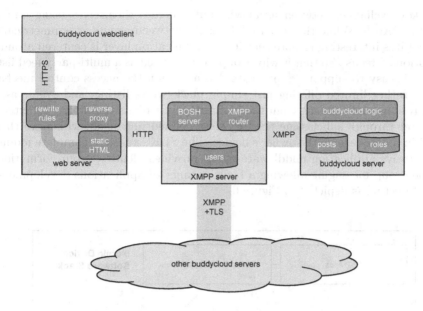

Fig. 5. buddycloud Architecture Overview

instances can communicate while it is still preserving the traditional online social networking paradigm where all the data is stored on the server. It is lacking
of any mature client API for mobile devices thus applications build on top of
the platform will reside on the server as plugins. The data model is rather limited but enough for its purpose containing groups, asymmetric user relationship,
messaging support (only 1 - 1), contents which can be attached to groups. The
data and policy model are extensible only through server side plugins while from
the authentication perspective it provides a powerful pluggable authentication
module (PAM) which allows the implementation of any sort of authentication.

Privacy and Access Control. Users can control the visibility of profile information, posts or groups so that the data can be private, accessed by friends, logged
in users or even public. By making use of plugins, enhanced authentication mechanisms can be added such as logging in using a Twitter account or even LDAP
credentials.

3.4   Decentralized

Decentralized networks are federated social networks which do not depend on
any central authority in order to function. Consequently, user data is completely
out of the cloud residing on user's devices (which can be one or many).

Musubi. As a mobile social networking platform Musubi [34] offers a comprehensive peer-to-peer (P2P) encryption mechanism, both 1 to 1 but also multiple

peers key exchange, between users who authenticate themselves using e-mail but also OAuth. While the social relationship between agents is symmetrically mapped it is interesting to note that its communication layer is centered around the notion of 'feeds'. So that is why groups are modeled as a multi-party feed list, making it easy to support group chats. Even though the access control mechanism is rather limited offering just simple black/white listing, and events as a social resource are missing from the basic model, it offers the ability to extend the latter through subclassing the Obj class defined in Musubi which are then stored in a database on the owner's device. The SDK exposes a complete mobile collaborative application middleware which provides identity, group formation, reliable group messaging allowing a facile manner of applications development. Its architecture is depicted in Figure 6.

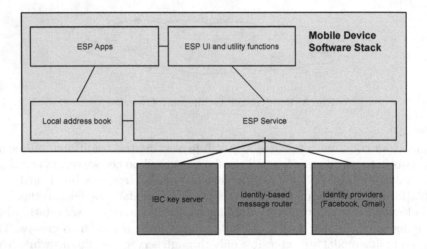

Fig. 6. Musubi's Egocentric Social Platform (ESP) Architecture Overview

Privacy and Access Control. Though the current platform depends on reliable but not fully trusted traffic relay services to achieve P2P communication over the Web, it provides encryption on data transfer, key management, as well as it describes a Trusted Group Chat Protocol which involves a multi-peers key exchange. The access control mechanism is simplistic thus error prone, but it does not protect against data re-sharing.

Yarta. Yarta [35] is a flexible decentralized mobile social platform (see Figure 7) which keeps all of users data out of the cloud, on their devices in a semantic manner (RDF) which offers a high level of information re-usability across applications built on top of the platform by using the inherited inference from ontology models. Moreover all these data is shared using a semantic aware access control manager which allows the creation of complex policy models which can

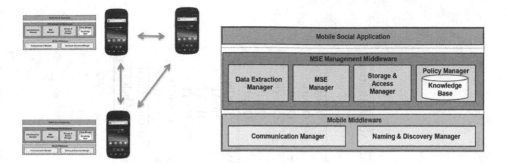

Fig. 7. Yarta Architecture Overview

also include context information which are gathered from mobile sensors. As for the authentication Yarta currently provides an OAuth example but this can be easily replaced with any flavor of one's needs.

Privacy and Access Control. Yarta offers an extensible, powerful and comprehensive semantic based access control mechanism [36] allowing the description of semantically defined policy rules which sits at the gate of owner's device before sharing any data. Still there is the problem of data re-sharing, since another peer which gathered the data might either not be aware of the sensitivity of that information nor it should be trusted.

4 Recommendations for a Privacy-Aware Federated Social Networking Architecture

Based on our survey above, we believe that there is a need for clear identification of the components needed to create federated social networking platforms, with a special emphasis on privacy and access control. Notably, in a federated social ecosystem each entity participating in the production or consuming information should comply to open standards which will further allow the integration of heterogeneous systems. To that end, we identify below the main components needed for a federated social network, as well as the currently existing solutions for each. The overall architecture is shown in Figure 8, and includes the following components:

- **Storage**: Whether it is present locally on the user's device or in a trusted federated server it is clear that the storage of a system needs to be done in such a fashion that will allow the description of existing social resources (e.g. person profiles, textual and multi-media contents, messages, etc.), but also allow the ability to extend the model through defining new concepts, complex data structure but also novel connections between these.
- **Access Control**: Users should be able to express rich policies in terms of their social context, links, groups and domain, which should be enforced before granting access to their data.

Table 1. Summary of major social networking platforms

Architecture	Network	Mobile	Groups	Person-Person links	Events	Storage	Access control	Authentication
Siloed	Facebook	Online	Yes	Symmetric	Yes	Fixed	Limited	OAuth
	Twitter	Online	No	Asymmetric	No	Fixed	Limited	OAuth
	Mosco	Online	Yes	Symmetric	No	Extensible	Extensible	OAuth
Social Networking-aaS	Google Plus	Online	Yes	Asymmetric	Yes	Fixed	Limited	OAuth
	Ning	Online	Yes	Symmetric	Yes	Fixed	Limited	OAuth
	Yammer	Online	Yes	Asymmetric	Yes	Extensible	Limited	OAuth
Federated	Status.net	Online	Yes	Asymmetric	Yes	Extensible	Extensible	Apache
	Friendica	Online	Yes	Symmetric	Yes	Fixed	Limited	LDAP
	Diaspora	Online	Yes	Asymmetric	No	Fixed	Extensible	HTTP
	buddycloud	Online	No	Asymmetric	No	Extensible	Extensible	HTTP
	OneSocialWeb	Online	No	Asymmetric	No	Extensible	Extensible	OpenID
	ELGG	Online	Yes	Asymmetric	No	Extensible	Extensible	PAM
Decentralized	Musubi	Mobile	Yes	Symmetric	No	Extensible	Limited	OAuth, Email
	Yarta	Mobile	Yes	Asymmetric	Yes	Extensible	Extensible	OAuth

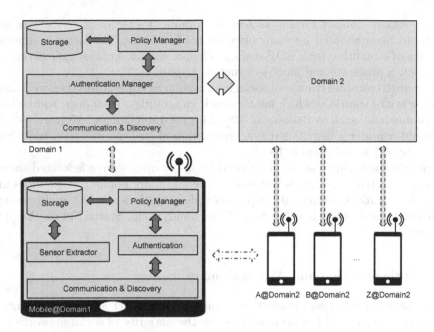

Fig. 8. Federated architecture which identifies the main components on the server side together with those present on client side devices along with the interaction which can happen between different peers

- **Authentication**: Authentication should be enabled whenever any peer communicates with a different one, allowing the problem of 'to whom I am speaking with' to be solved in an easy manner offering trust and security through an advanced cryptographic system.
- **Communication**: The communication module can be either part of the system itself or an independent external module but should enable the communication of any two peers which have social connections. In case the communication is an external third party component then it is imperative to employ adequate security measures to ensure data integrity as well as user-anonymity, when needed.
- **Discovery**: This is an essential mechanism to allow resources be defined over the web and also enables their discovery.

We discuss below the alternative solutions —both open source and commercial— which can be adopted for each component in part, noting that according to W3C's Federated Social Web group [37] the main trends towards federation would be to adopt open standards.

4.1 Storage

In terms of storage current social networking trends are moving towards extensible mechanisms such as mapping social resources as ontologies or JSON based actor - action - object format as seen in Yammer's case or ActivityStrea.ms which has been adopted by many open source platforms. The latter is similar, in terms of semantics, with RDF storage schema, since it implies the existing of a subject, a predicate and an object such as triples.

If we are to consider storage of social information as triple stores then we would have plenty of solutions which enables such capabilities, both open source but also commercial, such as Parliament [38], AllegroGraph [39] and Mulgara [40]. If we would consider a distributed synchronization of such models then tools like RDFSync [41] would come in handy.

One standard which has been adopted by many open source federated social networks, ActivityStrea.ms is becoming more and more popular. It provides an extensible manner of activity description. Implementations can be found in many open source projects such as OneSocialWeb, buddycloud, Status.Net or eXo [42] platform.

4.2   Authentication and Access Control

From the authentication perspective OAuth and OpenID are becoming more and more popular and has been adopted by the majority of social networks for which there exists several implementation for both server and clients. Source code in most popular programming languages can be found on each protocol's website. It we are considering federated authentication and authorization then Shibboleth [43] and Gluu [44] are two interesting tools which we might consider working with, noting that they both offer an open source implementation of SAML protocol.

Access control have become an important aspect of nowadays social ecosystem. As seen in [45], if we are to consider social networks as a SaaS, then both the provider and the tenant should be able to express their privacy policies in a secure manner since the latter has to disclose sensitive information. Access control mechanisms should be able to describe both traditional policies but also complex ones making use of context information as well. For simple access mechanism one can choose an open source implementation of Access Control List (ACL) protocols, more advanced ones such as XACML[2] or an implementation of the semantics-based policies of [36] which provides a highly extensible, generic yet expressive access control policy management solution. In order to approach the problem of re-sharing information one should consider sticky security policies solutions described in works such as [46,47].

4.3   Communication and Discovery

For communication various open protocols can be adopted such as XMPP, Salmon, PubSubHubbub or OStatus to achieve federation since those have been adopted by many open source social networking platforms. More, one can make

---

[2] Open Source XACML: http://sunxacml.sourceforge.net/

use of faster, light-weight communication middlewares such as MQTT [48], iBI-COOP [49] which provides transportation relays between devices over the Internet.

Coupled with the above, there are options for discovery which include open ones such as WebFinger which has been adopted by Diaspora and Status.net, XEP from XMPP, mDNS protocol which can be found in the Bonjour commercial software, or even UPnP media discovery and of course iBICOOP.

5   Future Directions

It is evident that the future will see increased adoption of social networking, and it will not all be managed by a single entity. Consequently, support for federation among social networks emerges as a necessary functionality, something that currently available systems are not able to provide in a comprehensive manner. We believe that in order to enable the federated social networking platforms of the future, empowered with strong privacy and access-control policies, the community should *i*) Adopt open standards for the necessary components as much as possible, in order to prevent reinventing the wheel and speed-up adoption; *ii*) Use semantic techniques for modeling of social knowledge, enabling the easy and extensible re-use of data, both by applications executing on these platforms and other social networking providers; and *iii*) provide rich privacy and access-control mechanisms, preferably semantically-based sticky policies so as to provide adequate protection to the users' and organizations' sensitive information. Following the above should lead to interoperable social networking platforms which will gain wide acceptance.

References

1. European Commission: Commission proposes a comprehensive reform of the data protection rules,
   http://ec.europa.eu/justice/newsroom/data-protection/
   news/120125_en.htm (accessed January 2014)
2. Microsoft: Microsoft to Acquire Yammer,
   http://www.microsoft.com/en-us/news/press/2012/jun12/
   06-25msyammerpr.aspx (accessed January 2014)
3. Ho, R.: Google+ is now available for Google Apps,
   http://googleenterprise.blogspot.it/2011/10/
   google-is-now-available-with-google.html (accessed January 2014)
4. Hinchcliffe, D.: Today's Collaboration Platforms for Large Enterprises,
   http://www.zdnet.com/the-major-enterprise-collaboration-
   platforms-and-their-mobile-clients-7000018519/ (accessed January 2014)
5. Narayanan, A., Toubiana, V., Barocas, S., Nissenbaum, H., Boneh, D.: A critical look at decentralized personal data architectures. CoRR abs/1202.4503 (2012)
6. Esguerra, R.: An introduction to the federated social network,
   https://www.eff.org/deeplinks/2011/03/
   introduction-distributed-social-network (accessed January 2014)

7. Facebook: Online Social Networking Platform, `https://www.facebook.com/` (accessed January 2014)
8. OAuth: Secure authorization open protocol, `http://oauth.net/` (accessed January 2014)
9. Twitter: Online Social Networking and Microblogging Service, `https://twitter.com/` (accessed January 2014)
10. Redis: Open source advanced key-value store, `http://redis.io/` (accessed January 2014)
11. Tuan Anh, D.T., Ganjoo, M., Braghin, S., Datta, A.: Mosco: A privacy-aware middleware for mobile social computing. Journal of Systems and Software (2013)
12. XACML: eXtensible Access Control Markup Language (XACML) Version 3.0, `http://docs.oasis-open.org/xacml/3.0/xacml-3.0-core-spec-os-en.html` (accessed January 2014)
13. Ning: Build and cultivate your own community, `http://www.ning.com/` (accessed January 2014)
14. Foundation, O.: OpenSocial protocol, `http://opensocial.org/` (accessed January 2014)
15. Yammer: Enterprise Social Network, `https://www.yammer.com/` (accessed January 2014)
16. SAML: Security Assertion Markup Language (SAML) v2.0, `https://www.oasis-open.org/standards#samlv2.0` (accessed January 2014)
17. Status.net: Free and open source social software, `http://status.net/` (accessed January 2014)
18. Identi.ca: Open source social networking service, `https://identi.ca/` (accessed January 2014)
19. pump.io: Open source social stream server, `http://pump.io/` (accessed January 2014)
20. WebFinger: Personal web discovery protocol, `https://code.google.com/p/webfinger/wiki/WebFingerProtocol` (accessed January 2014)
21. Appcelerator: Portable software development platform, `http://www.appcelerator.com/` (accessed January 2014)
22. OpenID Foundation: The Internet Identity Layer, `http://openid.net/` (accessed January 2014)
23. Macgirvin, M.: DFRN - The Distributed Friends and Relations Network, `https://macgirvin.com/spec/dfrn2.pdf` (accessed January 2014)
24. Zot: Secure decentralised communications framework, `https://github.com/friendica/red/wiki/zot` (accessed January 2014)
25. Wahl, M., Howes, T., Kille, S.: Lightweight Directory Access Protocol, `https://www.ietf.org/rfc/rfc2251.txt`
26. Friendica: Red design documentation, `https://github.com/friendica/red/wiki/red` (accessed January 2014)
27. Diaspora: The Community-run, Distributed Social Network, `http://www.joindiaspora.com/` (accessed January 2014)
28. Salmon: Real-time Commenting Protocol, `http://www.salmon-protocol.org/` (accessed January 2014)
29. OneSocialWeb: Creating a free, open, and decentralized social networking platform, `http://onesocialweb.org/` (accessed January 2014)
30. buddycloud: Federated social network, `http://buddycloud.com/` (accessed January 2014)
31. XMPP: XMPP standards foundation, `http://xmpp.org/about-xmpp/xsf/` (accessed January 2014)

32. XMPP: XMPP extension protocols, `http://xmpp.org/extensions/xep-0001.html` (accessed January 2014)
33. Elgg: Open Source Social Networking Engine, `http://elgg.org/` (accessed January 2014)
34. Dodson, B., Vo, I., Purtell, T., Cannon, A., Lam, M.: Musubi: Disintermediated interactive social feeds for mobile devices. In: Proceedings of the 21st International Conference on World Wide Web, pp. 211–220. ACM (2012)
35. Toninelli, A., Pathak, A., Issarny, V.: Yarta: A Middleware for Managing Mobile Social Ecosystems. In: Riekki, J., Ylianttila, M., Guo, M. (eds.) GPC 2011. LNCS, vol. 6646, pp. 209–220. Springer, Heidelberg (2011)
36. Hachem, S., Toninelli, A., Pathak, A., Issarny, V.: Policy-based Access Control in Mobile Social Ecosystems. In: Proceedings of the IEEE International Symposium on Policies for Distributed Systems and Networks, Pisa, Italy. IEEE computer society (June 2011)
37. W3C: Federated social web community group, `http://www.w3.org/2005/Incubator/federatedsocialweb/wiki/Main_Page` (accessed January 2014)
38. Parliament: High-performance triple store, `http://parliament.semwebcentral.org/` (accessed January 2014)
39. AllegroGraph: RDFStore Web 3.0's Database, `http://franz.com/agraph/allegrograph/` (accessed January 2014)
40. Mulgara: Open source scalable rdf database, `http://www.mulgara.org/` (accessed January 2014)
41. Tummarello, G., Morbidoni, C., Bachmann-Gmür, R., Erling, O.: RDFSync: Efficient remote synchronization of rdf models. In: Aberer, K., et al. (eds.) ASWC 2007 and ISWC 2007. LNCS, vol. 4825, pp. 537–551. Springer, Heidelberg (2007)
42. eXo: Open Source Enterprise Social Network, `http://www.exoplatform.com/` (accessed January 2014)
43. Shibboleth: Federated identity solutions, `http://shibboleth.net/` (accessed January 2014)
44. Gluu: Open source access management, `http://www.gluu.org/` (accessed January 2014)
45. Decat, M., Lagaisse, B., Van Landuyt, D., Crispo, B., Joosen, W.: Federated authorization for software-as-a-service applications. In: Meersman, R., Panetto, H., Dillon, T., Eder, J., Bellahsene, Z., Ritter, N., De Leenheer, P., Dou, D. (eds.) ODBASE 2013. LNCS, vol. 8185, pp. 342–359. Springer, Heidelberg (2013)
46. Mont, M.C., Pearson, S., Bramhall, P.: Towards accountable management of identity and privacy: Sticky policies and enforceable tracing services. In: IEEE Proceedings of the 14th International Workshop on Database and Expert Systems Applications, pp. 377–382 (2003)
47. Fatema, K., Chadwick, D.W., Lievens, S.: A multi-privacy policy enforcement system. In: Fischer-Hübner, S., Duquenoy, P., Hansen, M., Leenes, R., Zhang, G. (eds.) Privacy and Identity 2010. IFIP AICT, vol. 352, pp. 297–310. Springer, Heidelberg (2011)
48. MQTT: Machine to machine connectivity protocol, `http://mqtt.org/` (accessed January 2014)
49. Bennaceur, A., Singh, P., Raverdy, P.G., Issarny, V.: The iBICOOP middleware: Enablers and services for emerging pervasive computing environments. In: IEEE International Conference on Pervasive Computing and Communications, PerCom 2009, pp. 1–6. IEEE (2009)

Engineering Trust-Awareness and Self-adaptability in Services and Systems

Francisco Moyano[1], Carmen Fernandez-Gago[1], Benoit Baudry[2],
and Javier Lopez[1]

[1] Department of Computer Science
University of Malaga, 29071 Malaga, Spain
{moyano,mcgago,jlm}@lcc.uma.es
[2] INRIA Rennes Bretagne-Atlantique, Campus de Beaulieu, 35042 Rennes, France
Certus Software V&V Center, SIMULA RESEARCH LAB., Lysaker, Norway
benoit.baudry@irisa.fr

Abstract. The Future Internet (FI) comprises scenarios where many heterogeneous and dynamic entities must interact to provide services (e.g., sensors, mobile devices and information systems in smart city scenarios). The dynamic conditions under which FI applications must execute call for self-adaptive software to cope with unforeseeable changes in the application environment. Models@run.time is a promising model-driven approach that supports the runtime adaptation of distributed, heterogeneous systems. Yet frameworks that accommodate this paradigm have limited support to address security concerns, hindering their usage in real scenarios. We address this challenge by enhancing models@run.time with the concepts of trust and reputation. Trust improves decision-making processes under risk and uncertainty and constitutes a distributed and flexible mechanism that does not entail heavyweight administration. This chapter introduces a trust and reputation framework that is integrated into a distributed component model that implements the models@run.time paradigm, thus allowing software components to include trust in their reasoning process. The framework is illustrated in a smart grid scenario.

1 Introduction: The Need for Trust and Self-adaptability

The Future Internet (FI) scenarios are bringing two important changes in the Information and Communication Technology (ICT) world. On the one hand, the uprising of the service-oriented vision enables the on-the-fly improvement of the features offered to users. Applications become more dynamic, which calls for rapid adaptation strategies in order to meet new requirements or respond to environmental changes. On the other hand, the coming of age of the Internet of Things (IoT) entails that sensors and actuators are embedded in physical and daily life objects, which are linked in networks and can produce a vast amount of data that flow to services. This seamless integration between the physical and the virtual worlds brings new challenges in terms of dynamicity, since both

M. Heisel et al. (Eds.): Engineering Secure Future Internet Services, LNCS 8431, pp. 180–209, 2014.

services and systems as a whole must adapt to dynamic changes in hardware, firmware and software, including the unpredictable arrival or disappearance of devices and software components. Figure 1 illustrates this situation.

The aforementioned changes blur boundaries between design and runtime [9] as they prevent designers from envisioning all possible circumstances that might appear during the execution of an application. The widespread adoption of FI systems requires addressing three main concerns: complexity, dynamicity and security.

As for complexity, the software engineering community has proposed several approaches framed within the model-driven engineering paradigm, where high-level abstractions of systems are created and refined until reaching a final running system. These abstractions allow reasoning about system properties and functionality without the need to understand every tiny detail.

As part of the model-driven engineering approaches, *models@run.time* [1] is gaining relevance. It consists of keeping an abstract representation of a running system. This representation is always synchronized with the system, in such a way that when the former is changed, the latter adapts itself to match the new configuration. This fosters complexity reduction as well as allowing dynamicity reasoning, enabling the building of self-adaptive systems: a running system can be changed either manually by designers or automatically by adaptation rules that are executed upon environmental changes.

The complexity, dynamicity and distributed nature of FI systems call for new security approaches that do not require heavyweight administration and that can evolve automatically as a result of system dynamics. Addressing security in these systems requires that trust relationships among users, components, and system environments are not taken for granted; they must be explicitly declared, monitored and changed according to the system evolution. The security community has focused on developing methods and frameworks for traditional security requirements, that is: confidentiality, integrity, and availability. Authorization has also been a relevant field of study and some approaches like Role-Based Access Control (RBAC) are nowadays a standard in industry. However, the new conditions of the FI precludes the use of this approach and call for new flexible and dynamic ways of managing security, in general, and access control in particular [25].

In this chapter, we discuss the design and implementation of a trust and reputation development framework, together with its integration into a platform for self-adaptive, distributed component-based systems. This framework aims to help designers and developers in building highly dynamic, self-adaptive and trust-aware systems, enhancing the models@run.time paradigm with the inclusion of trust and reputation notions.

The structure of the chapter is the following. Section 2 reviews how the software engineering community has traditionally approached trust, specially during the initial phases of the Software Development Life Cycle (SDLC). A conceptual framework and some foundations of trust and reputation are discussed in Section 3. Models@run.time and Kevoree, a component-based development platform

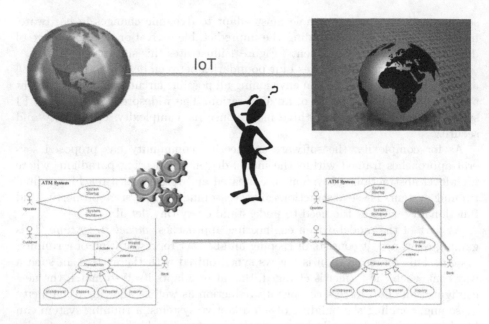

Fig. 1. Developers are confronted with the complexity of IoT and with the need to update system functionality once it is already deployed and running

that accommodates this paradigm, are presented in Section 4. The trust framework implementation and its integration in Kevoree are described in Section 5, whereas the use of the framework is illustrated in a smart grid scenario in Section 6. Finally, Section 7 concludes the chapter and provides hints for future research.

2   Trust in Software Development Life Cycle

This section reviews existing research from two different angles. Section 2.1 discusses contributions that consider trust during the initial phases of the Software Development Life Cycle (SDLC). Section 2.2 explains how trust and reputation have been used as decision enablers in Service-Oriented and Component-Based Architectures.

2.1   Trust in Software Engineering

The software engineering and security communities have focused on specifying traditional security requirements, such as confidentiality or authorization. In this direction, Jürjens [15] presents UMLsec, a UML profile for secure system development that allows designers to annotate diagrams with security information. On the other hand, Lodderstedt, Basin and Doser [16] present SecureUML, which uses the Object Constraint Language (OCL) to specify authorization constraints.

Other works focus on detecting possible attacks on the system. Sindre and Opdahl [27], and McDermott and Fox [18] propose using misuse cases and abuse cases, respectively. These methods aim to capture use cases that may be initiated by attackers or even stakeholders in order to harm the system. In a similar direction, Schneier [26] presents a formal and methodical way of capturing different types of attacks that can be performed in a system by means of attack trees.

The contributions mentioned up to now focus on hard security requirements, but they lay trust aside. There are, however, other works that focus on trust. On the one hand, we find policy languages for distributed trust management. Three remarkable examples are SULTAN [10], PolicyMaker [2] and REFEREE [4]. Abstracting away their differences, these policy languages specify the conditions under which entities of the system can be granted permission to a resource. These entities must present some so-called credentials to prove that they satisfy the conditions to be trusted.

Some methodologies aim to build secure systems by taking relationships between actors and agents into account. Mouratidis and Giorgini [20] present Secure Tropos, a methodology that extends the Tropos methodology in order to enable the design of secure systems. Actors in Tropos may depend on other actors in order to achieve a goal. Thus, Tropos captures the social relationships in the system by specifying the dependencies between actors using the notions of depender, dependum and dependee, and by modeling the actors and agents in the organization. In a similar direction, Lamsweerde and Letier presents KAOS [29], a comprehensive goal-oriented methodology to elicit the requirements of a sociotechnical system. All these contributions put forward the idea of capturing social aspects, but the notion of trust and its influence on the information systems is barely explored. This is partially covered by Pavlidis, Mouratidis and Islam [24], who extend the Secure Tropos modeling language in order to include some trust-related concepts.

The work by Chakraborty and Ray [3] bridges a gap between traditional security requirements modeling and soft-security considerations by incorporating the notion of trust levels into the traditional Role-Based Access Control model. These levels are measured by means of a trust vector, where each component in the vector is a factor that influences trust, such as knowledge or experience.

Moyano, Fernandez-Gago and Lopez [22], and Uddin and Zulkernine [28] present UML profiles that allow characterizing trust relationships and trust information in more detail than previous contributions during the initial phases of the SDLC. The former allows specifying reputation and trust dynamics (e.g. how trust is updated), whereas the latter is more focused on defining trust scenarios.

In spite of the works on specifying trust or social information, developers are unarmed when it comes to implementing trust models and integrating them into business applications.

2.2 Trust Decisions in Service-Oriented and Component-Based Architectures

In Service-Oriented Architecture (SOA) environments, trust is used for either protecting providers from potentially malicious clients or for shielding clients against potentially malicious providers (e.g. providers that publish a higher Quality of Service (QoS) than offered). As an example of the first situation, Conner et al. [5] present a feedback-based reputation framework to help service providers to determine trust in incoming requests from clients. As an example of the second approach, Crapanzano et al. [6] propose a hierarchical architecture for SOA where there is a so-called super node overlay that acts as a trusting authority when a service consumer looks for a service provider. When a client makes a service invocation, the service provider records it together with its feedback and a set of application-specific attributes, in such a way that this information can be used by other service providers to determine whether they should grant access to a future request from the same client.

Haouas and Bourcier [11] present a runtime architecture that allows a service-oriented system to meet a dependability objective set up by an administrator. System dependability is computed by aggregating ratings provided by service consumers regarding QoS attributes. Then, a reconfiguration manager may look up other available services to meet the dependability objective. Dependability of the system is computed by the aggregation of the dependability of each service. This, in turn, is computed by aggregating a weighted average of ratings provided by service consumers regarding QoS attributes (e.g. response time) of service providers. Then, a reconfiguration manager is in charge of querying the service broker to find the available services that can meet the dependability objective.

Yan and Prehofer [30] discuss a procedure to conduct autonomic trust management in Component-Based Architectures (CBA). Several quality attributes can be used to rate the trustee's trustworthiness, such as availability, reliability, integrity or confidentiality. Assessing these attributes requires defining metrics and placing monitors to measure their parameters. Finally, trust is assessed at runtime based on the trustor's criteria and is automatically maintained.

Herrmann and Krumm [12] propose using security wrappers to monitor components. The intensity of the monitoring activity by these wrappers is ruled by the component's reputation. This scheme was enhanced by Herrmann [13] in order to take the reputation of components' users into account so as to prevent deliberate false feedbacks.

3   Trust Foundations

There has been a huge amount of different definitions of trust over the years. This is due to mainly two factors: first, trust is very context dependent, and each context has its own particularities. Second, trust spans across many disciplines, including psychology, economics and law, and has different connotations in each of them. Finally, there are many factors that influence trust, and it is not straightforward to identify them all.

The singularity about trust is that everyone intuitively understands its underlying implications, but an agreed definition has not been proposed yet due to the difficulties in putting them down in words. The vagueness of this term is well represented by the statement made by Miller [19]: "trust is less confident than know, but also more confident than hope".

We define trust as *the personal, unique and temporal expectation that a trustor places on a trustee regarding the outcome of an interaction between them*. This interaction comes in terms of a task that the trustee must perform and that can negatively influence the trustor. The expectation is personal and unique because it is subjective, and it is temporal because it may change over time.

3.1 Trust and Reputation

According to the Concise Oxford dictionary, reputation is "what is generally said or believed about a person or the character or standing of a thing". This definition, and more concretely, the word *generally*, implies that reputation is formed by an accumulation of opinions. This accumulation of information makes reputation a more objective concept than trust.

We advocate that there exists a bidirectional relationship between trust and reputation, in the sense that each one may build upon the other. A good approximation to the relationship between trust and reputation was suggested by Jøsang [14], who made the following two statements: 'I trust you because of your good reputation and 'I trust you despite your bad reputation'. In this sense, reputation can be considered as a building block to determine trust but, as stated by the second statement, reputation has not the final say. One could either trust someone with low reputation or could distrust someone with high reputation, because there are other factors that may have a bigger influence on trust determination, such as the trustor's (the entity which places trust) disposition to believe in the trustee (the entity onto which trust is placed), the trustor's feelings, or above all, the trustor's personal experiences with the trustee.

3.2 Trust Models and Classification

The concept and implications of trust are embodied in the so-called trust models, which define the rules to compute trust and update trust relationships. There are different types of trust models, each one considering trust in different ways and for different purposes. The origins of trust management date back to the nineties, when Marsh [17] proposed the first comprehensive computational model of trust based on social and psychological factors. Two years later, Blaze [2] coined the term *trust management* as a way to simplify the two-step authentication and authorization process into a single trust decision.

These two seminal contributions reveal the two main branches or categories of trust models that have been followed until today, and which are further described in [21]. On the one hand, and following Marsh's approach, we find evaluation models, where factors that influence trust are identified, quantified and then aggregated into a final trust score. Uncertainty and evaluation play an important role in these models, as one entity is never completely sure whether it should trust another entity, and a quantification process is required to evaluate the extent to which one entity trusts another one.

On the other hand and following Blaze's approach, we find decision models, which are tightly related to the authorization problem. An entity holds credentials and a policy verify whether these credentials are enough to grant access to certain resources. Here, trust evaluation is not so important in the sense that there are no degrees of trust (and as a consequence, there is not such a big range of uncertainty), and the outcome of the process is often a binary answer: access granted or access denied.

A remarkable issue about trust and reputation models is that they often present high coupling with the application context, as they are designed as ad-hoc mechanisms that are plugged into existing applications, which in turn limits their reusability [7]. Therefore, one of the goals of our approach is allowing developers to implement different types of trust models. We achieve this by identifying high level concepts that form trust and reputation metamodels, and which abstract away from concrete instances.

3.3   Trust Conceptual Model

We are particularly interested in evaluation models, and this section presents the most important concepts related to these trust models, which are summarized in Figure 2 and Figure 3. These concepts were identified surveying relevant literature and finding commonalities and variations in the definition of different models. This conceptual model constitutes the basis for building a trust metamodel that underlies the trust framework, as we discuss in Section 5.1.

A trust model aims to compute trust in a given setting. This setting should have, at least, two entities that need to interact. An entity plays one or more roles. The basic roles are trustor (the entity that places trust) and trustee (the entity on which trust is placed). Once there is a trustor and a trustee, we claim that a trust relationship has been established. A trust relationship has a purpose, which can be for example controlling the access or provision of a resource, or ensuring the identity of an entity. It may also serve to establish trust in the infrastructure (e.g. devices, hardware, etc). In the very end, the purpose of a trust model is to assist in decision making. At the higher level, it is a trust decision in the sense of answering the question: would this entity behave as expected under this context? At a lower level, an entity trusts a property of another entity. For instance its capability to provide a good quality of service. A trust model also makes some assumptions, such as "entities will provide only fair ratings" and follows a modeling method.

Evaluation models often follow a trust life cycle with three phases. In the bootstrapping or initialization phase, initial trust values are assigned to the trust relationships of the entities of the system. Then, some monitoring is performed to observe a set of factors. Finally, a trust assessment process is done in order to assign values to these factors and to aggregate them into a final trust evaluation.

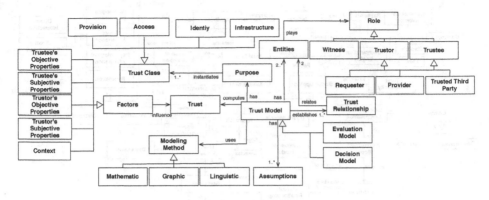

Fig. 2. Concepts for Evaluation Models (i)

Trust relationships are tagged with a trust value that describe to what extent the trustor trusts the trustee. This trust value has semantics and dimension, which might be simple or a tuple. Trust values are assigned during trust assessment through trust metrics, which receive a set of variables as input and produce a measure of one or several attributes using a computation engine. There exists several computation engines, ranging from the most simple ones such as summation engines, to complex ones that entail probability distributions or fuzzy logic.

There are several sources of information that can feed a trust metric. The most common one is the direct interaction of the entity with the trustee. Other possible sources of information, although less frequent, are sociological information (e.g. considering the roles of entities or their membership to a group) and psychological information (e.g. prejudice).

Reputation models can be, in turn, another source of information where opinions of a given trustee by different entities are made public and are used to compute a score. Reputation can be centralized or distributed, depending on whether reputation scores are computed and stored in a central location or individually by each entity. Reputation models build upon the notion of reputation statement, which is a tuple consisting of a source entity, a claim made by this source entity, and the claim's target entity.

4   Kevoree: A Models@Runtime Platform

Traditionally, the Model-Driven Development area has primarily focused on using models at design, implementation and deployment phases of the Software Development Life Cycle (SDLC). However, as systems become more adaptable, reconfigurable and self-managing, they are also more prone to failures, which demands putting in place appropriate mechanisms for continuous design and runtime validation and monitoring.

In this direction, model-driven techniques can also be used to model and reason about a runtime system, leading to the models@runtime paradigm [1],

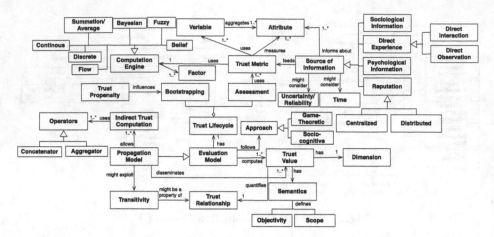

Fig. 3. Concepts for Evaluation Models (ii)

which brings some important benefits, as it is providing a richer semantic base for runtime decision-making on adaptation and monitoring. Models@runtime refers to model-driven approaches that aim to tame the complexity of software and system dynamic adaptation, pushing the idea of reflection one step further.

Section 4.1 discusses Kevoree, a component model for building distributed applications. Section 4.2 and Section 4.3 present how to develop and deploy applications in Kevoree, respectively.

4.1 Kevoree: Component Model

Kevoree[1] is an open-source dynamic component model that relies on models at runtime to properly support the design and dynamic adaptation of distributed, long-living systems [8]. Six concepts constitute the basis of the Kevoree component metamodel, as shown in Figure 4. A node models a device on which software components can be deployed, whereas a group defines a set of nodes that share the same representation of the reflecting architectural model. A port represents an operation that a component provides or requires. A binding represents the communication between a port and a channel, which in turn models the semantics of communication. The core library of Kevoree implements these concepts for several platforms such as Java, Android or Arduino.

Kevoree adopts the models@run.time paradigm, enabling the so-called continuous design and the building of self-adaptive systems. Kevoree boils down the reconfiguration process to moving from one configuration, represented by a current model, to another configuration represented by a target model. This transition consists of several steps, as depicted in Figure 5. First, the target model is checked and validated to ensure a well-formed system configuration. Then the target model is compared with the current model and this comparison

---

[1] http://kevoree.org

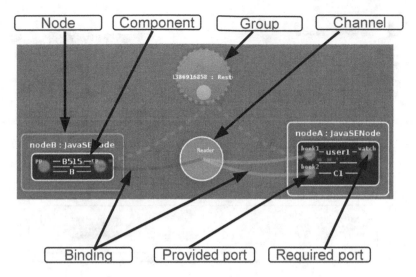

Fig. 4. Kevoree Architectural Elements

generates an adaptation model that contains a set of abstract primitives that allow the transition from the current model to the target model. The adaptation engine instantiates the primitives to the current platform (e.g. Android) and executes them. If an action fails, the adaptation engine rollbacks the configuration to ensure system consistency. Otherwise, all the nodes belonging to the same group are informed about the changes, ensuring that they share a common view and understanding about the current system.

Developing a system in Kevoree entails two steps. First, business components are developed in the Java language using the Kevoree core library. Second, a physical architecture consisting of nodes is designed, components are deployed in these nodes and wired together through channels that connect their ports.

4.2   Development in Kevoree

Kevoree components are created by extending from *AbstractComponentType*, which is an abstract component provided by the Kevoree core library. This component gives access to a set of useful methods that allow managing the component life cycle and that acts as an interface to the reflection layer.

Components can have *dictionary attributes*, which are properties of components instances that can be changed at runtime. Additionally, components can provide and require ports, which correspond to provided or required functionality. There are two types of ports: message ports and service ports. The former model asynchronous communication semantics through messages exchange, whereas the latter represent synchronous service invocations defined in service contracts.

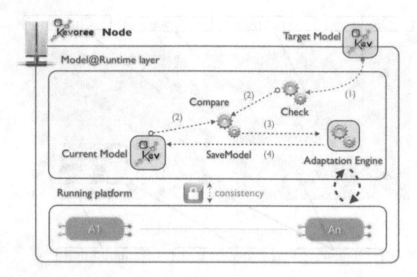

Fig. 5. Adaptation in Kevoree

The following code defines a *Console* component with one required port, one provided port and one dictionary attribute. The required port is a message port that allows sending a text to other consoles, whereas the provided port, also a message port, allows receiving and showing text from other consoles. The dictionary attribute determines the appearance of the console frame and can be changed easily at any time both from the editor and with Kevscript, a script language provided by Kevoree.

```
@Provides({
    @ProvidedPort(name="showText", type=PortType.MESSAGE)
})
@Requires({
    @RequiredPort(name="textEntered", type=PortType.MESSAGE,
    optional=true)
})
@DictionaryType({
    @DictionaryAttribute(name="singleFrame", defaultValue="true",
    optional=true)
})
public class Console extends AbstractComponentType
```

Kevoree makes a distinction between component types and component instances. Each component type can be deployed several times over the same or different nodes, leading to different component instances. Component instances have an auto-generated string identifier (which can be manually modified). Components on the same node need to have different identifiers, whereas components in different nodes can have the same identifier. Therefore, a component remains uniquely identified by the name of the instance and the name of the node where it is deployed.

Kevoree offers the possibility to query the system model programmatically through an EMF[2] auto-generated Application Programming Interface (API). Developers can therefore iterate over the Kevoree metamodel and extract valuable information about the current configuration, such as which components are connected through a given port. The following code snippet shows how to find the name of all component instances of a given component type *componentType* running in a node with name *nodeName*.

```
static List<String> getComponentInstanceName(ContainerRoot model, String
    componentType, String nodeName)
{
    List<String> components = new ArrayList<String>();
    for (ContainerNode node : model.getNodes()) {
        if (node.getName().equals(nodeName)) {
            for(ComponentInstance component : node.getComponents()) {
                if
(component.getTypeDefinition().getName().equals(componentType)) {
                    components.add(component.getName());
                }
            }
        }
    }
    return components;
}
```

4.3   Deployment in Kevoree

Once business components are developed, they can be deployed in nodes and connected through ports. This deployment phase can be realised through the Kevoree editor or by *Kevscript*, which is a script language provided by Kevoree.

Kevoree editor provides a set of basic, built-in libraries (e.g. nodes, basic components and channels) and allows loading custom libraries. It provides drag and drop functionality and a visual representation of the system architecture, as illustrated in Figure 6. The editor models are converted to Kevscript instructions under the hood, being possible to save the model as a *.kevs* file containing these instructions.

As the complexity of the system increases, the editor may end up overloaded with too much information. In these cases, it is possible to deploy the system by manually specifying Kevscript instructions. Figure 7 shows an excerpt of this script language.

As part of the deployment, components dictionary attributes must be given values, which can be changed at any time during the system execution. Also, required and provided ports of different components are connected through service

---

[2] Eclipse Modelling Framework: http://www.eclipse.org/modeling/emf/

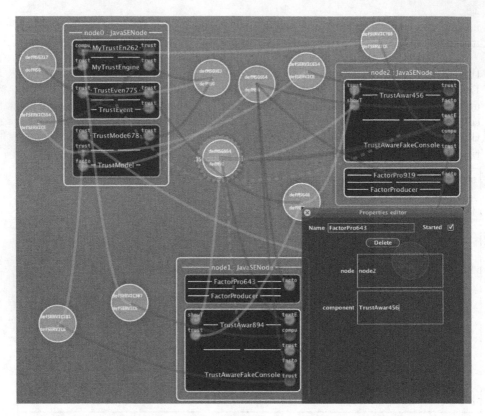

Fig. 6. Kevoree editor with three nodes. Three components are deployed in *node0* and two in *node1* and *node2*. Components communicate through channels (orange circles) that bind their ports. Dictionary attributes can be set for each component (bottom-right grey dialog).

```
   addComponent TrustEven158@node0 : TrustEvent {}
   addComponent TimeToRes401@node0 : TimeToResponseGenerator
addChannel defMSG178 : defMSG {}
addChannel defMSG46 : defMSG {}
addChannel defMSG677 : defMSG {}
addChannel defSERVIC771 : defSERVICE {}
addChannel defSERVIC340 : defSERVICE {}
addChannel defMSG880 : defMSG {}
addChannel defMSG477 : defMSG {}
addChannel defMSG948 : defMSG {}
addChannel defSERVIC168 : defSERVICE {}
addChannel defMSG899 : defMSG {}
bind TimeToRes401.factorAddition@node0 => defMSG477
bind TrustAwar274.trustRelationUpdate@node0 => defMSG677
bind TrustAwar274.trustEntityNotification@node0 => defMSG880
```

Fig. 7. Kevscript instructions. This script language can be used to both deploy the system and change it at runtime.

and message channels, depending on whether the ports are service or message ports respectively.

Kevoree platform does not support reasoning about security concerns, therefore any architectural element such as a node or a software component can join the system without further checks. Also, there is no criteria to guide the runtime changes. Our goal is to provide components with trust and reputation capabilities, which in turn can enable better decision-making on reconfigurations.

5   Trust Meets Models@Runtime: A Trust Framework for Self-adaptive Systems

In this section we explain how the notions of trust and reputation are integrated into Kevoree in order to enhance models@run.time with trust-awareness. This integration is performed in the form of a framework that enriches the component model of Kevoree and which consists of an API for developers, some base components that can be extended or directly deployed on the Kevoree runtime, and deployment guidelines on how to wire components together. The class diagram for the framework is presented in Figure 8.

The rest of this section describes the most important aspects of the framework implementation and its integration in the Kevoree component model.

5.1   Trust and Reputation Metamodels

We use EMF to create metamodels for trust and reputation. These metamodels gather a set of concepts and relationships among these concepts that abstract away from the particularities of different trust models, in such a way that different metamodels instantiations yield different models. The main source of information for elaborating these metamodels is the trust conceptual framework discussed in Section 3.3. The trust metamodel is shown in Figure 9, and the reputation metamodel in Figure 10.

The trust metamodel includes the concept of *TrustRelationship*, which is a tuple of a *Trustor, Trustee* and *TrustValue*. *Trustors* use *Metrics* to evaluate their trust in *Trustees*. *Metrics* use a set of *Factors*, which in turn have a *FactorValue*. Different trust models are created by instantiating the entities that play the trustor and trustee roles, the factors that are considered and the way these factors are combined in a metric.

The core concept of a reputation metamodel is a *ReputationStatement*, which is a tuple containing a *Source* entity, a *Target* entity and a *Claim*, which has a *ClaimValue*. A *ReputationMetric* is used in order to aggregate *Claims*. Reputation models are created by instantiating the entities that play the source and target roles, the way claims are generated and their type, and the way the metric combines the claims.

In both metamodels, other important concepts from the conceptual framework are included as attributes, like *Context* and *Time*. Other concepts from the conceptual framework that are not presented explicitly in the metamodel are included

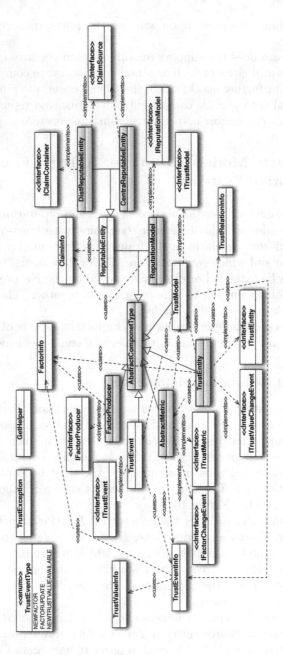

Fig. 8. Class Diagram of the Trust and Reputation Framework. In grey, the Kevoree component from which the rest of components inherits; in green, components that provide some extension points for developers.

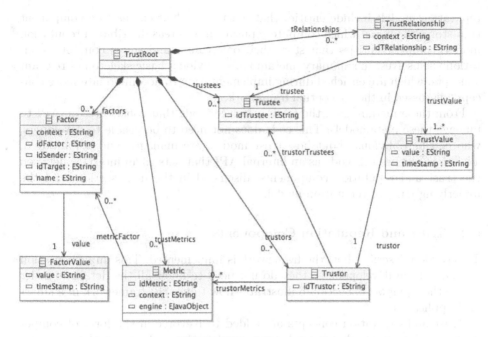

Fig. 9. Trust Metamodel

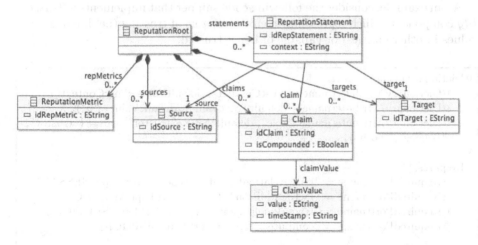

Fig. 10. Reputation Metamodel

implicitly in the implementation. For example, factors can be objective and subjective, but the difference is only made at the implementation level with methods available to entities, such as `addSubjectiveFactor`. We consider that *Engine*s are concrete implementations of *Metric*s. Another example concerns centralized and distributed reputation models. As we see in the next section, centralized

reputation models include entities that must send their claims to a component that stores them and which compute reputation, whereas distributed reputation models comprise entities that store their own claims and which compute reputation themselves. In summary, metamodels provide a basic skeleton of relevant concepts, which are enriched during implementation to accommodate more concepts discussed in the conceptual framework.

From these metamodels, the EMF generates code that constitutes an API to manage these metamodels. This code does not need to be visible to developers, who can be oblivious about how trust models are managed and instantiated. Therefore, we use this code as an internal API that acts as an interface between the trust and reputation components, discussed in the next section, and the underlying trust or reputation model.

5.2   Trust and Reputation Components

This section describes how the framework is implemented. This implementation is hidden from developers, as they do not need to know all the details in order to use the framework. Section 6 illustrates how to use the framework in a smart grid application.

Trust and reputation concepts are added to Kevoree in the form of components, dictionary attributes, and data structures passed among these components. These components, attributes and data structures are concepts of the trust and reputation metamodels.

As an example, consider the following code snippet that implements a *TrustEntity* component, which represents an entity capable of trusting (i.e. holding trust values in other entities) or capable of being trusted.

```
@DictionaryType({
    @DictionaryAttribute(name="trustContext", defaultValue="myContext"),
    @DictionaryAttribute(name="defaultTrustValue", defaultValue="0"),
    @DictionaryAttribute(name="role", defaultValue="trustor", vals= {"trustor",
    "trustee", "both"})
})
@Requires({
    @RequiredPort(name = "trustRelationUpdate", type = PortType.MESSAGE),
    @RequiredPort(name = "factorAddition", type = PortType.MESSAGE)),
    @RequiredPort(name = "trustManagement", type = PortType.SERVICE),
    @RequiredPort(name = "compute", type = PortType.SERVICE)
})
@Provides({
    @ProvidedPort(name="trustEntityNotification", type=PortType.MESSAGE)
})
public abstract class TrustEntity extends AbstractComponentType
        implements ITrustEntity, ITrustValueChangeEvent
```

The role played by the entity can be *trustor*, *trustee* or *both*, and this role can be specified by a dictionary attribute associated to this component. Other dictionary attributes are *default value*, which determines the initial trust values for all trust relationships of the entity, and *trust context*, which specifies the context under which the entity establishes its relationships.

TrustEntity requires two service ports and two message ports. Trust entities playing the trustor role use the service port *trustManagement* in order to initialize trust relationships and retrieve trust values. These services are provided in the service contract defined by the interface *ITrustModel*[3]. The other service port used by trust entities is *compute*, which computes trust of the trust entity (in case it is a trustor) in another trust entity. We want this port to be synchronous because this service is typically invoked prior to making a trust decision. Trust entities use the *factorAddition* message port to add subjective factors about itself (e.g. disposition to trust in a given trustee) in the trust model. The message port *trustRelationUpdate* is used by trust entities to update the model with new trust relationships.

The initialization of trust entities is performed in the **start()** method provided by the *AbstractComponentType* Kevoree component. The following code snippet shows the initialization of trust entities, which is performed in the **start()** method provided by the *AbstractComponentType* Kevoree component:

```
public void start() throws TrustException
{
    if (getDictionary.get("role").equals("trustor") ||
        getDicitionary.get("role").equals("both"))
    {
        if (!isPortBound("compute"))
        {
            //throw trust exception
        }
        getPortByName("trustManagement", ITrustModel.class).
            initializeTrustRelationships
            (
                getDictionary.get("trustContext").toString(),
                getModelElement().getName(),
                getDictionary.get("defaultTrustValue").toString()
            );
    }
}
```

If the entity is a trustor, its trust relationships are initialized through the service **initializeTrustRelationships** provided by *ITrustModel*. The arguments for this service are the name of the context where this relationship takes place, the name of the current trust entity, and the default value of all trust relationships of this particular entity. The following code depicts how the actual trust initialization is performed in the *TrustModel* component:

---

[3] In general, all elements whose name start with *I* are interfaces that define a contract with which the associated component must comply.

```
@Port(name="trustManagement", method="initializeTrustRelationships")
public void initializeTrustRelationships(String context, String trustor,
    String defaultValue)
{
    Map<String, List<String>> trustees =
        GetHelper.getTrusteesInstanceName
        (
        getModelService().getLastModel(),
        context
        );
    for (String nodeName: trustees.keySet()) {
            //... get the list of trustees running on that node
            idTrustee.addAll(trustees.get(nodeName));
    }
    //Create necessary entities in the trust metamodel
    for (String t : idTrustee) {
        addTrustRelationship(context, trustor, t, defaultValue);
    }
}
```

First, we need to retrieve all the trustees of the trustor. This is done through the static method `getTrusteesInstanceName` of the auxiliary class *GetHelper*, which we developed in order to provide an interface to the reflection layer of Kevoree. This means that we can use this class to query the system model and to extract certain information. The method `getModelService().getLastModel()`, provided by *AbstractComponentType*, allows us to retrieve a reference to the last deployed model, which can be queried by iterating over nodes and their components. We identify trustees of the trustor according to the following rule: a component is trustee of another component if the role of the former is *trustee* and its context is the same as the context of the latter. Once we have all the trustees, we create a trust relationship for each of them in the model through the API generated by EMF (see Section 5.1). This is what the method `addTrustRelationship` does.

As another example, consider the following code, which declares a *FactorProducer* component:

```
@DictionaryType({
    @DictionaryAttribute(name = "node", optional = false),
    @DictionaryAttribute(name = "component", optional = false),
    @DictionaryAttribute(name = "updateRate", optional = false)
})

@Requires({
        @RequiredPort(name = "factorAddition", type = PortType.MESSAGE,
            optional = false)
})
@ComponentType
@Library(name = "Trust")
public class FactorProducer extends AbstractComponentType
    implements IFactorProducer
```

Factor producers are entities capable of producing trust factors about a given target entity. The target entity of a factor producer is specified by means of the dictionary attributes *node* and *component*. The rate at which factor producers generate factors for their target entities is given by the dictionary attribute *updateRate*. Factor producers require one message port, which they use to send the factor to the *TrustModel* component. It also provides a method to retrieve the target, abstracting developers away from dictionary management.

The rest of implemented components and a brief description are shown in Table 1. We provide more insight about other components in Section 6.

Table 1. Trust Framework Components

Trust Component	Description
TrustModel	Encapsulation and information hiding. It provides interface to EMF trust metamodel.
TrustEntity	Base class for any trust-aware business logic component.
AbstractMetric	Base class for any trust engine.
TrustEvent	Entities and metric notification about changes in the model.
FactorProducer	It yields trust factors used by the engines.
Reputation Components	**Description**
ReputationModel	Encapsulation and information hiding. It computes reputation scores.
ReputableEntity	Entity that can be source or target in reputation statements.
DistReputableEntity	Reputable entity that stores its own claims and which computes reputation.
CentralReputableEntity	Reputable entity that sends claims to the reputation model. It uses *ReputationModel* to compute reputation scores.

The following section discusses two important concepts of the framework: data structures and trust events.

5.3 Trust Events and Data Structures

Fault-tolerant designs foster the use of asynchronous communication, as it allows components to continue their execution even if other components fail. Therefore, most of the framework components communicate through asynchronous message exchanges. These messages are data structures with trust or reputation information. For example, *FactorInfo* stores the identification of the sender (which may be an instance of a *FactorProducer* or a *TrustEntity*), the factor name, the context where that factor must be interpreted, the factor value, and the target entity to which the factor refers. Table 2 summarizes other data structures.

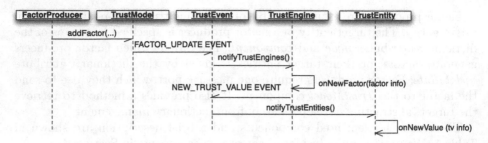

Fig. 11. Sequence Diagram of Trust Events

Trust events represent changes in the trust model and it is the way in which trust engines and trust entities are notified of changes that may require their attention. The process starts when a new factor is introduced in the model. The model sends a notification to the *TrustEvent* component, which forwards it to the trust engines. Upon receiving this notification, trust engines can either send notifications to trust entities through the *TrustEvent* component or capture these notifications and only send them when some application-specific condition occurs. When trust entities receive notifications, they know that a new trust value for at least one of its relationships is available, and they can take actions. The typical action is to update this trust relationship in the model. These steps are depicted in Figure 11.

Table 2. Data Structures Exchanged by Components

Data Structure	Description
FactorInfo	Factor information, including the sender, the context and the value.
TrustEventInfo	Event information, including the type of the event and extra information (e.g. factor information).
TrustRelationship	Trust relationship information, including context, trustor, trustee and the value.
TrustValueInfo	Information about trust values, including context, the sender (i.e. engine) and the value itself.
Claim	Information about a claim, including the context, the source and the target.

The next section illustrates how the trust framework can be used by developers to implement trust-aware and self-adaptive systems in a smart grid scenario.

6 Case Study: Smart Grid Scenario

Smart grids use Information and Communication Technology (ICT) to optimise the transmission and distribution of electricity from suppliers to consumers, allowing smart generation and bidirectional power flows [23]. The smart grid is one of the addressed scenarios in NESSoS[4].

The scenario is depicted in Figure 12. *Consumers* want to retrieve electric consumption information from their Controllable Local Systems (*CLS*), which are devices that can be controlled using the network communication technology of the grid. The interaction between consumers and the CLS go through a Smart Metering Gateway (*SMG*), the actual responsible for collecting and processing meter data, and for providing communication and security capabilities for devices. Authorized External Entities (*AEEs*) can also access the CLS for billing or maintenance purposes through the *SMG*.

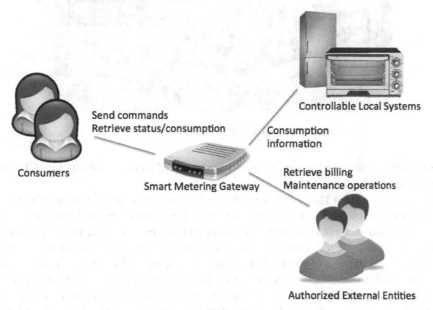

Fig. 12. Smart Grid Scenario

We want to implement this system in Kevoree. The first step is to map the scenario to nodes and business components according to the component model of Kevoree, resulting in the system depicted in Figure 13. In this configuration, there are four nodes: the consumer node, which models the device with which the consumer wants to control the CLS; the SMG node, which represents the SMG; the AEE nodes, which model devices used by AEEs in order to access CLS; and a CLS node, which represents CLS.

The consumer node hosts a component that communicates with the *SMG-Manager* component deployed on the SMG. The latter offers services to the consumer for receiving electricity consumption information from CLS, and for forwarding commands to the CLS. *CLSManager* component on CLS provide services to control the CLS and to send electricity consumption information about the CLS. The *CLSConfiguration* component on the AEE node allows AEEs to

---

[4] http://www.nessos-project.eu

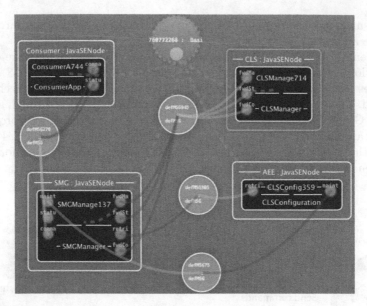

Fig. 13. Smart Grid Scenario in Kevoree

obtain billing information and to analyse status information about the CLS for maintenance purposes.

We want to enrich this system model with trust awareness by using the trust framework discussed in the previous section. First, we need to define the trust and reputation models that we want to implement. In this case, the trust model uses a trust engine that considers three factors: consumer's *disposition to trust* in the CLS, *reputation* of the CLS, and *time to response* of the CLS. Trust values are computed by adding the former two factors, and dividing the addition by the latter factor. The rationale is that the higher the disposition to trust and the CLS reputation, and the lower the time to response of the CLS, the higher the trust that the consumer places on the CLS.

Consumer's disposition to trust is provided by the consumer itself at installation time[5]. CLS reputation is computed by averaging the satisfaction ratings provided by AEEs after each interaction. CLS time to response can be measured by performing regular *pings* on the CLS.

Once we define the trust and reputation models, we need to implement them and to integrate them with the system depicted in Figure 13. The final trust-aware system is illustrated in Figure 14.

The reputation model is implemented by adding one new component, *MyReputationModel*, which is hosted by the SMG, and by specifying that the *CLSConfiguration* component is a centralized reputable entity[6]. The following code snippet shows this latter component:

---

[5] We can assume that the *SMGManager* component provides a service for setting this value for each installed CLS.

[6] We decide to use a centralized reputation model.

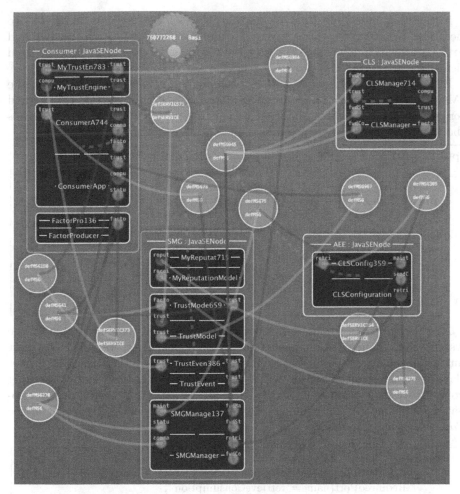

Fig. 14. Trust-Aware Smart Grid Scenario in Kevoree

```
public class CLSConfiguration extends CentralKevReputableEntity
{
    ...
    public Status getStatus()
    {
        //Obtain status of CLS through dedicated port
        //Check status
        Dialog d = createDialog("Please enter a  satisfaction  number between 0
    and 10: ")
        claim = d.readTextFromDialog();
        makeClaim("repContext", getTarget("status"), claim);
    }
}
```

Notice that inheriting from *CentralKevReputableEntity* gives access to two methods: `makeClaim`, which sends a claim to the reputation model; and `getTarget`, which determines the target of the claim by inspecting an associated dictionary attribute.

Regarding the *MyReputationModel* component, which is deployed on the SMG, developers must inherit from *ReputationModel* and override the method `computeReputation`, which in this case calculates an average of all the claims about a given target, as depicted in the following code:

```
public final class ReputationEngine extends ReputationModel
{
    @Override
    public String computeReputation(String context, String idTarget) {

        List<Claim> claims = getClaims(context, idTarget);
        for (Claim c : claims)
            res += Float.parseFloat(c.getClaimValue()) / claims.size();

        return String.valueOf(res);
}
```

At this point, the reputation model is implemented and integrated in the system. Now we need to implement the trust model. First, we define the trust entities in the system, which are *ConsumerApp* and *CLSManager*. The former plays the trustor role, whereas the latter is a trustee. This is done by inheriting from *TrustEntity* component and by defining the appropriate role in its associated dictionary. As an example, the following code shows an excerpt of the *ConsumerApp* component:

```
@Requires({
        @RequiredPort(name="commandEntered", type=PortType.MESSAGE),
        @RequiredPort(name="retrieveConsumption",
    type=PortType.MESSAGE)
})
@DictionaryType({
        @DictionaryAttribute(name = "singleFrame", defaultValue = "true")
})
public class ConsumerApp extends TrustEntity
{
    public void start() throws TrustException
    {
        // Initialize  trust  relationships
        super.start();
        createUserInterface();
    }

    public void onSendCommandButtonPressed()
    {
        String command = textField.readString();
```

```
        sanitized (command);
        getPortByName("commandEntered", MessagePort.class).
            process(command);
    }
    ...
}
```

This component requires two ports which are provided by the SMG: *commandEntered*, to send a command to the CLS through the *SMGManager* component, and *retrieveConsumption*, to receive electricity consumption from the CLS. It also defines a dictionary attribute that determines the appearance of the user interface. The code shows that when the user presses the button *Send Command*, the command written in a text field is read, sanitized and asynchronously sent through the *commandEntered* port. At deployment time, the *role* dictionary attribute must be set to trustor.

Regarding *CLSManager* component, it must inherit from *TrustEntity* and its role must be set to trustee. The *context* dictionary attribute of both the *ConsumerApp* and *CLSManager* components must have the same value. This way, when *ConsumerApp* initializes its trust relationships, it will identify *CLSManager* as its trustee (see Section 5.2).

Other trust application-specific components are the trust engine and the factor producer. The following code shows an excerpt of the former:

```
public class MyTrustEngine extends AbstractMetric
{
    @Override
    public Object compute(String idTrustor, String idTrustee) {
        Factor disp = getFactor("myContext", "disposition", idTrustor);
        Factor ttr = getFactor("myContext", "timeToResponse", idTrustee);
        Object reputation = getReputation("myContext", idTrustee);
        return (disp + reputation) / ttr;
    }
}
```

The trust engine must inherit from the *AbstractMetric* component and override the `compute` method. Inheriting from *AbstractMetric* provides access to two methods: `getFactor` and `getReputation`, which allows the engine to retrieve any factor and the reputation, respectively, from the trustor or the trustee. The trust engine behaves as we explained in the description of the model: it adds trustor's *trust disposition* and trustee's *reputation*, and divide this addition by the trustee's *time to response*.

The next step is creating the factor producer that generates the time to response of CLS. Factor producers are classes that inherit from the *FactorProducer* component. Given that we want factor producers to generate factors at a rate expressed by the *updateRate* attribute, factor producers must create a thread at start-up and implement the *run()* method of the *Runnable* interface. In the *run()* method, the factor producer executes a *PingService*[7] to its target by using *ExecutorService*[8], and adds a factor with the *time to response* obtained from the service. The following code snippet shows this factor producer, although we omit some details for simplicity:

```
public class TimeToResponseProducer extends FactorProducer
    implements Runnable
{
    public void start()
    {
        thread = new Thread(this);
        alive = true; thread.start();
    }

    public void run()
    {
        while (alive)
        {
            executorService.execute(new PingService(map_time,
                node.getName(), getModelService().getLastModel()));
            addFactor("chatContext", "timeToResponse",
                map_time.get(getTargetNode()), getTargetNode());
        }
        Thread.sleep(getUpdateRate());
    }
}
```

Note that there are two trust components that the developer does not need to develop, but which must be deployed: *TrustEvent*, to enable events notifications between the model, the engine, and the trust entities; and *TrustModel*, which provides the interface to store and retrieve trust information according to the underlying metamodel discussed in Section 5.1.

Enriching the system model with trust relationships and reputation information provides two advantages. First, trust entities are empowered with new information that can help them to make decisions at certain points during their execution. Second, as this trust integration is done in a models@run.time platform, it allows the adaptation engine to make reconfiguration decisions based on trust and reputation values.

As an example of the first case, consider the following code in the *Consumer-App* component, where now the component can decide whether to send commands or retrieve status information from a CLS depending on its trust in it.

---

[7] We develop *PingService* as a wrapper over *jpingy*(https://code.google.com/p/jpingy/), an existing library for performing pings to hosts.

[8] http://docs.oracle.com/javase/7/docs/api/java/util/concurrent/ExecutorService.html

```
public void onSendCommandButtonPressed()
{
    String command = textField.readString();
    if (getTrustValue("myContext", trustee) > THRESHOLD)
    {
        getPortByName("commandEntered", MessagePort.class).
            process(command);
    }
}
```

A more powerful mechanism is the automatic reconfiguration of the system in terms of trust and reputation values. Reconfiguration is realized through Kevscript instructions. In this scenario, one possible reconfiguration would take place when the reputation of a CLS falls below a given threshold. Under this condition, a Kevscript script would execute in order to remove the CLS from the system. Another possible reconfiguration would entail adding new components. For example, if the trust of the *ConsumerApp* in a CLS falls below a given threshold, the current *CLSManager* component could be removed and substituted by a new one. Also, new components could be deployed in order to encrypt commands before being sent and to decrypt them before being executed.

7 Conclusions and Future Work

As the complexity of software increases, self-adaptability and security become first-class requirements and the software engineering and security communities must join efforts in order to tackle the new challenges that arise. The highly distributed nature of FI systems and their increasing dimensions and heterogeneity limit the use of traditional security measures that often require heavyweight administration, and more flexible and self-controlled mechanisms are required. We advocate that trust and reputation fit nicely in this context, and therefore we integrate these notions together with self-adaptability in a component-based development framework that adopts the models@run.time paradigm.

We have learned that this kind of integration must overcome several technical challenges. First, a robust identity management system must be in place in order to uniquely identify trust and reputation entities, and to allow access at any moment to these identities. In our case, we could use the reflection layer of Kevoree to access this information. Second, more research on declarative reconfiguration policies is required. Current models@run.time platforms lack usable procedures to specify advanced reconfiguration policies. Third, as systems become more complex, visual editors become less useful, as they end up being overloaded with too much information. Therefore, there is a clear need for development of usable declarative languages to specify the architectural elements of these systems, like nodes and components.

Regarding the trust framework, there is enough room for further improvements, specially with regards to the API usability. One direction is allowing policy-based development of trust and reputation models. This would reduce the amount of code that developers must write, would provide a better decoupling of business logic and trust logic, and would foster the separation of duties; the business expert could be oblivious to the trust requirements and the trust expert would not need to understand the business needs. Achieving these goals, and pushing this research forward, requires a tight and continuous cooperation between software and security engineers.

Acknowledgements. This work has been partially funded by the European Commission through the FP7/2007-2013 project NESSoS (www.nessos-project.eu) under grant agreement number 256980. The first author is funded by the Spanish Ministry of Education through the National F.P.U. Program.

References

1. Blair, G., Bencomo, N., France, R.B.: Models@ run.time. Computer 42(10), 22–27 (2009)
2. Blaze, M., Feigenbaum, J., Lacy, J.: Decentralized Trust Management. In: Proceedings of the 1996 IEEE Symposium on Security and Privacy, SP 1996, p. 164. IEEE Computer Society, Washington, DC (1996)
3. Chakraborty, S., Ray, I.: Trustbac: Integrating trust relationships into the rbac model for access control in open systems. In: Proceedings of the Eleventh ACM Symposium on Access Control Models and Technologies, SACMAT 2006, pp. 49–58. ACM, New York (2006)
4. Chu, Y.-H., Feigenbaum, J., LaMacchia, B., Resnick, P., Strauss, M.: REFEREE: Trust management for Web applications. In: Selected Papers From the Sixth International Conference on World Wide Web, pp. 953–964. Elsevier Science Publishers Ltd., Essex (1997)
5. Conner, W., Iyengar, A., Mikalsen, T., Rouvellou, I., Nahrstedt, K.: A trust management framework for service-oriented environments. In: Proceedings of the 18th International Conference on World Wide Web, WWW 2009, pp. 891–900. ACM, New York (2009)
6. Crapanzano, C., Milazzo, F., De Paola, A., Re, G.L.: Reputation Management for Distributed Service-Oriented Architectures. In: 2010 Fourth IEEE International Conference on Self-Adaptive and Self-Organizing Systems Workshop (SASOW), pp. 160–165 (2010)
7. Farmer, R., Glass, B.: Building Web Reputation Systems, 1st edn. Yahoo! Press, USA (2010)
8. Fouquet, F., Barais, O., Plouzeau, N., Jézéquel, J.-M., Morin, B., Fleurey, F.: A Dynamic Component Model for Cyber Physical Systems. In: 15th International ACM SIGSOFT Symposium on Component Based Software Engineering, Bertinoro, Italie (July 2012)
9. Ghezzi, C.: The fading boundary between development time and run time. In: Zavattaro, G., Schreier, U., Pautasso, C. (eds.) ECOWS, p. 11. IEEE (2011)
10. Grandison, T.: Trust management for internet applications. PhD thesis, University of London (July 2002)
11. Hanen, H., Bourcier, J.: Dependability-Driven Runtime Management of Service Oriented Architectures. In: PESOS - 4th International Workshop on Principles of Engineering Service-Oriented Systems - 2012, Zurich, Suisse (June 2012)

12. Herrmann, P., Krumm, H.: Trust-adapted enforcement of security policies in distributed component-structured applications. In: Proceedings of the Sixth IEEE Symposium on Computers and Communications, pp. 2–8 (2001)
13. Herrmann, P.: Trust-Based Protection of Software Component Users and Designers. In: Nixon, P., Terzis, S. (eds.) iTrust 2003. LNCS, vol. 2692, pp. 75–90. Springer, Heidelberg (2003)
14. Jøsang, A., Ismail, R., Boyd, C.: A survey of trust and reputation systems for online service provision. Decision Support Systems 43(2), 618–644 (2007)
15. Jürjens, J.: UMLsec: Extending UML for Secure Systems Development. In: Jézéquel, J.-M., Hussmann, H., Cook, S. (eds.) UML 2002. LNCS, vol. 2460, pp. 412–425. Springer, Heidelberg (2002)
16. Lodderstedt, T., Basin, D., Doser, J.: SecureUML: A UML-Based Modeling Language for Model-Driven Security. In: Jézéquel, J.-M., Hussmann, H., Cook, S. (eds.) UML 2002. LNCS, vol. 2460, pp. 426–441. Springer, Heidelberg (2002)
17. Marsh, S.: Formalising Trust as a Computational Concept. PhD thesis, University of Stirling (April 1994)
18. McDermott, J., Fox, C.: Using Abuse Case Models for Security Requirements Analysis. In: Proceedings of the 15th Annual Computer Security Applications Conference, ACSAC 1999, p. 55. IEEE Computer Society, Washington, DC (1999)
19. Miller, K.W., Voas, J., Laplante, P.: In Trust We Trust. Computer 43, 85–87 (2010)
20. Mouratidis, H., Giorgini, P.: Secure Tropos: A Security-Oriented Extension of the Tropos Methodology. International Journal of Software Engineering and Knowledge Engineering 17(2), 285–309 (2007)
21. Moyano, F., Fernandez-Gago, C., Lopez, J.: A conceptual framework for trust models. In: Fischer-Hübner, S., Katsikas, S., Quirchmayr, G. (eds.) TrustBus 2012. LNCS, vol. 7449, pp. 93–104. Springer, Heidelberg (2012)
22. Moyano, F., Fernandez, C., Lopez, J.: Towards engineering trust-aware future internet systems. In: Franch, X., Soffer, P. (eds.) CAiSE Workshops 2013. LNBIP, vol. 148, pp. 490–501. Springer, Heidelberg (2013)
23. NESSoS. Initial version of two case studies, evaluating methodologies. Deliverable 11.3: http://www.nessos-project.eu/ (October 2012)
24. Pavlidis, M., Mouratidis, H., Islam, S.: Modelling Security Using Trust Based Concepts. IJSSE 3(2), 36–53 (2012)
25. Roman, R., Zhou, J., Lopez, J.: On the features and challenges of security and privacy in distributed internet of things. Computer Networks 57, 2266–2279 (2013)
26. Schneier, B.: Attack Trees: Modeling Security Threats. Dr. Dobb's Journal (1999)
27. Sindre, G., Opdahl, A.L.: Eliciting security requirements with misuse cases. Requir. Eng. 10(1), 34–44 (2005)
28. Uddin, M.G., Zulkernine, M.: Umltrust: Towards developing trust-aware software. In: Proceedings of the 2008 ACM Symposium on Applied Computing, SAC 2008, pp. 831–836. ACM, New York (2008)
29. van Lamsweerde, A., Letier, E.: Handling Obstacles in Goal-Oriented Requirements Engineering. IEEE Trans. Softw. Eng. 26(10), 978–1005 (2000)
30. Yan, Z., Prehofer, C.: Autonomic Trust Management for a Component-Based Software System. IEEE Transactions on Dependable and Secure Computing 8(6), 810–823 (2011)

Validation of Access Control Systems*

Antonia Bertolino[1], Traon Yves Le[2], Francesca Lonetti[1], Eda Marchetti[1],
and Tejeddine Mouelhi[2]

[1] Istituto di Scienza e Tecnologie dell'Informazione "A. Faedo"
CNR, Pisa, Italy
{firstname.lastname}@isti.cnr.it

[2] Interdisciplinary Centre for Security, Reliability and Trust (SnT)
University of Luxembourg, Luxembourg
{firstname.lastname}@uni.lu

Abstract. Access Control is among the most important security mechanisms to put in place in order to secure applications, and XACML is the de facto standard for defining access control policies. Due to the complexity of XACML language it is important to perform efficient testing to identify potential security flaws and bugs. However, in practice, exhaustive testing is impossible due to budget constraints. Test cases selection and prioritization are two well-known solutions to maximize the effectiveness of the test suite in terms of discovered faults, reducing as much as possible the required effort for tests execution and results analysis. In this chapter, after providing a survey on validation approaches for XACML based access control systems, we present a coverage based selection strategy and a similarity based test prioritization solution, both applied to XACML test cases. Then we compare the effectiveness of the two approaches in terms of mutation score and number of test cases. Experimental results show that coverage based selection outperforms similarity based prioritization, hinting to future improvements of the proposed approaches.

Keywords: testing, access control, XACML language, test cases selection, test cases prioritization, coverage criterion, similarity.

1 Introduction

In the modern pervasive ICT systems, in which resources and data are continuously exchanged and shared, security is becoming a crucial feature. Thus appropriate mechanisms that guarantee the confidentiality, integrity, and availability (the so-called CIA triad) must be put in place to protect data and resources against unauthorized, malicious, improper, or erroneous usage.

Among security mechanisms, one of the most important components is the *access control system*, which mediates all requests of access to protected data, ensures that only the intended (i.e., authorized) users are given access and provides them with the level of access that is required to accomplish their tasks.

---

* This work has been supported by the EU-NoE project NESSoS, GA 256980.

M. Heisel et al. (Eds.): Engineering Secure Future Internet Services, LNCS 8431, pp. 210–233, 2014.
© Springer International Publishing Switzerland 2014

In the access control systems, the eXtensible Access Control Markup Language (XACML) [22] is today the de facto standard for specifying access control policies. It is an XML-based language which is platform-independent and specifies the access control system architecture: incoming access requests are transmitted to the Policy Decision Point (PDP) that grants or denies the access based on the defined XACML policies. However, XACML policies themselves may be complex, distributed and subject to continuous change. Any fault in the policies or in the engine evaluating them could lead to security flaws, by either denying accesses that should be allowed or even worse allowing accesses to non authorized users. To guarantee the correctness of the policies specification and their implementation a careful testing activity is needed. The basic approach for testing XACML based systems consists of probing the PDP with a set of XACML requests and checking its responses against the expected decisions.

In this chapter we first provide a survey of validation approaches for XACML based access control systems focusing on the test cases generation problem. Most of the testing approaches for XACML policies are based on combinatorial techniques [3, 18], then the generated number of test cases can rapidly grow to cope with the policy complexity. Executing a huge number of test cases can drastically increase the cost of the testing phase, mainly due to the effort of checking the test oracle's results. As a matter of fact, in the context of access control systems this step is usually performed manually, because the complexity of the XACML language prevents the use of automated support. Considering the strict constraints on testing budget, a challenge of software testing is to maximize the effectiveness of the test suite in terms of discovered faults reducing as much as possible the required effort for tests execution and results analysis. To address this issue two different solutions have been proposed in the literature: selection and prioritization of test cases. Test case selection aims to identify the test cases that are more relevant according to some defined criteria. Test case prioritization aims at defining a test execution order according to some criteria, e.g., coverage, fault detection, so that those tests that have a higher priority are executed before the ones having a lower priority. Both approaches have been proven efficient to get the maximum effectiveness of the test suite [31]. However, their applicability and performance are dependent on the target language and context [25]. In this chapter we want to compare the effectiveness of selection and prioritization solutions applied to XACML test cases. Specifically, first we present: i) a selection strategy named *XACML smart coverage* that relies on an XACML rule coverage criterion; and ii) a test prioritization approach based on similarity of XACML requests. Then we provide a comparison of the proposed approaches in terms of fault detection effectiveness and size of the derived test suites. By means of mutation analysis we inject faults into the XACML policy and challenge the tests to detect these seeded faults. The goal is to end up with an effective test suite able to minimize both the number of test cases and the loss in mutation score with respect to the overall test suite. The experimental results on six real policies show that with the same number of test cases the *XACML smart coverage* selection approach outperforms similarity based prioritization in terms of fault detection effectiveness. Moreover, to get the same mutation score similarity based prioritization requires a higher number of test cases than *XACML smart coverage* selection.

The remainder of this chapter is organized as follows. Section 2 introduces the XACML language. Section 3 presents the results of a survey on access control systems validation. Then, Section 4 details the *XACML smart coverage* selection and similarity based prioritization approaches while their comparison is presented in Section 5. Finally, Section 6 provides discussion and conclusions.

2 XACML Language

XACML [22] is a de facto standard specification language that defines access control policies and access control decision requests/responses in an XML format. An XACML policy defines the rules regulating the users access to the system resources. When an XACML request is evaluated, the XACML policy is used to find which rules match that given request, which contains subject, resource, action, and environment attributes. The access decision is computed based on the matching rule and the access is then either granted or denied. More specifically, the XACML specification defines an access control system architecture interacting with the XACML policy. The main entities of this architecture are the Policy Enforcement Point (PEP) and the Policy Decision Point (PDP). A PEP intercepts a user's request, transforms it into an XACML request and transmits it to the PDP. The PDP evaluates the request against the rules in the policy and returns the access response (Permit/Deny/NotApplicable) according to the specified XACML policy. The main elements of an XACML policy are:

Policy Set. A policy set contains one or more policy sets or one or more policies. It includes a policy-combining algorithm, which states which policy (policy set) to consider when several policies (policy sets) are applicable to a given request. It also contains a target to be matched from a request before considering the policies (policy sets) in that policy set to be applicable.

Policy. A policy includes a set of rules and a rule-combining algorithm that states which rule decision to return in case the request is applicable to more than one rule. It also contains a target to be matched from a request before considering the rules in that policy to be applicable.

Rule. A rule contains a decision type (Permit or Deny) and a target. When the request matches the target then the request is applicable to the rule. In that case the decision type is to be returned. A rule might also contain a condition element, which is a boolean function that is used to specify constraints on the subjects, resources, actions, and environments values so that if the condition evaluates to true, then the rule's decision type is returned.

Target. A target contains four parameters: a set of subjects, a set of resources, a set of actions and finally a set of environments. A request is matching a target, if the subject, resource, action, and environment of the request are included in the corresponding target sets.

Combining Algorithms. A combining algorithm selects which policy (policy-combining algorithm) or rule (rule-combining algorithm) is to be considered in case the request matches more than one policy (or rule). For instance, the first-applicable combining algorithm will select the first applicable policy (or rule).

At the decision making time, the Policy Decision Point evaluates an access request against a policy, by comparing all the attributes in an access request against the attributes in all the *target* and *condition* elements of the *policy set*, *policy* and *rule* elements. If there is a match between the attributes of the request and those of the policy, the *effect* of a matching rule is returned, otherwise the *NotApplicable* decision is drawn.

```
1    <PolicySet PolicySetId="policySetExample"
2    PolicyCombiningAlgId="first-applicable">
3    <Target/>
4    <Policy PolicyId="policyExample" RuleCombiningAlgId="permit-overrides">
5      <Target><Resource><ResourceMatch MatchId="anyURI-equal">
6        <AttributeValue DataType="anyURI">
7          books
8        </AttributeValue>
9       <ResourceAttributeDesignator AttributeId="resource-id" />
10       </ResourceMatch></Resource></Target>
11     <Rule RuleId="ruleA" Effect="Deny">
12      <Target><Resources>
13      <Resource><ResourceMatch MatchId="anyURI-equal">
14        <AttributeValue DataType="anyURI">
15        books
16        </AttributeValue>
17        <ResourceAttributeDesignator AttributeId="resource-id"/>
18      </ResourceMatch></Resource>
19      <Resource><ResourceMatch MatchId="anyURI-equal">
20        <AttributeValue DataType="anyURI">
21        documents
22        </AttributeValue>
23        <ResourceAttributeDesignator AttributeId="resource-id" />
24      </ResourceMatch></Resource></Resources>
25      <Actions><Action><ActionMatch MatchId="string-equal">
26        <AttributeValue DataType="string">
27        read
28        </AttributeValue>
29      <ActionAttributeDesignator AttributeId="action-id" />
30       </ActionMatch></Action></Actions></Target></Rule>
31     <Rule RuleId="ruleB" Effect="Permit">
32      <Target><Subjects><Subject><SubjectMatch MatchId="string-equal">
33        <AttributeValue DataType="string">
34        Julius
35        </AttributeValue>
36      <SubjectAttributeDesignator AttributeId="subject-id" />
37       </SubjectMatch></Subject></Subjects>
38      <Actions><Action><ActionMatch MatchId="string-equal">
39        <AttributeValue DataType="string">
40        write
41        </AttributeValue>
42      <ActionAttributeDesignator AttributeId="action-id" />
43       </ActionMatch></Action></Actions>
44     </Target></Rule></Policy></PolicySet>
```

Listing 1.1. An XACML Policy

Listing 1.1 shows an example of a simplified XACML policy for library access. The policy set target (line 3) is empty, which means that it applies to any subject, resource, action, and environment. The policy target (lines 5-10) says that this policy applies to any subject, any action, any environment and the "books" resource. This policy has a first rule (*ruleA*) (lines 11-30) with a "deny" decision and with a target (lines 12-30) specifying that this rule applies only to the access requests of a "read" action of "books" and "documents" resources with any environment. The effect of the second rule (*ruleB*) (lines 31-44) is *Permit* when the subject is "Julius", the action is "write", the resource is also "books" (inherited from the policy target) and any environment.

```
1   <Request xmlns="urn:oasis:names:tc:xacml:2.0:context:schema:os">
2    <Subject>
3     <Attribute AttributeId="subject-id1" DataType="string">
4      <AttributeValue>Julius</AttributeValue>
5     </Attribute>
6    </Subject>
7    <Resource>
8     <Attribute AttributeId="resource-id" DataType="string">
9      <AttributeValue>books</AttributeValue>
10    </Attribute>
11   </Resource>
12   <Action>
13    <Attribute AttributeId="action-id" DataType="string">
14     <AttributeValue>write</AttributeValue>
15    </Attribute>
16   </Action>
17   <Environment/>
18  </Request>
```

Listing 1.2. First XACML request

```
1   <Request xmlns="urn:oasis:names:tc:xacml:2.0:context:schema:os">
2    <Subject>
3     <Attribute AttributeId="subject-id1" DataType="string">
4      <AttributeValue>Julius</AttributeValue>
5     </Attribute>
6    </Subject>
7    <Resource>
8     <Attribute AttributeId="resource-id" DataType="string">
9      <AttributeValue>documents</AttributeValue>
10    </Attribute>
11   </Resource>
12   <Action>
13    <Attribute AttributeId="action-id" DataType="string">
14     <AttributeValue>read</AttributeValue>
15    </Attribute>
16   </Action>
17   <Environment/>
18  </Request>
```

Listing 1.3. Second XACML request

Listing 1.2 shows an example of a simple request specifying that the subject Julius wants to write the "books" resource while the request in Listing 1.3 says that Julius wants to read the "documents" resource.

3   Survey of Testing Techniques and Tools for Access Control Systems

In this section we provide a survey on validation approaches for access control systems focusing on test cases generation and assessment of the derived tests suites. Specifically, the work presented in this chapter spans over the following research directions: model-based test cases derivation; XACML policy-based test cases derivation; test cases selection and prioritization; assessing the test suite effectiveness.

3.1   Model-Based Test Cases Derivation

In model-based testing, the test cases are automatically (or semi-automatically) derived from a model. This model can be a model of the application, of the policy or a combination of both. Among the available proposals that rely on a model, combining the application and the policy, the approach promoted by Xu et al. [30] is based on high level petri-nets. Moreover, there is the work done by Pretschner et al. [23], which presents a new approach which relies on a model of RBAC based access control and enables as well an automated generation of test cases. These two approaches are presented in detail in the following.

Petri-Net Based Access Control Testing. The strategy presented in [30] aims at considering the whole system and the access control security mechanisms in it as a black box. To validate these security mechanisms, the tester should create test cases that test the system functions using scenarios that will trigger the access control mechanisms and enforce all the rules. The abstract policy is thus taken into consideration when constructing the model of the system under test. In this case, it is important to take into account all the rules defined in the XACML policy. More concretely, this approach generates executable access control tests from a MID (Model-Implementation Description) specification, which consists of an access control test model and a MIM (Model-Implementation Mapping) description. The underlying test model, represented by a Predicate/Transition (PrT) net [10], is constructed from the given access control rules and functional requirements. This model is build according to the way the SUT (System Under Test) is designed and implemented. PrT nets are high-level Petri nets, a well-studied formal method for system modeling and verification. Contracts are used (preconditions and post-conditions) to construct test models for two main reasons. First, design by contracts [20] is a widely accepted approach to functional specification. Second, access control rules, as security constraints on system functionality, cannot be tested without involving system functionality. Access control testing requires understanding the preconditions and post-conditions of the related activities. Let us consider, testing for instance, the rule that a student is allowed to return books on working days. The test cannot be performed unless the functional precondition "book is borrowed" is satisfied. The accurate test oracle cannot be determined without knowing its post-condition "book becomes available". For test generation purposes, declarative access control rules and contracts are integrated into an operational PrT net. For code generation purposes, a MIM description is created by mapping the elements in a test model to the implementation constructs based on the SUT programming interface. The generated code can then be executed with the SUT. This approach has been implemented in MISTA[1], a framework for automated generation of test code in a variety of languages, including Java, C, C++, C#, and HTML/Selenium IDE (a Firefox plugin for testing web applications). Experiments were performed using two Java based applications. To assess the fault detection capability of the proposed approach, mutation analysis of access control implementation was applied. Mutants were created by seeding faulty rules in the policy implementation. For each case study, the authors constructed the access control test models in the subject program, generated executable tests from the test models, and executed the tests against the mutants. The experiments show that the proposed approach is highly effective in detecting policy violations since the generated tests killed a large percentage of mutants.

Policy Model Based Access Control Testing. The approach in [23] focuses on the access control policy to select the test targets by relying on pair-wise testing. A test target is an abstract test case, which is related to an access control request to be tested. The approach creates concrete tests for testing the scenarios based on these selected test targets. More precisely, it proposes to proceed in two steps. In a first step, it generates abstract tests. Test targets represent classes of actual requests. They are generated (1) regardless of any policy, i.e., by only taking into account roles, permissions, and contexts; (2) by considering all the rules in a given policy, that is the model; and (3) completely at random. Relying on a fault model that considers incorrect decisions of the PDP to be a consequence of n-wise interactions of rule elements, combinatorial testing is used to automatically generate a test suite of manageable size. In a second step, concrete tests are derived (code) from these abstract test targets. Because this involves application-specific program logic and usually also a particular state of the application, this activity can in general not be fully automated and we need to rely on an application model (for instance sequence diagrams, class diagrams etc.).

3.2   XACML Policy Based Test Cases Derivation

Testing Access Control Systems is a critical issue and the complexity of the XACML language specification prevents the manual specification of a set of test cases capable of covering all the possible interesting critical situations or faults. This implies the need of automated test cases generation for testing on one side the XACML policy specification and on the other that the PDP behavior conforms to the policy specification. Among the available proposals, the Targen tool [18]

---

[1] A release of MISTA can be downloaded from
http://www.homepages.dsu.edu/dxu/research/MBT.html

generates test inputs using combinatorial coverage of the truth values of independent clauses of XACML policy values. This approach has been proven to be more effective than random generation strategy in terms of structural coverage of the policy and fault detection capability [18]. A more recent tool is X-CREATE [3,4,6] that provides different strategies based on combinatorial approaches of the subject, resource, action and environment values taken from the XACML policy for deriving the access requests. Experimental results presented in [6] show that the fault detection effectiveness of X-CREATE test suites is similar or higher than that of Targen test suite. Specifically, three main generation strategies are defined into X-CREATE: *i)* the *Simple Combinatorial* testing strategy [3] that derives an XACML request for each of the possible combinations of the subject, resource, action and environment values taken from the policy; *ii)* the *XPT-based* testing strategy [3, 6] that generates requests using the structures obtained applying the *XPT* strategy [5] to the XACML Context Schema [22]; *iii)* the *Multiple Combinatorial* strategy that relies on combinations of more than one subject, resource, action and environment values for generating XACML requests. This last strategy automatically establishes the number of subjects, resources, actions and environments of each request according to the complexity of the policy structure, and targets the policy rules in which the effect is simultaneously dependent on more than one constraint [4]. A detailed comparison of X-CREATE test generation strategies in terms of fault detection is presented in [3, 4]. Among the X-CREATE generation strategies we select in this chapter the *Simple Combinatorial* one for deriving test suites used to empirically validate the effectiveness of the proposed selection and prioritization approaches. This strategy is simple and easy-to-apply and at the same time able to reach the coverage of the policy input domain represented by the policy values combinations. More detail about this strategy are presented in the Section 5.1.

3.3   Test Cases Selection and Prioritization

The work in [33] provides a survey on test adequacy criteria presenting code coverage as a good criterion for test cases selection and test suite effectiveness evaluation. Many frameworks for test coverage measurement and analysis have been proposed dealing with different programming languages. The proposal of [19] provides a first coverage criterion for XACML policies defining three structural coverage metrics targeting XACML policies, rules and conditions respectively. These coverage metrics are used for reducing test sets and the effects of test reduction in terms of fault detection are measured. The authors of [1] integrate and extend the coverage approach proposed in [19], also addressing the policy set and proposing the Rule Target Set concept and the inclusion of the request values in that Rule Target Set as selection criterion. However, differently from the approach presented in [19], the solution of [1] does not require the policy execution and PDP instrumentation to be applied, then reducing the effort for coverage measurement.

Many proposals address test cases selection for regression systems. The work in [31] presents a survey of selection techniques able to identify the test cases that are relevant to some set of changes and addresses the emerging trends in the field. The main proposal for regression testing of access control systems is the work done by Xie et al. [12], in which they promote a new approach that aims at selecting a superset of fault-revealing test cases, i.e., test cases that reveal faults due to the policy modification. This approach includes three regression-test selection techniques: the first one based on mutation analysis, the second one based on coverage analysis, and the third one based on recorded requests evaluation. The first two techniques are based on correlation between test cases and rules R_{imp} where R_{imp} are rules being involved with syntactic changes across policy versions. The first technique selects a rule r_i in P and creates Ps mutant $M(ri)$ by changing r_is decision. This technique selects test cases that reveal different policy behaviors by executing test cases on program code interacting with P and $M(r_i)$, respectively. However, if a test case is correlated with r_i, the test case may reveal different system behaviors affected by modification of r_i in P. This first technique is considered to be costly because it requires at least $2n$ executions of each test case to find all correlations between test cases and rules where n is the number of rules in P. The second technique uses coverage analysis to establish correlations between test cases and rules by monitoring which rules are evaluated (i.e., covered) for requests issued from program code. Compared with the first technique, this technique substantially reduces cost during the correlation process because it requires execution of each test case once. The third one first captures requests issued from program code while executing test cases. This technique evaluates these requests against P and P', respectively, then selects only test cases that issue requests evaluated to different decisions. According to experiments the third technique reveals to be better in terms of performance and efficiency. The above described test selection techniques can be applied to XACML based systems and can reveal regression faults caused by policy changes, thus reducing the number of test cases. Differently from the work in [12], the selection approach proposed in this chapter does not target regression systems and does not require the execution of test cases against the security policy for selecting test cases, then reducing cost and time effort of the overall testing process.

Another solution for increasing test suite effectiveness reducing the size of the test set is represented by tests case prioritization. It relies on test cases re-ordering techniques to improve fault detection rate at a given test execution time [26]. In [8], the authors have conducted a series of controlled experiments to evaluate test case prioritization techniques based on time constraints and fault detection rate. Their results have been in favor of applying heuristics when the software contains considerable faults number and when the testing process has no time constraints. In [9, 27], the authors have conducted experimental studies to show the effectiveness of prioritization techniques to improve fault detection rate in the context of regression testing. While most of the techniques that have been introduced in the literature rely on code coverage to achieve prioritization [14, 15, 29] some recent approaches have adopted different metrics: in [28], the authors use system models and system behavior to prioritize test cases, they have compared this approach with other prioritization techniques and have shown its effectiveness in early fault detection; the authors in [32] have used expert knowledge to achieve pair-wise comparison of test cases and have proposed similarity metrics between test cases clusters to achieve test case prioritization. Differently from existing works, the prioritization approach proposed in this chapter addresses XACML access control systems and provides similarity metrics between XACML requests.

3.4   Assessing the Test Suite Effectiveness

In software testing mutation analysis [13] is commonly used to assess the effectiveness of a test suite. It aims at introducing single faults in a given program and running tests to assess their capability to detect the faults. Mutation analysis has been applied on access control policies [2, 17, 21] to qualify security tests. By means of mutation operators, the policy under test is modified to derive a set of faulty policies (mutants) each containing a fault. A mutant policy is killed if the response of an XACML request executed on the mutant policy differs from the response of the same request executed on the original policy. In [17] the authors define a fault model for access control policies and a set of mutation operators manipulating the predicates and logical constructs of target and condition elements of an XACML policy. They have used mutation analysis applied on access control policies to assess coverage criteria for test generation and test selection in terms of fault-detection capability. In [21] the authors try to extend the mutation operators of [17], focusing on the use of a metamodel that allows to simulate the faults in the security models independently from the used role-based formalism (RBAC or OrBAC). Finally, the work in [2] includes and enhances the mutation operators of [17] and [21] addressing specific faults of the XACML 2.0 language and providing a tool, called XACMUT, for the derivation of XACML mutation operators and their application to XACML policies. In this chapter, we use the XACMUT tool to generate mutants of XACML policies and assess the effectiveness of the proposed selection and prioritization approaches.

4   Maximize Test Suite Effectiveness for Access Control Systems

Testing XACML access control systems is a critical activity and many solutions have been proposed to generate XACML tests, including Targen [18] and X-CREATE [3, 4, 6]. The main limitation of these approaches is that, as for any strategy that relies on combinatorial techniques, the generated test suites tend to grow in size as policy complexity increases, often making it too costly to execute entire test suites and check if the test results are correct or not. Different approaches have been studied to maximize the effectiveness of the obtained test suite, among them we focus on selection and prioritization. Test case selection seeks to select the test cases that are relevant according to some defined criteria. Test case prioritization aims to order test cases in such a way that early fault detection is maximized. In this chapter we provide a comparison of two approaches for improving the effectiveness of an XACML test suite: the former is a selection strategy named *XACML smart coverage* that relies on an XACML rule coverage criterion, the latter is an access control test prioritization approach based on similarity. In the following we describe both approaches while in Section 5.3 we compare their effectiveness in terms of mutation score and size of the test suite.

4.1 *XACML Smart Coverage* Selection

In this section we present the *XACML smart coverage* selection approach [7]. It relies on an XACML rule coverage criterion and an algorithm developed to select a set of requests that achieve this coverage criterion. We first provide some generic definitions concerning the policy (Definitions 1 and 2) and request elements (Definition 3) and then we define the XACML rule coverage criterion (Definition 4). Finally, the selection algorithm is presented.

Definition 1 (Target Tuple). *Given a Rule R, a Policy P, a PolicySet PS, with R ∈ P and P ∈ PS, and given the set of XACML Elements, called XE = {xe : xe is PS or P or R}, the Target Tuple of an xe ∈ XE, called TT_{xe}, is a 4-tuple (S, Res, A, E), where: S (Res, A, E) is a finite set of subjects (resources, actions, environments) in the XACML target of xe.*

Definition 2 (Rule Target Set). *Given a Rule R, its Target Set is a set of Target Tuple, ordered by the XACML hierarchy elements relation, defined as*

$$TS_R = \left\{ TT_{xe} : TT_{xe} = \begin{cases} TT_{PS} & if\,R \in PS \\ TT_P & if\,R \in P \\ TT_R & otherwise \end{cases} \right\}.$$

Definition 3 (Request Target Tuple). *Given a request Req, the Request Target Tuple, called TT_{req} is a 4 tuple (S_r, Res_r, A_r, E_r) where S_r, Res_r, A_r, E_r are the subject, resource, action and environment belonging to the request Req.*

Definition 4 (XACML Rule Coverage). *Given a rule R, the condition C of R, the Rule Target Set TS_R, and the request Req with Request Target Tuple TT_{req}=(S_r, Res_r, A_r, E_r), Req covers R if and only if*

- *for each Target Tuple TT_E =(S, Res, A, E) ∈ TS_R such that TT_E is a TT_{PS}, TT_P or TT_R, S_r ∈ S or S is ∅, Res_r ∈ Res or Res is ∅, A_r ∈ A or A is ∅, and E_r ∈ E or E is ∅.*
- *C is evaluated to True or False against TT_{req}[2].*

---

[2] Note that only the condition is evaluated against the request values, without having policy execution.

Considering the policy of Listing 1.1, according to Definition 2, the Target Set of $ruleA$ is

$TS_{RuleA} = \{TT_{PS_{policySetExample}}, TT_{P_{policyExample}}, TT_{RuleA}\} = \{(\emptyset, \emptyset, \emptyset, \emptyset, \emptyset), (\emptyset,$
$\{books\}, \emptyset, \emptyset), (\emptyset, \{books, documents\}, \{read\}, \emptyset)\}$

while the Target Set of $ruleB$ is

$TS_{RuleB} = \{TT_{PS_{policySetExample}}, TT_{P_{policyExample}}, TT_{RuleB}\} = \{(\emptyset, \emptyset, \emptyset, \emptyset, \emptyset), (\emptyset,$
$\{books\}, \emptyset, \emptyset), (\{Julius\}, \emptyset, \{write\}, \emptyset)\}$.

Considering the XACML request of Listing 1.2, according to Definition 3, the Request Target Tuple of this request is $TT_{requestExample} = (\{Julius\}, \{books\}, \{write\}, \emptyset)$.

According to Definition 4, the request of Listing 1.2 covers $ruleB$ but it does not cover $ruleA$ since the action of the request ($write$) is not included in the Target Set of $RuleA$.

In a nutshell, the defined XACML rule coverage criterion involves selecting tests that match the Rule Target Sets. The Rule Target Set is the union of the target of the rule, and all enclosing policy and policy sets targets. The main idea is that, according to the XACML language, in order to match the rule target, requests must first match the enclosing policy and policy sets targets (note that there could be several enclosing policy sets). For instance, if a rule contains no condition, and it has a target containing the elements Subject1, Action1, Resource1, and the policy and policy set targets which it belongs to are both empty, then in order to match that rule a request should contain exactly these three elements. If the rule target has several subjects, resources, actions, and environments and the enclosing policy and policy set targets are empty, to cover the rule target the request should include a subject contained in the target subjects set, a resource contained in the target resources set, an action contained in the target actions set, an environment contained in the target environments set. Finally, if the Rule Target Set of a rule is empty and its condition is evaluated to True or False, all requests are covering this rule.

Algorithm 1 is used to select the test cases. Roughly, it takes as input the Rule Target Sets and a set of requests. Then, it loops through the requests and selects those ones that match one Rule Target Set. Once a Rule Target Set is matched, it is removed from the set of Rule Target Sets. This prevents selecting all requests for empty Rule Target Sets.

Algorithm 2 allows all Rule Target Sets and Rule Conditions to be computed by taking into consideration the rule and its enclosing policy and policy sets. In addition, when a target contains more than one subject, action or resource, the algorithm divides that target into several targets, each having only one of these elements. For instance, a target with 2 subjects, 1 action and 3 resources leads to creating 6 targets (each one with 1 subject, 1 action and 1 resource). In fact, according to the XACML language a rule containing for instance a target with 3 subjects is equivalent to three rules having a target with 1 subject. XACML offers this facility to avoid creating several rules, however for the sake of rule evaluation, it is safer to consider several rules having each a target with only one element. For test cases selection, having targets with one subject,

---

Algorithm 1. Coverage-Based Selection of Test Cases

```
1: input: S = {Req₁, ..., Reqₙ}                    ▷ Unordered set of n XACML requests
2: input: P                                         ▷ The XACML policy
3: output: Result                   ▷ Set of m selected XACML requests with m ¡ n
4: Result ← {}
5: TargetsConds ← computeAllRulesTargetsConds(P)
6: i ← 0
7: while size(TargetsConds) > 0 do            ▷ Loop until all targets are covered
8:     ContainsReq ← False
9:     j ← 0
10:    while doNot ContainsReq          ▷ Loop until a matching request is found
11:        ReqTargetⱼ ← extractReqTarget(Reqⱼ)
12:        if containsReq(TargetCondᵢ, ReqTargetⱼ) then
13:            Result ← Result ∪ {Reqⱼ}
14:            ContainsReq ← True
15:        end if
16:        j ← j + 1
17:        if j == n then          ▷ not matching request then leave loop and carry on
18:            Break
19:        end if
20:    end while
21:    i ← i + 1
22: end while
23: return Result
```

Algorithm 2. Compute All Targets and Conditions

```
1: input: P = {Rule₁, ..., Ruleₙ}                 ▷ XACML policy having n rules
2: output: L                          ▷ Set of n Targets with Condition
3: L ← {}
4: i ← 0
5: while i < n do
6:     TargCondᵢ ← {}
7:     EnclosingPol ← retrievePolForRule(Ruleᵢ)
8:     PolTargetᵢ ← extractPolicyTarget(EnclosingPol)
9:     TargCondᵢ ← L ∪ {PolTargetᵢ}
10:    EnclosingPolSet ← retrievePolSetForPol(EnclosingPol)
11:    PolSetTargetᵢ ← extractPolicySetTarget(EnclosingPolSet)
12:    TargCondᵢ ← L ∪ {PolSetTargetᵢ}
13:    while isPolicySetEnclosedInPolicySet(EnclosingₚolSet) do
14:        PolSet ← getParent(PolSet)
15:        PolSetTargetᵢ ← extractPolicySetTarget(EnclosingPolSet)
16:        TargCondᵢ ← L ∪ {PolSetTargetᵢ}
17:    end while
18:    TargCondᵢ ← TargCondᵢ ∪ {Condᵢ}
19:    L ← L ∪ {TargCondᵢ}
20: end while
21: return L
```

---

action, resource and environment enables us to select test cases covering all subjects, actions, resources and environments and helps improving the quality of test cases.

4.2 Similarity Based Test Cases Prioritization

In this section we present a new approach for access control test prioritization that relies on similarity [1]. Similarity is a heuristic that is used here to order access control requests (i.e. the test cases). Previous work on model-based testing, such as [11], has shown that dissimilar test cases bestow a higher fault detection power than similar ones. Analogously, the experimental results presented in [1] showed that two dissimilar access control requests are likely to find more access control faults than two similar ones. In the following, we consider a test suite of r access control requests $\{R_1, ..., R_r\}$. A similarity approach consists of two steps. The first step involves the definition of a metric d between any two access control requests R_i and R_j, where $1 \leq i, j \leq r$. This metric is used to evaluate the degree of similarity between two given requests: the highest the resulting distance, the most dissimilar are the two requests; a distance value equal to 0 means that two requests are identical. The second step is the ordering of these r requests. To this end, we first compute the distance between each pair of requests. Then, a selection algorithm uses the distances to select the most dissimilar requests, resulting in a list where the first selected requests are the most dissimilar ones.

Given two requests (R_i, R_j), a similarity metric (called *simple similarity*) $d_{ss}(R_i, R_j)$ is defined based on a comparison between the request attributes values. There are four attributes in each request, namely the *subject*, the *action*, the *resource*, and the *environment*. For each attribute, the *simple similarity* compares the values in the two requests (R_i, R_j). The distance increases each time a given attribute is different in the two requests. Since the evaluation is based on four attributes, the final distance varies between 0 and 4. Formally, the *simple similarity* is defined as follows:

$$d_{ss}(R_i, R_j) = \sum_{k=1}^{4} d_{attribute}^{k}(R_i, R_j)$$

where
$$d_{attribute}^{k}(R_i, R_j) = \begin{cases} 1 & R_i.attribute[k] \neq R_j.attribute[k] \\ 0 & \text{otherwise} \end{cases}.$$

For instance, considering the requests R_1 and R_2 shown in Listings 1.2 and 1.3 respectively, and obtained by the application of the *Simple Combinatorial* strategy (Section 5.1) to the policy of Listing 1.1, the $d_{ss}(R_1, R_2) = 2$ since both the *resource* and the *action* differ in the two requests.

The similarity distance values relative to a set of requests $\{R_1, ..., R_r\}$ are represented by $r \times r$ matrix, called Simple Similarity Matrix (SSM).

$$SSM : (R \times R) \longrightarrow \{0, 1, 2, 3, 4\}.$$

defined as:

$$[SSM]_{i,j} = d_{ss}(R_i, R_j) \quad i, j = 1, 2, ..., r \text{ and } i < j.$$

This matrix is the input of the following algorithm used for the prioritization of the requests.

Algorithm 3. Prioritization

1: **input:** $S = \{R_1, ..., R_n\}$, distMatrix
2: **output:** L ▷ Prioritized list of n XACML requests
3: $L \leftarrow []$
4: Select R_i, R_j **where** $max(distMatrix(R_i, R_j))$, $1 \leq i, j \leq n$
5:   ▷ Take the first ones in case of equality
6:    $L.add(R_i)$
7:    $L.add(R_j)$
8: $S \leftarrow S \setminus \{R_i, R_j\}$
9: **while** $\#S > 0$ **do**
10:     $s \leftarrow size(L)$
11:     Select $R_i \in S$ **where** $max\left(\sum_{j=1}^{s} distMatrix(R_i, L.get(j))\right)$, $1 \leq i \leq n$
12:   ▷ Take the first one in case of equality
13:     $L.add(R_i)$
14:     $S \leftarrow S \setminus \{R_i\}$ ▷ Remove R_i from S
15: **end while**
16: **return** L

The idea is to order the requests so that the first executed are those most dissimilar, i.e. the requests sharing the higher distance. Informally, the algorithm aims at selecting the request that is the most distant to all the requests already selected during the previous steps of the approach. It takes as input the set of XACML request $S = \{R_1, ..., R_n\}$ and the SSM distance matrix (distMatrix).Using the distances between the requests collected into the matrix, it first selects the two XACML requests having the highest distance (Algorithm 3, line 4). In case of equality the first couple of requests is selected. Then these two requests are removed from the set of XACML requests to be prioritized, i.e the set S (Algorithm 3, line 8). Among the remaining XACML requests, in the next step the algorithm considers that having the maximum of the sum of the distances with respect to all the already selected requests (Algorithm 3, line 11). In case of equality the first request is selected. As before the selected request is removed from the XACML requests to be prioritized (Algorithm 3, line 14) and this process is repeated until all requests are selected.

Table 1. Description of the six policies

Name	# Rul.	# S	# Res	# A	# E	# Pol.set	# Pol.
LMS	42	8	3	10	3	1	1
VMS	106	7	3	15	4	1	1
ASMS	117	8	5	11	3	1	1
pluto	21	4	90	1	0	1	1
itrust	64	7	46	9	0	1	1
continue-a	298	16	29	4	0	111	266

5 An Experimental Comparison

In this section we present an experimental comparison between the *XACML smart coverage* selection strategy (detailed in Section 4.1) that relies on an XACML rule coverage criterion, and the access control test prioritization approach based on similarity, presented in Section 4.2. The comparison has been performed to evaluate the effectiveness of the two proposals in terms of mutation score. In the following subsections we present: first the case study and the test cases generation strategy, then the mutation operators used for the test suites evaluation and finally the experimental results.

5.1 Setup

We consider in our experiment six real world policies, which differ from each other in terms of the complexity of their structure and the number of elements they include. This information is summarized in Table 1, which shows the size of the XACML policies in terms of the number of subjects, resources, actions and environments, and their structure in terms of rules, policy sets and policies.

Briefly, the policy labeled *LMS* rules a Library Management System, *VMS* represents a Virtual Meeting System and *ASMS* is conceived for an Auction Sales Management System. All these policies are relative to three Java-based systems, which have been used in previous works (e.g., [23]). *pluto* policy is used by the ARCHON system, a digital library management tool [16]; *itrust* policy is part of the iTrust system, a health-care management system [24]. The policy named *continue-a* [26] is used by the *Continue application*, a web-based conference management tool.

Test Cases Generation. A critical issue in testing XACML access control systems is the generation of an effective test suite. Most of the common approaches for generating XACML requests are based on combinatorial approaches, as surveyed in Section 3. In this chapter, among the proposals available for test cases generation we refer to the tool X-CREATE [3, 4, 6][3]. In particular, we use the

---

[3] A release of the X-CREATE tool is available at
`http://labse.isti.cnr.it/tools/xcreate`

Simple Combinatorial test strategy implemented in this tool for deriving the test suites used to empirically compare the effectiveness of the proposed approaches.

Before explaining the test case generation strategy, we need to define the notion of XACML test case:

XACML Test Case. A test case is an XACML request derived from an XACML policy. It is composed of four values, a subject, a resource, an action and an environment. The values and types of these four elements should be among the values and types defined by the policy rules or targets. For instance, Listings 1.2 and 1.3 are two examples of test cases derived from the policy of Listing 1.1.

The *Simple Combinatorial* strategy applies a combinatorial approach to the policy values. Specifically, four data sets called *SubjectSet*, *ResourceSet*, *Action-Set* and *EnvironmentSet* are defined. Those sets are filled with the values of elements and attributes referring to the `<Subjects>`, `<Resources>`, `<Actions>` and `<Environments>` of the policy respectively. These elements and attributes values are then combined in order to obtain the entities. Specifically, a *subject entity* is defined as a combination of the values of elements and attributes of the *SubjectSet* set, and similarly the *resource entity*, the *action entity* and the *environment entity* represent combinations of the values of the elements and attributes of the *ResourceSet*, *ActionSet*, and *EnvironmentSet* respectively. Then, an ordered set of combinations of *subject entities*, *resource entities*, *action entities*, and *environment entities* is generated in the following way:

- First, pair-wise combinations are generated to obtain the PW set
- Then, three-wise combinations are generated to obtain the TW set
- Finally, four-wise combinations are generated to obtain the FW set

These sets have the following inclusion propriety $PW \subseteq TW \subseteq FW$.

The maximum number of requests derived by this strategy is equal to the size of the FW set. The X-CREATE framework provides an ordered set of requests guaranteeing a coverage first of all pairs, then of all triples and finally of all quadruples of values entities derived by the policy. Since the *Simple Combinatorial* strategy relies only on the values entities specified in the policy, the derived test suite can be used either for testing the policy or the PDP. More details about this strategy are in [3].

5.2   Mutation Analysis

We compared the effectiveness of the selection and prioritization approaches in terms of fault detection. A mutation approach specifically conceived for XACML language has been used for introducing faults in the six XACML policies, then the selected and prioritized test suites have been run to asses their capability to detect the introduced faults. It is important to note that we do not consider the running time because for all the approaches, it took less than one second and therefore this running time can be neglected. In addition, the running time is

Table 2. Mutation Operators [2]

ID	Description
PSTT	Policy Set Target True
PSTF	Policy Set Target False
PTT	Policy Target True
PTF	Policy Target False
RTT	Rule Target True
RTF	Rule Target False
RCT	Rule Condition True
RCF	Rule Condition False
CPC	Change Policy Combining Algorithm
CRC	Change Rule Combining Algorithm
CRE	Change Rule Effect
RPT (RTT)	Rule Type is replaced with another one
ANR	Add a New Rule
RER	Remove an Existing Rule
RUF	Remove Uniqueness Function
AUF	Add Uniqueness Function
CNOF	Change N-OF Function
CLF	Change Logical Function
ANF	Add Not Function
RNF	Remove Not Function
CCF	Change Comparison Function
FPR	First the Rules having a *Permit* effect
FDR	First the Rules having a *Deny* effect

not an important factor because usually, prioritization is performed only once and testers can afford to wait for few seconds or even few minutes. In fact, the manual checking of the oracle that is done manually, will take much more time.

In this chapter we used XACMUT tool[4] [2] to generate mutant policies. To the best of our knowledge, XACMUT is currently the most complete tool for mutants derivation, since it combines together XACML mutants taken from the literature with new ones that have been conceived to address the specific features of XACML 2.0 policies. Specifically, Table 2 lists the XACMUT mutation operators. For instance, the Policy Set Target True (PSTT) removes the Target of each PolicySet ensuring that the PolicySet is applied to all requests while the Policy Set Target False (PSTF) modifies the Target of each PolicySet such that the PolicySet is never applied to a request. We refer to [2] for a complete description of these operators.

5.3 Results

As for any test strategy that relies on a combinatorial approach, the size of the test suite derived by the *Simple Combinatorial* strategy may rapidly grow up in

---

[4] A release of the XACMUT tool is available at http://labse.isti.cnr.it/tools/xacmut

relation with the policy complexity. As we discussed in Section 1, this may result into a huge increase of time and effort due to test execution and results analysis. To deal with this problem we propose in this chapter two different solutions: the former based on the *XACML smart coverage* selection approach, the latter relying on a test prioritization approach based on similarity. Here we provide some experimental results to answer to the following research questions:

- RQ1: Is the *XACML smart coverage* selection better than test prioritization based on similarity in terms of fault detection effectiveness?
- RQ2: Considering the same level of mutation score, is the difference in terms of number of test cases between *XACML smart coverage* selection and similarity based prioritization negligible?

To tackle these research questions we first derived for each policy in Table 1 the set of test cases by applying the *Simple Combinatorial* strategy provided by the X-CREATE tool. Table 3 third column shows the size of each derived test suite: as shown, the number of test cases has a large variation (from the 360 of *pluto* to the 2835 of *iTrust*) reflecting the differences in structures and values of the considered set of policies. Then for a fair comparison we applied the *XACML smart coverage* selection and the similarity based prioritization to the derived test suites, using the number of test cases selected from *XACML smart coverage* selection as a stopping criterion for the second one. The second column of Table 3 shows the size of the test suites selected using the *XACML smart coverage* selection criterion. As shown in the last column of the table, for most cases (except *pluto*) the number of selected tests is quite low (less than 12%) and the size of the reduced test suite remains manageable in terms of requests to be run and manually checked. This evidences a good performance of the *XACML smart coverage* selection approach in terms of test reduction. Finally, by means of the XACMUT tool, for each of the six policies we generated the respective set of mutants and used them for evaluating the test effectiveness of the various test suites.

To tackle RQ1, first we derived the number of mutants killed by the test suite selected using the *XACML smart coverage* criterion; then we applied to the overall test suite the prioritization based on similarity and we calculated the number of mutants killed by the subset of test cases having the same size of the test suite derived by the *XACML smart coverage* selection criterion; finally we computed the percentage of mutants killed by these two reduced sets with respect to the mutants killed by the overall test suite. It is out of the scope of this chapter to evaluate the effectiveness of the test strategy used in this experiment; the objective is the evaluation of the capability of the two presented approaches to provide a fault detection effectiveness as close as possible to that of the overall test suite (whatever its effectiveness). The results are shown in Table 4. In particular, the second column (labeled Cov.-Based) reports the number of mutants killed by the *XACML smart coverage* selection and summarizes

Table 3. Test Reduction of the Coverage Based Selection

Policy	# Selected Tests	# Tests	% Selected Tests
LMS	42	720	6%
VMS	106	945	11%
ASMS	130	1760	7%
pluto	175	360	49%
iTrust	61	2835	2%
continue-a	169	1382	12%

Table 4. Test suites effectiveness in terms of mutation results

Policy	Cov.-Based	Sim.-Based	# Killed Mutants
LMS	1357 (62%)	446 (20%)	2183
VMS	4031 (72%)	1151 (20%)	5550
ASMS	4771 (71%)	1440 (22%)	6649
pluto	13968 (94%)	8489 (58%)	14721
iTrust	11782 (98%)	8664 (72%)	11949
continue-a	1333 (76%)	783 (45%)	1741

in brackets the percentage of fault detection effectiveness reached by the reduced test suite with respect to the complete one; similarly the third column (labeled Sim.-Based) reports the number of mutants killed by the similarity based prioritization approach and in brackets the percentage. The fourth column of the same table (labeled # Killed Mutants) reports the number of mutants killed by the complete test suite. Considering column Cov.-Based, the loss in fault detection (except LMS) varies from the 29% to the 2% , with an average value of 18% while for Sim.-Based the loss varies from 80% to 28% with an average value of 60%. Thus using the number of test cases selected from *XACML smart coverage* selection as a stopping criterion for similarity based prioritization, the loss in fault detection of Sim.-Based is on average more than triple score of that of Cov.-Based. The data collected in this experiment give a positive answer to RQ1, i.e. *XACML smart coverage* is better than prioritization based on similarity in terms of fault detection effectiveness.

The second experiment focused on RQ2, i.e., we wanted to evaluate the difference in terms of derived number of test cases, between *XACML smart coverage* selection and similarity based prioritization, in order to obtain comparable values of fault detection effectiveness. Thus we repeated a similar experiment of the one performed for RQ1 considering as a stopping criterion for similarity based prioritization the mutation score obtained by the *XACML smart coverage* selection. The results are shown in Table 5. In particular, the second column (labeled #Sim.-Based TCs) reports the number of test cases necessary with the similarity based prioritization to get the mutation scores of *XACML smart coverage* selection reported in Table 4 second column (labeled Cov.-Based). For aim of

Table 5. Test cases of Sim.-Based to get Cov.-Based mutation score

Policy	# Sim.-Based TCs	# Cov.-Based TCs
LMS	234	42
VMS	555	106
ASMS	843	130
pluto	335	175
iTrust	2502	61
continue-a	674	169

completeness we duplicated in the third column of Table 5 (labeled #Cov.-Based TCs) the number of test cases selected with *XACML smart coverage* selection criterion. As shown in the table, for four of the considered policies, the number of test cases of the similarity based prioritization is in average more than 4 times the size of the test sets of *XACML smart coverage* selection. For *pluto* the size of the test suite selected by *XACML smart coverage* selection is around half of that of the similarity based prioritization, while for the remaining *iTrust* the difference between the two approaches is extremely high: the prioritization based on similarity requires a number of test cases more than 41 times that of the *XACML smart coverage* test suite. This second experiment evidenced that the difference in terms of number of test cases between *XACML smart coverage* selection and similarity based prioritization is not negligible and that *XACML smart coverage* selection outperforms in all the cases the prioritization approach. This negatively replies to RQ2.

6   Discussion and Conclusions

The results presented in the previous section show that the proposed coverage criterion is very effective in terms of fault detection and test reduction, when compared to similarity based prioritization. However, the main issue with this approach is that it is not possible to improve further the test suite. Once the test suite covering all rules is selected, there is no possibility to apply the criterion to choose more tests to improve further the mutation scores (simply because 100% coverage is reached). Especially in cases where testing resources are still available, it would be better to be able to run more requests. It is therefore important to provide a solution that enables to select more test cases. Moreover, the experiments show that similarity based prioritization approach gets a low mutation score evidencing that prioritizing requests according to a similarity metric which is policy-independent and involves comparing only the content of the requests does not allow to address the peculiarities and complex structure of XACML policies. A possible solution to this issue would be to rely on a better similarity based approach that takes into account the applicability of the requests to the XACML policy. This approach will be thus tailored to the policy under test and will be able to prioritize the requests triggering the rule decision of an XACML policy, leading then to better results.

The threats to external validity of our work mainly relate to the fact that the six policies used in the experiments may not be representative of true practice. Therefore further experiments on a larger set of policies may be required to reduce this threat. In fact, several other real policies were available to us. However, they included a quite small set of tests (they had 2 or 3 rules only). In those cases, test selection did not make much sense because the policies are quite small and they could easily be checked manually. On the other hand, our six policies have quite different structures. Some have relatively few rules, while others have a large number of rules. For some policies the number of resources is bigger than the number of subjects (while for others it is not the case). Therefore, we are confident in the general relevance of the results.

Furthermore, our current version of the coverage criteria does not take into consideration the combining algorithm, which plays an important role when it comes to selecting which rule applies in case of conflicts. Therefore, for some cases, it is important to consider the combining algorithm at policy and policy set level. It is therefore important to improve the coverage criterion by taking this into consideration. Nevertheless, it is unclear whether combining algorithms have an important impact on the quality of the selected test cases in terms of fault detection effectiveness. This issue should therefore be investigated by using other policies having many conflicts.

Finally, the effectiveness of the selection and prioritization approaches was evaluated based on mutation analysis. As always, when mutation is used, there is the issue whether the artificial faults represent or not real faults. However, in the presented work, we have combined three different sets of mutation operators, which are implemented by the XACMUT tool [2]. We are confident in the quality of the mutation operators even though it would be interesting to perform a large empirical study to assess the quality of access control mutation operators.

To conclude, we have presented in this chapter a survey on existing validation techniques of access control systems (focusing on XACML-based strategies for test cases generation and reduction). We also have showed a comparison between a test cases selection approach that relies on rule coverage and a similarity based prioritization approach. The experiments showed that the proposed coverage based selection approach is able to reach high mutation scores and to select a test suite with a higher fault detection capability than the similarity based prioritization approach. This evidenced that a better prioritization approach is needed for XACML test cases. In the future we plan to improve the similarity criterion taking into account, as in the *XACML smart coverage* selection approach, also the XACML policy and the applicability of the requests to the XACML policy. Moreover, we plan to extend the similarity-based prioritization in order to consider other test case generation strategies, also based on the combination of more than one subject, resource, action, environment.

References

1. Bertolino, A., Daoudagh, S., El Kateb, D., Henard, C., Le Traon, Y., Lonetti, F., Marchetti, E., Mouelhi, T., Papadakis, M.: Similarity testing for access-control. Submitted to Information and Software Technology (2013)
2. Bertolino, A., Daoudagh, S., Lonetti, F., Marchetti, E.: XACMUT: XACML 2.0 Mutants Generator. In: Proc. of 8th International Workshop on Mutation Analysis, pp. 28–33 (2013)
3. Bertolino, A., Daoudagh, S., Lonetti, F., Marchetti, E.: Automatic XACML requests generation for policy testing. In: Proc. of The Third International Workshop on Security Testing, pp. 842–849 (2012)
4. Bertolino, A., Daoudagh, S., Lonetti, F., Marchetti, E., Schilders, L.: Automated testing of extensible access control markup language-based access control systems. IET Software 7(4), 203–212 (2013)
5. Bertolino, A., Gao, J., Marchetti, E., Polini, A.: Automatic test data generation for XML schema-based partition testing. In: Proc. of Second International Workshop on Automation of Software Test (AST), pp. 4–10 (2007)
6. Bertolino, A., Lonetti, F., Marchetti, E.: Systematic XACML Request Generation for Testing Purposes. In: Proc. of 36th EUROMICRO Conference on Software Engineering and Advanced Applications (SEAA), pp. 3–11 (2010)
7. Bertolino, A., Le Traon, Y., Lonetti, F., Marchetti, E., Mouelhi, T.: Coverage-based test cases selection for XACML policies. In: Proc. of Fifth International Workshop on Security Testing, SECTEST (2014)
8. Do, H., Mirarab, S., Tahvildari, L., Rothermel, G.: The effects of time constraints on test case prioritization: A series of controlled experiments. IEEE Transactions on Software Engineering 36(5), 593–617 (2010)
9. Elbaum, S., Malishevsky, A.G., Rothermel, G.: Test case prioritization: A family of empirical studies. IEEE Transactions on Software Engineering 28(2), 159–182 (2002)
10. Genrich, H.J.: Predicate/transition nets. In: Brauer, W., Reisig, W., Rozenberg, G. (eds.) APN 1986. LNCS, vol. 254, pp. 207–247. Springer, Heidelberg (1987)
11. Hemmati, H., Arcuri, A., Briand, L.: Achieving scalable model-based testing through test case diversity. ACM Trans. Softw. Eng. Methodol. 22(1) (March 2013)
12. Hwang, J., Xie, T., El Kateb, D., Mouelhi, T., Le Traon, Y.: Selection of regression system tests for security policy evolution. In: Proc. of the 27th IEEE/ACM International Conference on Automated Software Engineering (ASE), pp. 266–269 (2012)
13. Jia, Y., Harman, M.: An analysis and survey of the development of mutation testing. IEEE Transactions on Software Engineering 37(5), 649–678 (2011)
14. Kaur, A., Goyal, S.: A genetic algorithm for regression test case prioritization using code coverage. International Journal on Computer Science and Engineering 3(5), 1839–1847 (2011)
15. Leon, D., Podgurski, A.: A comparison of coverage-based and distribution-based techniques for filtering and prioritizing test cases. In: Proc. of 14th International Symposium on Software Reliability Engineering (ISSRE), pp. 442–453. IEEE (2003)
16. Maly, K., Zubair, M., Nelson, M., Liu, X., Anan, H., Gao, J., Tang, J., Zhao, Y.: Archon - A digital library that federates physics collections
17. Martin, E., Xie, T.: A fault model and mutation testing of access control policies. In: Proc. of 16th International Conference on World Wide Web (WWW), pp. 667–676

18. Martin, E., Xie, T.: Automated Test Generation for Access Control Policies. In: Supplemental Proc. of 17th International Symposium on Software Reliability Engineering, ISSRE (November 2006)
19. Martin, E., Xie, T., Yu, T.: Defining and measuring policy coverage in testing access control policies. In: Ning, P., Qing, S., Li, N. (eds.) ICICS 2006. LNCS, vol. 4307, pp. 139–158. Springer, Heidelberg (2006)
20. Meyer, B.: Applying'design by contract'. Computer 25(10), 40–51 (1992)
21. Mouelhi, T., Fleurey, F., Baudry, B.: A generic metamodel for security policies mutation. In: Proc. of Software Testing Verification and Validation Workshop (ICSTW), pp. 278–286 (2008)
22. OASIS. extensible access control markup language (xacml) version 2.0 (February 1, 2005)
23. Pretschner, A., Mouelhi, T., Le Traon, Y.: Model-based tests for access control policies. In: Proc. of First International Conference on Software Testing, Verification (ICST), pp. 338–347 (2008)
24. Realsearch Group at NCSU. iTrust: Role-Based Healthcare,
    http://agile.csc.ncsu.edu/iTrust/wiki/doku.php
25. Rothermel, G., Harrold, M.J., Ostrin, J., Hong, C.: An empirical study of the effects of minimization on the fault detection capabilities of test suites. In: Proc. of International Conference on Software Maintenance, pp. 34–43 (1998)
26. Rothermel, G., Untch, R.H., Chu, C., Harrold, M.J.: Test case prioritization: An empirical study. In: Proc. of IEEE International Conference on Software Maintenance (ICSM), pp. 179–188. IEEE (1999)
27. Rothermel, G., Untch, R.H., Chu, C., Harrold, M.J.: Prioritizing test cases for regression testing. IEEE Transactions on Software Engineering 27(10), 929–948 (2001)
28. Tahat, L., Korel, B., Harman, M., Ural, H.: Regression test suite prioritization using system models. Software Testing, Verification and Reliability 22(7), 481–506 (2012)
29. Walcott, K.R., Soffa, M.L., Kapfhammer, G.M., Roos, R.S.: Timeaware test suite prioritization. In: Proc. of the 2006 International Symposium on Software Testing and Analysis, pp. 1–12. ACM (2006)
30. Xu, D., Thomas, L., Kent, M., Mouelhi, T., Le Traon, Y.: A model-based approach to automated testing of access control policies. In: Proc. of the 17th ACM Symposium on Access Control Models and Technologies (SACMAT), pp. 209–218 (2012)
31. Yoo, S., Harman, M.: Regression testing minimization, selection and prioritization: A survey. Softw. Test. Verif. Reliab. 22(2), 67–120 (2012)
32. Yoo, S., Harman, M., Tonella, P., Susi, A.: Clustering test cases to achieve effective and scalable prioritisation incorporating expert knowledge. In: Proc. of the 18th International Symposium on Software Testing and Analysis, pp. 201–212. ACM (2009)
33. Zhu, H., Hall, P.A.V., May, J.H.R.: Software unit test coverage and adequacy. ACM Comput. Surv. 29(4), 366–427 (1997)

Evaluation of Engineering Approaches in the Secure Software Development Life Cycle*

Marianne Busch, Nora Koch, and Martin Wirsing

Institute for Informatics
Ludwig-Maximilians-Universität München
Oettingenstraße 67, 80538 München, Germany
{busch,kochn,wirsing}@pst.ifi.lmu.de

Abstract. Software engineers need to find effective methods, appropriate notations and tools that support the development of secure applications along the different phases of the Software Development Life Cycle (SDLC). Our evaluation approach, called SecEval, supports the search and comparison of these artifacts. SecEval comprises: (1) a workflow that defines the evaluation process, which can be easily customized and extended; (2) a security context model describing security features, methods, notations and tools; (3) a data collection model, which records how data is gathered when researchers or practitioners are looking for artifacts that solve a specific problem; (4) a data analysis model specifying how analysis, using previously collected data, is performed; and (5) the possibility to easily extend the models, which is exemplarily shown for risk rating and experimental approaches. The validation of SecEval was performed for tools in the web testing domain.

1 Introduction

The development of software requires among others decisions regarding methods, notations and tools to be used in the different phases of the Software Development Life Cycle (SDLC). In the development of secure applications, such decisions might even be more relevant as new threats continuously appear and more and more methods, notations and tools are developed to increase the level of security. Therefore it is important to be able to identify, e.g., authentication-related threats that can be mitigated by a method and to find out which tools support this method. Furthermore, it is advantageous to know which tools can work together.

However, often the selection of methods, tools and notations is performed based on the experience of the developers, as all too frequent there is neither time to investigate on alternatives to the artifacts used so far, nor to document choices and lessons learned. In other cases engineers have to search in a time-consuming process for appropriate artifacts, decide about the relevant research

---

* This work has been supported by the EU-NoE project NESSoS, GA 256980.

M. Heisel et al. (Eds.): Engineering Secure Future Internet Services, LNCS 8431, pp. 234–265, 2014.

questions and repeat evaluations. What could help is a systematic way of collecting information on methods, tools and notations driven by specific research questions and a subsequent selection.

To ease the tasks of recording information and of getting an overview of existing artifacts the Common Body of Knowledge (CBK) [1] was implemented as a semantic Wiki within the scope of the EU project NESSoS [2]. It provides a useful knowledge base and underlying model, but leaves open the following questions: (a) How could security-related features also be included as first-class citizens in the knowledge base? (b) How can we use the approach not only for recording and comparing features of methods, notations and tools, but also for documenting the search process? (c) How is the process of data collection and data analysis specified, to make sure that emerging research results are comprehensible and valid?

The aim of our evaluation approach is to give answers to these questions and to provide software and security engineers with mechanisms to ease the selection and comparison of methods, tools and notations. Our conceptual framework for evaluating security-related artifacts is called SECEVAL [3,4]. We selected a graphical representation for SECEVAL, which comprises (1) a workflow that defines the evaluation process, which can be easily customized and extended; (2) a security context model describing security properties, vulnerabilities and threats as well as methods, notations and tools; (3) a data collection model, which records how data is gathered when researchers or practitioners do research to answer a question; and (4) a data analysis model specifying, how reasoning on the previously collected data, is done. However, we do not claim to provide a one-fits-all approach for IT-security (which would overload any model), instead we introduce an extensible basis.

In this chapter we focus on the evaluation process and its placement within the software development life cycle. Conversely to [3] in which we presented the architectural features of SECEVAL, we go into more details, concerning its requirements, the process supported by SECEVAL, and the case study. In addition, we show how the conceptual framework can be extended to cover approaches like the OWASP's Risk Rating Methodology [5] and Moody's method evaluation approach [6]. The applicability of an approach like SECEVAL is given by an appropriate tool support and the usability of its user interface. Therefore we plan an implementation of SECEVAL as an online knowledge base and present the requirements of such an implementation.

The remainder of this chapter is structured as follows: Section 2 discuss related work and background. Section 3 gives an overview of the SDLC for the development of secure software and systems. Section 4 describes our evaluation approach SECEVAL in detail, before Sect. 5 presents its extensions. In Sect. 6 we validate the approach by a case study in the area of security testing of web applications. We give an overview of the requirements for a future implementation of SECEVAL in Sect. 7 and conclude in Sect. 8.

2   Related Work

In this section, we discuss approaches that focus on security during the Software Development Life Cycle (SDLC). We continue with general evaluation approaches and conclude with security-specific evaluation frameworks.

Secure Software Development Life Cycles. Incorporating security into the SDLC means to add activities to ensure security features in every phase of SDLC. Adopting a secure SDLC in an organization's framework has many benefits and helps to produce a secure product. These approaches enrich the software development process by, e.g., security requirements, risk assessment, threat models during software design, best practices for coding, the use of static analysis code-scanning tools during implementation, and the realization of code reviews and security testing. Hereby, the concrete phases of the SDLC and how they are arranged is less important than the focus on security during all phases.

Therefore, many companies define their own secure SDLC in order to be able to ensure the software they developed has as few vulnerabilities as possible. A main contribution in this area is the Microsoft Security Development Lifecycle (SDL) [7]. It is a software development process used to reduce software maintenance costs and increase reliability of software concerning software security-related bugs. The SDL can be adapted to be used in a classical waterfall model, a spiral model, or an agile model.

Besides, cybersecurity standards, as ISO 27001 [8] can be applied. They go beyond software development and define an information security management system that requires the specification of security guidelines for policies, processes and systems within an organization. Important is that most standards do not define how to increase security, but which areas have to be taken into consideration in order to create meaningful security guidelines.

Another example for supporting secure development along the SDLC is the Open Web Application Security Project (OWASP). It comprises, beyond others, a set of guides for web security requirements, cheat sheets, a development guide, a code review and a testing guide, an application security verification standard (ASVS), a risk rating methodology, tools and a top 10 of web security vulnerabilities [9].

General Evaluation Approaches. Our approach is based on the so called "Systematic Literature Review" of KITCHENHAM et al. [10], which is an evaluation approach used in software engineering. Their aim is to answer research questions by systematically searching and extracting knowledge of existing literature. We go even further using arbitrary resources in addition to available literature, such as source code or experiments that are carried out to answer a research question. The systematic literature review is executed in three main steps: first, the review is planned, then it is conducted and finally results are reported (this process is depicted in deliverable D5.2 [11, Fig. 3.2]). In contrast to Kitchenham's approach, our data collection process is iterative, and more specific for a chosen domain as we specify a detailed structure of the context for which we pose the research questions.

The CBK (Common Body of Knowledge) [11] defines a model to collect and describe methods, techniques, notations, tools and standards. We use the CBK as a starting point for our SECEVAL's approach. However, in our model we do not consider standards and we aggregate the concepts of technique and method, as an instance model immediately shows whether actions (in our case called steps) are defined. In contrast to the CBK, SECEVAL focuses on security-related features providing a fine-grained model. In addition, it defines a process for the evaluation of methods, tools and notations. The CBK is implemented as a semantic Wiki [1] and serves as a knowledge base to which queries can be posted. Unlike the CBK, SECEVAL is not implemented yet.

SIQINU (Strategy for understanding and Improving Quality in Use) [12] is an approach defined to evaluate the quality of a product version. It is based on the conceptual framework C-INCAMI (Contextual-Information Need, Concept model, Attribute, Metric and Indicator), which specifies general concepts and relationships for measurement and evaluation. The latter consists of six modules: measurement and evaluation project definition, nonfunctional requirements specification, context specification, measurement design and implementation, evaluation design and implementation, and analysis and recommendation specification. Although C-INCAMI is used for the domain of quality evaluation, we recognized several properties we considered relevant for our approach. Regarding the framework specification technique SIQinU provides an evaluation strategy that is sketched as UML activity diagrams whereas C-INCAMI concepts and relationships are specified as a UML class diagram. We also stick to use UML for graphical representation of our approach and implemented separation of concerns through UML packages.

MOODY [6] proposes an evaluation approach which is based on experiments and centers the attention on practitioners' acceptance of a method, i.e. its pragmatic success, which is defined as "the efficiency and effectiveness with which a method achieves its objectives". Efficiency is related to the effort required to complete a task and effectiveness to the quality of the result. In [6] practitioners use methods and afterwards answer questions about perceived ease of use, perceived usefulness and intention to use. This approach is integrated into SECEVAL (cf. Sect. 5).

Security-Specific Evaluation Approaches. Security-related frameworks often consider concrete software systems for their evaluation. An example is the OWASP RISK RATING METHODOLOGY [5], where the risk for a concrete application or system is estimated. We added vulnerability-dependent features of the OWASP model to SECEVAL, as e.g., the difficulty of detecting or exploiting a vulnerability. Features that are related to a concrete system and the rating of a possible attack are introduced as an extension of SECEVAL, which can be found in Sect. 5.

The i* [13] metamodel is the basis of a vulnerability-centric requirements engineering framework introduced in [14]. The extended, VULNERABILITY-CENTRIC I* METAMODEL aims at analyzing security attacks, countermeasures, and requirements based on vulnerabilities. The metamodel is represented using UML class models.

Another approach that focuses on vulnerabilities is described by Wang et al. [15]. Their concept model is less detailed than the i* metamodel. They create a knowledge base that can be queried using the Semantic Web Rule Language (SWRL) [16]. Unlike our approach, they do not use graphical models.

Moyano et al. [17] provide a CONCEPTUAL FRAMEWORK FOR TRUST MODELS which is also represented using UML. As trust is an abstract concept, which emerges between communication partners, we do not consider it in SECEVAL.

3 Engineering Secure Software and Systems

In the NESSoS project, we address the development of secure software and systems starting from the early phases of the secure Software Development Life Cycle (SDLC). The life cycle on which this section is based [18], considers not only the traditional phases, such as requirements engineering, design, implementation, testing and deployment, but also stresses the relevance of service composition and adaptation. In addition, we have to ensure that the developed software is secure; therefore we include assurance as an orthogonal topic of paramount importance. Another aspect is risk and cost awareness, which is a key research direction we foresee also as transversal since it links security concerns with business.

Figure 1 gives an overview of tools, methods and notations for which information is available in the NESSoS Common Body of Knowledge (CBK) [1] relating them to the phases of the SDLC in which they can be used. The graphical representation includes both the traditional phases and the orthogonal ones mentioned above. On the left bottom corner Fig. 1 includes tools and methods that correspond to a metalevel as they help developers to build more secure software along the whole SDLC: On the one hand the Service Development Environment (SDE) and the CBK, which were already implemented and are available online. On the other hand two methods: our evaluation framework for security artifacts (SECEVAL) and the Microsoft Security Development Lifecycle (SDL) [7].

The CBK provides the descriptions of methods, tools, notations and standards in the area of engineering secure software; several of the tools described in the CBK are integrated in the SDE tool workbench, which allows for connecting and executing tools in a toolchain (see chapter [19]). The amount of these artifacts that support the different phases makes it difficult to select the appropriate ones for a project, lead to the development of the SECEVAL approach that provides a systematic evaluation and comparison of methods, notations and tools, which is further detailed in Sect. 4.

Security Requirements Engineering. The main focus of the requirements engineering phase is to enable the modeling of high-level security requirements of the system under construction. These requirements can be expressed in terms of concepts such as compliance, privacy or trust and should be subsequently mapped into more specific requirements that refer to technical solutions. Indeed, it is important that security requirements are addressed from a higher-level perspective, e.g., in terms of the actors' relationships with each other and by considering

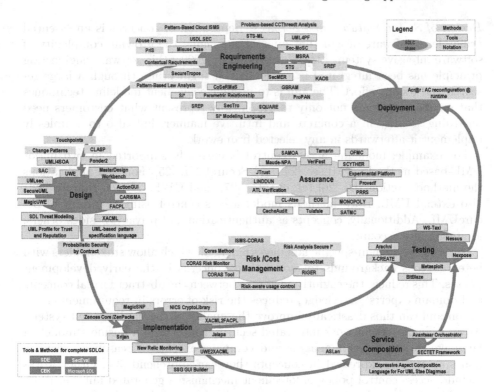

Fig. 1. Overview of Security-Related methods, notations and tools in the SDLC

security not only at the technological level. It is essential to analyze how security may impact on other functional and non-functional requirements, including Quality of Service/Protection (QoS/P), both at design-time and at run-time. In this respect, agent-oriented and goal-oriented approaches such as Secure Tropos [20] and KAOS [21] are currently well recognized as means to explicitly take the stakeholders' perspective into account.

Elicitation, specification – in particular modeling and documentation – and verification of security requirements is a major challenge and will be even more relevant in applications in the Future Internet (FI), as systems are becoming more autonomous [22]. A significant number of methods has been proposed to elicit and analyze security requirements, but there is a lack of empirical comparative evaluations that support decisions to favor one over another. The SECEVAL approach was developed to close this gap.

For the evaluation it is important to define the relevant research objectives, i.e. which are the criteria for a comparison and selection. For example: "Which methods exist that support the elicitation of security requirements for the embedded domain?" or "Which notations can be used for the specification of security requirements of web applications?"

Design of Secure Software and Services. Separation of concerns is an essential principle of software design that aims at managing the growing complexity of software intensive systems [23]. Since the early 2000's this software engineering principle has been integrated in model-driven engineering, through a large research and tooling effort. The aim is to provide convenient modeling techniques that enable developers not only to graphically represent what customers need regarding security in a concrete and intuitive manner, but also to seamlessly implement it afterwards in any selected framework.

For example, modeling access control is currently supported in two major UML-based methods: UMLsec [24] and SecureUML [25]. For web applications the methods ActionGUI [26] (cf. chapter [27]) and UWE [28] (cf. chapter [29]) also extend UML. Both methods model access control using a variant of SecureUML. Additionally, concepts as authentication and privacy, besides others, are taken into account.

Alternative domain-specific languages emerged, which allow stakeholders with heterogeneous backgrounds to model their concerns in the early development phases. This reduces the cognitive distance between the abstract formal concepts and domain experts' knowledge, reduces the risk of errors in requirements elicitation and can thus drastically improve the quality of the implemented system. As an example, recent work integrated security concerns in a business modeling language to let project managers and company executives reason on security issues on models expressed in concepts they can apprehend [30]. Other works include access control policy enforcement mechanisms generated automatically from high-level requirements models. The policies need to be submitted to checks in order to ensure security aspects being modeled are preserved in the code [31].

Effective methods and tools to deal with security concerns in design models are needed to manage the major threat of increasing cost to deploy, fix and maintain security mechanisms. If we are able to design abstract models for these concerns, they are much more difficult to understand at the code level, and even more difficult to maintain, because of all the technical details introduced at the code level.

The selection of appropriate methods and corresponding tools for the design of secure applications remains a crucial decision and definitely will influence other phases of the SDLC. A typical research question could be: "Are there any tools that support secure web engineering and that can be used by non-experts?" or "Which UML CASE tools support model-driven development with reduced learning effort?"

Implementation of Secure Applications. Many security vulnerabilities arise from programming errors that allow for their exploitation. For example, the OWASP top ten list [9] for web application security flaws, clearly shows how coding issues as injection, cross scripting and generally speaking wrong programming practices are major issues to be tackled. The aim is therefore to use languages and tools that minimize this threat. This can be partially achieved by emphasizing the use of well-known programming principles and best practices in secure software development. In particular, language extensions or security patterns can be used during development to guarantee adherence to best practices.

The main focus of this research area is not only language based security, secure coding principles and practices but also programming platforms enforcing security properties. Indeed, reliable programming environments are crucial to minimize the presence of exploitable vulnerabilities in software-based services. Research questions for selecting appropriate languages, methods and programming environments are: "What are common security flaws in applications implemented with C++?" and "Which methods and tools exists to harden the application against these vulnerabilities?"

Testing. The implemented software has to be tested in different ways; both if it fulfills the structural and functional goals, i.e. it has to be checked whether the requirements are all achieved and it has to be tested for bugs. In particular, security testing consists of verifying that data is safe and of ensuring functionality.

The following are typical research questions that could be defined for the selection of appropriate vulnerability scanners for web applications. "Which vulnerability scanners are available for testing security features of web applications?", "Can these scanners run on Microsoft Windows, be freeware or provide at least a free trial version and come with a command line or web interface?"

Deployment. When deploying applications at the end of the build process, this is the appropriate moment to evaluate runtime characteristics of the applications in the context of the real environment. Deployment reviews for security focus on evaluating security design and implementation and the configuration of the application and the network. The objective is to verify if the settings of the web server are correct like the configuration of file encryption, the use of authentication and the applied personalization issues. Within the scope of the Microsoft SDL, a checklist for the deployment reviews is provided, which includes, e.g., checks for latest patches, installed updates or strong passwords. A research question that arises in the deployment context is "Which methods support systematic deployment reviews?"

Service Composition and Adaptation. The capability to achieve trustworthy secure composition is a main requirement in security engineering. Building secure services that cannot be further composed is an inherent obstacle that needs to be avoided. The integration and interoperability of services in order to tailor and enhance new services require adapting the service interfaces at different levels, including the semantic level. Another aspect to consider include assessing the trustworthiness of composition of services.

Integration and interoperability of services, is achieved among others using techniques such as semantic annotations and secure adaptation contracts, as well as decentralized secure composition and distributed component models. Services and components need to be more open, with clearer interfaces and need to be easily accessible from known repositories. Moreover, a research question could investigate for example techniques that provide security measures for composed services [18].

Assurance. During the SDLC, there is a need to ensure security from many perspectives. On the one hand, the security design decisions and the choices of security mechanisms that are used must fulfil the identified security requirements. On the other hand, it is important that engineers are able to select the appropriate mechanisms for implementing required security features.

As shown in Fig. 1 many tools were implemented to check different security aspects of software that is under development. The focus of the assurance activities are: (1) Security support for service composition languages; (2) Run time and platform support for security enforcement; and (3) Security support for programming languages, aiming for verification. For example, tools such as Dafny [32] (for Dafny programs) and Verifast [33] (for C and Java programs) address assurance aspects in order to verify correctness, i.e. that software fulfills their requirements. A research question regarding methods and tools could be: "Which are helpful tools for assessing the trustworthiness of a system under development?"

Risk and Cost Management. The value of security solutions and their return on investment must be demonstrated from a business oriented perspective. Therefore, risk analysis plays an important role when selecting security solutions and implementing security measures. The integration of risk and cost analysis in the whole SDLC, and an extension of the overall approach towards execution time, is the necessary response to these needs.

The main objective of the identification and assessment of risks and the analysis of the costs of associated countermeasures is to exploit an engineering process that optimizes value-for-money in terms of minimizing effective risk, while keeping costs low and justified. A set of methods and tools are available in this context, among others those of the CORAS tool suite [34].

Relevant research questions in the area of security risk and associated cost management are: "What are most appropriate methodologies for performing risk management and cost assessment through the complete SDLC?" and "Which tools support conduction of risk management?"

4   Systematic Evaluation of Engineering Approaches

This section, which is an extension of [3], provides the description of SECEVAL, a conceptual evaluation framework for methods, notations and tools supporting the development of secure software and systems. The framework can be used to collect security-related data and to describe security-relevant metrics, using them for reasoning and obtaining the appropriate techniques for a specific project. An example for a simple evaluation is required to answer the question posted in the implementation phase: "Which library for authentication should be used?" A more elaborated one could be the evaluation of risks for a concrete software system, which is a question that is relevant for all SDLC phases.

The conceptual framework comprises a structural part and a behavioral part, defined as a model for evaluation and an evaluation process, respectively. For the graphical representation of the evaluation model a UML class diagram was chosen; the evaluation process is represented as a UML activity diagram. In the remainder of the section, we present the requirements engineering work done to elicit the main steps of the process, followed by the main concepts of SecEval.

4.1   Evaluation Process

We start by eliciting the requirements of such a framework, i.e. which stakeholders are involved, which concepts play a role in secure software and evaluation of methods, tools and notations, and how those concepts are related. Therefore, the first step was to name common stakeholders for secure software: security engineers (i.e. security designers and developers), normal users of the software and attackers. In some cases, users can attack software without being aware of it, e.g., when they have a virus installed on their computer. We consider those users also attackers, as well as developers which are, e.g., trying to smuggle malicious code into software. Figure 2 depicts stakeholders and use cases in a UML use case diagram.

We grouped use cases based on their purpose in evaluation and development use cases. The Evaluation package at the top contains all use cases related to collecting, reasoning and selecting, e.g., tools, whereas the package Development at the bottom of the diagram refers to security-related tasks within the SDLC, such as identification of security requirements, design and implementation of these security requirements, identification and patch of vulnerabilities. The «include» dependencies show the order these use cases have in the SDLC: implementing secure software requires having a design, and a design implies that requirements were elicited beforehand. Both, the attacker and the security engineer can identify vulnerabilities, whereas the former usually attacks them and the latter tries to patch them, which is modeled using an «extend» dependency. Those patches can then be installed by users (which also might happen by using an automatic update function).

From time to time, tasks within the development package require evaluation activities to respond for example to questions like "Which tool should be used for gathering security requirements or for designing secure web applications?". In fact, for security experts it is helpful to be aware of common security methods and tools that can be used for a specific task. For further examples of research questions related to the different SDLC phases the reader is referred to Sect. 3.

Figure 3 depicts the process of working with SecEval, which is represented as a UML activity diagram. The first step of the process is the data collection based on the defined research questions. Therefore different sources (as papers, reports, websites, ...) are gathered, which are then analyzed in the second step. This analysis process consists of extracting information from the data collected, activating some reasoning activities and expressing the results using SecEval's security context model. Notice that this process has to be adapted (and usually simplified) for a specific evaluation. Writing down the exact process might not always be necessary, as many tasks can be executed in parallel or in any order (indicated by horizontal bars).

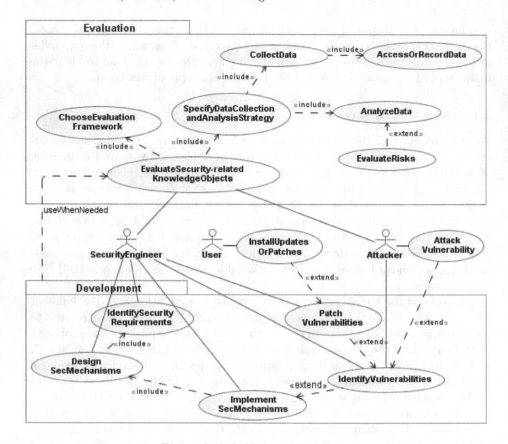

Fig. 2. Stakeholders and Use Cases

In practice the basic ingredients of the evaluation process are a set of tasks that has to be performed and information pieces relevant for these tasks. Tasks are represented as UML activities like select queries, execute search/experiments and define filters. Information pieces are represented as objects in the UML model showing which input is required for a task and which are the results. Examples for identified objects are: research question, used resource, query, filter and criterion.

4.2 Systematic Evaluation – Model Overview

The use cases from our requirements analysis and the objects of the evaluation process were a starting point to identify relevant concepts related to security for using and evaluating methods, notations and tools during the software engineering process. We clustered these concepts in three packages: Security Context, Data Collection and Data Analysis. Figure 4 shows the model represented as a UML class diagram that can be instantiated with concrete methods, tools and notations whenever needed.

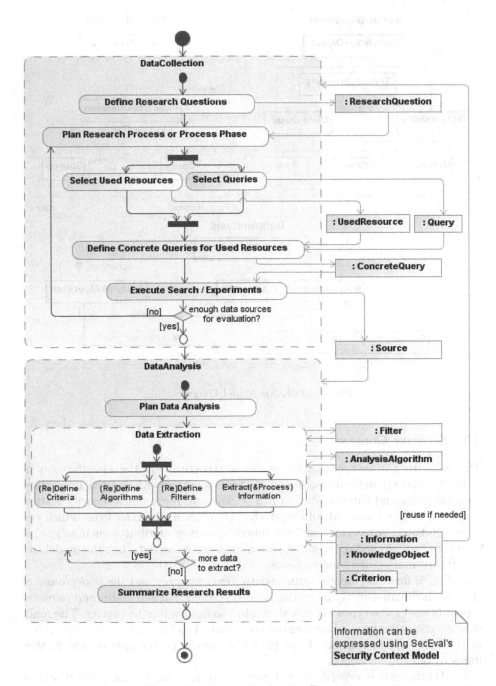

Fig. 3. SECEVAL's Evaluation Process

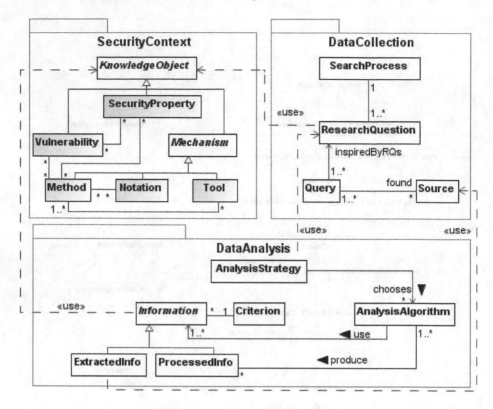

Fig. 4. SecEval: Model Overview [3]

4.3 Security Context

The Security Context package provides a structure for the classification of (security-related) methods, notations and tools together with security properties, vulnerabilities and threats. Within this package we represent a security feature as a class element and introduce an abstract class `Mechanism` from which the classes `Method`, `Notation` and `Tool` inherit common attributes such as `goals`, `costs`, `basedOnStandards`, etc. We focus on security aspects, but the model can also record non-security mechanisms.

In Fig. 5, for convenience enumerations' texts are grey and the background of classes which can directly be instantiated is colored. All attributes and roles are typed; however the types are not shown in the figures due to brevity. The main characteristics of the class `Mechanism` are specified as boolean types (can.., has.., is..). In an implementation of our model, it should be possible to add further items to the enumerations.

A Mechanism is described by a problem statement, by the goals it strives for, by its costs and by the consequences it implies. Mechanisms can be based on standards or be standardized themselves. Before applying a mechanism, the preconditions that are necessary for using it have to be fulfilled. Furthermore, an

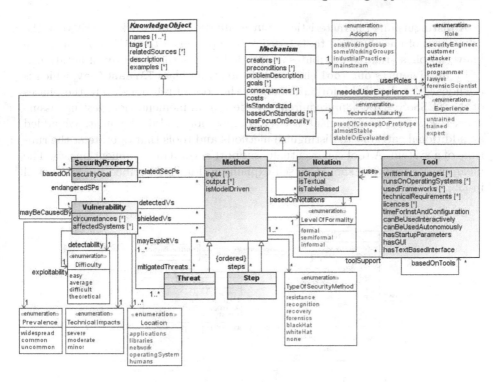

Fig. 5. SECEVAL: Security Context [3]

estimation regarding technical maturity and adoption in practice should be given. Several levels of usability can be stated indicating the experience users need in order to employ a mechanism, e.g., they need to be experts.

The classes METHOD, TOOL and NOTATION inherit all these properties from the class **Mechanism** and have their own characteristics defined by a set of specific attributes. For example, a METHOD has some general attributes, such as input, output and if it is model-driven. These attributes are used to describe the method at a high level of abstraction. Note that a method or step can be supported by notations or tools. These facts are represented in the model with corresponding associations between the classes.

For a NOTATION, we consider characteristics such as whether the notation is graphical, textual or based on a tabular representation. We also added a level of formality, which ranges from informal to formal. Notations can be based on other notations, for example many context-specific extensions for UML exist.

The description of a TOOL is given among others by the information of languages it is written in, operating systems it supports, frameworks it uses and licenses under which it is released. A tool can be based on other tools, which is the case when libraries are used or when plugins are written.

A distinguishing characteristic of our evaluation framework SECEVAL is the refinement of methods and tools based on the phases of the SDLC. As far as we know, no phase-related attributes are needed to describe features of notations.

Figure 6 depicts our `Tool` class and the abstract class `TAreasOfDev`, which is a wildcard for detailed information about the tool in relationship to the phases of the NESSoS SDLC [35]: requirements, design, implementation, testing, assurance, risk & cost management, service composition and deployment. We added an additional category to distinguish methods and tools that operate at the runtime of a system. A tool can eventually support several development phases. The meaning of attributes should be self-explaining, but is described in more detail in [36].

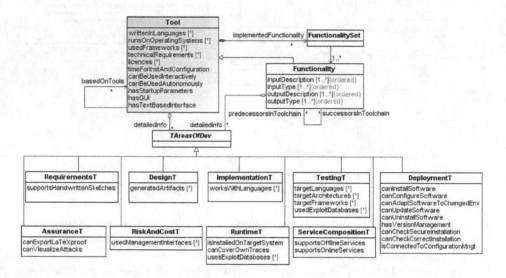

Fig. 6. Security Context: Details of Tools

Similarly, a method can be redefined according to the phases in the SDLC it covers, as depicted in Fig. 7. For example a method, such as Microsoft's Security Development Lifecycle [7], can be used as a basis for designing secure applications, but also covers other phases. In this case, the attributes of the classes `DesignM` and `ImplementationM` and others would be used to describe this method.

As seen before, a tool supports a certain method. However, we have not yet defined the quality of this support. Does the tool fully support the method? Does it provide partial support? Which features are not supported? We add this information to the model using the association class `ToolSupportedMethod`, as depicted in Fig. 8 with a dotted line. The association class itself is inherited from the class `Method`, thus can redefine its attributes. For instance, a design tool can partly support a model-driven method (e.g., by facilitating

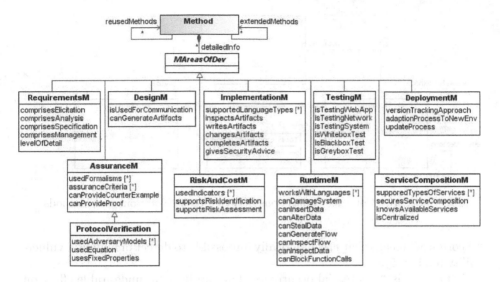

Fig. 7. Security Context: Details of Methods [3]

the modeling process), although it cannot generate artifacts. In this case, DesignM.canGenerateArtifacts (cf. Fig. 7) would be set to false.

A method can extend other methods, which means it might also change them. In this case the role **extendedMethods** should be further specified, we recommend to add an association class which inherits from the class **Method** (similar to the association between method and tool). In this way, it can be exactly described if and how the original methods are modified. It is also possible that other methods are used without any changes (role **usesMethods**).

We adopted the abstract class KNOWLEDGEOBJECT which is used in the CBK as a super class for all elements which are described by SECEVAL. In SECEVAL, we applied separation of concerns so that only very general descriptions remain as attributes in a knowledge object, which can be applied to all elements (cf. Fig. 5). Therefore, the class **KnowledgeObject** has associated names, tags and related sources, which could be any kinds of sources, as publications or URLs. We represent security issues, such as confidentiality, integrity and privacy by the class SECURITY PROPERTY. The attribute **SecurityGoal**, which is denoted by a string, describes the goal of the property. For instance "integrity refers to the trustworthiness of data or resources" [37].

A VULNERABILITY is "a weakness that makes it possible for a threat to occur" [37]. Thus, it endangers security properties. Examples are XSS, SQL Injection, Buffer Overflows, etc. The objective of certain methods is to detect vulnerabilities or shield them from being exploited by a threat. Every vulnerability is located at least in one location (which is modeled as a UML enumeration). Furthermore, we include the categorization scheme from OWASP TOP 10 [9] (which is adapted from the OWASP Risk Rating Methodology [5]) using prevalence, impact level, detectability and exploitability. Regarding the latter two roles, the **Difficulty**

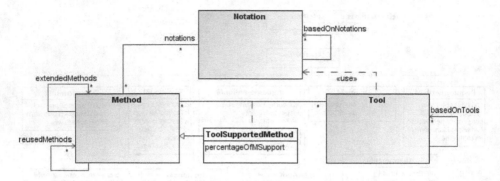

Fig. 8. Security Context: Connections between Tools, Notations and Methods

"theoretical" means that it is practically impossible to detect or exploit a vulnerability (cf. Fig. 5).

A THREAT is "a potential occurrence that can have an undesirable effect on the system assets or resources" [37, p.498]. We treat a threat as a kind of method which is vicious. At least one vulnerability has to be involved, otherwise a threat is not malicious (and the other way around), which is denoted by the multiplicity [1..*]. Additionally, threats can be mitigated by other methods.

4.4 Data Collection

High-quality data is the basis needed to obtain good evaluation results. Therefore we create a rigorous schema which describes a set of properties that have to be defined before starting collecting data. The model we build contains all the relevant features needed during data collection. It is a approach based on Kitchenham's systematic literature review [10]. Conversely to Kitchenham's approach, we do not restrict ourselves to reviewing literature; we also include information about tools which cannot always be found in papers, but on websites and on information which is obtained from benchmarks or experiments.

Data collection comprises among others a search process that can be performed in different ways, e.g., the search can be automated or not, or it can be a depth-first or a breadth-first search (c.f. Fig. 9). Depth-first means, that the aim of a search is to extract a lot of detail information about a relatively small topic, whereas a breadth-first search is good to get an overview of a broader topic.

Similar to Kitchenham's literature review, research questions are used to define the corner stones and the goals of the search. Please note that for us the term "research" does not necessarily refer to *scientific* research. Queries can be derived from research questions. As different search engines support different types of queries, concrete queries are specific for each resource, as e.g., Google Scholar. Queries can also refer to questions which are used as a basis for experiments (cf. Sect. 6). In addition, resources that will serve as data sources for the evaluation need to be chosen. If a concrete query matches sources, as papers, websites or personal answers, we classify the source at least by author and

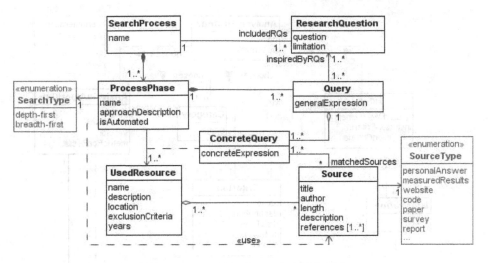

Fig. 9. SECEVAL: Data Collection [3]

description (as an abstract) and provide information about the type of source and at least one reference where to find it. The process of data collection and data analysis is depicted in Fig. 3.

In Fig. 9 the use of an association class for `ConcreteQuery` (depicted by a dashed line) denotes that for each pair of `ProcessPhase` and `UsedResource`, the class `ConcreteQuery` is instantiated. The concrete search expression is derived from a general search expression.

For example, the general search expression could be "recent approaches in Security Engineering" and we want to ask Google Scholar and a popular researcher. For Google Scholar we could use ""Security Engineering" 2012..2013" as a concrete search expression and the concrete expression for asking a researcher could read: "I'm interested in Security Engineering. Which recent approaches in Security Engineering do you know?"

4.5   Data Analysis

Data is collected with the purpose to obtain an answer to research questions based on the analysis of the data.

Figure 10 depicts relevant concepts for analyzing data. First, we have to specify which type of strategy we want to use. Are we limited to quantitative analysis or do we focus on qualitative analysis? Accordingly, one can later refer to Kitchenham's checklists for quantitative and qualitative studies [10] to ensure the quality of the own answers to the research questions.

The analysis strategy defines which algorithm is employed and makes sure that the result of the algorithm fits to a criterion regarding meaning and metric. The algorithm does not have to be executable on a computer, but it might be implemented by a tool.

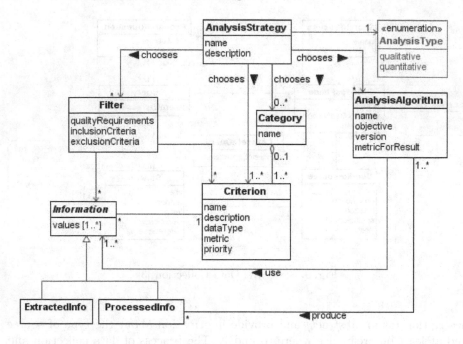

Fig. 10. SecEval: Data Analysis [3]

Criteria can be grouped by categories. A criterion gives more information about data values as it defines the data type (string, list of booleans, ..) and the metric (milliseconds, ..). In addition, a priority can be defined which is useful when methods, tools or notations should be compared.

Information can be extracted from the sources which were found in the data collection phase (see «use» dependency starting from the class ExtractedInfo in Fig. 4), or they can be processed using an analysis algorithm.

For example, a relation IsCompatible_NxN_ToolIO can be seen as instances of an analysis algorithm. It expresses that "two notations are compatible if there exists a tool chain that can transform the first given notation into the second one" [35]. In this case, the algorithm might contain the depth-first search for a tool-chain consisting of tools where the output of one tool serves as input for the second one. The automation of such an algorithm is challenging, because in- and output of tools may differ.

Besides, a filter can be specified to disqualify results according to certain criteria as costs or quality. This filter is finer grained than the filter that is defined by UsedResource's attribute exclusionCriteria used in the data collection, which only can be based on obvious criteria, such as the language the source is written in. In addition to this, the filter for data analysis accesses information as well as criteria and thus can exclude, e.g., methods, tools or notations from the evaluation that do not meet a high-priority requirement.

A valid question is how information, criteria and the security context model fit together. This is shown in Fig. 4: information can be stored in an instance of our security context model, which provides a sound basis when collecting data about methods, tools and notations. Consequently, the attributes `name` and `dataType` of a `Criterion` can be left blank when information is stored in an instance of our model, as attributes have a name and are typed. However, these attributes are needed when describing information which is not directly related to an instance of an artifact or not meaningful without their connection to a concrete analysis process.

Contrary to the context model, neither the collection of data nor the data analysis are security specific and thus can be applied in the same way to other domains.

5   Extensions of SecEval

As stated in the introduction, the core of SECEVAL cannot include all attributes which could be needed in the future. Therefore, SECEVAL's models are extensible, which means that users can add classes and attributes for their domain of research. In this section, we introduce an extension to show how SECEVAL can be enhanced in order to support OWASP's Risk Rating Methodology [5]. In addition, we provide an extension for Moody's method evaluation approach [6].

OWASP's Risk Rating. To rate risks for concrete IT systems is a common task for security engineers. OWASP's Risk Rating Methodology provides categories and terms for this task. Figure 11 depicts the extended model whereby added connections use thick line linkings.

The class `Threat`, known from the basic context model, inherits its features to a concrete `Attack`. The severity of the risk (which is an attribute of `Threat`) can be calculated by likelihood multiplied with impact. The likelihood is derived from the factors which describe the vulnerabilities and the threat agents, whereas the impact is determined by the concrete technical and business-related consequences. Therefore, each enumerations' literal is mapped to a likelihood rating from 0 to 9. For more information the interested reader is referred to [5].

Moody's Method Evaluation Approach. Experimental approaches are used to evaluate the success of using a method in practice. Our extension of SECEVAL to express Moody's concepts is shown in Fig. 12: we introduce a `Test` class that is connected to at least one method and vice versa. The test uses the method on at least one example and is executed by `TestingParticipants`. Each participant assesses the method using Moody's evaluation criteria:

- "Actual Efficiency: the effort required to apply a method.
- Actual Effectiveness: the degree to which a method achieves its objectives.
- Perceived Ease of Use: the degree to which a person believes that using a particular method would be free of effort.

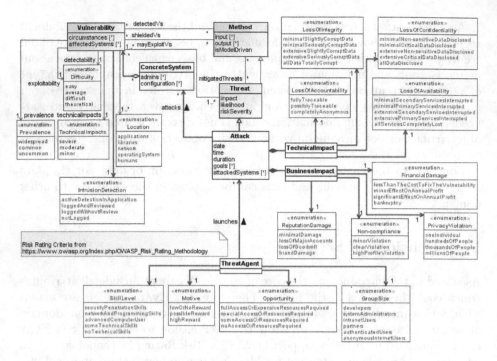

Fig. 11. Inclusion of basic risk evaluation approach

- Perceived Usefulness: the degree to which a person believes that a particular method will be effective in achieving its intended objectives.
- Intention to Use: the extent to which a person intends to use a particular method.
- Actual Usage: the extent to which a method is used in practice" [6].

Usually, the average value of the participants' results is used as final evaluation result for the method under test.

6   Validation of the Evaluation Approach

The soundness of our SECEVAL evaluation approach is proved by a case study on security testing of web applications.

Web applications are the focus of many attacks. Thus, many methods such as "penetration testing" or "vulnerability scanning" are used to identify security flaws. These methods are supported by many commercial and open-source tools and frequently it is not easy to decide which one is the more suitable for the tests to be performed. In this section, we use our SECEVAL approach to evaluate vulnerability scanners for web applications.

Data Collection. According to the SECEVAL approach the first step consists of specifying the data that should be collected. This is done by an instance model as

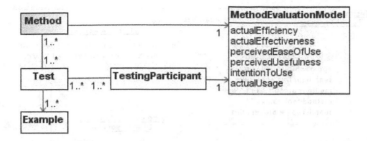

Fig. 12. Method extension using Moody's method evaluation approach

shown in Fig. 13, which depicts instances of the classes we have already defined in Fig. 9. For example, instances of the class `ResearchQuestion` define two research questions, a high-level and a concrete one. We used identical background colors for instances of the same classes and omitted all `name` attributes in case a name (e.g., `p3`) is given in the header of an instance.

Research question `q1` ("Which security-related tools and methods are available and how do they compare?", cf. Fig. 13) is very general. In the first process phase `p1`, 13 methods and 18 tools were selected [38]. More detailed information was gathered in the second process phase `p2` about: vulnerability scanning, penetration testing, fuzzing and the classification into black- grey- and white-box testing. Examples for tools are WSFuzzer, X-Create and WS-Taxi, just to mention a few. As we already added most of the methods and tools we found to the CBK [1], we focus on `q2` in this section.

Research question `q2` ("Which vulnerability scanners are available for testing security features of web applications?") is a typical question which could be asked by security engineers working in a company. The "sources" (i.e., tools) we selected for analysis were [39]: a) Acunetix Web Vulnerability Scanner[1], b) Mavituna Security - Netsparker[2], c) Burp Scanner[3], d) Wapiti[4], e) Arachni[5], f) Nessus[6], g) Nexpose[7] and h) Nikto[8].

The instance `experienceWithTestScenario` describes how the data is gathered by testing the vulnerability scanners. Please note that SECEVAL does not impose the completion of the data collection phase before the data is analyzed. This means that the tests were partly executed on tools which were later classified as inappropriate. This becomes clear when we think of how evaluation works in practice: sometimes we have to collect a bunch of data before we observe information which, e.g., leads to the exclusion of a tool from the result set.

---

[1] Acunetix. http://www.acunetix.com

[2] Netsparker. https://www.mavitunasecurity.com/netsparker

[3] Burp Scanner. http://portswigger.net/burp/scanner.html

[4] Wapiti. http://www.ict-romulus.eu/web/wapiti

[5] Arachni. http://www.arachni-scanner.com

[6] Nessus. http://www.tenable.com/de/products/nessus

[7] Nexpose. https://www.rapid7.com/products/nexpose

[8] Nikto. http://www.cirt.net/Nikto2

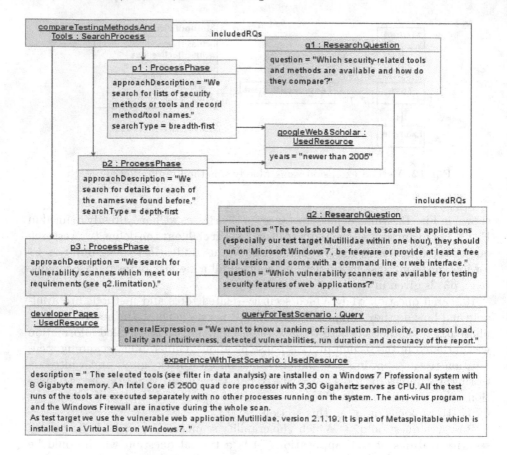

Fig. 13. Case Study: Data Collection

Data Analysis. The analysis phase consists in defining the analysis strategy and selecting a filter that enforces the requirements (`limitations`) defined for question q2. Figure 14 depicts instances of the data analysis model we defined in Fig. 10.

Before going into detail about particular results of our experiments, we first take a look at the overall result regarding our research question q2. Figure 14 thus depicts an instance of the class `ProcessedInfo`, which is called `weightedResult Values`.

Only four tools passed our filter: Arachni and Nikto, which provide command-line interfaces and Nessus and Nexpose, which also provide web interfaces. From our list of tools from above, the trial of *a*) only allows to scan predefined sites. Tools *b*) and *c*) do not support a command line or web interface in the versions that are free. A run of tool *d*) on our test target Multidae[9] took six hours.

---

[9] NOWASP (Mutillidae). http://sourceforge.net/projects/mutillidae

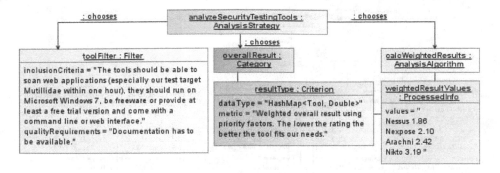

Fig. 14. Case Study: Data Analysis – Results [3]

Apart from information available online, we experimented with the tools that passed the filter, in order to obtain data for our tool evaluation (q2). We evaluated the following criteria (and weighted them as indicated in the brackets, cf. `queryForTestScenario`):

- Installation simplicity (0.5)
  Do any problems occur during installation?
- Costs (1)
  How much do the tool cost? Is it a one-time payment or an annual license?
- Processor load (1)
  How high is the CPU load while running the scanner
- Clarity and intuitiveness (1)
  Is the tool easy to understand, clearly structured and user-friendly
- Run duration (1)
  How long does a scan take?
- Quality of the report (2)
  How detailed is the report of the scan? Which information does it contain?
- Number of detected vulnerabilities (4)
  How many vulnerabilities does the tool detect on our test environment?

As we can see in Fig. 14, an algorithm is involved, which calculates results according to a rating. The rating is depicted in Fig. 15.

Lower factors of a criterions' priority denote that we consider the criterion less important. Table 1 contains the measured results as well as the average[10] and weighted[11] results.

In addition, we show how intermediate values of our tests could be described in our data analysis model in Fig. 16, as e.g., the costs of the tools or the operating systems it runs on. Concrete instances of `Information` classes are not depicted; the interested reader is referred to [39].

---

[10] AVG: average

[11] WAVG: weighted average according to ratings

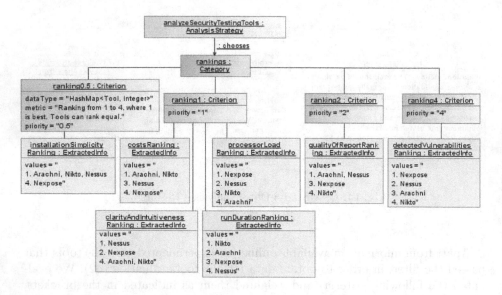

Fig. 15. Case Study: Data Analysis – Ratings

Table 1. Case Study: Final Tool Ranking (adapted from [39])

Tool	Inst.	Costs	CPU	Clarity	Time	Vuln.	Report	AVG[10]	WAVG[11]
Nessus	1	2	2	1	4	1	2	1,86	1,86
Arachni	1	1	4	4	2	1	3	2,29	2,42
Nexpose	4	4	1	2	3	3	1	2,57	2,10
Nikto	1	1	3	4	1	4	4	2,57	3,19

Security Context Model. We integrated all four tools into the NESSoS tool work-bench, called SDE [40]. If they are executed from within the SDE, URL and port of the web application under test have to be provided by the user. To try out the vulnerability scanners it is possible to use Multidae as a target, as we did above. Multidae comes with Metasploitable[12], an intentionally vulnerable Linux virtual machine. Therefore, the default configuration for the integrated SDE tools point to a local Multidae instance, but can be changed at any time.

As SECEVAL's context model is more detailed, we modeled the context of vulnerability scanning of web applications and two of the tested tools: Nessus and Nikto. Figure 17 shows an instance diagram of the context model, which we have already depicted in Fig. 5. The association between vulnerabilities, as well as further supported methods are not depicted in Fig. 5; the interested reader is referred to the model example that can be downloaded [36].

---

[12] Metasploitable.
   http://www.offensive-security.com/metasploit-unleashed/Metasploitable

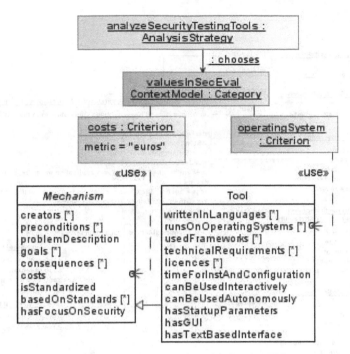

Fig. 16. Case Study: Data Analysis – Values

The vulnerabilities that are modeled are the top 3 from OWASP's top 10 project 2013 [9]. Vulnerabilities may be caused by other vulnerabilities, for example invalidated input can lead to injection vulnerabilities.

We recommend using additional classes for extensions, such as a class to detail a test run, using attributes as run duration or processor load. Although building the instance model was straight forward, our experience with SECEVAL and the UML CASE tool MagicDraw showed us that the layout is not inviting to read the containing information. Consequently, we are looking forward to a future implementation of SECEVAL as a kind of semantic Wiki, as described in the following section.

7   Towards an Implementation of SecEval

Currently, we are implementing the concept of SECEVAL as a flexible web application. The aim is to provide a Wiki-like knowledge base for software and security engineers as well as for developers. Advantages of a web-based implementation of SECEVAL would be that connections to existing elements (like other methods or vulnerabilities), can be added without building the knowledge base from scratch and that data sets of previous evaluations remain available for future research.

The SECEVAL Wiki will support the following use cases: (1) viewing Knowledge Objects (knowledge objects), (2) editing knowledge objects, (3) importing external information and (4) searching for information to answer research

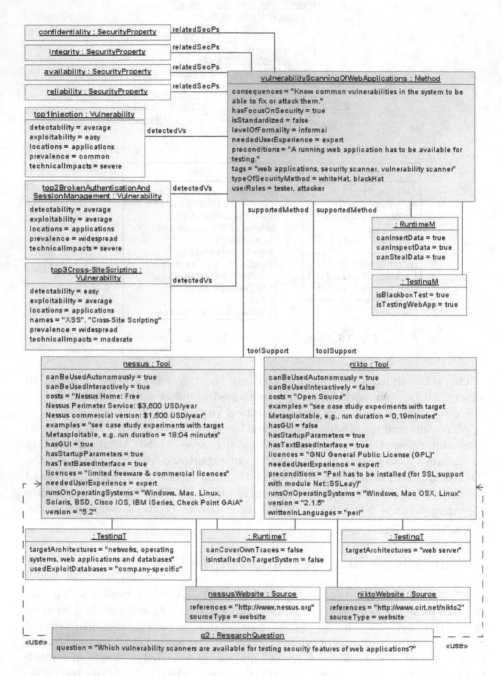

Fig. 17. Case Study: Instances of the Context Model (excerpt) [3]

questions, which can result in executing a tool-supported SECEVAL evaluation process.

Viewing knowledge objects. For the implementation of SECEVAL's context model, we experiment with a system that provides three views on each knowledge object:

- A *tabular view* that shows attributes' values, grouped by classes (presented as boxes) of SECEVAL's models. Which attributes are shown can be defined by the user. This view is especially useful for comparing knowledge objects.
- A *UML view* that presents an instance model of SECEVAL's UML model. The advantage of this view is that it is easy to examine links between several knowledge objects.
- A view that shows *continuous text*, enriched by boxes that can be placed between paragraphs or beside the text, similar to Wikipedia[13].

The user should be able to switch between these views at any time.

Editing knowledge objects. When creating a new element in the Wiki, the page is empty at first and shown in the *continuous text view* so that text can by written and structured by headings and paragraphs immediately, like in most Wikis. Additionally, on the side of the screen, common attributes are presented in a sidebar which can be dragged onto the Wiki page in order to fill them with actual values and to arrange them within the text or in boxes. These attributes correspond to attributes from SECEVAL models. For example, the user can specify some attributes of the `Tool` class, as technical requirements, licenses or the language the tool is written in.

Usually, information about knowledge objects has already been stored in continuous text form. In such a case, the application should allow to easily mark text and to click on an attribute on the sidebar. The attribute is then linked to the text so that it changes automatically when the text is altered. It is important to store previous versions not only for continuous text, but also for attributes, as both can easily be changed or deleted.

For the sidebar (which is resizable up to full-screen) it is also useful to implement different views, for example:

- a *UML view*, showing the full SECEVAL class diagrams for experts. This is the counterpart to the instance view for a concrete entry of the Wiki.
- an *auto-suggestion view* in which single attributes are shown according to an attribute-based suggestion system. This system can then recommend attributes which seem to be useful in the current context, as e.g., attributes of testing tools, as soon as it becomes clear that a user describes a tool from the domain of testing.

Recommendation includes that the system needs to explain rules inferred by SECEVAL , as e.g. that it is useful to describe a tool and a corresponding notation in two separate entries, even if the notation has only been used by this tool so

---

[13] Wikipedia. `https://www.wikipedia.org/`

far. A focus is on the connection between several knowledge objects in our SEC-
EVAL system and on the possibility to add data which is not only associated
with one knowledge object, as e.g., evaluation results.

Importing external information. Another useful feature is syndication, i.e. to be
able to insert text from other web pages, as from Wikipedia or from vulnerability
management systems, which are correctly cited and updated automatically. This
task could be eased by step-by-step wizards and good attribute recommendation
according to the attributes selected so far and the information provided. For
example, if the user inserts the URL of a Wikipedia article, the article is displayed
in a window that allows selecting passages and to transfer them to the SECEVAL
system immediately, along with a linked cite.

Another requirement is the import of text from PDF files. Hereby, a challenge
is to deal with licensed books or papers, because citing small passages is usually
allowed, whereas publishing the whole document in the web is prohibited.

Searching for information to answer research questions. In addition to the implementation of SECEVAL's context model, the application should support the
process of collecting and analyzing data to answer a concrete research question.

Simple questions can be answered using a full-text search. More complex
questions can involve several knowledge objects and their attributes, so that the
search function has to be able to rely on the associations between knowledge
objects stored in the knowledge base.

If the requested information cannot be found in the knowledge base, a wizard
might suggest using SECEVAL's process to collect and analyze information. Ideally, the wizard allows jumping between several process steps while offering to
record information for SECEVAL's data collection and data analysis models. The
users can decide whether their research question should be public[14]. At the end
of a complex evaluation process, artifacts as research questions, used sources and
the concrete approach of a research can be published to save time and money in
case a similar question will arise again in the future.

A general requirement for our implementation is the usability of the interface.
For example, the CBK provides a complex search function, but it turned out that
it is rarely used, because attributes have to be selected by using their technical,
short names. For SECEVAL, it might be helpful to present descriptions and to
suggest attributes according to a catalogue that learns how users tend to name
a concept. Ideally, this search does not require a complex interface, but supports
the user with auto-completion or wizards when typing a query into a text box.

8   Conclusions

We presented a conceptual framework, called SECEVAL, for the structured evaluation of so-called knowledge objects – methods, tools, notations, security properties,

---

[14] Discussions can also help to answer a research question, therefore it is desirable to
connect the Wiki with question/answer systems as, e.g., Stackoverflow
`http://stackoverflow.com/`.

vulnerabilities and threats – in the area of secure software. SECEVAL is based on the structured literature review by Kitchenham et al. [10] and inspired by the C-INCAMI framework of Becker et al. [12], to name a few. Our approach is designed to ease the process of doing research or obtaining pragmatic answers in the area of security whether the research question aims at scientific or engineering issues.

SECEVAL is represented as a UML model and follows the separation of concerns principles. These concerns are:

- *An evaluation process* that specifies the set of tasks and information pieces needed to evaluate methods, tools and notation in the security area.
- *A security context model* for describing features of the security-relevant knowledge objects.
- *A data collection model* that records the way how data is gathered. It mainly comprises the research question, collection process, used resources and the queries for finding sources that might be used to answer the question.
- *An analysis model* which defines the analysis strategy and the filters and algorithms it uses on the collected sources. Furthermore, the data structure for information is exactly specified, regardless of whether the data is to be stored in the security context model or not.

An advantage of our context model is that it can describe tools and methods according to their placement within the software development life cycle. In case SECEVAL does not provide all attributes for expressing elements of related domains, it can easily be extended, as demonstrated for Moody's method evaluation approach and OWASP's Risk Rating Methodology.

To validate our SECEVAL approach, we performed a case study about methods and tools from the area of security focusing on a research question about the selection of vulnerability scanners for web applications. For the case study all elements were presented as UML objects. To improve the practicability of our approach, we envisioned how an implementation of a SECEVAL knowledge base might look like and which requirements might be important.

Summarizing, SECEVAL provides a sound basis for evaluating research questions related to secure software engineering. This might ease the process of doing research in the area of security no matter whether a research question aims at scientific or engineering issues. In the future we plan to evaluate further research questions using SECEVAL, describing knowledge objects that are security-related and those that are related to other domains. Besides, it would be interesting to implement SECEVAL as a smart and flexible knowledge base and to execute empirical studies to measure the utility of our framework.

References

1. CBK: Common Body of Knowledge (2013), http://nessos-project.eu/cbk
2. NESSoS: Network of Excellence on Engineering Secure Future Internet Software Services and Systems (2014), http://nessos-project.eu/
3. Busch, M., Koch, N., Wirsing, M.: SecEval: An Evaluation Framework for Engineering Secure Systems. In: MoK 2014 (2014)

4. Busch, M., Koch, N.: NESSoS Deliverable D2.4 – Second release of Method and Tool Evaluation (2013)
5. OWASP Foundation: OWASP Risk Rating Methodology (2013), https://www.owasp.org/index.php/OWASP_Risk_Rating_Methodology
6. Moody, D.L.: The method evaluation model: A theoretical model for validating information systems design methods. In: Ciborra, C.U., Mercurio, R., de Marco, M., Martinez, M., Carignani, A. (eds.) ECIS, pp. 1327–1336 (2003)
7. Lipner, S., Howard, M.: The Trustworthy Computing Security Development Lifecycle. Developer Network - Microsoft (2005), http://msdn.microsoft.com/en-us/library/ms995349.aspx#sdl2_topic2_5
8. ISO/IEC: 27001: Information technology – Security techniques – Information security management systems – Requirements. Technical report, International Organization for Standardization (ISO) and International Electrotechnical Commission, IEC (2013)
9. OWASP Foundation: OWASP Top 10 – 2013 (2013), http://owasptop10.googlecode.com/files/OWASPTop10-2013.pdf
10. Kitchenham, B., Charters, S.: Guidelines for performing Systematic Literature Reviews in Software Engineering. Technical Report EBSE 2007-001, Keele University and Durham University Joint Report (2007)
11. Beckers, K., Eicker, S., Heisel, M. (UDE), W.S.: NESSoS Deliverable D5.2 – Identification of Research Gaps in the Common Body of Knowledge (2012)
12. Becker, P., Papa, F., Olsina, L.: Enhancing the Conceptual Framework Capability for a Measurement and Evaluation Strategy. In: 4th International Workshop on Quality in Web Engineering (6360), pp. 1–12 (2013)
13. RWTH Aachen University: i* notation, http://istar.rwth-aachen.de/
14. Elahi, G., Yu, E., Zannone, N.: A vulnerability-centric requirements engineering framework: analyzing security attacks, countermeasures, and requirements based on vulnerabilities. Requirements Engineering 15(1), 41–62 (2010)
15. Wang, J.A., Guo, M.: Security data mining in an ontology for vulnerability management. In: International Joint Conference on Bioinformatics, Systems Biology and Intelligent Computing, IJCBS 2009, pp. 597–603 (2009)
16. RWTH Aachen University: SWRL: A Semantic Web Rule Language Combining OWL and RuleML (2004), http://www.w3.org/Submission/SWRL/
17. Moyano, F., Fernandez-Gago, C., Lopez, J.: A conceptual framework for trust models. In: Fischer-Hübner, S., Katsikas, S., Quirchmayr, G. (eds.) TrustBus 2012. LNCS, vol. 7449, pp. 93–104. Springer, Heidelberg (2012)
18. Fernandez, C., Lopez, J., Moyano, F.: NESSoS Deliverable D4.2 – Engineering Secure Future Internet Services: A Research Manifesto and Agenda from the NESSoS Community (2012)
19. Bertolino, A., Busch, M., Daoudagh, S., Lonetti, F., Marchetti, E.: A Toolchain for Designing and Testing Access Control Policies. In: Heisel, M., Joosen, W., Lopez, J., Martinelli, F. (eds.) Engineering Secure Future Internet Services. LNCS, vol. 8431, pp. 266–286. Springer, Heidelberg (2014)
20. Giorgini, P., Mouratidis, H., Zannone, N.: Modelling Security and Trust with Secure Tropos. In: Integrating Security and Software Engineering: Advances and Future Vision (2006)
21. Dardenne, A., Fickas, S., Van Lamsweerde, A.: Goal-directed Requirements Acquisition 20(1-2), 3–50 (1993)
22. Bresciani, P., Perini, A., Giorgini, P., Giunchiglia, F., Mylopoulos, J.: Tropos: An agent-oriented software development methodology. Autonomous Agents and Multi-Agent Systems 8(3), 203–236 (2004)

23. Gedik, B., Liu, L.: Protecting Location Privacy with Personalized k-anonymity: Architecture and Algorithms 7(1), 1–18 (2008)
24. Jürjens, J.: Secure Systems Development with UML. Springer (2004)
25. Basin, D., Doser, J., Lodderstedt, T.: Model Driven security: From UML Models to Access Control Infrastructures. ACM Trans. Softw. Eng. Methodol. 15(1), 39–91 (2006)
26. Basin, D., Clavel, M., Egea, M., Garcia de Dios, M., Dania, C.: A model-driven methodology for developing secure data-management applications. IEEE Transactions on Software Engineering PP(99), 1 (2014)
27. de Dios, M.A.G., Dania, C., Basin, D., Clavel, M.: Model-driven Development of a Secure eHealth Application. In: Heisel, M., Joosen, W., Lopez, J., Martinelli, F. (eds.) Engineering Secure Future Internet Services. LNCS, vol. 8431, pp. 97–118. Springer, Heidelberg (2014)
28. Busch, M., Knapp, A., Koch, N.: Modeling Secure Navigation in Web Information Systems. In: Grabis, J., Kirikova, M. (eds.) BIR 2011. LNBIP, vol. 90, pp. 239–253. Springer, Heidelberg (2011)
29. Busch, M., Koch, N., Suppan, S.: Modeling Security Features of Web Applications. In: Engineering Secure Future Internet Services. LNCS, vol. 8431, pp. 119–139. Springer, Heidelberg (2014)
30. Goldstein, A., Frank, U.: Augmented Enterprise Models as a Foundation for Generating Security-related Software: Requirements and Prospects. In: Model-Driven Security Workshop in Conjunction with MoDELS 2012 (MDsec 2012). ACM Digital Library (2012)
31. Busch, M., Koch, N., Masi, M., Pugliese, R., Tiezzi, F.: Towards Model-Driven Development of Access Control Policies for Web Applications. In: Model-Driven Security Workshop in Conjunction with MoDELS 2012 (MDsec 2012). ACM Digital Library (2012)
32. Microsoft: Dafny (2014),
    https://research.microsoft.com/en-us/projects/dafny/
33. Jacobs, B., Smans, J., Piessens, F.: VeriFast (2013),
    http://www.cs.kuleuven.be/~bartj/verifast/
34. CORAS method: CORAS tool (2013), http://coras.sourceforge.net/
35. Busch, M., Koch, N.: NESSoS Deliverable D2.1 – First release of Method and Tool Evaluation (2011)
36. Busch, M.: SecEval – Further Information (2014),
    http://www.pst.ifi.lmu.de/~busch/SecEval
37. Bishop, M.: Computer Security: Art and Science, 1st edn. Addison-Wesley Professional (2002)
38. Schreiner, S.: Comparison of Security-related Tools and Methods for Testing Software, Bachelor Thesis (2013)
39. Lacek, C.: In-depth Comparison and Integration of Tools for Testing Security features of Web Applications, Bachelor Thesis (2013)
40. Busch, M., Koch, N.: NESSoS Deliverable D2.3 – Second Release of the SDE for Security-Related Tools (2012)

A Toolchain for Designing and Testing Access Control Policies*

Antonia Bertolino[2], Marianne Busch[1], Said Daoudagh[2], Francesca Lonetti[2], and Eda Marchetti[2]

[1] Institute for Informatics, Ludwig-Maximilians-Universität München
Oettingenstraße 67, 80538 München, Germany
`busch@pst.ifi.lmu.de`
[2] Istituto di Scienza e Tecnologie dell'Informazione "A. Faedo", CNR
via G. Moruzzi 1, 56124, Pisa, Italy
`{firstname.lastname}@isti.cnr.it`

Abstract. Security is an important aspect of modern information management systems. The crucial role of security in this systems demands the use of tools and applications that are thoroughly validated and verified. However, the testing phase is an effort consuming activity that requires reliable supporting tools for speeding up this costly stage. Access control systems, based on the integration of new and existing tools are available in the Service Development Environment (SDE). We introduce an Access Control Testing toolchain (ACT) for designing and testing access control policies that includes the following features: (i) the graphical specification of an access control model and its translation into an XACML policy; (ii) the derivation of test cases and their execution against the XACML policy; (iii) the assessment of compliance between the XACML policy execution and the access control model. In addition, we illustrate the use of the ACT toolchain on a case study.

1 Introduction

Security is a crucial aspect of modern information management systems; when stored data and other resources are sensitive, a proper support must be put in place to protect them against unauthorized, malicious, improper or erroneous usage. In this context access control systems allow for the specification of access control policies, which rule various protection aspects such as: the level of confidentiality of data, the procedures for managing data and resources, the classification of resources and data into category sets with different access controls.

Software and security engineers constantly make decisions about which technology should be used for testing and verifying access control behavior. Unfortunately due to time and effort constraints, often there is no possibility to investigate on either the best choice of tools and applications to be used in the different stages of testing process or on how chosen tools work together.

---

* This work has been supported by the EU-NoE project NESSoS, GA 256980.

M. Heisel et al. (Eds.): Engineering Secure Future Internet Services, LNCS 8431, pp. 266–286, 2014.

In this chapter, considering in particular the XACML [1] language, which has become the *de facto* standard for specifying access control policies in many application domains, we focus on solving two issues of access control systems development: the designing and testing XACML policies. To tackle the problem of selecting compatible tools for the prefixed purpose we rely on the Service Development Environment (SDE) [2], a tool workbench that allows to combine functions of integrated tools into toolchains. Toolchains execute tools' functionalities in a row in order to improve the process of software development.

Concerning the policy creation the most critical steps are (1) the definition of the access control constraints and conditions a subject needs to comply with accessing a resource in a given environment and (2) the subsequent translation of access control constraints into the XACML language, as the complexity of the XACML language makes this a difficult and error prone process. In recent years, the adoption of model-driven approaches that abstract from the complexity of the XACML language by, e.g., using graphical access control models, has been proposed as a possible solution.

However, the simplified view proposed by model-driven approaches, sometimes hides security inaccuracies, due to an inappropriate use of graphical modeling constructs. Consequently, testing of the derived XACML policies becomes a necessary step for discovering possible weaknesses and avoiding security flaws. Unfortunately, the available model-driven proposals rarely provide facilities for verifying the derived policy against the requirements expressed in the model [3,4].

The testing approach of this chapter, which expands our work presented in [5], is inspired by the conformance testing process. It uses XACML-based testing strategies for generating appropriate test cases that are able to validate functional aspects, constraints, permissions and prohibitions of the XACML policy. The test cases are generated independently from the structure of the graphical access control model and the generated XACML policy, so that their execution could provide (partial) input/output traces of XACML policy behavior. These traces, categorized into different sets called *traces sets*, can be used for verifying the compliance of the XACML policy behavior with the access control requirements expressed in the graphical model.

The innovation of our proposal is based on two aspects: the exploitation of a testing process for deriving the actual policy behavior (the traces sets); and the use of typical model assessment techniques for discovering possible gaps between the access control design model and the traces sets.

All tools that support our approach can work together as a toolchain, the so-called Access Control Testing toolchain (ACT), which includes three main components: *model-driven policy design* for developing the graphical specification of access control requirements and converting it into an XACML policy; *test case generation and execution* for deriving test cases and executing them on the XACML policy; *trace analysis and model compliance* for analyzing the requests execution results and assessing their compliance with the access control model.

The ACT toolchain is a proposal of tool integration for designing and testing access control policies. Different application scenarios can be considered:

1. Detecting policy errors: the ACT toolchain can be used to find errors in the policy. Differences between the policy executor's response and the graphical model will be highlighted in the graphical model and reported in the toolchain's log. As long as all tools work correctly, no errors occur.
2. Replacing tools in the toolchain: for instance another transformation tool can be used to transform graphical access control specifications into an XACML policy or another tool for executing the policies can be employed. In these cases the testing facilities provided by ACT toolchain can be exploited for testing the tool integration.
3. Deriving the graphical model: if an XACML policy is already available and a graphical access control model should be created, e.g., for documentation purposes, the ACT toolchain toolchain can be used for testing that the created model conforms to the XACML policy. This can help developers to get a clearer idea of the constraints and permissions expressed in the policy and to ease improvements or modifications. Additionally, the traces of XACML policy behavior help the modeler to design a correct graphical model.

In this chapter we focus on the first two scenarios.

The remainder of this chapter is structured as follows: Section 2 introduces background information about notations we use and about the SDE. In Sect. 3 we present our ACT toolchain and its underlying functions, while a case study shows how to use the different components of the toolchain in Sect. 4. Section 5 outlines related work regarding the graphical modeling of access control policies and regarding the generation of test cases for XACML policies. Finally Sect. 6 concludes and sketches future work.

2   Background

In this section, we show how to model access control using the graphical modeling notation called UWE (UML-based Web Engineering) and we introduce the XACML policy language. In addition, we present the Service Development Environment (SDE), which is used to connect the functions of our toolchain.

2.1   UML-Based Web Engineering (UWE)

UML-based Web Engineering (UWE) [6] is the chosen security-aware engineering approach. It focuses on modeling web applications and supports access control. One of the cornerstones of UWE is the "separation of concerns" principle using separate models for different views. In this chapter, we focus on three views:

Content Model contains the data structure used by the application.
UWE Role Model describes a hierarchy of roles to be used for authorization and access control issues. It is usually part of a *User Model*, which specifies basic structures, as e.g. that a user can take on certain roles simultaneously, which is also allowed in this work.

Basic Rights Model describes access control policies, i.e., it is the graphical access control model we use in this chapter. It constrains elements from the *Content Model* and from the *Role Model*.

We use UML class diagrams to model all mentioned views. In addition, the UWE Profile adds a set of stereotypes, tag definitions and constraints, which can be downloaded from the UWE website [7]. Stereotypes can then be applied to UML model elements and values can be assigned to tags. UML tags are always associated to a stereotype and stereotypes can inherit tags from other stereotypes. A UWE modeling example can be found in Sect. 4. Further information about UWE is provided in chapter [8].

2.2   eXtensible Access Control Markup Language (XACML)

XACML [1] is a platform-independent XML-based language for the specification of access control policies.

A policy consists of a target, a set of rules and a rule combining algorithm. The target specifies the subjects, resources, actions and environments on which a policy can be applied. Each subject, resource, action and environment contains two main attributes that are `<AttributeId>` and `<DataType>` and an `<AttributeValue>` element that specifies the associated value. If a request satisfies the target of the policy, then the set of rules of the policy is checked, else the policy is skipped.

The rule is composed of a target, which specifies the constraints of the requests to which the rule is applicable; a condition which is a boolean function evaluated when the rule is applicable to a request. If the condition is evaluated to true, the result of the rule evaluation is the rule effect (*Permit* or *Deny*), otherwise a *NotApplicable* result is given. If an error occurs during the application of a policy to the request, *Indeterminate* is returned.

The rule combining algorithm specifies the approach to be adopted to compute the decision result of a policy when more than one rule may be applicable to a given request. For instance, the *permit-overrides* algorithm specifies that *Permit* takes the precedence regardless of the result of evaluating any of the other rules in the policy, then it returns *Permit* if there is a rule that is evaluated to *Permit*, otherwise it returns *Deny* if there is at least a rule that is evaluated to *Deny* and all other rules are evaluated to *NotApplicable*. If there is an error in the evaluation of a rule with *Permit* effect and the other policy rules with *Permit* effect are not applicable, the *Indeterminate* result is given.

The access decision is given by a so-called Policy Decision Point (PDP) while considering all attribute and element values describing the subject, resource, action and environment of an access request and comparing them with the attribute and element values of a policy.

2.3   Service Development Environment (SDE)

The NESSoS project uses a service-oriented tool integration approach, which enables developers to loosely integrate their tools as services to a workbench named

Service Development Environment (SDE). We used the SDE's functionality to connect the tools we work with to the ACT toolchain. The following description of the SDE is adapted and abridged from [9, p.5]; integrated NESSoS tools can be downloaded from [2]. The SDE was developed within the SENSORIA project [10], a FET initiative funded by the EU from 2005 to 2010. It is currently maintained and extended by LMU within the scope of the NESSoS and the ASCENS [11] projects.

The SDE is an Integrated Development Environment (IDE) based on a Service-Oriented Architecture (SOA) approach, where each tool is represented as a service. Technically, the service-oriented OSGi framework in Eclipse [12] is used. OSGi is based on so-called bundles, which are components grouping a set of Java classes and metadata providing among other things name, description and version. An OSGi bundle may provide arbitrary services to the platform and therefore all tools are integrated as bundles which offer certain functions for invocation by the SDE platform. Furthermore, it provides the ability to compose new tools out of existing ones, by building toolchains (called "orchestration"). The main features of the tool workbench are:

- The SDE Browser that contains a categorized listing of all available tools.
- The SDE Function Browser that provides the description of the tool and its functions.
- The SDE Blackboard which stores Java object values in-between service invocations when executing tool's functions.
- The SDE Shell which is an orchestrator that can be used to employ JavaScript to call tool functions.
- The SDE Orchestrator which provides graphical interface for creating toolchains by linking functions of (different) tools in order to create a new service that manages these tools, functions, inputs and outputs.

Tools to be used as part of the SDE must be implemented as OSGi bundles and contain a declarative description of the entry points of their functionality but are otherwise unlimited in their implementation. For the ACT toolchain, we integrated our tools into the SDE so that it is possible to use the SDE Orchestrator for building the toolchain, as detailed in the following section.

3   The Access Control Testing Toolchain "ACT"

In this section we present the proposed Access Control Testing toolchain "ACT", which includes the following main functionalities:

Model-driven Policy Design: The possibility to design a graphical specification of access control requirements and to convert the model into an XACML policy.

Test Case Generation and Execution: The selection of different testing strategies useful for deriving test cases and the possibility of executing them on the XACML policy.

Trace Analysis and Model Compliance: The analysis of test results and consequent derivation of the *traces sets*, i.e. the execution of test cases execution on the XACML policy. The assessment of the compliance of the *traces sets* with the graphical access control model is also included.

For realizing the ACT toolchain different tools were integrated into the SDE. Within the SDE, the tools are represented as services. In Fig. 1 the toolchain is depicted in the SDE's graphical orchestrator.

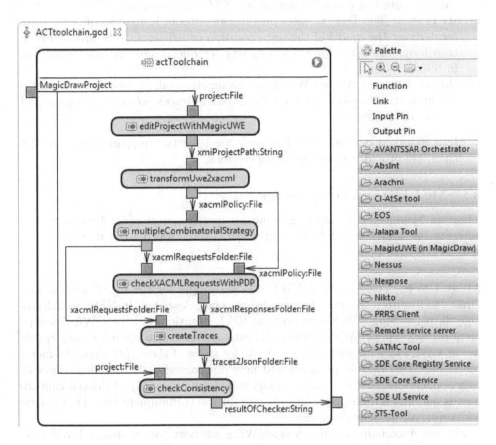

Fig. 1. SDE: toolchain for designing and testing access control policies

As shown in Fig. 1, different activities are considered, each one involving a tool available in the SDE. In the following we list orchestrator activities and briefly describe the corresponding services (tools) that implement them:

editProjectWithMagicUWE: MagicDraw[13] this is a modeling framework for specifying access control requirements, i.e. a graphical access control model, to simplify the designing of authorization constraints. MagicUWE [6] is integrated as a plugin into MagicDraw.

transformUwe2xacml: UWE2XACML [14] provides an automatic translation of the graphical access control model into an XACML policy to avoid common errors and problems of manually written XACML policies.

multipleCombinatiorialStrategy: The X-CREATE tool [15,16,17] enables automatic tests generation (i.e. XACML request generation) according to different testing strategies to speed up and improve the verification by reducing as much as possible time and effort due to test cases specification.

checkXACMLRequestWithPDP: The Sun PDP [18] is used to automatically execute test cases. Its output are XACML responses.

createTraces: The Trace Creator provides an automatic analysis of test results for deriving the model of the test execution called *traces sets*, followed by a transformation of the *traces sets* into sets of requests and responses expressed in the JSON format.

checkConsistency: MagicUWE offers this function (also called the "Checker") to automatically assess the compliance of the *traces sets* with the graphical access control model.

More technical details about the tools used for the implementation of the toolchain are provided in the following sections.

3.1 Model-Driven Policy Design

The tool MagicUWE allows to graphically specify access control requirements whereas the tool UWE2XACML automatically transforms the derived model into an XACML policy.

MagicUWE. The tool MagicUWE [19] is a plugin for the CASE tool Magic-Draw [13], written in Java. As has already been described in NESSoS deliverable [9, p.45], MagicUWE supports the UWE notation and the UWE development process. MagicUWE comprises (1) extensions of the toolbar for comfortable use of UWE elements including shortcuts for some of them, (2) a specific menu to create UWE default packages and new diagrams for the different views of web applications, and to execute model transformations, (3) additional context menus not only within diagrams, but also for the containment tree, i.e. the tree containing all modeling elements.

For our toolchain, we use MagicUWE's support for modeling UWE diagrams [6]. In particular, the toolchain first opens an existing UML project for modeling access control using the Basic Rights model of UWE. When the user finished modeling, he or she uses MagicUWE's menu to export the project as XMI [20]. In the same step, a link to the exported project is sent back to the SDE so that the toolchain can continue with the transformation to XACML.

UWE2XACML. The prototype UWE2XACML [14] is a tool for transforming role based access control policies modeled in the UML-based Web Engineering (UWE) language into XACML policies. UWE2XACML is written using the transformation language XPand [21] with Java extensions.

The input for UWE2XACML is an XMI-formatted UML model of an application modeled using the UWE profile. UWE2XACML iterates over the available roles while taking the role hierarchy into account. Additionally, the UML dependencies between the roles and the constrained elements are examined, i.e., the allowed actions are extracted. While iterating over the structure of the UML model, the XACML policy is written. In the end it is formatted automatically according to the nesting of XML tags.

In our toolchain, UWE2XACML is immediately followed by X-CREATE for generating XACML requests for the newly generated XACML policy.

3.2 Test Case Generation and Execution

The automatic test cases generation and execution is implemented by means of the tool X-CREATE and the use of an available access control system implementation (Sun PDP).

X-CREATE. The XACML policy derived by the tool UWE2XACML is then used for deriving a set of test cases. For this we relied on the tool X-CREATE (XaCml REquests derivAtion for TEsting) [15,16,17], which implements different strategies for deriving XACML requests from an XACML policy. These strategies are based on combinatorial analysis [22] of the values specified in the XACML policy with the aim of testing both policy evaluation engines and access control policies.

In the toolchain implementation among the various X-CREATE proposals, we decided to use the *Multiple Combinatorial* test strategy, because it provides a good compromise between test effectiveness and cost reduction [23]. In particular, for each policy, four sets are generated, the SubjectSet, the ResourceSet, the ActionSet, and the EnvironmentSet, containing the values of elements and attributes of the subjects, resources, actions and environments respectively. Random entities are also included in each set so that the resulting test plan could be used also for robustness and negative testing purposes. The entities are then combined to derive the XACML requests.

However, to avoid the possibility of an exponential cardinality of requests X-CREATE allows to fix the number of entities to be considered in each subset. Indeed the necessary condition for an XACML request to be applicable on a field of the XACML policy (rule, target, condition) is that this request simultaneously includes all entities that are specified in that policy field. Thus X-CREATE exploits the minimum and maximum number of entities of the same type that have to be included in a request for reducing the set of generated test cases. The XACML requests are then generated by combining the subject, resource, action and environment subsets applying first a pair-wise, then a three-wise, and finally a four-wise combination, obtaining all possible combinations. In this process X-CREATE automatically eliminates the duplicated combinations. For more details we refer to [15,16,17].

Sun PDP. This component integrates a Policy Decision Point (PDP) engine (specifically the Sun PDP [18]) which provides a support for parsing both policy and request/response documents, determining applicability of policies, and evaluating requests against policies giving the corresponding response (*Permit, Deny, NotApplicable* or *Indeterminate*).

In ACT we included the Sun PDP engine, which is an open source implementation of the OASIS XACML standard, written in Java. This choice was not mandatory and different PDP implementations could be considered. We decided for Sun's PDP engine because it is currently one of the most mature and widespread used engine for XACML policy implementation, which provides complete support for all the mandatory features of XACML as well as a number of optional features. This engine supports also all the standard attribute types, functions and combining algorithms and includes APIs for adding new functionalities as needed.

3.3 Results Analysis and Verdicts Generation

The XACML requests and the corresponding PDP responses are used to trace the policy execution and to assess the compliance of the derived policy with the graphical access control model. Consequently, possible inconsistencies in the access control model due to an inappropriate / misinterpreted use the UWE modeling elements or errors in the XACML generation can be detected. The report supports debugging in order to avoid security flaws. Details of the SDE components used in this stage are provided in the following.

Trace Creator. The Trace Creator gets as input the set of XACML requests and the corresponding responses from the Sun PDP components and derives the *traces sets*. For this different methodologies for classify the couples (request, response) are available, which rely on the opportune combination of the subjects, resources, actions, environments and the corresponding responses. In our ACT toolchain we consider the classification according to the PDP responses. Thus the couples (request, response) are divided into three groups: those having *Permit* as response (i.e. the *Permit set*), those having *Deny* as response (i.e. the *Deny set*), and those having either *NotApplicable* or *Indeterminate* (the *Other set*) as response.

To simplify the validation process the elements of the *traces sets* are translated into JavaScript Object Notation (JSON)-formatted couples. The choice of the JSON language instead of XML was made because JSON is a lightweight format that is easier to read and parse than XML language[1]. Moreover, in the development of the ACT toolchain the JSON format turned out to be very useful for manual debugging.

MagicUWE Checker. The final element of our toolchain is the MagicUWE Checker, which validates the compliance of the elements of the *traces sets* against the original graphical access control model, i.e. the UWE Basic Rights model.

---

[1] Comparisons of JSON and XML. http://www.json.org/xml.html

The main function of the MagicUWE Checker is `checkConsistency`, which takes two arguments: the UML project and the JSON-formatted traces sets. The checker's functionality is implemented as a part of MagicUWE. If the MagicDraw project is already open when executing the checker function within our tool-chain (e.g., because it was opened during the first step of the ACT toolchain), it is not re-opened.

Considering the elements of the three sets distinguished by the Trace Creator, the Checker tests if each couple (request, *Permit*) of the *Permit set* can be associated to stereotyped dependencies between roles and concepts expressed in the model. In particular if a request contains a user that has more than one role, the Checker verifies if there exists at least one stereotyped dependency between one of the mentioned roles and concepts expressed in the model.

Additionally, each couple (request, *Deny*) is tested, to make sure that there is an action in the request which does *not* appear in the UWE model. If a user requested more than one action the Checker verifies if at least one of these actions is not shown in the UWE model (i.e. denied in the model).

The elements belonging to the *Other* set of traces are not considered in the current version of the toolchain implementation.

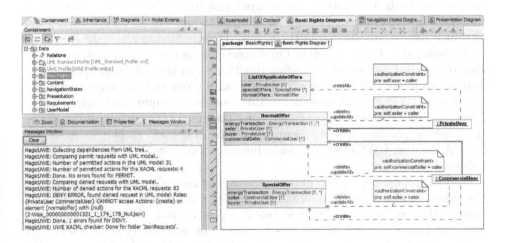

Fig. 2. Output of MagicUWE Checker

As depicted in Fig. 2, MagicDraw provides three main windows: on the right, a UWE Basic Rights diagram is shown, which will be covered in our case study (cf. Sect. 4, Fig. 4). On the top left, the element tree of the model is depicted, together with the root of the UML profile and UWE profile. On the lower left, the log of MagicUWE's Checker provides details of the requests under test. There, it is indicated if the PDP allows a request that is not permitted in the model or the PDP denied a request that is modeled in the Basic Rights diagram. In the latter case, the Checker also flags mistakenly denied dependencies in the graphical model. These bold, (red) dependencies and the Checker's log can then be used for debugging.

In the end, the log is automatically handed back to the SDE where it is shown as result of the ACT toolchain. In the future, new tools could extend our toolchain, as e.g., a dashboard tool that parses the log to show a green light if the checker reported no errors.

3.4   Toolchain Integration

Technically, the assembly of our toolchain is done in three steps: first, we identified the tools which had already been integrated into the SDE. Second, we created a SDE wrapper for tools that were not integrated and third, we connected them to a toolchain using SDE's graphical Orchestrator.

MagicDraw, UWE2XACML and X-CREATE had already been integrated into the SDE, however a function for MagicDraw's new Checker had to be added. Furthermore, X-CREATE did not provide a return value, which also had to be changed in the wrapper.

Creating a SDE wrapper for tools that had not been integrated, is done using the demo wrapper that is described in the SDE Tutorial [24]. We just had to execute our tools from within the wrapper and to return their results back to the SDE. Additionally, we created an Eclipse update site [2] for each wrapper, so that it can be installed using the Eclipse Update Manager.

As depicted in Fig. 1, the SDE Orchestrator is easy to use: we created a new *Function*, called "actToolchain" using the *Palette* on the right hand side. Using drag & drop, we added an input and an output pin and the tools' functions (e.g. MagicUWE: checkConsistency). After connecting inputs and outputs with *Link*s, the toolchain can be executed using the green play-button on the upper right corner. At the moment, there is a minor drawback, as plugins based on XPand, such as UWE2XACML, only function when they are executed in the Eclipse development mode.

In practice, developers can also get the advantages of parts of the toolchain. For example, already existing XACML policies can be modeled with UWE, as long as they are restricted to role based access control (cf. third scenario in Sect. 1). This might help developers to regain an overview of their policy and to debug it. In this case, a part of our toolchain would be used, starting with the tool X-CREATE. The UWE Basic Rights model, which is needed by the Checker, would then be the new model of which the developers want to know if it is yet compliant to the XACML policy they provided. If it is not, the Checker's log provide hints to missing or misplaced modeling elements.

4   Case Study

In this section we apply the ACT toolchain on a Smart Grid application, which allows offers to be created and bought. Offers can be bought from a list of offers, which is generated individually for each user. Offers are connected to energy transactions, i.e. an amount of energy that is provided. Two types of offers exist: normal offers and special offers. Special offers are promoted, which means they are advertised at the beginning of the list of offers. Special offers can only be created by commercial users that provide a great quantity of energy, as owners of power stations do. Normal offers can be submitted by commercial users as well as by private households, which e.g., want to sell surplus energy from their solar panels. We assume that a concrete user can play one or both roles at the same time.

Our case study comprises two scenarios: in the former we describe a run of the toolchain from the design of the policy to the successful assessment of its consistency. In the latter we show the use of the toolchain for debugging. In the following subsections more details are provided.

4.1   First Scenario: Clean Run

In this section we detail the use of the ACT toolchain, by showing all the proposed steps from the derivation of the access control model to the final verification of the policy compliance.

Step 1: modeling Access Control. In the first step of our toolchain, we use Magic-Draw with MagicUWE installed to model the classes and their associations, as shown in Fig. 3. It is noticeable that `Role` and its subclasses are located in UWE's role model and are just shown in the Content diagram in order to present the connection between roles and content.

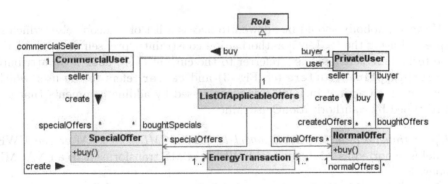

Fig. 3. UWE: Content Model, also containing roles from the Role Model

The Basic Rights Model constrains classes, attributes or methods from the Content Model by connecting them with role instances using stereotyped UML dependencies. Actions can be read, update, execute, create and delete. Figure 4 depicts the Basic Rights diagram (i.e. the access control model) of our Smart Grid case study. For example a user with the role `PrivateUser` is allowed to read all attributes of an instance of `ListOfApplicableOffers`, which refers to the customized list of energy offers that is presented to a user. The stereotype «readAll» is a shortcut, which allows a dependency to point to a class instead of pointing to each attribute of that class. (Additionally, {except} tags can be used to exclude specific attributes.)

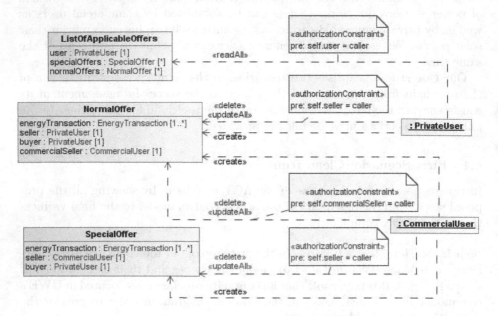

Fig. 4. UWE: Basic Rights Model

However, nobody should be allowed to access a list of someone else, which is expressed using the OCL [25] authorization constraint: "pre: self.user = caller". The term `self` is defined as a referrer to the current class, `user` is an attribute of `ListOfApplicableOffers` (cf. Fig. 3) and `caller` refers to the user which is executing an action. In UML this is expressed by adding comments that are stereotyped by «authorizationConstraint».

Step 2: transforming the UWE model to an XACML policy. After the UWE model is exported as XMI, the tool UWE2XACML transforms it to an XACML policy.

According to [14], the transformation intuitively works as follows: It generates an XACML *PolicySet* for each role, each of which contains one *Policy* for any class connected to the considered role. Furthermore, a single *Policy* is used to deny access to all resources not specified in the *PolicySet*, which is the default behavior of UWE's basic rights models.

Attributes targeted by **All* actions are divided into a set of *Resources*, omitting those from the {*except*} tag. OCL constraints inside UML comments with *authorizationConstraint* stereotype are transformed to a *Condition*. The condition is located within a *Rule* representing the appropriate action. For the time being, we have implemented only a few basic OCL constraints.

Generally XACML policies generated by UWE2XACML are structured as follows (in brackets we show the policy for the uppermost «readAll» dependency in Fig. 4, which connects `PrivateUser` and the class `ListOfApplicableOffers`):

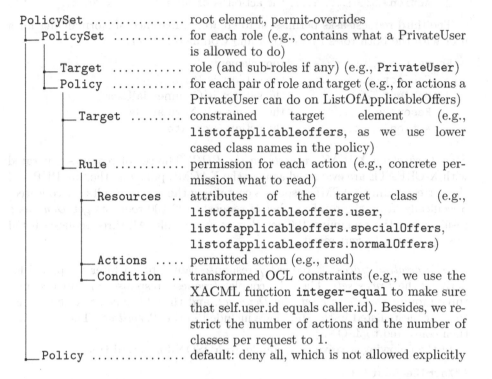

```
PolicySet ................ root element, permit-overrides
 └─PolicySet ............ for each role (e.g., contains what a PrivateUser
   │                      is allowed to do)
   ├─Target ............ role (and sub-roles if any) (e.g., PrivateUser)
   └─Policy ............ for each pair of role and target (e.g., for actions a
     │                   PrivateUser can do on ListOfApplicableOffers)
     ├─Target ........ constrained      target      element      (e.g.,
     │                 listofapplicableoffers, as we use lower
     │                 cased class names in the policy)
     └─Rule ........... permission for each action (e.g., concrete per-
       │               mission what to read)
       ├─Resources .. attributes  of   the   target   class   (e.g.,
       │             listofapplicableoffers.user,
       │             listofapplicableoffers.specialOffers,
       │             listofapplicableoffers.normalOffers)
       ├─Actions ..... permitted action (e.g., read)
       └─Condition .. transformed OCL constraints (e.g., we use the
                     XACML function integer-equal to make sure
                     that self.user.id equals caller.id). Besides, we re-
                     strict the number of actions and the number of
                     classes per request to 1.
 └─Policy ................ default: deny all, which is not allowed explicitly
```

Step 3: generating requests for the XACML policy. Using the tool X-CREATE a set of XACML requests is derived starting from the XACML policy. Specifically, 192.290 XACML requests are generated using the *Multiple Combinatorial* testing strategy provided by X-CREATE (see Sect. 3.2), which combines all the possible values of elements and attributes of the subjects, resources, actions and environments respectively. As described in Sect. 3.2, by construction the derived requests can have more then one subject, resource, action or environment.

In the following, we present three request examples. The former two denote that a user with the role of PrivateUser (or CommercialUser) wants to create an instance of the class `NormalOffer`.

```
Request .................. root element
 └─Subject .............. the subject is PrivateUser
 └─Resource ............ the resource is NormalOffer
 └─Action ............... the action is create
```

```
Request ................ root element
 └─Subject ............. the subject is CommercialUser
 └─Resource ........... the resource is NormalOffer
 └─Action ............... the action is create
```

The third request asks permission to create an instance of NormalOffer for a user with the both roles PrivateUser and CommercialUser.

```
Request ................ root element
 └─Subject ............. the subject is PrivateUser
 └─Subject ............. the subject is CommercialUser
 └─Resource ........... the resource is NormalOffer
 └─Action ............... the action is create
```

Step 4: checking XACML requests on the PDP. The set of requests generated with X-CREATE are evaluated against the XACML policy on the Sun PDP and the corresponding XACML responses containing the access results are collected. Specifically, from the total number of requests 192.100 requests get *Deny* as a result, while the remaining 190 get *Permit* as a result. All three requests listed in step 3 get a *Permit* result.

Step 5: creating traces. A request / response values based filter is applied for deriving the *traces sets*. Then the couples (request, response) are divided into three groups: the *Permit set*, the *Deny set*, and the *Other set*. Specifically, all three requests listed in the step 3 are included in the *Permit set*. The traces are then converted to JSON.

In the following we give an example for a JSON-formatted trace.

```
{"XacmlRequest":{
  "Attributes":[],
  "InstanceIDs":{"self.seller.id":"94","self.caller.id":"94"},
  "Classes":["normaloffer"],
  "Decision":"Permit",
  "Actions":["delete"],
  "Roles":["PrivateUser"]}
}
```

Step 6: checking consistency of responses and initial model. The resulting differences between the XACML responses and the initial model are logged, if any. Additionally, actions which are denied by the PDP, but permitted in the model are highlighted in bold (and red) in the model. Considering in particular the requests presented in step 3. The Checker confirms the conformance between all the requests and the access control model. Indeed the access control model of Fig. 2 shows a create association between PrivateUser and NormalOffer and between the CommercialUser and NormalOffer. This means that the access control system has to authorize a user with role PrivateUser (CommercialUser) who wants to create a NormalOffer. Because the Sun PDP responses corresponding to the three requests of step 3 are *Permit* as required by the access control model no violation or inconsistency is detected and the requests are compliant with the model.

4.2 Second Scenario: Error Detection

The second scenario demonstrates how the ACT toolchain can be used for testing and debugging an access control policy. We considered the case in which a developer uses the toolchain to design the policy of our case study, but this time, errors are found while testing. In the following more details about all steps are provided:

Step 1: modeling Access Control. As in the previous section the we use Magic-Draw with MagicUWE installed to derive the access control model.

Step 2: transforming the UWE model to an XACML policy. In this case we simulate the use of a faulty transformation tool by simply providing a modified version of the XACML policy derived in the step 2 of Sect. 4.1. In particular we alter the policy so that it is not allowed to create normal offers.

Step 3: generating requests for the XACML policy. As in Sect. 4.1 we use the tool X-CREATE to derive the set of XACML requests from the modified XACML policy. The requests shown in the Step 3 of the previous section are still generated by the X-CREATE tool.

Step 4: checking XACML requests on the PDP. Again the set of requests are evaluated against the XACML policy on the Sun PDP. In this case, the first two requests listed in Step 3 of Sect. 4.1 get a *Permit* result while the last one gets a *Deny* result.

Step 5: creating traces. The couples (request, response) are divided into three groups: the *Permit set*, the *Deny set*, and the *Other set*. In this case the first two requests listed in Step 3 of Sect. 4.1 are included in the *Permit set* while the last one is included in the *Deny set*.

Afterwards, the requests are transformed into JSON-formatted traces.

Step 6: checking consistency of responses and initial model. In this case considering the requests presented in Step 3 of Sect. 4.1, the Checker:

- confirms the conformance between the first two requests and the access control model, similar to the previous scenario.
- detects an inconsistency between the access control model and the last request of step 3 of the previous scenario. Indeed the execution on the Sun PDP of this request having a user with the roles `PrivateUser` and `CommercialUser`, action `create` and resource `NormalOffer` provides as response *Deny*. However, in the access control model of Fig. 4 users are authorized to create a normal offer. Consequently, an inconsistency is detected and highlighted with a bold (and red) line in the access control model (see Fig. 2).

Consequently, the developer can start debugging by studying the checker's log which points to the faulty trace file(s). Backtracking along the toolchain is easy, as the intermediate data that is handed over from one tool to the next is saved locally. Errors might occur, e.g., because: (a) the Basic Rights model was exchanged during the run of the toolchain, e.g., to compare changes to a previous version; (b) the transformation from UWE to XACML or the PDP produced an incorrect output. The latter is especially interesting if UWE2XACML or the Sun PDP were replaced in the toolchain, as the need to replace tools often arises due to discontinuation of tool support, as it is the case with Sun PDP.

As evidenced by this simple case study the ACT toolchain can help developers to create thoroughly tested XACML policies. In particular, it contributes to avoid possible inconsistencies in the access control models since inappropriate / misinterpreted use XACML constructs can be highlighted.

5   Related Work

In this chapter, we first introduce related work for modeling access control policies graphically. Then, we provide information about approaches for generating test cases for XACML policies.

5.1   Modeling Access Control Policies Graphically

Security-aware modeling approaches are briefly introduced in the following and compared to the UWE approach (cf. Sect. 2.1) that we have chosen for our toolchain [description adapted from [26]].

SECUREUML [27] is a UML-based modeling language for secure systems. It provides modeling elements for role-based access control and the specification of authorization constraints. A SecureUML dialect has to be defined in order to connect a system design modeling language as, e.g., ComponentUML to the SecureUML metamodel, which is needed for the specification of all possible actions on the predefined resources. In UWE's Basic Rights model, we specify role-based execution rights to methods using dependencies instead of the SecureUML association classes, which avoids the use of method names with an access related return type. However, UWE's Basic Rights models can easily be transformed into a SecureUML representation.

A similar approach to SecureUML is UACML [28] which also comes with a UML-based meta-metamodel for access control, which can be specialized into various meta-models for, e.g., role-based access control (RBAC) or mandatory access control (MAC). Conversely to UWE, the resulting diagrams of SecureUML and UACML are overloaded, as SecureUML uses association classes instead of dependencies and UACML does not introduce a separate model to specify user-role hierarchies.

ACTIONGUI [29] is an approach for generating complete, but simplified, data-centric web applications from models. E.g, web applications using nested menus are not supported yet. Functionality of a web application has to be modeled using the formal language OCL. Access control is modeled using SecureUML.

UMLsec [30] is an extension of UML with emphasis on secure protocols. It is defined in form of a UML profile including stereotypes for concepts like authenticity, freshness, secrecy and integrity, role-based access control, guarded access, fair exchange, and secure information flow. In particular, the use of constraints gives criteria to evaluate the security aspects of a system design, by referring to a formal semantics of a simplified fragment of UML. UMLsec models, compared to UWE models, are extremely detailed and therefore quickly become very complex. Tool support is only partly adopted from UML1.4 to UML2. However, the new tools have not been updated for almost two years.

5.2   Generating Test Cases for XACML Policies

Testing of access control systems is a critical issue and the complexity of the XACML language prevents the manual specification of a set of test cases capable of covering all the possible interesting critical situations or faults. This implies the need of automated test cases generation.

Some existing approaches consider the policy values in the test cases derivation. In particular, [31] presents the Targen tool that derives the set of requests satisfying all the possible combinations of truth values of the attribute id-value pairs found in the subject, resource, and action sections of each target included in the policy under test. A different approach is provided by Cirg [32] that is able to exploit change-impact analysis for test cases generation starting from policies specification. In particular, it integrates the Margrave tool [33] which performs change-impact analysis so to reach high policy structural coverage. The X-CREATE tool [34,16,17] exploits the potentiality of the XACML Context schema defining the format of the test inputs, and also applies combinatorial approaches to the policy values. In [34] a comparison between X-CREATE and the tool Targen [31] has been performed in terms of fault-detection capability, and the obtained results showed that X-CREATE has a similar or superior fault detection effectiveness, and yields a higher expressiveness, as it can generate requests showing higher structural variability. In [16,17] we present the advantages in terms of fault detection effectiveness of the testing strategies implemented into X-CREATE tool. Our proposal here consists in a new testing strategy and its application for testing the XACML PDP used by a real-world Trusted Service Provider in the healthcare domain.

The authors of [35] address testing of the XACML PDP by running different XACML implementations for the same test inputs and detecting not correctly implemented XACML functionalities when different outputs are observed. Differently from our proposal, this approach randomly generates requests for a given policy and requires more PDP implementations for providing an oracle facility by means of a voting mechanism. Our focus is on test cases derivation for PDP testing and not on oracle definition. A different solution for testing a PDP is presented in [36] where the authors provide a fault model and a test strategy able to highlight the problems, vulnerabilities and faults that could occur during the PDP implementation. The authors also provide a testing framework for the automatic generation of a test suite that covers the fault model. This approach deals with a specific authorization system supporting usage control and history-based control and is specifically conceived for PolPA language.

Other approaches target the testing of XACML policy and are based on the representation of policy implied behavior by means of models [37,38,39,4]. Usually, these approaches provide methodologies or tools for automatically generating abstract test cases that have to be then refined into concrete requests for being executed.

6   Conclusion

In this chapter, considering the specific context of access control systems, we presented a toolchain, called Access Control Testing toolchain (ACT) that can be used for designing access control policies as well as for testing their execution against the initial graphical access control models. ACT has been realized using a set of tools available in the SDE framework and includes the following features: (i) a modeling framework for specifying a graphical access control model; (ii) an automatic translation of this model into an XACML policy; (iii) an automatic tests generation and execution and (iv) an automatic assessment of the compliance of the XACML policy execution with the graphical access control model. Furthermore, we presented how to employ the ACT toolchain on a case study.

Preliminary test results obtained from the case study confirm the effectiveness of the ACT toolchain in evidencing possible security problems and inconsistencies between the model and the derived policy. Of course the trustworthiness of validation results depends on the correctness of the used testing tools. Indeed as a side effect the realization of this toolchain, caused the discovery of several inconsistencies between the input/output of the different components. These have been detected and improvements have been realized.

The most critical part in our toolchain is the prototype UWE2XACML, especially the part which parses the OCL should be improved to be able to parse arbitrary OCL constraints. In particular although XACML is a standard, several PDPs interpret the policies in different ways. Therefore the translation of the access control model into an XACML policy could be improved taking into consideration the various differences. As the toolchain allows to simply replace UWE2XACML by other transformation tools, according to our experience, we suggest to base a future transformation on Acceleo [40] instead of XPand as it is more flexible and programs are easier to maintain.

References

1. OASIS: eXtensible Access Control Markup Language (XACML) Version 2.0 (2005),
   http://docs.oasis-open.org/xacml/2.0/
   access_control-xacml-2.0-core-spec-os.pdf
2. SDE: Service Development Environment (2014),
   http://www.nessos-project.eu/sde

3. Massacci, F., Zannone, N.: A model-driven approach for the specification and analysis of access control policies. In: Proc. of the OTM Confederated International Conferences, CoopIS, DOA, GADA, IS, and ODBASE, pp. 1087–1103 (2008)
4. Pretschner, A., Mouelhi, T., Le Traon, Y.: Model-based tests for access control policies. In: Proc. of ICST, pp. 338–347 (2008)
5. Bertolino, A., Busch, M., Daoudagh, S., Koch, N., Lonetti, F., Marchetti, E.: A Toolchain for Designing and Testing XACML Policies. In: Proceedings of ICST 2013, Poster (2013)
6. Busch, M., Knapp, A., Koch, N.: Modeling Secure Navigation in Web Information Systems. In: Grabis, J., Kirikova, M. (eds.) BIR 2011. LNBIP, vol. 90, pp. 239–253. Springer, Heidelberg (2011)
7. LMU. Web Engineering Group: UWE Website (2014), http://uwe.pst.ifi.lmu.de/
8. Busch, M., Koch, N., Suppan, S.: Modeling Security Features of Web Applications. In: Heisel, M., Joosen, W., Lopez, J., Martinelli, F. (eds.) Engineering Secure Future Internet Services. LNCS, vol. 8431, pp. 119–139. Springer, Heidelberg (2014)
9. Busch, M., Koch, N.: NESSoS Deliverable D2.3 – Second Release of the SDE for Security-Related Tools (2012)
10. Sensoria Project: Software Engineering for Service-Oriented Overlay Computers (2011), http://www.sensoria-ist.eu/
11. ASCENS: Autonomic Service Component Ensembles (2012), http://www.ascens-ist.eu/
12. Eclipse Foundation: Eclipse Modeling Project (2014), http://eclipse.org/modeling/
13. No Magic Inc.: Magicdraw (2014), http://www.magicdraw.com/
14. Busch, M., Koch, N., Masi, M., Pugliese, R., Tiezzi, F.: Towards model-driven development of access control policies for web applications. In: Model-Driven Security Workshop in Conjunction with MoDELS 2012. ACM Digital Library (2012)
15. Bertolino, A., Lonetti, F., Marchetti, E.: Systematic XACML request generation for testing purposes. In: Proceedings of the 36th EUROMICRO Conference on Software Engineering and Advanced Applications (SEAA), Lille, France, September 1-3, pp. 3–11 (2010)
16. Bertolino, A., Daoudagh, S., Lonetti, F., Marchetti, E.: The X-CREATE framework: a comparison of XACML policy testing strategies. In: Proceedings of 8th International Conference on Web Information Systems and Technologies (WEBIST), Porto, Portugal, April 18-21 (2012)
17. Bertolino, A., Daoudagh, S., Lonetti, F., Marchetti, E.: Automatic XACML Requests Generation for Policy Testing. In: Proceedings of IEEE Fifth International Conference on Software Testing, Verification and Validation (ICST), pp. 842–849 (2012)
18. Sun Microsystems: Sun's XACML Implementation (2006), http://sunxacml.sourceforge.net/
19. Busch, M., Koch, N.: MagicUWE — A CASE Tool Plugin for Modeling Web Applications. In: Gaedke, M., Grossniklaus, M., Díaz, O. (eds.) ICWE 2009. LNCS, vol. 5648, pp. 505–508. Springer, Heidelberg (2009)
20. OMG.: XMI 2.1 (2005), http://www.omg.org/spec/XMI/
21. Eclipse: XPand (2013), http://wiki.eclipse.org/Xpand
22. Cohen, D.M., Dalal, S.R., Fredman, M.L., Patton, G.C.: The AETG system: An approach to testing based on combinatorial design. IEEE Trans. on Soft. Eng. 23(7), 437–444 (1997)

23. Bertolino, A., Daoudagh, S., Lonetti, F., Marchetti, E., Schilders, L.: Automated testing of extensible access control markup language-based access control systems. IET Software 7(4), 203–212 (2013)
24. SDE.: Tutorial (2012), http://sde.pst.ifi.lmu.de/trac/sde/wiki/Tutorial
25. OMG.: OCL 2.0 (2011), http://www.omg.org/spec/OCL/2.0/
26. Busch, M.: Secure Web Engineering supported by an Evaluation Framework. In: Modelsward 2014. Scitepress (2014)
27. Lodderstedt, T., Basin, D., Doser, J.: SecureUML: A UML-Based Modeling Language for Model-Driven Security. In: Jézéquel, J.-M., Hussmann, H., Cook, S. (eds.) UML 2002. LNCS, vol. 2460, pp. 426–441. Springer, Heidelberg (2002)
28. Slimani, N., Khambhammettu, H., Adi, K., Logrippo, L.: UACML: Unified Access Control Modeling Language. In: NTMS 2011, pp. 1–8 (2011)
29. Basin, D., Clavel, M., Egea, M., Schläpfer, M.: Automatic Generation of Smart, Security-Aware GUI Models. In: Massacci, F., Wallach, D., Zannone, N. (eds.) ESSoS 2010. LNCS, vol. 5965, pp. 201–217. Springer, Heidelberg (2010)
30. Jürjens, J.: Secure Systems Development with UML. Springer (2004), Tools: http://carisma.umlsec.de/
31. Martin, E., Xie, T.: Automated Test Generation for Access Control Policies. In: Supplemental Proc. of 17th International Symposium on Software Reliability Engineering, ISSRE (2006)
32. Martin, E., Xie, T.: Automated test generation for access control policies via change-impact analysis. In: Proc. of Third International Workshop on Software Engineering for Secure Systems (SESS), pp. 5–12 (2007)
33. Fisler, K., Krishnamurthi, S., Meyerovich, L., Tschantz, M.: Verification and change-impact analysis of access-control policies. In: Proc. of ICSE, pp. 196–205. ACM, New York (2005)
34. Bertolino, A., Lonetti, F., Marchetti, E.: Systematic XACML Request Generation for Testing Purposes. In: Proc. of 36th EUROMICRO Conference on Software Engineering and Advanced Applications (SEAA), pp. 3–11 (2010)
35. Li, N., Hwang, J., Xie, T.: Multiple-implementation testing for XACML implementations. In: Proc. of TAV-WEB, pp. 27–33 (2008)
36. Bertolino, A., Daoudagh, S., Lonetti, F., Marchetti, E., Martinelli, F., Mori, P.: Testing of PolPA Authorization Systems. In: Proc. of AST, pp. 8–14 (2012)
37. Traon, Y., Mouelhi, T., Baudry, B.: Testing security policies: going beyond functional testing. In: Proc. of ISSRE, pp. 93–102 (2007)
38. Mallouli, W., Orset, J.M., Cavalli, A., Cuppens, N., Cuppens, F.: A formal approach for testing security rules. In: Proc. of SACMAT, pp. 127–132 (2007)
39. Li, K., Mounier, L., Groz, R.: Test generation from security policies specified in or-BAC. In: Proc. of COMPSAC, pp. 255–260 (2007)
40. Eclipse: Acceleo (2014), http://www.eclipse.org/acceleo/

Verification of Authorization Policies Modified by Delegation

Marina Egea[1] and Fabian Büttner[2]

[1] Atos, Research & Innovation, Madrid
marina.egea@atos.net
[2] Database Systems Group, University of Bremen
green@tzi.de

Abstract. Delegation is widely used in large organizations where access to systems needs to be controlled and often depends on the role of a user within the organization. Delegation allows to grant access rights under certain, often temporal conditions. Usually, a delegation policy specifies the authority to delegate, and an administrative delegation operation performs the changes in the authorization policy accordingly. Unfortunately, the consequences of these changes are not checked in common practice before delegation is 'in-effect.' In this work, we present a systematic, automated approach to verify, before the actual enforcement in the system, whether a subject has the right to perform delegation, and that this delegation will not introduce Separation of Duties' (SoD) conflicts. We implement the delegation operation as an ATL transformation and apply our previous work on automatic transformation verification to check an authorization policy that is modified by a delegation policy. Our approach allows us to check, following an automated process: i) that delegation is only performed when conditions, for legitimate delegation, that we formalize using OCL, hold; ii) that the output of our transformation is always a valid authorization policy when it is obtained by executing the delegation operation using as input a valid authorization and delegation policy; iii) the absence of SoD' conflicts in the resulting authorization policy, for which we provide patterns that can be instantiated following policy's rules, as we illustrate.

1 Introduction

Delegation is widely used in large organizations where access to systems needs to be controlled and often depends on the role of a subject within the organization. Delegation allows to grant or to transfer access rights under certain, often temporal conditions. Delegation may occur in two forms [10]: administrative delegation and subject delegation. An administrative delegation allows an administrator to assign access rights to a subject and does not, necessarily, require that the subject possesses these access rights. In contrast, a subject delegation allows a subject to assign a subset of its available rights to another subject. In the latter form of delegation, a delegation policy contains the authority to delegate and an administrative delegation operation performs the changes in the authorization policy accordingly. In this chapter we only consider subject delegation. We work with a delegation language that supports delegation of actions from one

M. Heisel et al. (Eds.): Engineering Secure Future Internet Services, LNCS 8431, pp. 287–314, 2014.

subject to another, optionally under certain conditions. Yet, we note that the concept of delegation cannot substitute the permanent assignment of permissions to subjects by administrators. Access control policies must be modified to cover this need, instead. The subject who performs a delegation is referred to as a 'grantor' and the subject who receives a delegation is referred to as a 'grantee'. The delegation of rights from one subject to another needs to be controlled since not always a subject is allowed to delegate them. These controls are called in the literature *delegation legitimacy conditions* [1]. Who and when can delegate certain permissions to another subject is a critical issue in systems allowing cascade delegation of access rights. Yet, one step delegation may already create conflicts in the security policies, e.g. separation of duties' rules violations. In this chapter, we will focus on one-step delegation, but we plan to extend our approach to cascade delegation of rights in the future. Also, delegation of privileges may be classified into (at least) two kinds: grant and transfer [4]. A grant delegation model, following a successful delegation operation, allows a delegated access right to be available to both the grantor and the grantee. In contrast, in transfer delegation models, following a successful delegation operation, the ability to use a delegated access right is transferred to the grantee and it is no longer available to the grantor. In this work, we follow the grant model since, in our experience, it is more used in an organization environment, while the transfer of rights would be usually performed by a change in the access control policy.

As we have already mentioned, in subject delegation a delegation policy specifies the authority to delegate and an administrative delegation operation performs the changes in the authorization policy accordingly. Unfortunately, the consequences of these changes are not checked in common practice before delegation is 'in-effect'. In this work, we present a systematic approach to verify, before the actual enforcement in the system, that a subject has the right to perform delegation and that this delegation will not introduce authorization conflicts. We implement the delegation operation as an Atlas Transformation Language (ATL) transformation [15] and apply our previous work on automatic transformation verification [9] to analyze an authorization policy that is modified by a delegation policy. This work is contextualized in the area of Model Driven Security (MDS) [6], where models constitute pivotal elements of the security software to be built. These models can serve, for instance, to specify the vocabulary of a domain and the domain knowledge, to elicit the security requirements and as a basis for different types of verification, e.g. model based testing or monitoring, satisfiability checking, etc.. Moreover, if models of security policies are well specified, model transformations can be employed for various purposes, e.g., by model refinement to get the designs close to code, or to directly enforce the security policies in code. Yet, the confidence on these model-to-model transformations not to lose or mix important information in their execution needs of assurance techniques to be reliable and adopted by developers. In our approach, we translate rule-based model-to-model transformations into a constraint-based representation (in OCL) and apply automatic bounded satisfiability checking (using SAT solving) to this representation. This methodology allows us to advance the state of the art by supporting the automated checking of the following properties, namely, i) that delegation is only performed when conditions for legitimate delegation hold; ii) that the output of our transformation is always a valid authorization policy when it is obtained by executing the delegation operation using as input a valid authorization and delegation policy; iii) the absence of separation of duties' conflicts in the resulting authorization policy, that often arise after the delegation of different actions by various subjects is performed. When the resulting authorization policies are shown valid and conflict free for the requirements of interest, they are ready to be enforced at runtime in the final system.

Organization. Section 2 provides some background about the Ponder language that we primarily followed to specify authorization and delegation policies. Section 3 describes the authorization and delegation metamodels that we use to specify authorization and delegation policies (respectively). In Section 4 we propose patterns that allow detection of separation of duties' conflicts in our policies; we also explain how they are used with a running example. Section 5 explains the ATL transformation that is implemented to perform the delegation operation. Section 6 explains how our verification method works in practice while and shows the results of applying the verification method to the ATL delegation operation. We summarize related work in Section 7. We outline future work and conclusions in Section 8.

2 Background

Our work is inspired by the Ponder language [11]. Ponder is a declarative, object-oriented language for the specification of security and management policies in networks and distributed systems. Ponder policies relate to system objects and control the activities between them through authorization, obligation, refrain, and delegation policies within a defined set of constraints. In this chapter we focus on Ponder authorization and delegation policies.[1]Ponder authorization policies are essentially access control policies to protect resources from unauthorized access. A positive authorization policy (indicated by the header inst auth+, see Fig. 1) defines the actions that subjects are permitted to perform on target objects. We do not consider negative authorization policies (indicated by the header inst auth−) that deny subjects access to certain resources since delegation of prohibitions does not make sense. Positive delegation policies allow subjects to grant privileges, which they must possess (due to an existing authorization policy) to grantees, so that they can perform the delegated actions on their behalf. For example, the botton-left part of Fig. 1 shows a Ponder authorization policy in the banking domain that allows a teller to perform the actions input, and modify on target deposit accounts during weekdays. The bottom-right part of Fig. 1 also shows a Ponder delegation policy in which a customer service representative intends to delegate to a teller the actions create and delete on target deposit accounts during weekdays (and this delegation would expire in 15 days).

Ponder is the language of our choice for various reasons: i) it supports separation of concerns, i.e., the authorization and the delegation policy are written separately; ii) it supports the main concepts that can be found in existing works on authorization and

---

[1] To the best of our knowledge, Ponder2 only adds to Ponder authorization policies the concept *'focus' that tells the policy that it is protecting the target object(s) indicated* [28]. Delegation policies are not revised in Ponder2.

delegation policies' modeling; iii) it has shown a broad applicability in different settings where Ponder authorization policies are known to be mappable onto a variety of heterogeneous security platforms and mechanisms [28,11]. We have built a metamodel that allows us to model Ponder authorization and delegation policies. Their syntax is shown in the top part of Figure 1. Our metamodel leverages the use of model analysis techniques for the verification of these policies. However, the approach could be similarly applied to other authorization and delegation languages.

Authorization policy syntax

inst (auth + |auth−) $policyName$ '{'
subject   ([⟨$type$⟩] $domainScopeExp$;)
target   ([⟨$type$⟩] $domainScopeExp$;)
action   ($actionList$;)
[when $constraintExp$;] '}'

****

Authorization policy example

inst auth+ $bankAuthEx$ {
subject $teller$;
target $depositAccount$;
action $input, modify$;
when $weekdays$; }

Delegation policy syntax

instdeleg+ '(' $refAuthPolicy$')' $policyName$ '{'
grantee   ([⟨$type$⟩] $domainScopeExp$;)
subject   ([⟨$type$⟩] $domainScopeExp$;)
target   ([⟨$type$⟩] $domainScopeExp$;)
action   ($actionList$;)
[when $constraintExp$;]
[valid $constraintExp$;] '}'

****

Delegation policy example

instdeleg+ ($bankAuthEx$) $delegEx$ {
grantee $teller$;
subject $customerServiceRep$;
target $depositAccount$;
action $create, delete$;
when $weekdays$;
valid 15 $days$; }

Regarding Ponder syntax, we note that choices are enclosed in (and) separated by |, optional elements are specified with square brackets [ ] and repetition is specified with braces { }. Constraints are optional in all types of policies.

Fig. 1. Ponder syntax and examples of authorization and delegation policies

To the best of our knowledge, there have not been previous works on the automated verification of delegation legitimacy conditions for Ponder policies prior to the enforcement of the rules in the final system. Neither, the resulting authorization policy for a system that takes delegation rules into account has been systematically analyzed. However, for Ponder policies it is explicitly described that when a delegation operation is executed, a separate authorization policy should be created turning the grantee into the subject [11]. This is exactly the idea that we follow when executing the transformation that automatically performs the delegation operation in our approach.

3   A Metamodel to Specify Authorization and Delegation Policies

In this section, we present the metamodel that we have specified in order to leverage the use of model analysis techniques, in particular our work in [9], for the verification of Ponder authorization and delegation policies. The metamodel is supported as an Ecore metamodel in the Eclipse Modeling Framework [13]. Ecore modelling supports a sub-set of Meta Object Facilities (MOF) [21] elements which suffice for our purpose of specifying authorization and delegation policies. In particular, the modeling elements that we employ are metaclasses, attributes, and associations.

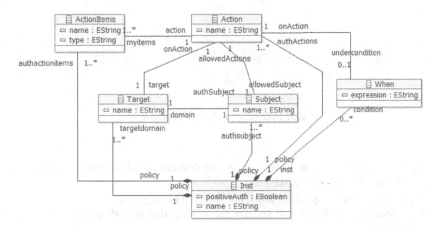

Fig. 2. Authorization policy metamodel

The Authorization Policy Metamodel (APM), shown in Figure 2, contains six meta-classes to specify a (positive) authorization policy, mirroring the Ponder syntax elements.

- *Inst* is the root Ecore metaclass that brings together all the other metaclasses that are needed to specify and authorization policy. Thus, this metaclass is linked to:
  - *authactionitems[1..*]:ActionItem*, to specify action items;
  - *authactions[1..*]:Action*, to specify action holders;
  - *targetdomain[1..*]:Target*, to specify domains;
  - *authSubject[1..*]:Subject*, to specify authorized subjects;
  - *condition[1]:When* to optionally specify conditions for the authorization rules.
- *Subject* is the metaclass that is used to specify the role with granted access. This metaclass is linked to:
  - *policy[1]:Inst*, to specify the policy to which the subject belongs;
  - *allowedAction[1]:Action*, to specify the category of actions which the subject has access to;
  - *domain[1]:Target*, to specify the domain which the subject has access to;

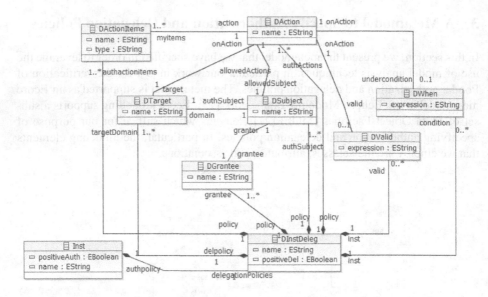

Fig. 3. Delegation policy metamodel

- *Target*, is the metaclass used to specify the domain on which the actions are performed. This metaclass is linked to:
  - *policy[1]:Inst*, to specify the policy which it belongs to;
  - *authSubject[1]:Subject*, to specify the subject that is authorized to access this domain;
  - *onAction[1]:Action*, to declare the category of actions that can be performed on this domain;
- *Action*, is the metaclass that is used as an action holder, to group action items;
  - *policy[1]:Inst*, to specify the policy which it belongs to;
  - *myitems[1..*]:ActionItem*, to specify the action items that belong to each action group;
  - *target[1]:Target*, to specify the domain on which each action group can be performed;
  - *allowedSubject[1]:Subject*, to specify the subject that can perform each action group;
  - *undercondition[0..1]:When*, to optionally specify the constraints under which the action group can be performed;
- *ActionItem*, is the metaclass that holds each action item that is granted to a subject through an action holder. This metaclass is linked to:
  - *policy[1]:Inst*, to specify the policy which it belongs to;
  - *action[1]:Action*, to specify the action group which the item belongs to;
- *When*, is the metaclass used to specify the conditions under which the policy applies. This metaclass is linked to:
  - *policy[1]:Inst*, to specify the policy which it belongs to;
  - *onAction[1]:Action*, to specify the action group that the condition constrains.

Note that our metamodel contains many multiplicity constraints that restrict its valid instances. Interestingly, that the authorization policies are well formed in Ponder syntax (cf. Figure 1) are captured by these multiplicity constraints and the OCL constraints shown in Figure 4. Hence, we will consider that an instance of the APM is valid if it fulfills both metamodel multiplicy constraints and the OCL constraints shown in Figure 4. Essentially, these constraints ensure that there is just one authorization policy instantiated, i.e., only one instance of the metaclass *Inst* is allowed. We note that the metaclass *Inst* is acting as an aggregating class for all the authorization rules that may be involved in the authorization policy. The *Inst* instance may have associated many triple of instances' names ⟨*Subject, Target, Action*⟩, the latter optionally linked to a *When* metaclass' name to express a condition. Of course, each action instance is linked to their items, as it is enforced by the corresponding multiplicity constraint. Notice that the metaclasses Subject, Target, and Action act a references – there may be more than one instances of each sharing the same name. This way we can authorize the same subject to access different actions while keeping the metamodels as closer as possible to the structure of Ponder textual policies. Also because of this design decision we require that two equally named action holders own either the same items or a subset of them. This enables granting different subjects access to distinct items in the same group of actions, e.g., the administrator may be authorized to create and delete a database, while a supervisor may be authorized to create and delete database tables, all being action items grouped as database actions.

```
inv AuthIntegrity1:                                -- there is only one
Inst.allInstances()->size()=1                      -- auth.policy, i.e.,
                                                   -- Inst has just one instance

inv AuthIntegrity2:
Action.allInstances()->forAll(a,a1 | (a<>a1 and    -- if an instance of an action
a.name=a1.name and                                 -- holder appear more than once
a.myitems->size()>=a1.myitems->size())             -- in a policy, the items
implies a1.myitems->forAll(i1| a.myitems           -- linked to them must have
->exists(i| i.name=i1.name and i.type=i1.type)))   -- the same name and type
```

Fig. 4. OCL constraints to follow Ponder syntax with metamodel instances

The Delegation Policy Metamodel (DPM), shown in Figure 3, contains the metaclasses *DSubject, DAction, DActionItem, DTarget, DWhen* that are similar to those already described for the APM. Moreover, DPM's root metaclass is called *DInstDeleg*, and it also contains:

- *DGrantee*, that is the metaclass used to specify the role to whom access rights are delegated. This metaclass is linked to:
  - *policy[1]:DInstDeleg*, to specify the delegation policy which the grantee belongs to;
  - *grantor[1]:DSubject*, to specify the subject who delegates some of its rights to the grantee.

- *DValid*, is the metaclass used to specify validity conditions under which the delegation holds. These are typically temporal conditions. This metaclass owns the links:
  - *inst[1]:DInstDeleg*, to specify the delegation policy to which the grantee belongs;
  - *onAction[1]:DAction*, to specify the delegated group of actions. The opposite association end is *valid[0..1]:Valid*, to optionally specify a validity condition (in addition to the when-condition) to further restrict the access to a group of delegated actions.

Again, the rules for writing delegation policies in Ponder syntax (please, recall Figure 1) are captured by the metamodel multiplicity constraints, and similar OCL constraints to those shown in Figure 4, but contextualized by the delegation metamodel. Hence, we will consider that an instance of the DPM is valid if it fulfills both metamodel multiplicy constraints and the OCL constraints shown in Figure 4. Yet, we note that although the grantee element is the only element that is mandatory in the specification of a Ponder delegation policy, we are also requiring the developer to specify the other modeling elements for the delegation policy, so as to be able to check the legitimacy constraints and potential separation of duties' conflicts directly, before running the delegation transformation. As we do for the authorization metamodel, we assume that these tuples contain a reference by name to other domain metamodel that defines the subject, potential grantee, action and domain's objects. Thus, in this metamodel, those instances having the same name are the same instance.

Essentially, the constraints imposed on the DPM ensure that there is just one delegation policy instantiated (only one instance of the metaclass *InstDeleg* is allowed). Note that the metaclass *InstDeleg* is acting as an aggregating class for all the delegation rules that may be involved in a delegation policy. The *InstDeleg* instance may own many 4-tuples of names ⟨*Grantee, Subject, Target, Action*⟩, the latter optionally linked to a *When* metaclass' name to express an authorization condition. Moreover, it can be also optionally linked to a *Valid* metaclass to express the condition under which the delegation is valid. Finally, since a delegation policy refers to an authorization policy (please, recall Figure 1), we introduce a one-to-one link from *Inst* to *InstDeleg* metaclasses so this reference gets specified. This link is also shown in Figure 2. Thus, we obtain just one metamodel that allows the specification of an authorization and a delegation policy (APM+DPM). The ATL transformation that we define to perform the delegation operation in section 5, takes as input instances of the APM+DPM metamodel and outputs instances of a final APM only.

4   Patterns to Check Separation of Duties in Authorization Policies

In this section, we define patterns that help to detect Separation of Duties (SoD) conflicts that may exist in an authorization policy or that delegation may introduce in an authorization policy.

The patterns shown in Figure 5 allow us to check Separation of Duty's conflicts at different levels:

- Pattern 1 checks that a subject is not granted access on two conflicting domains T_1 and T_2, e.g., in a bank office a teller is not granted access into loan accounts, and deposit accounts.

– Pattern 2 checks that a subject is not granted access on two conflicting groups of actions A_1 and A_2, e.g., authoring and reviewing actions are not granted to the same teller;
– Pattern 3 checks that a subject is not granted access on two conflicting action items I_1 and I_2, e.g., create and delete a loan account are not granted to the same teller.
– Pattern 4 checks that a subject with access to a domain T_2 does not get rights on a conflicting domain T_1 by delegation. E.g., a teller who can access to loan accounts cannot get access to deposit accounts by delegation.
– Pattern 5 checks that a subject with access to certain group of actions A_1 does not get rights on a conflicting group of actions A_2 by delegation. E.g., a teller who is in charge of authoring reports does not get access to reviewing reports by delegation.
– Pattern 6 checks that a subject with access to a specific action item I_2 does not get rights on a conflicting action item I_1 by delegation. E.g., a teller who is in charge of creating loan accounts does not get rights to delete loan accounts by delegation.
– Pattern 7 checks that two subjects with access to conflicting domains T_1 and T_2 cannot delegate on the same grantee.
– Pattern 8 checks that two subjects with access to conflicting actions A_2 and A_2 cannot delegate on the same grantee.
– Pattern 9 checks that two subjects with access to conflicting action items I_1 and I_2 in certain domains T_1 and T_2 cannot delegate on the same grantee.

Patterns are instantiated to be of practical use. Instances of patterns 1 to 3 can be checked over an authorization model instance, and instances of patterns 4 to 9 can be checked over a delegation model instance. In section 4.1, we introduce a banking example partially borrowed from [25]. We model this example and illustrate how patterns can be instantiated to detect SoD conflicts in this setting. Later, in section 6, we will show how we integrate patterns instances in the analysis of the delegation operation that we perform, and the results of the analysis itself.

4.1   Banking Application Example

Let us consider a banking application that allows bank officers to perform transactions on customer deposit accounts and customer loan accounts, and to generate and verify financial account data. The roles in the banking system contain teller, customer service representative, loan officer, and accountant. The actions that may be assigned to these roles include (a) create, delete, input, or modify customer deposit accounts, (b) create, or modify customer loan accounts, (c) create general ledger report, and (d) modify, or verify ledger posting rules. Figure 6 shows the authorization model instance that correspond to the following participating roles and actions granted to each role in the banking system:

1. teller – input and modify customer deposit accounts during weekdays.
2. customerServiceRep – create and delete customer deposit accounts during weekdays.
3. loanOfficer – create and modify loan accounts (Monday-to-Thursday).
4. accountant – create general ledger reports on Fridays.

```
Pattern 1: a subject cannot access two conflicting domains, T1 and T2,
in the auth. policy
  not(Inst.allInstances().authSubject->exists(s, s1 |
  s.name=s1.name and
  s.domain.name ='T1' and s1.domain.name='T2')),  T1<>T2

Pattern 2: a subject cannot access two conflicting action groups, A1 and A2,
in the auth.policy
  not(Inst.allInstances().authSubject->exists(s, s1 |
  s.name=s1.name and
  s.allowedActions.name = 'A1' and s1.allowedActions.name = 'A2')), A1<>A2

Pattern 3: a subject cannot access two conflicting action items, I1 and I2,
from certain domain, T1 and T2, in the auth.policy
  not(Inst.allInstances().authSubject->exists(s, s1 |
  s.name=s1.name and
  s.domain.name='T1' and s1.domain.name='T2' and
  s.allowedActions.myitems->exists(i| i.name='I1') and
  s1.allowedActions.myitems->exists(i1| i1.name='I2')))

Pattern 4: A subject with access to a domain  'T2' cannot get delegation
of rights on a conflicting domain 'T1'
  context Subject inv:
  self.domain= 'T2' implies
  not(self.policy.delegationPolicies.authSubject->exists(s|
  s.grantee.name=self.name and s.domain='T1')

Pattern 5: Actions of certain type 'A2' cannot be delegated to a subject
with access to actions of a conflicting type 'A1'
  context Subject inv:
  self.allowedActions.name='A1' implies
  not(self.policy.delegationPolicies.authSubject->exists(s|
  s.grantee.name=self.name and s.allowedActions.name='A2')

Pattern 6: specific actions 'I2' cannot be delegated to a subject with
access to specific actions 'I1'
  context Subject inv:
  self.allowedActions.myitems.name->includes('I1') implies
  not(self.policy.delegationPolicies.authSubject->exists(s|
  s.grantee.name=self.name and s.allowedActions.myitmes.name->includes('I2'))

Pattern7: two subjects with access to conflicting domains cannot delegate
on the same grantee
inv: not DSubject.allInstances()->exists(s,s1| s<>s1 and s.domain.name='T1' and
     s1.domain.name='T2' and s.grantee.name=s1.grantee.name), with 'T1' and
     'T2' conflicting domains.

Pattern8: two subjects with access to conflicting actions cannot delegate
on the same grantee
inv: not DSubject.allInstances()->exists(s,s1| s<>s1 and
     s.allowedActions.name='A1' and s1.allowedActions.name='A2' and
     s.grantee.name=s1.grantee.name), with 'A1' and 'A2' conflicting actions.'

Pattern 9: two subjects with access to conflicting action items of certain
     domains cannot delegate  on the same grantee
inv: not DSubject.allInstances()->exists(s,s1| s<>s1 and  s.domain.name='T1'
     and s1.domain.name='T2' and s.allowedActions.myitems->exists(i
     i.name='I1') and s1.allowedActions.myitems->exists(i1|i1.name ='I2') and
     s.grantee.name=s1.grantee.name), with 'I1' and 'I2' conflicting actions
     items on domains 'T1' and 'T2' (respectively)
```

Fig. 5. Separation of Duty's constraints patterns

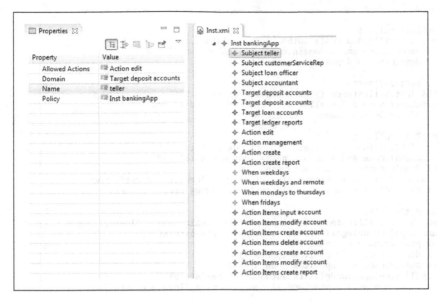

Fig. 6. Banking application authorization policy (excerpt)

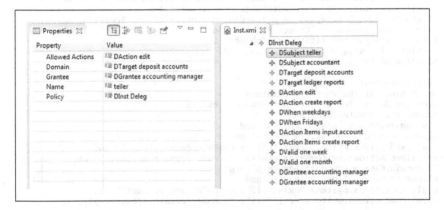

Fig. 7. Delegation model instance for the banking example

In the banking application, several organizational authorization rules need to be enforced to support common security principles such as separation of duties. We exemplify these rules next:

- Rule 1: There must not be a bank officer who can interact with both domains 'loan accounts' and 'deposit accounts'.
- Rule 2: There must not be a subject who can both edit deposit accounts and create ledger reports.
- Rule 3: The operations create loan account and create deposit account cannot be performed by the same subject. (This rule is a weaker alternative to Rule 1)
- Rule 4: The teller and accountant privileges cannot be delegated to the same grantee.

```
inv Pattern1Inst:
 not Inst.allInstances().authsubject->exists(s,s1|
 s.name=s1.name and s.domain.name = 'loan accounts' and
 s1.domain.name='deposit accounts')

inv Pattern2Inst:
 not Inst.allInstances().authsubject->exists(s,s1|
 s.name=s1.name and s.allowedActions.name = 'Edit' and
 s1.allowedActions.name = 'Create Report')

inv Pattern3Inst:
 not Inst.allInstances().authsubject->exists(s,s1|
 s.name=s1.name and s.domain.name='loan accounts' and
 s1.domain.name='deposit accounts' and
 s.allowedActions.myitems->exists(i| i.name='create account') and
 s1.allowedActions.myitems->exists(i1| i1.name='create account')

inv Pattern4Inst:
 not Subject.allInstances()->exists(s| (s.domain.name = 'loan accounts'
 and s.policy.delegationPolicies.authSubject->exists(s1|
 s1.grantee.name = s.name and
 s1.domain.name = 'deposit accounts')) or
 (s.domain.name = 'deposit accounts' and
 s.policy.delegationPolicies.authSubject->exists(s1|
 s1.grantee.name = s.name and s1.domain.name = 'loan accounts')))

inv Pattern5Inst:
 not Subject.allInstances()->exists(s| (s.allowedActions.name='Edit' and
 s.policy.delegationPolicies.authSubject->exists(s1 |
 s1.grantee.name=s.name and s1.allowedActions.name='Create Report')) or
 (s.allowedActions.name='Create Report' and
 s.policy.delegationPolicies.authSubject
 ->exists(s1 | s1.grantee.name=s.name and
 s1.allowedActions.name='Edit')))

inv Pattern6Inst:
 not Subject.allInstances()->exists(s |
 s.policy.delegationPolicies.authSubject->exists(s1|
 s.name = s1.grantee.name and
 ((s.domain.name = 'loan accounts' and
 s1.domain.name = 'deposit accounts' and
 s.allowedActions.myitems->exists(i| i.name='create account') and
 s1.allowedActions.myitems->exists(i1| i1.name='create account')) or
 (s.domain.name = 'deposit accounts' and
 s1.domain.name = 'loan accounts' and
 s.allowedActions.myitems->exists(i| i.name='create account') and
 s1.allowedActions.myitems->exists(i1| i1.name='create account')))))

inv Pattern7Inst:
 not DSubject.allInstances()->exists(s,s1| s<>s1  and
 s.domain.name='loan accounts' and s1.domain.name='deposit accounts' and
 s.grantee.name=s1.grantee.name)

inv Pattern8Inst:
 not DSubject.allInstances()->exists(s,s1| s<>s1 and
 s.allowedActions.name='Edit' and s1.allowedActions.name='Create
 Report' and s.grantee.name=s1.grantee.name)

inv Pattern9Inst:
 not DSubject.allInstances()->exists(s,s1| s<>s1
 and s.domain.name='loan accounts' and
 s1.domain.name='deposit
 accounts' and s.allowedActions.myitems->exists(i|i.name='create
 account') and s1.allowedActions.myitems >exists(i1|i1.name
 ='create account') and s.grantee.name=s1.grantee.name)
```

Fig. 8. Instances of Patterns 1-9 that detect violation of Rules 1-4

The patterns formalized in Figure 5 are instantiated in Figure 8 to enable checking of rules 1-3 (respectively).[2] Rule 4 is illustrating another source of SoD violation, i.e., two subjects with access to conflicting domains, actions or action items delegate their rights on a grantee who originally does not own access rights conflicting with any of its grantors. In delegation literature, this type of constraints are usually called pre-requisite constraints. They can be checked in the delegation policy by using constraints like the following at subject-level. For instance, the following constraint would check Rule 4 in the source DPM instance.

```
prereq: two conflicting subjects cannot delegate on the same grantee
   not DSubject.allInstances()->exists(s,s1 |s.name='accountant' and s1.name='teller'
   and s.grantee.name=s1.grantee.name)
```

However, to prevent this situation attending to the protected resources, we have included patterns 7-9 that impede that two different subjects with access to conflicting domains, actions, or action items delegate on the same grantee.

If any of these patterns is not applied and subjects are allowed to delegate on the same grantee, this is a potential source of conflict on the resulting authorization policy that the transformation *delegationExecution* generates. Fortunately, the conflict would be detected by evaluating appropriate instances of patterns 1, 2, or 3, on the resulting the authorization policy. For instance, in the model shown in Figure 7 a teller and an accountant delegate their rights on the accounting manager for certain periods of time. The evaluation of the instance of Pattern 2 of Figure 8 on the resulting authorization policy obtained by modifying the initial policy shown in Figure 6 by the delegation transformation specified in Figure 10, would detect violation of Rule 2. Prior to delegation, if patterns 2, 5 and 8 are enforced in the original policy, they ensure that the conflicting actions 'Edit' and 'Create Report' are not delegated on the same grantee, i.e., they make Rule 2 to hold in the target policy after the delegation is executed.

5   An ATL Transformation to Perform the Delegation Operation

ATL (ATL Transformation Language) is a model transformation language and toolkit [13] that provides ways to produce a set of target models from a set of source models. In this section, we explain first the structure and execution semantics of ATL matched rules which we use to define the delegation transformation and are the main constructs of ATL. Then, we continue by introducing the ATL transformation shown in Figure 10. This is the transformation that we implemented to perform the delegation operation. It is composed only of matched rules.

5.1   ATL Matched Rules

A matched rule is composed of a source pattern and a target pattern (i.e., the from and to-clauses in the rules of Fig. 10). The source pattern specifies a set of objects of the source metamodel and uses, optionally, an OCL expression as a filtering condition, that is enclosed in parenthesis after the from-clause that contains the source objects patterns. The target pattern specifies a set of objects of the target metamodel plus a set

---

[2] Notice that patterns 3-6 are instantiated commutatively, in both forms that could lead to a separation of duty's violation for pairs of conflicting domains, actions, and action items.

of bindings, that are also enclosed in parenthesis after the to-clause and separated by commas. The bindings describe assignments to features (i.e., attributes, references, and association ends) of the target objects. The interested reader can find the precise rule pattern that we consider in [9]. The execution semantics of matched rules can be described in three steps: First, the source patterns of all rules are matched against input model elements. Second, for every matched source pattern, the target pattern is followed to create objects in the target model. The execution of an ATL transformation always starts with an empty target model. In the third step, the bindings of the target patterns are executed. These bindings are performed straight-forwardly with one exception: An implicit resolution strategy is applied as follows when assigning a value to a property of an object of the output model (i.e., to an object created by one of the rules). If the value is referencing an object value of the source model, and this object has been matched by a matched rule (more exactly, by a rule having a single input pattern element), then the object value of the first output pattern element of this rule is assigned instead. By default, the ATL execution engine would report an error if no or multiple of such matches exist.[3]

5.2   An ATL Delegation Transformation

The ATL transformation *delegationExecution* shown in Figure 10 takes as input instances of the APM+DPM metamodel presented in section 3, and outputs instances of a final APM metamodel. The ATL transformation always copies the source authorization policy instance to the target authorization metamodel. In addition, it creates new access rights in the target authorization policy according to the source delegation policy instance, but only if what we have called legitimacy constraints are met. The legitimacy constraints that apply to our case are itemized next (based on the description provided in [11]). We show our formalization of these legitimacy constraints as an OCL helper called *checkDelegation()* in Figure 9. After each of the following items, we indicate the number of line that contains its formalization in Figure 9.

```
1   helper context DSubject def: checkDelegation() : Boolean =
2     not(self.grantee.oclIsUndefined()) and
3       self.policy.authpolicy.authsubject->exists(s |
4       s.name=self.name and s.allowedActions.name=
5       self.allowedActions.name and
6       s.domain.name=self.domain.name and
7       s.allowedActions.target.name=
8       self.allowedActions.target.name and
9       self.allowedActions.myitems->forAll(i |
10      s.allowedActions.myitems->exists(i1 |
11      i1.name=i.name and i1.type=i.type)) and
12      self.allowedActions.undercondition.expression  =
13      s.allowedActions.undercondition.expression);
```

Fig. 9. checkDelegation() helper definition

---

[3] We note that we only consider executions of a transformation that actually yield a target model.

- each grantor must exist as a subject in the authorization policy [line 2];
- each grantor must have access as a subject in the authorization policy to the action holder that she wants to delegate and in exactly that target domain [lines 3–8];
- each grantor must also have access as subject in the authorization policy to the particular action items that she wants to delegate [lines 9–11];
- each grantor must have access as a subject in the authorization policy to the actions that she wants to delegate and under the same circumstances in which she wants to delegate them [lines 12–13].

Only if the helper *checkDelegation()* returns true for the rules that map the source delegation policy instance to the target authorization policy instance, these rules will carry out their work. If this helper did not have evaluated prior to the transformation execution, several inconsistencies may arise, e.g., one subject could delegate privileges that she does not own. Next, we explain the rules that compose the *delegationExecution* transformation that is shown in Figure 10:

- the rule *Inst2FInst* maps a source authorization policy's root instance to a target authorization policy's root instance. More concretely, this rule maps an instance of *Inst* to an instance of *FInst*; [4]
- the rule *Grantee2FSubject* maps a grantee of the source delegation policy to a subject in the target authorization policy only if the grantor fulfills the legitimacy constraints. More concretely, this rule maps an instance of *DGrantee* to an instance of *FSubject*, only if the grantee is linked to a grantor for whom the helper *checkDelegation()* returns true. This rule also links to the new subject created in the target policy those actions that were linked to the grantor in the source policy;
- the rule *DAction2FAction* maps an action holder of the source delegation policy to an action holder in the target authorization policy, only if the grantor fulfills the legitimacy constraints. More concretely, this rule maps an instance of *DAction* to an instance of *FAction* only if the helper *checkDelegation()* returns true for the *allowed subject* that is linked to the action group instance in the source delegation policy;
- the rule *DActionItem2FActionItem* maps an action item of the source delegation policy to an action item in the target authorization policy, only if it is linked to an action group for which the allowed subject fulfills the legitimacy constraints. More concretely, this rule maps an instance of *DActionItem* to an instance of *FActionItem* only if the helper *checkDelegation()* returns true for the *allowed subject* linked to the action group instance in the source delegation policy which the action item belongs to;
- the rule *DTarget2FTarget* maps a domain of the source delegation policy to a domain in the target authorization policy, only if the source domain can be accessed by a grantor that fulfills the legitimacy constraints. More concretely, this rule maps an instance of *DTarget* to an instance of *FTarget* only if the helper *checkDelegation()* returns true for the grantor instance that is linked to the source domain instance.

---

[4] Notice that the target authorization policy's (i.e., APM) metaclasses are prefixed by '*F*', for clarity.

- the rule *Conditions2FWhen* maps *when* and *valid* conditions of the source delegation policy to a target when condition for which its expression is the conjunction of
  the expressions held by both types of source conditions. But these conditions are
  mapped only if they restrict an action group for which the allowed subject fulfills
  the legitimacy constraints. More concretely, this rule maps an instance of *When* and
  an instance of *Valid* to an instance of *FWhen* only if the helper *checkDelegation()*
  returns true for the grantor linked to the action group instance constrained by both
  types of conditions.
- the rule *When2FWhen* is triggered instead of the rule *Conditions2FWhen* when
  a validity condition is not specified in the delegation policy for a given group of
  actions. It maps a when condition of the delegation policy that is constraining an
  action group for which the allowed subject fulfills the legitimacy constraints to a
  when condition in the target policy. More concretely, this rule maps an instance of
  When to an instance of *FWhen* if validity conditions are not specified on the action
  group that is constrained by the source when-condition, and its allowed subject
  fulfills the legitimacy constraints.
- the rule *MapSubject* maps a subject of the source authorization policy to a subject
  in the target authorization policy. More concretely, this rule maps an instance of
  Subject to an instance of *FSubject* and links to the target subject the transformed
  properties from those linked to the source subject, i.e., name, policy, domain and
  allowed actions.
- the rule *MapAction* maps an action of the source authorization policy to an action in
  the target authorization policy. More concretely, this rule maps an instance of *Action*
  to an instance of *FAction* and links to the target action the transformed properties
  from those linked to the source action, i.e., name, policy and target domain.
- the rule *MapTarget* maps a target of the source authorization policy to a target in the
  resulting authorization policy. More concretely, this rule maps an instance of *Target*
  to an instance of *FTarget* and links to the target instance the transformed properties
  from those linked the source instance, i.e., name and policy.
- the rule *MapActionItem* maps an action item that belongs to an action of the source
  authorization policy to an action item belonging to the corresponding action in
  the target authorization policy. More concretely, this rule maps an instance of *ActionItem* to an instance of *FActionItem* and links to the target instance the transformed properties from those linked to the source instance, i.e., name, type, action
  and policy.
- the rule *MapWhen* maps a when condition of the source authorization policy to a
  when condition in the resulting authorization policy. More concretely, this rule maps
  an instance of *When* to an instance of *FWhen* and links to the target instance the
  transformed properties from the source instance, i.e., expression, onAction and inst.

In short the rules named following the pattern '*name2name*' turn the source delegation policy, i.e., a DPM instance, into a final APM instance. The remaining rules copy
the source authorization policy, i.e., APM instances, to final APM instances.

```
module delegationExecution;
create OUT : fauthPolicy from IN1 : auth-delegPolicy;

rule Inst2FInst {
from ds: Inst  (ds.delegationPolicies.authSubject->exists(f|
                  f.checkDelegation()))
to aps: FInst (name<-ds.name, positiveAuth<-ds.positiveAuth)  }

rule Grantee2FSubject {
from s: DGrantee, ds: DSubject (s.policy = ds.policy and
                  ds.grantee=s and ds.checkDelegation())
to aps: FSubject (name<-s.name, policy<-ds.policy.authpolicy,
                  allowedActions<-ds.allowedActions, domain<-ds.domain)
                  }

rule DAction2FAction {
from a: DAction (a.allowedSubject.checkDelegation())
to  fa: FAction (name<-a.name, policy<-a.policy.authpolicy,
   target<-a.target)  }

rule DActionItem2FActionItem {
from ai: DActionItems, a: DAction (a.myitems->includes(ai) and
                  a.allowedSubject.checkDelegation())
to  fai: FActionItems (name<-ai.name, type<-ai.type, action<-a,
                  policy<-a.policy.authpolicy)  }

rule DTarget2FTarget {
from t: DTarget  (t.authSubject.checkDelegation())
to  ft: FTarget (name<-t.name,policy<-t.delpolicy.authpolicy)  }

rule Conditions2FWhen {
from w: DWhen, v: DValid, a:DAction, ds:DInstDeleg
                  (not(a.valid.oclIsUndefined()) and
                  a.undercondition=w and a.valid= v and w.inst=ds and
                  a.allowedSubject.checkDelegation())
to  fw: FWhen (expression<-w.expression.concat(' and ' + v.expression),
                  onAction<-a, inst<-ds.authpolicy) }

rule DWhen2FWhen {
from w: DWhen,  ds: DInstDeleg, a: DAction (a.valid.oclIsUndefined() and
                  a.undercondition=w  and w.inst=ds and
                  a.allowedSubject.checkDelegation())
to  fw: FWhen (expression<-w.expression, inst<-ds.authpolicy,
                  onAction<-w.onAction)}

rule MapSubject {
from s: Subject
to fs: FSubject (name<-s.name, policy<-s.policy, domain<-s.domain,
                  allowedActions<-s.allowedActions)}

rule MapAction {
from a: Action
to fa: FAction (name<-a.name,policy<-a.policy,target<-a.target)}

rule MapActionItem {
from ai: ActionItems, a: Action (a.myitems->includes(ai))
to  fai: FActionItems (name<-ai.name,type<-ai.type,action<-a,
   policy<-a.policy)}

rule MapTarget {
from t: Target
to  t1: FTarget (name<-t.name,policy<-t.policy)}

rule MapWhen {
from w: When, a: Action (a.undercondition=w)
to  fw: FWhen (expression<-w.expression, onAction<-a, inst<-w.inst)}
```

Fig. 10. ATL transformation to modify an authorization policy by delegation

6 Verification of the ATL Delegation Transformation

In the previous sections we have provided metamodels and well-formedness rules for Ponder authorization and delegation policies, OCL patterns to capture separation of duty constraints, and an ATL transformation to actually perform the delegation operation. Next, we explain how we can automatically check the Hoare-style notion of partial correctness of our ATL transformation with respect to these various OCL constraints using a verification methodology that is based on constraint-satisfiability checking. More specifically, we check the notion of correctness that we formalized in [9]. Verifying the correctness of our transformation will involve checking the properties of our interest, namely, i) that delegation is only performed when conditions for legitimate delegation hold; ii) that the output of our transformation is always a valid authorization policy when it is obtained by executing the delegation operation using as input a valid authorization and delegation policy; iii) the absence of separation of duties' conflicts, in the resulting authorization policy, that often arise after the delegation of different actions by various subjects is performed.

6.1 Verification Methodology

Our verification approach is based on *transformation models*. Transformation models are a specific kind of what is commonly called a 'trace model'. Given an ATL transformation, a transformation model MM_T is a metamodel that integrates the source and target metamodels of the transformation and includes additional structural modelling elements and constraints that capture the execution semantics of the transformation. We apply the automated verification methodology presented in [9] to the transformation specified in Figure 10. In a nutshell, the procedure that we follow is described next: We first generate from the ATL transformation T, its source metamodel MM_{src}, and its target metamodel MM_{tar}, a *transformation model* MM_T, consisting of the elements of MM_{src} and MM_{tar}, and additional model elements that represent the transformation rules specified. Moreover, a set Sem of OCL constraints is generated for the combined model that characterizes the execution semantics of the ATL rules. For declarative ATL rules without recursion, the constraints describe the ATL semantics one-to-one, i.e., each valid instance of the transformation model corresponds to an execution of the transformation and vice-versa. In [9] the interested reader can find the general algorithm that we use to derive transformation models for ATL transformations; the formalization of the Hoare-style notion of partial correctness that we consider, and a discussion about the validity and limitations of our translation to verify this notion of partial correctness of T using off-the-shelf model finders.

Using this representation we can check partial correctness of the transformation with respect to properties specified as OCL constraints over the source and/or the target model, by checking if there exists a counterexample within a specific scope (i.e., maximum number of objects per class). More specifically, for a set of transformation preconditions (or assumptions) $Pre_1, \ldots, Pre_n$ and a set of postconditions (or assertions) $Post_1, \ldots, Post_m$, we want to show that for each instance M of the transformation model, the following formula

$$\left(Sem_1 \text{ and } Sem_2 \text{ and} \ldots \text{and } Sem_k \text{ and } Pre_1 \text{ and } Pre_2 \text{ and} \ldots \text{and } Pre_n\right)$$
$$\text{implies } \left(Post_1 \text{ and } Post_2 \text{ and} \ldots \text{and } Post_m\right) \tag{1}$$

holds. This formula can be expressed equivalently as follows: For each postcondition $Post_i$ $(1 \leq i \leq m)$, the formula (2) must be unsatisfiable (i.e., there is no model M that makes it '*true*'):

$$Sem_1 \text{ and} \ldots \text{and } Sem_k \text{ and } Pre_1 \text{ and} \ldots \text{and } Pre_n \text{ and not}(Post_i) \tag{2}$$

Figure 11 illustrates the transformation model generated for our transformation. Notice that the transformation model contains a new class for each rule declared in the *delegationExecution* transformation. Each of these new classes contains associations to the source and target classes of the rule, which target multiplicy 1 to force the instantiation of these classes for each instantiation of a rule-based class. Notice that the associations' multiplicities from the original source and target metamodels have been weakened to 0..1 and 0..*. For our analysis purpose, we turn them into explicit OCL constraints and include them in the sets *Pre* and *Post*, in order to check whether they are fulfilled. The same procedure is followed with the composition relationships.

The additional set of constraints *Sem* that characterizes the transformation execution semantics contains four kinds of elements:

– *Matching Constraints*. These constraints characterize the matching of ATL rules in the source model – every combination of input model objects that would be matched by an ATL rule has to be connected to the corresponding rule-based object in the transformation model, and no additional rule-based objects may exist. For example, for the rule *Grantee2Subject*, the following constraints are generated:

```
context DGrantee inv MATCH_Grantee2Subject:
```

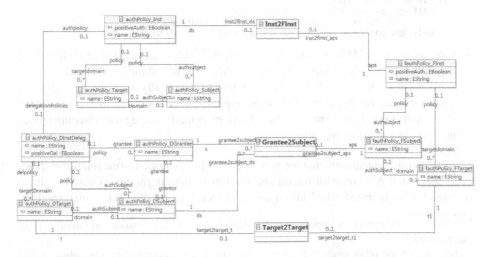

Fig. 11. The transformation model generated for our transformation (excerpt)

```
DGrantee.allInstances()->forAll(l_s:DGrantee |
  DSubject.allInstances()->forAll(l_ds:DSubject |
    l_s.policy = l_ds.policy and
    l_ds.grantee = l_s and
    l_ds.checkDelegation() implies
    Grantee2Subject.allInstances()->one(l_Grantee2Subject:Grantee2Subject |
      l_Grantee2Subject.s = l_s and l_Grantee2Subject.ds = l_ds)))

context Grantee2Subject inv MATCH_Grantee2Subject_COND:
self.s.policy = self.ds.policy and self.ds.grantee = self.s and
self.ds.checkDelegation()
```

– *Creation constraints*. These constraints control the existence of objects in the target model – a target object may only exist if it is created by an ATL rule (hence, only if it is connected to a corresponding rule-based object)[5], and target objects cannot be 're-used' between different rules. A creation constraint like the following is added for each class type in the target metamodel of the transformation:

```
context fauthPolicy_FSubject inv CREATE_fauthPolicy_FSubject:
    self.oclIsTypeOf(fauthPolicy_FSubject) implies
        self.grantee2subject_aps->size() = 1
```

– *Binding Constraints*. The constraints characterize the binding (each assignment of a property of an output object) of the ATL rules. In ATL, the new values for property assignments are expressed as OCL expressions. These OCL expressions are the basis for the corresponding source-target constraints on the transformation model. They are, however, further modified to capture the implicit resolution semantics of ATL. The first of the following two constraints illustrates a simple case where a primitive type value is bound. In the second case, we can see how the binding *(policy <– ds.policy)* of the rule *Grantee2FSubject* is transformed into an OCL expression that explicitly follows the navigation via the *Inst2FInst* rule to resolve the Inst type (which is the result type of *ds.policy* to an *FInst* type. [6]

```
context Grantee2Subject inv BIND_Grantee2FSubject_aps_name:
    self.aps.name = self.s.name

context Grantee2FSubject inv:
    self.aps.policy.oclIsUndefined() =
        self.ds.policy.authpolicy.oclIsUndefined() and
    self.aps.policy = self.ds.policy.authpolicy.inst2finst_ds.aps
```

– *Overlapping-avoid Constraints*. In general, ATL rules can overlap in their pattern types, but each tuple of input objects can only be matched once (ATL raises an execution error otherwise). Hence, for each pair of potentially overlapping ATL rules (i.e., each pair having compatible input types), a corresponding mutual exclusion constraint is required. However, the ATL transformation *delegationExecution* does not have any overlapping rules.

The semantics constraints that we generate establishes a one-to-one relationship between the actual ATL transformation and its transformation model. Whenever an input model M_{src} is transformed into a target model M_{trg} by the ATL transformation,

---

[5] Unlike Query/Views/Transformations (QVT) Relations [20], ATL assumes an initially empty target model.

[6] There are several other kinds of binding shapes that can be processed by our approach. We refer the interested reader to [9] for a detailed discussion.

an instance of the transformation model exists that is valid with respect to the semantics constraints and that comprises M_{src} and M_{trg} (connected by rule-based objects). The converse holds, too. Because of this one-to-one relationship, the transformation model and the semantics constraints can be used as a surrogate to verify the actual transformation.

In order to verify that some constraint $Post_i$ is implied by the transformation (given some other constraints as preconditions), we have to check that Eq. (2) is unsatisfiable. This can be tested using a metamodel satisfiability checker, or *model finder*, such as the UML Software Engineering (USE) Validator [17] which is publicly available [12]. The USE Validator translates the UML model and the OCL constraints into a relational logic formula and employs the SAT-based solver Kodkod [27] to check the unsatisfiability of Eq. (2) for each of the post-conditions $Post_i$ within a given scope.

6.2 Tooling

We have integrated the whole chain as a verification prototype (Fig. 12). We have implemented the ATL-to-OCL transformation [9] as a higher-order ATL transformation [26], i.e., a transformation from Ecore and ATL metamodels to Ecore (transformation) metamodels (ATL-to-TM),where the Ecore model can contain OCL constraints as annotations. Our implementation automatically generates the *Sem* constraints from the ATL transformation as well as *Pre* and *Post* constraints from the structural constraints of the source and target metamodels (further constraints to be verified can be added manually). Since the USE validator has a proprietary metamodel syntax, we had to create a converter from Ecore to generate a *USE specification*. We also generate a default search space configuration, which is a file specifying the scopes and ranges for the attribute values. In the search configuration file, we can disable or negate individual invariants or constraints. This prototype has also shown its applicability and scalability in our previous work on the industrial automotive domain [22]. For this reason, we are quite confident on its performance for the analysis of larger authorization and delegation policies.

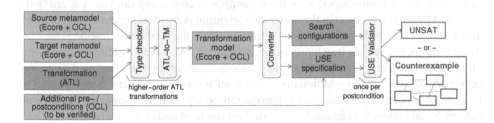

Fig. 12. The tool chain used to perform the transformation verification

To check Eq. (2) for a postcondition, we have to negate the respective postcondition and disable all other postconditions in the generated *search configuration* file (Fig. 12) and then run USE. If USE reports 'unsat', this means that there is no input model in the search space for which the transformation can produce an output model that violates the postcondition. If there exists a counterexample, USE provides the object diagram of the counterexample which can be analyzed using many browsing features of the tool.

6.3 Results

We now present the results that we have obtained from the integrated prototype that supports the application of the verification methodology described to the *delegationExecution* transformation and the constraints presented earlier. Table 1 shows several selections of pre- and postconditions and, for each line, whether the USE model validator could find a counter-example for the corresponding instance of formula 2 or not. The structure of the table has two parts. The first part is focused on the integrity of the generated authorization policy model. Hence, it contains the results of checking under which conditions the ATL transformation guarantees the well-formedness constraints from Fig. 4 and the APM multiplicity constraints for the resulting models. As explained before, our tool automatically turns all multiplicity constraints other than 0..1 and 0..∗ into OCL invariants before they are checked. In particular, the first part of the table shows that the integrity constraints are established by the transformation. Interestingly, fulfillment of some of the multiplicity constraints on the output models require more that just valid multiplicities on the input models. For example, Fig. 13 illustrates a counter-example that we get if the constraint `AuthIntegrity1` is not assumed as a precondition. It shows that the transformation could not generally handle input models with more than one *Inst* object: In the counter-example, the object *ftarget2* is generated without an associated subject because it is connected to a grantee in the source side which belongs to an authority instance which is not mapped. However, if we assume the constraint `AuthIntegrity1` as a precondition for the transformation, all multiplicity postconditions hold. Like the multiplicity constraints, all other constraints from Fig. 4 are established by the transformation on the output, too.

The second part of Table 1 considers the three separation of duty pattern instances from Fig. 8 on the final authorization policy. In all three cases, just assuming the pattern on the initial authorization policy does not guarantee that the same pattern holds after delegation. Fig. 14 illustrates this for the separation of conflicting domains pattern (pattern 1): Although no subject in the initial authorization policy had access to both deposit and loan accounts, a domain conflict is introduced into the final authorization policy by delegation for the subject (randomly) named 'String2'. We have to additionally assume an instance of pattern 4 and pattern 7 to guarantee pattern 1 on the final authorization policy. Also, we have to additionally assume an instance of pattern 5 and pattern 8 to guarantee pattern 2 on the final authorization policy; and to assume an instance of pattern 6 and pattern 9 to guarantee pattern 3 on the final authorization policy.

6.4 A Remark on Scalability

While our approach is per se independent from a specific model finder for OCL, we have only applied the USE Model Validator [17] to a larger extent. The USE Model Validator is based on Kodkod, which is based on a configurable SAT solver. Thus, we have to consider several tool layers when discussing scalability and limitations of this

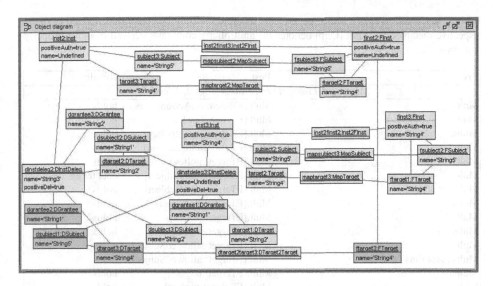

Fig. 13. Counter-example for multiplicity constraint FTarget::authSubject when the constraint AuthIntegrity1 is not assumed. Only objects of relevant classes shown. The highlighted objects illustrate the problem: The object ftarget3 is not connected to any FSubject, because the corresponding object dgrantee2 is connected to dsubject1 that comes from a different delegation policy.

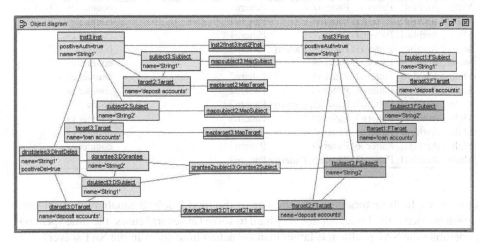

Fig. 14. Counter-example showing a violation of pattern 1 in the final authorization policy, even when pattern 1 holds for the initial authorization policy. Only objects of relevant classes shown.

(bounded) verification approach [9]. From a user-perspective, both solving time and space consumption of the tool chain are, in practice, mainly dependent on two factors: (1) The size of the search space in terms of the number of instances per metamodel class (which reflects in the relation size on the level of the relational logic solver Kodkod), and (2) the complexity of the OCL constraints in terms of nested (implicit and explicit)

Table 1. Verification results. Mults. denotes the set of all multiplicity constraints derived from the respective metamodels. Mult.[C::p] denotes the multiplicity constraint derived from the property p of class C.

Pre	Post	Result
Metamodel integrity constraints (Figs 2, 3, and 4)		
Mults.	Mult.[FWhen::onAction]	holds
Mults.	Mult.[FWhen::inst]	holds
Mults.	Mult.[FActionItems::policy]	holds
Mults.	Mult.[FActionItems::action]	holds
Mults.	Mult.[FTarget::policy]	holds
Mults.	Mult.[FTarget::authSubject]	counter ex. (Fig. 13)
Mults., AuthInt1	Mult.[FTarget::authSubject]	holds
Mults.	Mult.[FTarget::onAction]	holds
Mults.	Mult.[FTarget::policy]	holds
Mults.	Mult.[FTarget::myitems]	holds
Mults.	Mult.[FTarget::allowedSubject]	counter ex.
Mults., AuthInt1	Mult.[FTarget::allowedSubject]	holds
Mults.	Mult.[FTarget::target]	holds
Mults.	Mult.[FSubject::policy]	holds
Mults.	Mult.[FSubject::allowedActions]	holds
Mults.	Mult.[FSubject::domain]	holds
Mults., AuthInt1	AuthIntegrity1	holds
Mults., AuthInt2	AuthIntegrity2	holds
Separation of duty constraints (Fig. 8)		
Mults., AuthInt1, Pattern1, Pattern7	Pattern1	counter ex.(Fig. 14)
Mults., AuthInt1, Pattern1, Pattern4	Pattern1	counter ex.
Mults., AuthInt1, Pattern4, Pattern7	Pattern1	counter ex.
Mults., AuthInt1, Pattern1, Pattern4, Pattern7	Pattern1	holds
Mults., AuthInt1, Pattern2, Pattern8	Pattern2	counter ex.
Mults., AuthInt1, Pattern2, Pattern5	Pattern2	counter ex.
Mults., AuthInt1, Pattern5, Pattern8	Pattern2	counter ex.
Mults., AuthInt1, Pattern2, Pattern5, Pattern8	Pattern2	holds
Mults., AuthInt1, Pattern3, Pattern9	Pattern3	counter ex.
Mults., AuthInt1, Pattern3, Pattern6	Pattern3	counter ex.
Mults., AuthInt1, Pattern6, Pattern9	Pattern3	counter ex.
Mults., AuthInt1, Pattern3, Pattern6, Pattern9	Pattern3	holds

quantifiers. Both factors influence the size of the final Boolean satisfiability problem, which is often quite large, but not very hard to solve (in several cases, the time spent on generating the SAT problem is larger than the actual time spent in the SAT solver).

For the presented case study, the checks in Table 1 that report *unsat* (i.e., find no counter-example), all run in less than one second using a search scope of up to 4 objects per metaclass and in less than ten seconds for a search scope of up to 5 objects per metaclass[7]. Larger search spaces require larger search times, and the growth is exponential.

While the specific maximum number of objects per class that can be solved in reasonable time (say, less than a minute) is dependent on the case study, it is always comparably low (say, less than ten). This is independent on the number of classes in the

---

[7] Conducted on typical office laptop, running Kodkod 2.0 bundled with MiniSat.

metamodel, which can be often be quite high (say, several hundreds [22]), as long as the number of objects per class remains low.

7   Related Work

In this section we primarily focus on works that fall within a Model Driven Development (MDD) scope in which our work is also contextualized. Yet, we include some other works from a formal ground that either have influenced much our vision of this chapter, or seem particularly interesting as delegation languages or analysis methods. In this area, there have been many works that have proposed or employed models to specify role-based access control policies. Some prominent approaches are, e.g., [23,2,5,16,24]. None, of them, however, allow the modeling of delegation policies or the analysis of how delegation would modify access rights.

There are also MDD approaches focused on delegation policies modeling and administration. The work most related to ours is [19] where they present a model driven security method to transform RBAC policies by delegation rules, which they execute using an ATL transformation. Their approach also supports validation of OCL invariants over the source and target models. However, they do not investigate conflicts that may arise from the delegation of rights, e.g., separation of duties' conflicts, or verify that the policies resulting from the execution of their ATL transformation are valid from any valid input policies. Namely, they do not apply a verification process similar to ours to their ATL transformation.

In [25], they present a UML-based Domain Specific Languages (DSL) to model role based delegation and revocation. They can also validate OCL constraints, e.g., SoD constraints, on object diagrams using the USE tool. Yet, they do not execute any administrative operation to perform the delegation. In [3] they propose an extension of RBAC models to deal with delegation and revocation of privileges, but they do not perform any automated analysis on their models. In [18], they present a validation mechanism for delegation and revocation of roles assignments to users under specific conditions. They execute USE state manipulation commands to perform the administrative delegation operation that enables checking pre- and post-conditions for the policies. However, their metamodel does not suffice to deal with fine-grained delegation policies that may give access to a grantee only to subsets of roles' actions.

There are other works that study delegation of rights using a more formal ground. In [1] they discuss a language to capture delegation and revocation of rights' processes and point out the need of the verification of these processes. In particular, (1) delegation legitimacy verification when a delegation request is submitted, and (2) policy consistency verification when the policy is updated. However, they are not able to perform any kind of verification analysis due to the lack of tool support for their language. In [7] they introduce a self-administrative formal model to deal with delegation and revocation of rights in access control policies. They also present a prototype for the management of the policies, but it does not support a verification process for the delegation operation similar to the one that we have explained in this chapter. The same difference applies to [10] and [29]. In the former, they use a formal model to study the impact of the transference and grant of access rights by user delegation. In the latter, they propose a rule based delegation language that considers, in particular, the effects of delegation in presence of role hierarchies, which is a feature that we would have liked to integrate in our work but since they were not included in the Ponder policies of our study, we will leave it for future work. Finally, the work presented in [14] consider delegation in relation to the tasks a user has to perform, which we find very interesting. However, although they check that delegation meets global policy constraints, they do not support a verification process for the delegation operation.

8   Conclusion and Future Work

In this work, we have presented an approach that eases the verification of user delegation by using an ATL transformation that transforms an input authorization and delegation policy into an authorization policy (that is modified to attend the delegation policy specification). Prior to the execution of our transformation, we are able to validate delegation legitimacy constraints in OCL on the source authorization and delegation models, and we provide a set of OCL constraints' patterns that can be instantiated to check Separation of Duties' conflicts that may exist in the authorization policy or may have been introduced by delegation in the resulting authorization policy. As its core, our analysis is based on a previous work of us [9] that translates an ATL transformation into a transformation model, which is a constrained metamodel that can be used as a surrogate for the verification of partial transformation correctness w.r.t. to the constraints of the input and output metamodels.

The verification approach is of practical use for two reasons. First, it employs an automated translation from ATL and its constrained metamodels to relational logic. Actually, this mapping is composing three different translations: from ATL to an OCL constrained metamodel [9], from OCL to relational logic [17], and from relational logic to SAT [27]. Finally, we employ a SAT solver to check the existence of counterexamples. The approach provides a fully automated verification of the generated translation that seems reliable since, even when applied to a realistic case study [22], it scaled to a scope that was large enough to strongly suggest that the analysis does not overlook bugs in the transformation due to the boundedness of the underlying satisfiability solving approach. Second, regarding the coverage of ATL, our previous work [9,22] translates a substantial subset of ATL for verification, i.e., all rules except for imperative blocks, recursive lazy rules and recursive query operations other than relational closures. Thus, the approach takes advantage of the ways declarative, rule-based transformation languages (e.g., ATL) provide to iterate over the input model without requiring recursion or looping. This simplifies verification by, for instance, obviating the need for loop invariants. Although this subset of ATL is not Turing-complete, it can be used to implement many non-trivial transformations. We want to emphasize that the verification process can be automated as a 'black box' technology, since the idea is that the user specifying a delegation would only write a Ponder-like policy that can be automatically mapped to an instance of our delegation metamodel, under legitimacy conditions our ATL transformation would be executed obtaining a well formed final authorization policy that can be checked free of SoD conflicts, before being mapped again to a Ponder policy and enforced in the system at runtime. Thus, the user is in contact only with the simple Ponder syntax and is not aware of the analysis performed before delegation takes place. In the future, we want to apply a similar validation of delegation policies in the context of a health care scenario, where transfer of rights on a personal health record is needed from one physician to another (not only granting) when, e.g., the patient is moved from one hospital department to another due to his diagnosis. On the side of verification, we hope that we will be also able to perform unbounded verification of delegation tranformations using Satisfiability Modulo Theories (SMT) solvers by applying also our previous work [8]. Another further line of work will be to extend our transformation to deal with revocation of rights and obligation policies, and perform our analysis taking into account the interleaving of all these kinds of policies, which may easily lead to different types of conflicts. Finally, let us note that the analysis of the conditions contained in both authorization and delegation policies is particularly important and would usually require a logic able to deal with temporal conditions. It should allow, e.g., to check that loan officers are only eventually delegating their right to create loan accounts in any of the days of the time frame (Monday-to-Thursday) in which they are allowed to execute this action. This line of work seems also very interesting to us.

References

1. Abassi, R., Fatmi, S.G.E.: Delegation management modeling in a security policy based environment. In: Bouhoula, A., Ida, T., Kamareddine, F. (eds.) SCSS. EPTCS, vol. 122, pp. 85–95 (2013)
2. Alam, M., Hafner, M., Breu, R.: Constraint based role based access control in the sectet–framework model-driven approach. Journal of Computer Security 16(2), 223–260 (2008)
3. Barka, E., Sandhu, R.: Role-based delegation model/hierarchical roles (rbdm1). In: 20th Annual Computer Security Applications Conference, pp. 396–404 (2004)
4. Barka, E., Sandhu, R.S.: Framework for role-based delegation models. In: 16th Annual Computer Security Applications Conference (ACSAC 2000), December 11-15. IEEE Computer Society, New Orleans (2000)
5. Basin, D., Clavel, M., Doser, J., Egea, M.: A metamodel-based approach for analyzing security-design models. In: Engels, G., Opdyke, B., Schmidt, D.C., Weil, F. (eds.) MODELS 2007. LNCS, vol. 4735, pp. 420–435. Springer, Heidelberg (2007)
6. Basin, D.A., Clavel, M., Egea, M.: A decade of model-driven security. In: Breu, R., Crampton, J., Lobo, J. (eds.) Proceedings of the 16th ACM Symposium on Access Control Models and Technologies, SACMAT 2011, June 15-17, pp. 1–10. ACM (2011)
7. Ben-Ghorbel-Talbi, M., Cuppens, F., Cuppens-Boulahia, N., Bouhoula, A.: A delegation model for extended rbac. Int. J. Inf. Sec. 9(3), 209–236 (2010)
8. Büttner, F., Egea, M., Cabot, J.: On verifying atl transformations using 'off-the-shelf' smt solvers. In: France, R.B., Kazmeier, J., Breu, R., Atkinson, C. (eds.) MODELS 2012. LNCS, vol. 7590, pp. 432–448. Springer, Heidelberg (2012)
9. Büttner, F., Egea, M., Cabot, J., Gogolla, M.: Verification of atl transformations using transformation models and model finders. In: Aoki, T., Taguchi, K. (eds.) ICFEM 2012. LNCS, vol. 7635, pp. 198–213. Springer, Heidelberg (2012)
10. Crampton, J., Khambhammettu, H.: Delegation in role-based access control. In: Gollmann, D., Meier, J., Sabelfeld, A. (eds.) ESORICS 2006. LNCS, vol. 4189, pp. 174–191. Springer, Heidelberg (2006)
11. Damianou, N., Dulay, N., Lupu, E.C., Sloman, M.: The ponder policy specification language. In: Sloman, M., Lobo, J., Lupu, E.C. (eds.) POLICY 2001. LNCS, vol. 1995, pp. 18–38. Springer, Heidelberg (2001)

12. Database Systems Group–University of Bremen: UML-based Specification Enviroment (2013), http://sourceforge.net/projects/useocl/
13. Eclipse Community: Eclipse modeling project – Kepler release (2013), http://www.eclipse.org/modeling/
14. Gaaloul, K., Zahoor, E., Charoy, F., Godart, C.: Dynamic authorisation policies for event-based task delegation. In: Pernici, B. (ed.) CAiSE 2010. LNCS, vol. 6051, pp. 135–149. Springer, Heidelberg (2010)
15. Jouault, F., Allilaire, F., Bézivin, J., Kurtev, I.: Atl: A model transformation tool. Sci. Comput. Program. 72(1-2), 31–39 (2008)
16. Jürjens, J.: UMLsec: Extending uml for secure systems development. In: Jézéquel, J.-M., Hussmann, H., Cook, S. (eds.) UML 2002. LNCS, vol. 2460, pp. 412–425. Springer, Heidelberg (2002)
17. Kuhlmann, M., Gogolla, M.: From UML and OCL to Relational Logic and Back. In: France, R.B., Kazmeier, J., Breu, R., Atkinson, C. (eds.) MODELS 2012. LNCS, vol. 7590, pp. 415–431. Springer, Heidelberg (2012)
18. Memon, M.A., Hashmani, M., Sohr, K.: Validation of temporary delegation and revocation of roles with uml and ocl. International Journal of Computer Theory and Engineering 2(1), 1793–8201 (2010)
19. Nguyen, P.H., Nain, G., Klein, J., Mouelhi, T., Traon, Y.L.: Model-driven adaptive delegation. In: AOSD, pp. 61–72 (2013)
20. OMG: Meta Object Facility (MOF) 2.0 Query/Views/Transformation Specification v1.1). Object Management Group, Inc. (2011), Internet: http://www.omg.org/spec/QVT/1.1
21. OMG: Meta Object Facility (MOF) Core Specification 2.4.1 (Document formal/2013-06-01). Object Management Group, Inc. (2013), Internet: http://www.omg.org/spec/MOF/2.4.1/PDF
22. Selim, G.M.K., Büttner, F., Cordy, J.R., Dingel, J., Wang, S.: Automated verification of model transformations in the automotive industry. In: Moreira, A., Schätz, B., Gray, J., Vallecillo, A., Clarke, P. (eds.) MODELS 2013. LNCS, vol. 8107, pp. 690–706. Springer, Heidelberg (2013)
23. Shin, M.E., Ahn, G.J.: Uml-based representation of role-based access control. In: IEEE International Workshops on Enabling Technologies: Infrastructure for Collaborative Enterprises (WETICE 2000), pp. 195–200. IEEE Computer Society (2000)
24. Sohr, K., Ahn, G.-J., Gogolla, M., Migge, L.: Specification and validation of authorisation constraints using uml and ocl. In: di Vimercati, S.d.C., Syverson, P.F., Gollmann, D. (eds.) ESORICS 2005. LNCS, vol. 3679, pp. 64–79. Springer, Heidelberg (2005)
25. Sohr, K., Kuhlmann, M., Gogolla, M., Hu, H., Ahn, G.J.: Comprehensive two-level analysis of role-based delegation and revocation policies with uml and ocl. Information & Software Technology 54(12), 1396–1417 (2012)
26. Tisi, M., Jouault, F., Fraternali, P., Ceri, S., Bézivin, J.: On the use of higher-order model transformations. In: Paige, R.F., Hartman, A., Rensink, A. (eds.) ECMDA-FA 2009. LNCS, vol. 5562, pp. 18–33. Springer, Heidelberg (2009)
27. Torlak, E., Jackson, D.: Kodkod: A Relational Model Finder. In: Grumberg, O., Huth, M. (eds.) TACAS 2007. LNCS, vol. 4424, pp. 632–647. Springer, Heidelberg (2007)
28. Twidle, K.P., Dulay, N., Lupu, E., Sloman, M.: Ponder2: A policy system for autonomous pervasive environments. In: Calinescu, R., Liberal, F., Marín, M., Herrero, L.P., Turro, C., Popescu, M. (eds.) Fifth International Conference on Autonomic and Autonomous Systems, ICAS 2009, Valencia, Spain, April 20-25, pp. 330–335. IEEE Computer Society (2009)
29. Zhang, L., Ahn, G.J., Tseng Chu, B.: A rule-based framework for role-based delegation and revocation. ACM Trans. Inf. Syst. Secur. 6(3), 404–441 (2003)

ISMS-CORAS: A Structured Method for Establishing an ISO 27001 Compliant Information Security Management System

Kristian Beckers[1], Maritta Heisel[1], Bjørnar Solhaug[2], and Ketil Stølen[2,3]

[1] Paluno, University of Duisburg-Essen, Germany
[2] SINTEF ICT, Norway
[3] Dep. of Informatics, University of Oslo, Norway
{kristian.beckers,maritta.heisel}@paluno.uni-due.de,
{bjornar.solhaug,ketil.stolen}@sintef.no

Abstract. Established standards on security and risk management provide guidelines and advice to organizations and other stakeholders on how to fulfill their security needs. However, realizing and ensuring compliance with such standards may be challenging. This is partly because the descriptions are very generic and have to be refined and interpreted by security experts, and partly because they lack techniques and practical guidelines. In previous work we showed how existing security requirements engineering methods can be used to support the ISO 27001 information security standard. In this chapter we present ISMS-CORAS, which is an extension of the CORAS method for risk management that supports the ISO 27001 standard. ISMS-CORAS comes with techniques and guidelines necessary for establishing an Information Security Management System (ISMS) compliance with the standard, as well as the artifacts that are needed for the required documentation. We validate the method by applying it to a scenario from the smart grid domain.

Keywords: Information security, risk analysis, security standard compliance, ISO 27001, CORAS.

1 Introduction

The management of security and risk, as well as identifying and fulfilling the security needs, is challenging for many organizations and other stakeholders. Fortunately, several security standards, such as ISO 27001 [19], offer ways to attain this goal in a structured and systematic way. The mentioned standard prescribes a process for establishing and maintaining an Information Security Management System (ISMS), which tailors security to the specific needs of any kind of organization. However, several ambiguities in the standard need to be handled, and the organizations need to understand and decide how to operationalize the standard, and how to document the ISMS.

This security standard is ambiguous on purpose, because it should serve a multitude of different domains and stakeholders. The ambiguity is nevertheless

M. Heisel et al. (Eds.): Engineering Secure Future Internet Services, LNCS 8431, pp. 315–344, 2014.

a problem for the stakeholders who have to choose a method for security analysis that is compliant with the standard. The stakeholders moreover need to decide the abstraction level for the required documentation without any support from the standard. For example, security experts have to describe the business, processes, actors and roles, technologies, etc., and decide on their own what is the most relevant scope elements to consider. In addition, the security experts have to find a method that allows them to achieve completeness of identifying stakeholders, security objectives, assets and other elements within the desired scope. Moreover, the standard does not provide any techniques or methods for assembling the necessary information, or a pattern or template for structuring and documenting this information. The importance of these steps becomes apparent when one realizes that essential further steps of ISO 27001 depend upon them, including the identification of threats, vulnerabilities and security controls.

In this chapter we propose an extension of the CORAS method [28] to support the establishment of an ISO 27001 compliant ISMS. In previous work we analyzed the relations between different security requirements engineering and risk analysis methods [7], and our results showed that the ISO 27001 standard has a significant focus on risk analysis. It describes how to build an ISMS, and CORAS already supports many of these steps due to its focus on risk management. A further motivation for building on CORAS is that the method is based on the ISO 31000 [18] risk management standard, which is also the basis for the information security risk management process of ISO 27005 [20]. The latter standard refines the risk management process described in the ISO 27001.

In addition, the ISO 27001 standard demands legal aspects (such as laws, regulations, contracts and legally binding agreements) to be considered. CORAS provides support for this during the risk analysis by an extension called *Legal CORAS* [28]. CORAS also comes with tool and modeling support for all phases of the process. The approach moreover facilitates the reporting of the results by a formal mapping of its diagrams to English prose, which is useful for generating the documentation that is required by ISO 27001.

In summary, we use CORAS as a basis because of its structured method for risk management, its compliance to ISO 31000, the consideration of legal aspects, the tool support and the support for document generation. The CORAS approach has moreover undergone thorough industrial validation in many different domains over more than a decade [28].

We refer to the CORAS extension presented in this report as *ISMS-CORAS*. We show how we extend CORAS, and we present a mapping from the resulting ISMS-CORAS artifacts to the ISMS documentation compliant with ISO 27001. We apply our method to a smart grid scenario provided by the industrial partners of the NESSoS project [35].

Compared to standard CORAS, which is a method for risk analysis in general, there are a number of novel features and artifacts of ISMS-CORAS. First of all, ISMS-CORAS comes with diagrams and templates to support all documentation requirements of the ISO 27001 standard. This documentation support goes well beyond the modeling support of CORAS. It moreover comes with a classification of attacker types, templates for attacker description, and attacker overview diagrams to facilitate the attacker identification. It has support for identification of attacker motivation and entry points, and for modeling this information in the threat diagrams. These and other novelties in combination provide a systematic support for establishing and documenting an ISMS in compliance with the standard.

The outline of this chapter is as follows. In Section 2 we describe the background to ISMS-CORAS, and in Section 3 we describe the method, the documentation artifacts and how ISMS-CORAS supports the ISO standard. In Section 4 we demonstrate and exemplify ISMS-CORAS by using the smart grid scenario. The section also describes in more details the documentation artifacts introduced in Section 3. Related work is presented in Section 5 before we conclude in Section 6.

The presentation of ISMS-CORAS in this chapter is a shortened version of a technical report with the same title [10]. We refer the reader to the report for the full description of ISMS-CORAS and for a more detailed description of all the documentation artifacts. The report also gives more detailed references to the ISO 27001 demands, as well as a more elaborated presentation of the application of ISMS-CORAS to the smart grid scenario.

The security and risk terminology that we use in this chapter is based on both CORAS and the above mentioned standards. The technical report comes with an appendix with a comparison of the respective terminologies and a clarification of the underlying terminology of ISMS-CORAS.

2   Background

In this section we briefly describe the main background to the ISMS-CORAS method, namely the CORAS method and its extension Legal CORAS [28], as well as the ISO 27001 standard [19].

2.1   CORAS

CORAS is a model-driven approach to risk analysis that follows the process defined by the ISO 31000 risk management standard [18]. The approach consists of three tightly integrated artifacts, namely the CORAS method, the CORAS language and the CORAS tool. The method comes with techniques and practical guidelines, and the language provides modeling and documentation support for all steps of the method. The tool is a diagram editor for creating any CORAS diagram. The overall process consists of the five following consecutive steps, which is also according to ISO 31000.

Establishing the context involves setting the scope and focus of the analysis, identifying the assets with respect to which risks are identified, and defining the risk evaluation criteria. The target of analysis is specified at the desired level of abstraction using a precise and well-understood notation, such as UML [36]. The documentation of the context establishment is used as input to and a basis for the subsequent risk assessment.

The risk assessment includes the three steps of *risk identification, risk estimation* and *risk evaluation.* Risk identification is to identify and document unwanted incidents, together with the threats and vulnerabilities that may cause them, using CORAS threat diagrams. The risk estimation involves the estimation of likelihoods and consequences for the unwanted incidents using the threat diagrams. In order to facilitate the risk estimation and to identify the most important sources of risk, likelihoods are estimated also for threats and threat scenarios. The results of the risk estimation are documented using CORAS *risk diagrams.* The risk evaluation involves comparing the identified risks with the risk evaluation criteria, and to determine which risks are unacceptable. In addition to structured brainstorming, a technique for risk identification and estimation that brings together people with different expert insight into the target of analysis, CORAS makes use of any other input such as statistics, security logs, questionnaires, and so forth.

Finally, the *risk treatment* is to identify means for mitigating unacceptable risks. This is also conducted by structured brainstorming, and is supported by CORAS *treatment diagrams.*

2.2 Legal CORAS

Legal CORAS is an extension of CORAS specifically for considering legal aspects and legal risk. The method elicits relevant legal aspects based on the target of analysis and the target description.

The source of legal risk is legal norms, which are norms that stem from a legal source such as laws, regulations, contracts and legally binding agreements. When assessing legal risk, there are two kinds of uncertainties that must be estimated. First, the legal uncertainty is the uncertainty of whether a specific norm actually applies to circumstances that may arise. Second, the factual uncertainty is the uncertainty of whether the circumstances will actually occur, and thereby potentially trigger the legal norm. It is by combining the estimates for these two notions of uncertainty that we can estimate the significance of a legal norm and its impact on the risk picture. Legal CORAS comes with the necessary analysis techniques and modeling support, but the involvement of a lawyer or other legal experts is usually required.

2.3 ISO 27001

The ISO 27001 standard is structured according to the Plan-Do-Check-Act (PDCA) model, which is referred to as the ISO 27001 process. In the Plan phase an ISMS is established, in the Do phase the ISMS is implemented and operated, in the Check phase the ISMS is monitored and reviewed, and in the Act phase the ISMS is maintained and improved.

We focus in our work on the Plan phase, because we provide a specific method for building an ISMS, and because it is during this phase that the security risk analysis is stressed the most. In future work we will also develop support for the other phases of the PDCA model.

Table 1. ISO 27001 documentation demands

#	Name
1.	The scope of the ISMS
2.	The ISMS policy statements that contain general directions towards security and risk
3.	Procedures and controls in support of the ISMS
4.	A description of the applied risk assessment methodology
5.	A risk assessment report
6.	A risk treatment plan
7.	Documented procedures to the effective planning, operation and control of the ISMS
8.	ISMS records
9.	Statement of applicability
10.	Management decisions

The Plan phase considers the scope and boundaries of the ISMS, its interested parties, the environment, and the assets. All the technologies involved are moreover defined, as well as the ISMS policies, risk assessments, evaluations, and controls. Controls in the ISO 27001 are measures to modify risk.

The ISO 27001 standard demands a set of documents for certification, which we introduce in Table 1. Note that the names of the ten documents are given by us to simplify the reference to them when presenting ISMS-CORAS throughout this chapter. The standard itself describes these documents only by their contents.

Document 8, the ISMS records, is for providing evidence of compliance to the requirements of the ISMS. This is out of the scope of ISMS-CORAS, which rather concerns the establishment of the ISMS, and is therefore not among the ISMS-CORAS documentation artifacts. ISMS-CORAS is also not providing document 4, since the risk assessment method is part of ISMS-CORAS itself. Document 9 is for describing the control objectives and controls that are relevant and applicable to the organization's ISMS, whereas document 10 provides support for establishing and maintaining an ISMS.

3   The ISMS-CORAS Method

The ISMS-CORAS method is conducted according to the five steps depicted to the left in Figure 1. These consecutive steps comprise the risk analysis process as defined by the ISO 31000 risk management standard that also CORAS complies with. ISMS-CORAS is defined as an extension of CORAS, and while keeping the names of the steps we focus in our description of ISMS-CORAS on the novel artifacts and the changes with respect to standard CORAS. We explain how our changes to CORAS are related to ISO 27001 and its documentation requirements as described in the previous section. The reader is referred to existing literature for details about standard CORAS [28].

Method   Artifacts

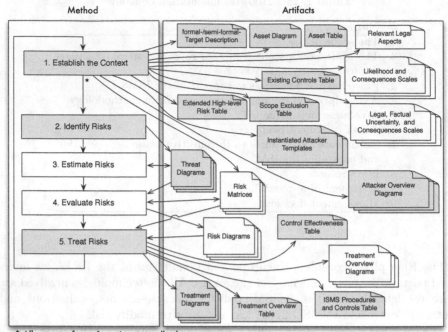

* All outputs of step 1 are inputs to all subsequent steps.

Fig. 1. ISMS-CORAS method and artifacts

The CORAS steps that we have modified are depicted in grey in Figure 1. The same is the case for the novel or modified documentation artifacts as depicted to the right. Note that the ISO 27001 standard does not have specific demands on the form of the documentation, as "documents and records may be in any form or type of medium" [19]. When introducing the ISMS-CORAS method in this section we explain the steps and tasks, as well as the documentation artifacts that are produced and used. We refer to Section 4 for examples of the artifacts.

Also note that in addition to the ISMS-CORAS documentation artifacts, the results should be documented by accompanying prose and textual documents. The main purpose of the artifacts is to support the method, structure the results in adequate ways, and ensure completeness of fulfilling the tasks and requirements of the ISO standard.

3.1 Step 1: Establish the Context

The first step of ISMS-CORAS is to establish the context of the ISMS. The main objective of this step is as for CORAS, namely to build the target description and to set the scope and focus of the analysis. There are, however, several extensions that are needed in order to fulfill the standard. We have also developed additional support for increasing the focus on information security as compared to CORAS, thereby facilitating the subsequent risk identification and threat modeling. Due to the extensions we have structured Step 1 of ISMS-CORAS into five sub-steps.

Step 1.1: Develop the Target Description. This task is to build the description of the target of analysis, including the relevant actors, roles, components, work processes, business processes, networks, etc. The description should include all parts of the system or organization that are included in the analysis and governed by the ISMS. It will serve as part of the basis of the subsequent risk identification and estimation, and it is therefore important that the level of abstraction reflects the desired level of details for the security risk analysis.

ISMS-CORAS requires an explicit description of the geographical location of the elements in the target description due to demands in the ISO 27001 standard. Such location information may also be important for the required identification of relevant legal issues. For example, according to the German Federal Data Protection Act, it is not allowed to store personal information outside of the European Union.

As for CORAS, ISMS-CORAS does not require a specific notation or language to be used for creating the target description. This is the decision of the customer and/or the risk analysts, but the description should be sufficiently precise or formal to avoid ambiguities and misunderstandings. Notations like UML [36] or similar are recommended.

A task that is specific for ISMS-CORAS is the justification of any exclusions from the scope of the ISMS. This is documented in a scope exclusion table that refers to target elements and provides the reason for the exclusion.

Step 1.2: Specify Security Objectives and Assets. The identification of the security objectives and the assets is an essential step in defining the focus of the analysis. CORAS is asset-driven, which means that all activities of the risk assessment are targeting these assets, which means that threats and vulnerabilities that are irrelevant for the identified assets are disregarded. The related task of characterizing the security objectives is required by the ISO standard.

The security objectives concern the protection of information security properties such as confidentiality, integrity and availability. An asset is anything of value to the organization for which the ISMS is established, and ISMS-CORAS focuses on information assets related to the target of analysis and the identified security objectives. The identified assets are documented using CORAS asset diagrams. ISMS-CORAS moreover requires a prioritization of assets, as well as the assignment of an asset owner to each asset, both of which are documented in an asset table. According to the ISO standard, the asset owner is the individual or entity responsible for the asset and its security, and is not an assignment of property right.

ISMS-CORAS requires also the documentation of existing controls for each of the identified assets using a table format. This is a detailing of the target description, and facilitates both the risk identification and the identification of any further necessary controls.

Step 1.3: Conduct High-Level Security Risk Analysis. In addition to the specification of the target of the analysis and the asset identification, CORAS recommends conducting a high-level risk analysis in order to identify the main concerns. ISMS-CORAS extends this activity with tasks specifically related to the security objectives and the preservation of security properties. For this purpose ISMS-CORAS provides three documentation artifacts, namely attacker templates, attacker overview diagrams and a high-level risk table.

The attacker template is a table format for describing attacker types, the assets and security properties they may threaten, the attack entry points and paths, attacker skills and motivation, as well as further relevant information. The instantiation of these templates not only serves as a basis for the subsequent and more detailed risk identification; it also documents attackers that are excluded from the scope, including the justification. This will help focusing the risk analysis, and also facilitate future maintenance and management of the ISMS, in particular when there are any changes in the organization or in the security objectives.

An attacker overview diagram is a graphical and high-level representation of an instantiated attacker template. It gives an intuitive representation of the identified attackers, and is a useful means for checking completeness of the attacker description.

The high-level risk analysis is an initial identification of scenarios and incidents that can be caused by the attackers, the vulnerabilities that may be exploited, as well as the related security objectives. The results are documented in the high-level risk table which serves as a basis for structuring the risk identification.

Step 1.4: Define the Scales and the Risk Evaluation Criteria. This task is similar to CORAS and most other approaches to risk analysis. It involves defining the scales that are needed for estimating the risks, as well as developing the criteria for accepting risks.

Risks are estimated by estimating the likelihoods and consequences of unwanted incidents. Hence, the scales to be defined are for making and documenting these estimates. Both likelihoods and consequences can be specified quantitatively or qualitatively, and we can use intervals or continuous scales. ISMS-CORAS uses the risk matrix format for specifying the risk level of each combination of a likelihood and a consequence, and for defining the risk evaluation criteria.

Step 1.5: Identify Legal Aspects. All relevant legal issues must be considered during the context establishment of the ISMS-CORAS method due to requirements of the ISO 27001 standard. The identification of legal aspects can be achieved by using our law pattern method [8,14], methods for legal risk management [30], or by involving lawyers or other domain experts.

While taking legal aspects into account, the focus of ISMS-CORAS is still on information security. Hence, the legal aspects to consider are mostly those that can arise due to information related issues such as privacy and data protection.

However, it may also be related to other laws and regulations, and to contractual obligations or legally binding agreements.

ISMS-CORAS makes use of Legal CORAS where legal norms that may cause risks are identified and analyzed. This requires the specification of scales for estimating legal uncertainty.

Further Considerations. In addition to the five sub-steps of the context establishment, Step 1 of ISMS-CORAS cannot be concluded until a written management and resource commitment for the ISMS has been provided as demanded by the ISO 27001 standard. ISMS-CORAS moreover requires the decision makers to formally approve the documentation of the context establishment.

The standard finally requires the identification of risk assessment methodology that will be applied when establishing the ISMS. In our case, the method is ISMS-CORAS as it has been developed for conducting security risk assessment compliant with the standard.

3.2   Step 2: Identify Risks

The objective of this step is to identify the risks that must be managed by determining where, when, why and how they may occur. The risk identification is conducted by a systematic walkthrough of the target description in order to identify incidents that may arise with respect to the identified assets. Following CORAS, the risk identification may be conducted by structured brainstorming involving people from different backgrounds and with different expert insight into the target of analysis. The task may also be supported by historical data, statistics, available repositories and databases of known threats and vulnerabilities, etc.

The risk identification is supported by CORAS threat diagrams, which are designed to support on-the-fly risk modeling during brainstorming sessions. The diagrams moreover document the results of this step. In particular, threat diagrams model how threats may exploit vulnerabilities in order to cause threat scenarios that lead to unwanted incidents.

ISMS-CORAS makes use of the instantiated attacker templates and attacker overview diagrams from Step 1. The resulting threat diagrams are therefore refinements of the initial attacker descriptions and the high-level risk analysis. ISMS-CORAS moreover extends the CORAS threat diagram notation with support for specifying attacker types and relating elements of the threat diagram to the models from the target description. ISMS-CORAS also makes use of Legal CORAS to make legal aspects explicit in the analysis and in the threat diagrams.

3.3   Step 3: Estimate Risks

The objective of this step is to estimate the identified risks by estimating the likelihoods and consequences of the identified unwanted incidents. CORAS makes use of structured brainstorming and any available data also for this task, and the results are documented by annotating the threat diagrams. Likelihoods of threat scenarios as well as conditional likelihoods for one scenario to lead to another are estimated in order to provide a stronger basis for the risk estimation and to understand the most important sources of risk. The CORAS calculus supports the estimation, and can also be used for consistency checking.

ISMS-CORAS focuses on the likelihoods of misuses and exploits by considering the attacker types and attacker skills documented during Step 1, which is similar to the descriptions proposed by the Common Criteria [21].

3.4   Step 4: Evaluate Risks

The objective of the risk evaluation is to determine which risks are acceptable and which risks need to be evaluated further for possible treatment. The step is identical to CORAS, and involves using the risk evaluation criteria from Step 1 together with the results from the risk estimation.

3.5   Step 5: Treat Risk

The objective of this step is to identify cost-effective means to mitigate unacceptable risks by reducing the likelihood and/or the consequence of unwanted incidents. CORAS uses treatment diagrams for this tasks, where identified treatments are related to the risk elements that are treated. ISMS-CORAS extends the notation by relating treatments to the relevant part of the target of analysis.

A further requirement of ISMS-CORAS is that the treatment identification is restricted to the normative controls defined in Appendix A of ISO 27001. Additional support for treatment identification is provided by a mapping from the ISMS-CORAS attacker types to ISO 27001 controls. This mapping includes a description of the objective of each control, as well as the kinds of target elements that are relevant.

As part of the risk treatment step, the existing controls must be taken into account, and treatment responsibility assigned to the asset owner. The residual risks must be documented and approved by the management. The treatment plan should be made by use of cost-benefit reasoning, for example by using the CORAS extension we proposed in earlier work [46].

ISMS-CORAS moreover requires the justification for why any Appendix A control is left out. For this purpose the treatment documentation incudes filling out a treatment overview table. For each treatment, this table specifies the related asset, asset owner and security objective, as well as a reasoning of why the treatment is sufficient. A control exclusion table specifies for each Appendix A control the reason for excluding each control that is not considered.

A further demand is the documentation of how to measure the effectiveness of each control, which is supported in ISMS-CORAS by a control effectiveness measure table. Finally, an analysis of possible conflicts between the identified treatments on the one hand and legal, regulatory and contractual requirements on the other hand must be identified. For this purpose Legal CORAS can be applied.

The identified controls, the existing controls and the justification of excluded controls form the documentation that is required by the ISO standard to make the so-called statement of applicability.

3.6 Contribution to ISMS Documents

In Table 2 we give an overview of how the ISMS-CORAS documentation artifacts depicted in Figure 1 support the ISO 27001 demands on the documentation of the ISMS. The first column refers to the ISO 27001 documents listed in Table 1, the second column lists the ISMS-CORAS artifacts that provide the documentation, and the third column refers to the ISMS-CORAS method steps that produce the artifacts.

Recall from Section 2.3 that documenting the risk assessment method (document 4) and creating the ISMS records (document 8) are outside the scope of ISMS-CORAS. Note also that the ISMS-CORAS artifacts need to be accompanied with complementary written documentation whenever additional clarifications are needed. For the management decisions (document 10) such written documentation is required as there are no supporting ISMS-CORAS artifacts.

Table 2. ISMS-CORAS support for ISO 27001 documentation; the first column refers to the documents listed in Table 1

#	ISMS-CORAS artifacts	Steps
1.	Target description and model; Scope exclusion table	1
2.	High-level risk tables	1
3.	Existing controls table ISMS procedure and controls table	1, 5
4.	N/A	
5.	Asset diagrams; Asset tables; Attacker templates; Attacker overview diagrams; Likelihood and consequence scales; Risk matrices (criteria); Threat diagrams; Risk diagrams	1–4
6.	Treatment diagrams; Treatment overview diagrams;	5
7.	Treatment overview table; Control effectiveness table	5
8.	N/A	
9.	Treatment diagrams; Treatment overview table	5
10.	Prose	1,5

4 Applying the ISMS-CORAS Method to a Smart Grid Scenario

In this section we demonstrate and exemplify the use of ISMS-CORAS by applying the method to a smart grid scenario. The section also introduces in more detail the ISMS-CORAS modeling and documentation artifacts that we mentioned in the previous section. The example is a simplified and shortened presentation of the corresponding demonstration in the technical report [10].

A smart grid provides energy on demand from distributed generation stations to customers. The grid intelligently manages the behavior and actions of its participants using information and communication technology (ICT). One of the novelties as compared to existing energy networks is the two-way communication between consumers and electric power companies. The envisioned benefits of the smart grid include a more economic, sustainable and reliable supply of energy. However, significant security concerns arise due to the possible dangers of missing availability of energy for customers, as well as threats to the security of customer data. These concerns are of particular relevance for the smart grid, because energy grids have a significantly longer lifespan than telecommunication networks [4]. In addition, privacy concerns have risen due, for example, to the possibility of creating behavioral profiles of customers when their energy consumption is transmitted over the grid in small time intervals [27].

In the following we present each of the five steps of ISMS-CORAS in turn, focusing in particular on the tasks and artifacts that go beyond standard CORAS. The reader is referred to existing literature for details on the latter [28].

4.1   Step 1: Establish the Context

The context establishment includes understanding and documenting the target of analysis, setting the scope and focus, identifying the assets and security objectives, and specifying the risk evaluation criteria. We structure the presentation of this step according to the five sub-steps of this initial phase of ISMS-CORAS.

Step 1.1: Establish the Target Description. The smart grid scenario we use for the example is provided by the industrial partners of the NESSoS network of excellence [35]. It concerns a smart home, which in our example is a house that is divided into two living units of separate electricity consumers.

For the purpose of describing the target of analysis at the desired level of abstraction, we use UML class diagrams and activity diagrams. As shown in Figure 2, the class diagram includes information about geographical locations, which is demanded by ISMS-CORAS. In the following we present some of the details about two of the diagrams that we developed.

In the class diagram of Figure 2 the associations represent communication connections, as the focus of the analysis is on the communication and security of information. The elements within the indicated scope are inside the smart home, and the indicated locations are based on real smart grid experiments conducted in Germany [43].

The *ICT Gateway (ICTG)* is the connection between the smart home and the information systems of the *Energy Supplier (ES)*. The *Consumers (CO)* are the house dwellers who use *Smart Appliances (SA)*. SAs are connected to the internet via the ICTG. An SA may, for example, be a fridge that can be remotely configured to cool down to a specific temperature at a specified time. The parties can use services offered by the energy providers via a *Consumer Home Energy Display (CHED)*. A *Thermostat (TH)* measures the temperature of the home or

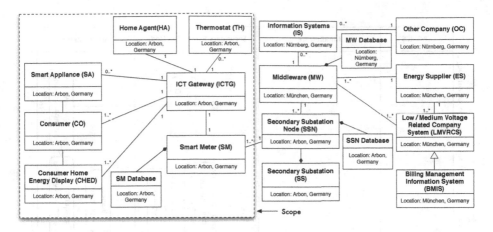

Fig. 2. Elements of the smart home scenario; the indicated scope (left part) includes the elements of the smart home, whereas the remaining elements (right part) belongs to the grid

of SAs. The temperature information is used, for example, for safety purposes, such as preventing a stove from overheating. They are also used by applications that control SAs. In addition, customers can use THs to configure SAs, for example to configure a heater to warm the smart home to a specific temperature during daytime. This information is used by the *Home Agent (HA)* to offer the CO a selection of different energy rates from different ESs [41]. Every consumer has its own *Smart Meter (SM)*, which is placed in the cellar of the smart home. The SM transfers the energy consumption/production data to the *Secondary Substation Node (SSN)*, which is part of the *Secondary Substation (SS)*.

The two consumers in this scenario share the cellar. The SM measures the energy consumption and sends the consumption information at specified intervals to the ES via the ICTG. Intermittently the energy consumption information is stored in the SM Database. Consumers can also produce energy and sell it to the ES. The SM measures this production and sends the information to the ES.

All of the communications in the smart grid are two-way and form the so-called *Advanced Metering Infrastructure (AMI)*. This scenario is in alignment with other European projects regarding smart grids [13,16,26,40].

Figure 3 shows one of the activity diagrams we specified in order to capture relevant behaviors of the target of analysis, namely the SM electricity reading for billing purposes. The SSN initiates the process every 24 hours, which is a configurable time interval. The SM receives the request, queries its internal database and sends the result back to the SSN. The process continues with some validation and verification checks before the LMVRCS eventually receives the reading. Note that we used three dots to simplify the diagram at places where activities are repeated. We refer to the technical report for the detailed description, and for the data structure model and further activity diagrams for the smart home scenario.

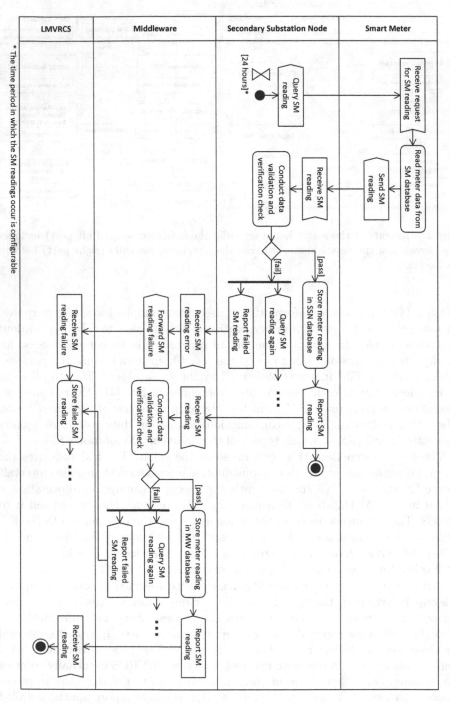

Fig. 3. Smart Meter reading process

Table 3. Scope exclusion table

Target element	Reason for scope exclusion
Secondary Substation (SS)	The SS is provided by the government and is protected by its security team
Secondary Substation Node (SSN)	The SSN is provided by the government and is protected by its security team
Middleware (MW)	The MW has a Common Criteria certification
...	...

Before concluding the description of the target, ISMS-CORAS requires the documentation and justification of any exclusions from the scope of the ISMS. This is documented in a scope exclusion table as exemplified in Table 3, which is an excerpt from the full table in the technical report.

Step 1.2: Specify Security Objectives and Assets. The client of the analysis (i.e. the commissioning party) is the energy supplier. Hence, the security risk analysis and the establishment of the ISMS is conducted for this party, and the security risks that we aim to identify are with respect to the security objectives and the assets of this party. However, the analysis is conducted from the viewpoint of the consumers in order to understand how security risks may arise due to the information processes involving the consumers and the smart homes.

The energy supplier is interested in analyzing privacy, integrity and confidentiality concerns of the consumers, and how these can be assured by establishing an ISMS. The following high-level security objectives are stated:

- The integrity, confidentiality, and availability of consumers' Home Agent configuration data shall be preserved
- The privacy of the consumers' energy consumption data shall be preserved
- The integrity, confidentiality, and availability of the consumers' Smart Appliances configuration data shall be ensured

The assets of the analysis are depicted in the CORAS asset diagram of Figure 4. The *Consumers' energy consumption data* shall be protected from attackers that may use this data for creating behavioral profiles. The value of the *Smart Appliances' configuration* to the consumer is essential, because without it the consumer loses control of the appliances in their home. For example, a stove could heat up during the night and cause a fire. The *Home Agents' configuration* states from/to which energy supplier the consumer buys/sells energy. An unauthorized change in the configuration could, for example, lead to the purchase of electricity at a too high price.

The arrows in the CORAS asset diagrams are so-called *harms* relations; a relation from one asset to another means that harm to the former may lead to harm to the latter. Hence harm to any of the three mentioned assets may cause harm to the *Consumers' security and privacy*.

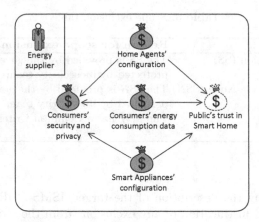

Fig. 4. Assets

In order to identify and assess risk, CORAS also includes so-called indirect assets. An indirect asset is an asset that, with respect to the target and scope of the analysis, is harmed only via harm to other assets. Hence, the risks are identified only with respect to the direct assets, but the risk estimation and evaluation also take into account the harm to the indirect ones. In our scenario the *Public's trust in Smart Home* is an indirect asset. We do not treat the indirect asset further in this chapter, and rather refer the reader to CORAS [28].

As a means to further focus the risk analysis, ISMS-CORAS requires the ranking of assets according to their relative importance. This is documented in an asset table as shown in Table 4, where 1 denotes the highest importance. The asset table also specifies the asset owner. Note that indirect assets are not included as risks with respect to these are identified via the direct assets, and the protection of these assets is the responsibility of the owners of the related direct assets.

Table 4. Asset table with ranking and owner

Asset	Rank	Owner
Consumers' energy consumption data	1	Mr. Jones
Smart Appliances' configuration	2	Mrs. Smith
Home Agents' configuration	3	Mr. Jones
Consumers' security and privacy	2	Mrs. Jackson

Existing controls for each asset are documented in the table format shown in Table 5, which is an excerpt from the corresponding table in the full technical report. These refer to controls implemented by the energy supplier, and are based on the controls specified by the ISO 27001 standard.

Table 5. Existing controls table

Asset	Existing Control
Consumers' energy consumption data	Secure communications between the SM and the SSN by encrypted data communication and encryption of all data on removable devices like SD-cards; data integrity by certificates and hash values
Home Agents' configuration	Access control: The prices and tariffs the SM can only be read by the customer; only the energy supplier is allowed to update prices and tariffs
...	...

Step 1.3: Conduct High-Level Security Risk Analysis. The high-level security analysis is conducted in order to get an initial understanding of the most important security risks, and to narrow down the scope of the analysis. The results are used to prioritize and structure the risk identification in Step 2. The attacker template and the attacker overview diagrams are ISMS-CORAS artifacts, whereas the high-level risk table is an extended version of the corresponding CORAS artifact. We have based the attacker template and attacker overview diagrams on the ideas behind misuse cases [37,44], which also rely on textual templates for describing misuse cases that attackers conduct, as well as corresponding UML use case diagrams [36]. The difference to our work is that ISMS-CORAS has a strong focus on security risk analysis, which is required for compliance with the ISO 27001 standard.

The ISMS-CORAS attacker template is shown in Table 6, and its instantiations give a structured way of describing attacker types, motivations, assumptions and resulting threat scenarios. The template consists of three parts, namely a *basic attacker description*, a *refined attacker description*, and *results*.

The basic attacker description starts with the definition of the attacker type, which is based on our previous work [6,9] where attackers are classified into the following categories. *Physical attackers* threaten the physical elements of the system, e.g., hardware or buildings that host computers. *Network attackers* threaten network connections within the target of analysis. *Software attackers* threaten software components of the system, e.g., the smart meter. *Social engineering attackers* threaten humans, e.g., the consumers. We reason about these types of attackers to determine whether they are relevant to our target of analysis, given its scope and assets. The reason for any exclusion of an attacker is that it cannot pose a threat to the target system and its assets. For example, if we analyze an autonomous system that has no humans in its scope, social engineering attackers do not need to be considered in the remaining analysis. All such reasons for exclusion of an attacker from the scope of the analysis have to be documented.

The usage of the template requires a statement about which assets are threatened by the attackers. The template has to be adjusted for each analysis according to the identified assets. We also state which of the security goals of confidentiality,

Table 6. Attacker template

Basic Attacker Description	
Attacker Type	□Physical Attacker □Network Attacker □Software Attacker □Social Engineering Attacker
Threatened Assets	□Asset 1 □Asset 2 □...
Threatened Security Goals	□Availability □Confidentiality □Integrity
	Reasoning
	– Explain why the selected security goals of an asset are threatened. – Reason also why the remaining security goals are excluded.
Entry Points	□Target Description Element 1 □Target Description Element 2 □...
	Reasoning
	– State why the selected elements are entry points for this attacker. – Reason why the remaining entry points are not relevant.
Attack Paths (possible vulnerabilities)	Describe all attack paths from the entry points to the assets.
Assumptions of the Target Description	□Target Description Element 1 □Target Description Element 2 □...
	Describe all assumptions about the target description.
Refined Attacker Description	
Required Attack Skills	State which kind of skills the attacker needs to succeed.
Attacker Motivation	□financial gain □self-interest □revenge □external pressure □curiosity
	Reasoning
	– Describe why the selected attacker motivations are relevant. – Explain also all exclusions of attacker motivations.
Required Resources	Describe the resources required for the attacker to conduct the attack.
Assumptions about the Attacker	Describe the assumptions about the motivation, skills, and resources of the attacker.
Insider / Outsider	Describe the difference if persons that are inside the scope and persons that are outside are the attacker.
Results	
Threats	Describe the high-level threats the attacker presents.
Reasons for Scope Exclusion	Describe the reasons for excluding the attacker or variants of the attacker from the scope of the threat analysis.

integrity, and availability that is/are threatened, and a reasoning of why any assets and security goals are selected or ruled out. The reasoning should be based on the attacker type.

The *entry points* and *attack paths* are based on Microsoft Threat Modeling [45]. This technique focuses on analyzing all interfaces of the target description elements to the outside world, and afterwards analyzing how an attacker can reach a particular asset from these entry points. A sequence of actions of an attacker leading him/her to the asset is a so-called *attack path*. An attack path without mitigating controls represents a vulnerability. Our attacker template has to be instantiated with the elements of the target description for each analysis.

A subsequent task is to reason about why an attacker can use an entry point or not, and to describe resulting attack paths. The last task for instantiating the first part of the attacker template is to specify assumptions about elements of the target description that reduce the number of entry points or attack paths.

The *refined attacker description* requires a description of the skills an attacker needs in order to succeed in harming the assets. The field *attacker motivation* is based on a study from the SANS Institute [3] that revealed four fundamental motivations of social engineering attackers: *Financial gain, self-interest, revenge,* and *external pressure*. We also added the motivation *curiosity*, which we identified in discussions with the industrial partners of the NESSoS project.

A subsequent task is to reason about why motivations are part of the scope of a particular attacker or why the motivations in regard to the attacker type and the threatened assets do not make sense. Existing threat classifications (such as the STRIDE classification [17]) can be used in combination with motivations to further facilitate the reasoning about attackers, in case threats do not come to mind immediately.

The *required resources* field describes the kind of resources, such as material and money, that the attacker requires to succeed in the attack. The instantiation of the template also involves the elicitation of *assumptions about the attacker*. The *insider/outsider* field shall invoke a reasoning of attackers that are part of the target description (insiders) and those that are not (outsiders). The *results* part of the template sums up the information collect about an attacker. This includes specifying the *threats* an attacker causes and also the *reasons for scope exclusions* of attackers.

In the technical report [10] we give examples of instantiated attacker templates for the smart home scenario for four kinds of attackers, namely a physical attacker, a network attacker, a software attacker and a social engineering attacker. Due to space constraints we omit these tables here, and show only the corresponding attacker overview diagram for the network attacker in Figure 5. Each such diagram always refers to one specific instantiation of the attacker template, and gives a brief and intuitive overview of the attacker, the attack entry points, the assets that may be harmed, as well as which of the security properties of confidentiality (C), integrity (I) and availability (A) that are affected. We have also identified a number of validation conditions to check the correctness and completeness of the attacker descriptions that are presented in the report.

The high-level security risk analysis takes into account the description of the target, the identified assets, and the instantiated attacker templates. The results serve as a means to further refine the scope and focus of the analysis, and to structure the risk identification of Step 2. The high-level risk table is exemplified with two entries in Table 7.

Note that there obviously are cases of attacks that involve the combination of attacker types. An attacker could, for example, target both network and software vulnerabilities at the same time. ISMS-CORAS allows for this by the possibility of considering more than one attacker type in the template. Such possible

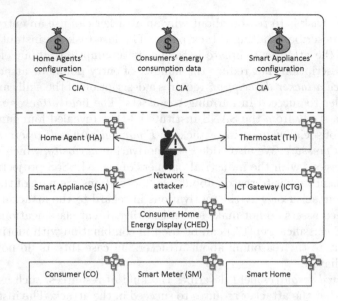

Fig. 5. Attacker overview diagram for network attacker

Table 7. High-level risk table

Who/what causes it?	What is the incident? What is harmed?	What makes it possible?	What are the security objectives?
Software attacker	Theft of energy consumption data	Insufficient malware detection	Consumers' privacy
Physical attacker	Housebreaking and destruction of Smart Meter	Insufficient physical protection	Availability of energy consumption data
...	...	...	...

combinations should also be identified and analyzed in more detail during the subsequent risk identification of Step 2.

Step 1.4: Define the Scales and the Risk Evaluation Criteria. This step is identical to CORAS, and includes the definition of scales for likelihoods and consequences. In the smart grid scenario we use qualitative scales of five values. In increasing order, the likelihoods are *rare*, *unlikely*, *possible*, *likely* and *certain*, whereas the consequences are *insignificant*, *minor*, *moderate*, *major* and *catastrophic*. We refer to the technical report for the more precise definition of the values since they are not important for the purpose of this chapter.

The risk evaluation criteria are shown in Figure 6, and distinguish between acceptable and unacceptable risks. The acceptable combinations of likelihoods and consequences are in light shading, whereas the unacceptable combinations are in dark shading.

Step 1.5: Identify Legal Aspects. The smart home scenario involves certain legal issues, and in our example both the German Energy Industry Act and the German Federal Data Protection Act (BDSG) apply. The latter refers to personal information, and according to [22,25,39], energy consumption data is personal information. We refer to the technical report for a detailed discussion of the implied legal issues, but mention only that the BDSG requires the informed consent of the person whose data is collected. In our scenario the metering data is collected once a day, and the shift to shorter intervals is an example of a possible violation.

In order to make the legal risk explicit in the analysis we introduce the asset of *Legal compliance*. We also define a consequence scale for this asset using the same terms as before, ranging from *insignificant* to *catastrophic*. See the technical report for further details.

4.2 Step 2: Identify Risks

The risk identification involves the identification and documentation of how threats and attackers may exploit vulnerabilities in order to initiate threat scenarios that lead to unwanted incidents. We give here a small and quite high-level example in order to illustrate the artefacts.

The risk identification refines the attacker descriptions and the high-level risk table by using CORAS threat diagrams. Figure 7 illustrates how ISMS-CORAS extends the CORAS threat diagram notation with the attacker motivation (depicted as a cloud) and the references from vulnerability to the target element that contains it. In our example a software attacker changes the Smart Meter configuration such that the frequency of readings is increased to every 15 minutes. A network attacker exploits a vulnerability in the ICT Gateway in order to steal energy consumption data.

In Figure 8 we show how Legal CORAS is used to take into account legal issues. As explained above, an increase in the frequency of Smart Meter readings may be

		Consequence				
		Insignificant	Minor	Moderate	Major	Catastrophic
Likelihood	Rare					
	Unlikely					
	Possible					
	Likely					
	Certain					

Fig. 6. Risk evaluation criteria; the light shading represents acceptable risk levels, while the dark shading represent unacceptable risk levels

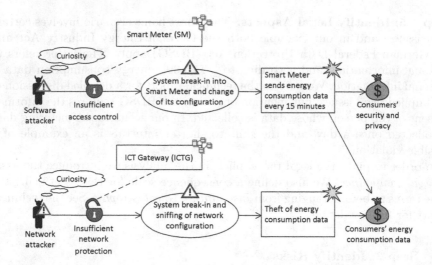

Fig. 7. Threat diagram

a violation of the BDSG. The diagram documents the legal norm that may apply when the incident *Smart Meter sends energy consumption data every 15 minutes* occurs. If the norm applies, this may lead to the incident of prosecution.

4.3   Step 3: Estimate Risks

This step is identical to CORAS, and involves the estimation of likelihoods and consequences of unwanted incidents. The results are documented by annotating the threat diagrams as illustrated in Figure 8. Legal uncertainties are also estimated and annotated on the identified legal norms. The latter is an estimate of the likelihood that the norm will actually apply under the identified circumstances. For the detailed explanation of the specific estimates we refer the reader to the full technical report.

4.4   Step 4: Evaluate Risks

The likelihood and consequence estimates are combined into risks using CORAS risk diagrams as exemplified in Figure 9. The risk levels (acceptable or unacceptable) are determined using the risk evaluation criteria as specified in the risk matrix of Figure 6. Note that because a risk is the combination of an unwanted incident and an asset, the incidents identified in Figure 8 represent four risks. In order to distinguish between them we give each risk a unique identifier (such as *SMS1* and *SMS2*). From Figure 9 and the filled in matrix in Figure 10 we see that there is one acceptable risk and three unacceptable.

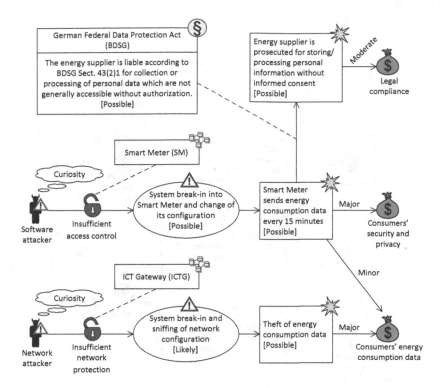

Fig. 8. Threat diagram with estimates

4.5   Step 5: Treat Risk

The unacceptable risks have to be evaluated for possible treatment. Appendix A of ISO 27001 describes a set of normative controls, and ISMS-CORAS requires these to be considered.

ISMS-CORAS provides support for the selection of controls by a mapping of controls to attacker types. Due to space constraints we do not present this mapping here, but rather refer to the full report. Each mapping refers to an ISO control (e.g. A.10.4 Protection against malicious and mobile code), an attacker type (e.g. software attacker), a control objective (e.g. integrity of software and information), and the relevant kind of target elements (e.g. critical software and services).

The identification and documentation of risk treatments are exemplified by the treatment diagram in Figure 11. The novelty of ISMS-CORAS is that the ISO 27001 controls have to be considered. The attacker motivation and related target elements are moreover specified, as for the extended threat diagram notation.

Each identified treatment points to the element of the threat diagram that it treats. The analyst may optionally annotate this relation with the treatment effect, which may be reduction of likelihood (*RL*) or reduction of consequence

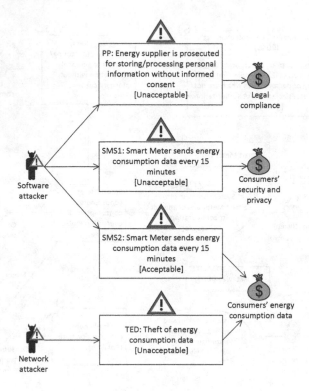

Fig. 9. Risk diagram

		Consequence				
		Insignificant	Minor	Moderate	Major	Catastrophic
Likelihood	Rare					
	Unlikely					
	Possible		SMS2	PP	SMS1 TED	
	Likely					
	Certain					

Fig. 10. Risk evaluation

(*RC*). In Figure 11, controls for the protection of the ICT Gateway have been identified where, for example, improved network protection control may reduce the likelihood of a system break-in by a network attacker. Further treatments and their explanations are given in the report.

For the example of the use of the treatment overview diagrams, the treatment overview tables, the control exclusion table, the control effectiveness measure table and the ISMS procedure and control table, we refer the reader to the

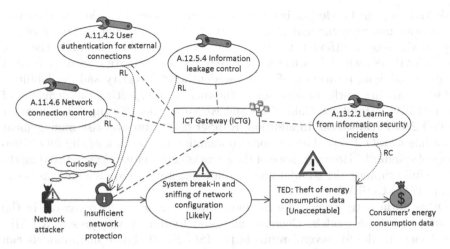

Fig. 11. Treatment diagram

full technical report. These documentation artifacts documents the rationale for the treatment selection, including the related assets and security objectives, the responsible entities, as well as the necessary procedures and controls.

5   Related Work

To the best of our knowledge no specific methods for security requirements engineering or security risk analysis exist that support the establishment of an ISO 27001 compliant ISMS, and that satisfies the standard's documentation demands as is the goal of ISMS-CORAS.

Looking at established standards and methods for security risk analysis, several alternatives could be considered for facilitating the establishment of an ISMS, but none of them provide systematic support for ISO 27001 compliance. OCTAVE [2] is a suite of tools, techniques and methods for risk-based information security assessment and planning. Although the security risk analysis process is similar to ISMS-CORAS, the aim of OCTAVE is not to create and document an ISMS. The same is the case for CRAMM [42]. Both CRAMM and OCTAVE are compliant with the BS 7799 information security standard, which was adopted by ISO 27001. However, the focus is still on the security risk analysis, and less on systematically fulfilling the standard's requirements to ISMS establishment and documentation. The CRAMM repositories of assets, threats and countermeasures could, however, support the ISMS-CORAS process.

EBIOS [1] is a method for assessing and treating risks related to information systems security, and is consistent with the ISO 31000, ISO 27001 and ISO 27005 standards. While consistent with these standards, the method is designed for security risk identification and mitigation and provides therefore only partial support for establishing an ISO 27001 ISMS. The Microsoft Security

Risk Management Guide [33] is developed to support organizations in the overall security management and risk assessment. The fulfillment of ISO 27001 is beyond the scope, although there are many overlaps. The similar is the case for FRAAP [38], which is a method for analysis of information security related issues, focusing on protection of data confidentiality, integrity and availability.

Other existing works provide some guidance in interpreting the demands of the ISO 27001 standard. Calder [11] and Kersten et al. [23] provide advice for an ISO 27001 realization. In addition, Klipper [24] focuses on risk management according to ISO 27005. The author also includes an overview of the ISO 27000 series of standards. However, none of these works consider using structured methods to fully support the standard and its documentation requirements, as is the aim of ISMS-CORAS.

Other authors try to capture the most important relations presented in the standard by using models. Cheremushkin and Lyubimov [12] present a UML-based meta-model for several terms of the ISO 27000. These meta-models can be instantiated and, thus, support the refinement process [29]. However, the authors do not present a holistic method to information security.

Some existing approaches aim at improving the establishment of an ISMS via automation. Montesino et al. [34] investigate possible automation of controls that are listed in the ISO 27001 and ISO 27002. Their work can complement our own by providing some automation, but does not provide a complete method for establishing and documenting an ISMS.

For the Common Criteria (CC) standard [21] there exists a security requirements engineering approach that uses the standard as a baseline for a method. Mellado et al. [31] created the Security Requirements Engineering Process (SREP), which is an iterative and incremental security requirements engineering process. In addition, SREP is asset-based, risk driven, and follows the structure of the Common Criteria [32]. The work differs from ours, because the authors do not support the ISO 27001 standard and also do not aim at security standard compliance or satisfying the Common Criteria documentation demands. In addition, Ardi and Shahmehri [5] extend the CC Security Target document with a section that considers knowledge of existing vulnerabilities. The authors aim at improving the CC and not at supporting its establishment.

6 Conclusion

In this chapter we have presented ISMS-CORAS, which is a structured method for establishing an information security management system (ISMS) that is compliant with the ISO 27001 standard. ISMS-CORAS is supported by techniques, modeling guidelines and documentation templates to ensure that all requirements to tasks and documentation are fulfilled. ISO 27001 defines the so-called Plan-Do-Check-Act (PDCA) model that specifies how to establish, implement, monitor and maintain an ISMS. ISMS-CORAS is developed to support the plan phase, and therefore focuses on the establishment and documentation of an ISMS.

Establishing an ISMS involves conducting a security risk analysis following a process similar to those defined by ISO 31000 and ISO 27005. Because CORAS is based on the former standard it already fulfills many of the ISO 27001 requirements to risk analysis and documentation. CORAS moreover comes with techniques, guidelines, modeling support and tool support that facilitate several parts of the ISO 27001 tasks. A further useful feature of CORAS in the ISMS context is the support for modeling and analyzing legal aspects.

ISMS-CORAS extends CORAS with the features, artefacts and techniques that are needed to provide complete support for establishing and documenting an ISMS. Some of the main novelties of ISMS-CORAS are the following. The method comes with detailed steps for asset identification, threat analysis, risk management and security reasoning; it is supported by attacker templates, classification of attacker types and attacker overview diagrams to facilitate and ensure completeness of attacker identification; it is supported by several kinds of diagrams for threat and risk modeling with attacker types, modeling of vulnerabilities and attacker entry points, as well as legal aspects; it provides a mapping between attacker types and ISO 27001 controls to facilitate treatment identification. These and other novelties in combination provide a systematic support for generating the required ISMS documentation in compliance with the standard.

As part of future work we plan to extend the approach to support all phases of the PDCA model, and not only the ISMS establishment of the plan phase. We will also conduct empirical studies to evaluate ISMS-CORAS and improve its usability. As part of the evaluation and validation, we moreover plan to compare ISMS-CORAS with alternative approaches to establish and document an ISO 27001 compliant ISMS. In particular, we will use publicly available tools such as verinice [47] and templates like the free ISO27k Toolkit [15] to create ISMS artifacts using the smart grid scenario presented in this chapter. The artifacts will serve as a basis for comparison and evaluation of ISMS-CORAS.

Acknowledgments. The research presented in this chapter was partially funded by the European Commission FP7 via the NESSoS (256980) network of excellence and the RASEN (316853) project.

References

1. Agence nationale de la sécurité des systèmes d'information: EBIOS 2010 – Expression of Needs and Identification of Security Objectives (2010) (in French)
2. Alberts, C.J., Dorofee, A.J.: OCTAVE Criteria. Tech. Rep. CMU/SEI-2001-TR-016, CERT (2001)
3. Allen, M.: Social engineering: A means to violate a computer system. SANS Institute Reading Room (2007)
4. Aloul, F., Al-Ali, A.R., Al-Dalky, R., Al-Mardini, M., El-Hajj, W.: Smart grid security: Threats, vulnerabilities and solutions. International Journal of Smart Grid and Clean Energy 1(1), 1–6 (2012)
5. Ardi, S., Shahmehri, N.: Introducing vulnerability awareness to Common Criteria's security targets. In: Fourth International Conference on Software Engineering Advances (ICSEA 2009), pp. 419–424. IEEE Computer Society (2009)

6. Beckers, K., Côté, I., Hatebur, D., Faßbender, S., Heisel, M.: Common Criteria CompliAnt Software Development (CC-CASD). In: Proceedings of the 28th Symposium on Applied Computing, pp. 937–943. ACM (2013)

7. Beckers, K., Faßbender, S., Heisel, M., Küster, J.-C., Schmidt, H.: Supporting the development and documentation of ISO 27001 Information Security Management Systems through security requirements engineering approaches. In: Barthe, G., Livshits, B., Scandariato, R. (eds.) ESSoS 2012. LNCS, vol. 7159, pp. 14–21. Springer, Heidelberg (2012)

8. Beckers, K., Faßbender, S., Küster, J.-C., Schmidt, H.: A pattern-based method for identifying and analyzing laws. In: Regnell, B., Damian, D. (eds.) REFSQ 2011. LNCS, vol. 7195, pp. 256–262. Springer, Heidelberg (2012)

9. Beckers, K., Hatebur, D., Heisel, M.: A problem-based threat analysis in compliance with Common Criteria. In: Proceedings of the International Conference on Availability, Reliability and Security (ARES 2013), pp. 111–120 (2013)

10. Beckers, K., Heisel, M., Solhaug, B., Stølen, K.: ISMS-CORAS – A structured method for establishing an ISO 27001 compliant information security management system. Tech. Rep. A25626, SINTEF ICT (2013)

11. Calder, A.: Implementing Information Security based on ISO 27001/ISO 27002: A Management Guide. Haren Van Publishing (2009)

12. Cheremushkin, D.V., Lyubimov, A.V.: An application of integral engineering technique to information security standards analysis and refinement. In: Proceedings of the 3rd International Conference on Security of Information and Networks (SIN 2010), pp. 12–18. ACM (2010)

13. Evaluation of general requirements according state of the art. OpenNode project deliverable D1.2 (2010)

14. Faßbender, S., Heisel, M.: From problems to laws in requirements engineering – Using model-transformation. In: International Conference on Software Paradigm Trends (ICSOFT 2013), pp. 447–458. SciTePress (2013)

15. FREE ISO27k Toolkit, http://www.iso27001security.com/html/iso27k_toolkit.html (accessed January 21, 2014)

16. Functional use cases. OpenNode project deliverable D1.3 (2010)

17. Howard, M., LeBlanc, D.: Writing Secure Code, 2nd edn. Microsoft Press (2003)

18. International Organization for Standardization: ISO 31000 – Risk management – Principles and guidelines (2009)

19. International Organization for Standardization / International Electrotechnical Commission: ISO/IEC 27001 – Information technology – Security techniques – Information security management systems – Requirements (2005)

20. International Organization for Standardization / International Electrotechnical Commission: ISO/IEC 27005 – Information technology – Security techniques - Information security risk management (2008)

21. International Organization for Standardization / International Electrotechnical Commission: ISO/IEC 15408 – Common Criteria for Information Technology Security Evaluation (2009)

22. Karg, M.: Datenschutzrechtliche Bewertung des Einsatzes von "intelligenten" Messeinrichtungen für die Messung von gelieferter Energie (Smart Meter). Tech. rep., Unabhängiges Landeszentrum für Datenschutz (ULD) (2009) (in German)

23. Kersten, H., Reuter, J., Schröder, K.W.: IT-Sicherheitsmanagement nach ISO 27001 und Grundschutz. Vieweg+Teubner (2011) (in German)

24. Klipper, S.: Information Security Risk Management mit ISO/IEC 27005: Risikomanagement mit ISO/IEC 27001, 27005 und 31010. Vieweg+Teubner (2010) (in German)
25. Knyrim, R., Trieb, G.: Smart metering under EU data protection law. International Data Privacy Law 1(2), 121–128 (2011)
26. Kreutzmann, H., Vollmer, S.: Protection profile for the gateway of a smart metering system (Smart meter gateway PP). Tech. Rep. BSI-CC-PP-0073, Federal Office for Information Security, version 1.2, Final Release (2013)
27. Lin, H., Fang, Y.: Privacy-aware profiling and statistical data extraction for smart sustainable energy systems. IEEE Transactions on Smart Grid 4(1), 332–340 (2013)
28. Lund, M.S., Solhaug, B., Stølen, K.: Model-Driven Risk Analysis – The CORAS Approach. Springer (2011)
29. Lyubimov, A., Cheremushkin, D., Andreeva, N., Shustikov, S.: Information security integral engineering technique and its application in ISMS design. In: Sixth International Conference on Availability, Reliability and Security (ARES 2011), pp. 585–590. IEEE Computer Society (2011)
30. Mahler, T.: Legal Risk Management – Developing and Evaluating Elements of a Method for Proactive Legal Analyses, With a Particular Focus on Contracts. Ph.D. thesis, University of Oslo (2010)
31. Mellado, D., Fernandez-Medina, E., Piattini, M.: A comparison of the Common Criteria with proposals of information systems security requirements. In: The First International Conference on Availability, Reliability and Security (ARES 2006), pp. 654–661. IEEE Computer Society (2006)
32. Mellado, D., Fernández-Medina, E., Piattini, M.: Applying a security requirements engineering process. In: Gollmann, D., Meier, J., Sabelfeld, A. (eds.) ESORICS 2006. LNCS, vol. 4189, pp. 192–206. Springer, Heidelberg (2006)
33. Microsoft Solutions for Security and Compliance and Microsoft Security Center of Excellence: The Security Risk Management Guide (2006)
34. Montesino, R., Fenz, S.: Information security automation: How far can we go? In: Sixth International Conference on Availability, Reliability and Security (ARES 2011), pp. 280–285. IEEE Computer Society (2011)
35. Network of Excellence on Engineering Secure Future Internet Software Services and Systems (NESSoS), http://www.nessos-project.eu/ (accessed December 19, 2013)
36. Object Management Group: OMG Unified Modeling Language (OMG UML), Superstructure. Version 2.3, OMG Document: formal/2010-05-03 (2010)
37. Opdahl, A.L., Sindre, G.: Experimental comparison of attack trees and misuse cases for security threat identification. Inf. Softw. Technol. 51, 916–932 (2009)
38. Peltier, T.R.: Information Security Risk Analysis, 3rd edn. Auerbach Publications (2010)
39. Raabe, O., Lorenz, M., Pallas, F., Weis, E.: Datenschutz im Smart Grid und in der Elektromobilität. Tech. rep., Karlsruher Institut für Technologie, KIT (2011) (in German)
40. Report on the identification and specification of functional, technical, economical and general requirements of advanced multi-metering infrastructure, including security requirements. OPEN meter project deliverable D1.1 (2009)
41. Rodden, T.A., Fischer, J.E., Pantidi, N., Bachour, K., Moran, S.: At home with agents: Exploring attitudes towards future smart energy infrastructures. In: Proceedings of the SIGCHI Conference on Human Factors in Computing Systems, CHI 2013, pp. 1173–1182. ACM (2013)

42. Siemens: CRAMM – The total information security toolkit,
    http://www.cramm.com/ (accessed: January 15, 2013)
43. Siemens: No longer a one-way street,
    http://www.siemens.com/innovation/apps/pof_microsite/
    _pof-spring-2011/_html_en/smart-grids.html (accessed December 19, 2013)
44. Sindre, G., Opdahl, A.L.: Templates for misuse case description. In: Procedings
    of the 7th International Workshop on Requirements Engineering, Foundation for
    Software Quality (REFSQ 2001), pp. 4–5 (2001)
45. Swiderski, F., Snyder, W.: Threat Modeling. Microsoft Press (2004)
46. Tran, L.M.S., Solhaug, B., Stølen, K.: An approach to select cost-effective risk
    countermeasures. In: Wang, L., Shafiq, B. (eds.) DBSec 2013. LNCS, vol. 7964,
    pp. 266–273. Springer, Heidelberg (2013)
47. verinice, http://www.verinice.org (accessed January 21, 2014)

Divide and Conquer – Towards a Notion of Risk Model Encapsulation

Atle Refsdal[1], Øyvind Rideng[2], Bjørnar Solhaug[1], and Ketil Stølen[1,3]

[1] SINTEF ICT, Norway
[2] Oilfield Technology Group, Norway
[3] Dep. of Informatics, University of Oslo, Norway
{atle.refsdal,bjornar.solhaug,ketil.stolen}@sintef.no,
oyvind.rideng@otg.no

Abstract. The criticality of risk management is evident when considering the information society of today, and the emergence of Future Internet technologies such as Cloud services. Information systems and services become ever more complex, heterogeneous, dynamic and interoperable, and many different stakeholders increasingly rely on their availability and protection. Managing risks in such a setting is extremely challenging, and existing methods and techniques are often inadequate. A main difficulty is that the overall risk picture becomes too complex to understand without methodic and systematic techniques for how to decompose a large scale risk analysis into smaller parts. In this chapter we introduce a notion of risk model encapsulation to address this challenge. Encapsulation facilitates compositional risk analysis by hiding internal details of a risk model. This is achieved by defining a risk model interface that contains all and only the information that is needed for composing the individual risk models to derive the overall risk picture. The interface takes into account possible dependencies between the risk models. We outline a method for compositional risk analysis, and demonstrate the approach by using an example on information security from the petroleum industry.

Keywords: Risk analysis, risk modeling, risk model encapsulation, risk composition, security, ICT.

1 Introduction

For most organizations, risk management is an indispensable part of the overall management process. Risk management is coordinated activities to direct and control an organization with regard to risk [11], and the objective is to systematically and proactively identify the current risk picture and to ensure that the necessary controls are in place to maintain risks at an acceptable level.

Risk management may be with respect to many different kinds of risk, such as financial, safety, operational, security and environmental damage. In this chapter we focus on (information) security [12]. The criticality of security is particularly evident when considering the information society of today, and the emergence of Future Internet technologies. Information systems and services become ever more

M. Heisel et al. (Eds.): Engineering Secure Future Internet Services, LNCS 8431, pp. 345–365, 2014.

complex, heterogeneous, dynamic and interoperable. Businesses, enterprises, governments, citizens and many other stakeholders rely more and more on the availability of services and information over the Internet, with Cloud services as a prominent example. Managing risks in such a setting is extremely challenging, and established methods and techniques are often inadequate. The main problems are that the overall risk picture becomes too complex to understand, and that the risk picture quickly and continuously changes and evolves.

Risk analysis is a core part of the risk management process, and should be conducted regularly in order to identify, assess and document risks, as well as identifying controls and means to mitigate risks. For most risk analyses only selected parts or aspects of a system or an organization are addressed. This is because it is infeasible or too costly to conduct a full analysis of the whole system or organization at the same time. For such risk analyses addressing selected parts or aspects we can make use of established methods and techniques (e.g. [1,2,6,11,15,16,19]). Such a traditional approach is fine when we can reach an adequate understanding of the risks by analyzing separate parts of the target in isolation. However, for large, complex systems or organizations we may need to consider all parts of the target in combination in order to adequately understand the full risk picture. Taking into account the infeasibility of addressing the full system or organization at once, we need novel techniques for sound and systematic composition of separate risk analyses in order to deduce an overall risk model.

The challenge we address in this chapter is how to facilitate a compositional [18] approach to risk analysis by applying the principle of *encapsulation*. Following a divide-and-conquer strategy we aim for an approach to risk management where separate parts of a system or organization can be analyzed individually. By risk model we mean any representation of risk information, such as threats, vulnerabilities, unwanted incidents and how they are related, as well as estimates of likelihoods and consequences. Compositional techniques should then enable the systematic and sound composition of the individual risk models in order to derive the overall combined result without having to reconsider the details of the individual models.

A compositional approach has several advantages. First, for systems or organizations that are to be analyzed from scratch, a compositional approach allows the analysis to be split-up top-down in manageable chunks in such a way that the details of each individual analysis do not have to be reconsidered when the results of the individual analyses are aggregated back into an overall risk model for the system or organization as a whole. Second, when there already are several risk analyses of different parts or aspects of some system or organization available, a compositional approach enables the overall risk picture to be derived bottom-up without re-analyzing what has already been analyzed. Third, if the target of one individual analysis is reused in another context, also the risk analysis for the target in question should be reusable in the new context. Fourth, when a system changes due to replacement or introduction of new parts, we should be able to deduce the risk level by re-analyzing only the modified parts.

In the example of this chapter we focus mainly on the first of these usage scenarios, namely the top-down one. The three others are however equally important but only partly addressed by the method presented in this chapter.

The contribution of the presented work is an approach to compositional risk analysis that is based on a new notion of risk model encapsulation. By encapsulation we mean that only the elements that are essential for the composition of risk models are externally observable via its interface. As already mentioned, we outline a method for compositional risk analysis from a top-down perspective where a large target is decomposed into sub-targets that are analyzed individually. We introduce techniques for risk model composition that make use of the risk interface of each individual risk model. We demonstrate the approach by using an example drawn from the petroleum industry.

The structure of the chapter is as follows. In Section 2 we present our notion of risk model encapsulation. In Section 3 we present the petroleum industry example that we use to illustrate our approach and techniques. In Section 4 we outline our method for compositional risk analysis, and in Section 5 to Section 7 we present and exemplify the method in more details. In Section 8 we discuss related work before we conclude in Section 9.

2   Risk Model Encapsulation

In this section we introduce and explain our notion of risk model encapsulation. The objective is to allow different risk models to be composed without having to know or understand all the interior details of the individual models. For this purpose we need to define a notion of risk model interface, where the interface contains all and only the information that is needed for risk model composition. Moreover, the resulting combined risk model should possess all the information that is needed for understanding the risk situation of the overall target.

A further challenge that needs to be tackled is how to take into account possible dependencies between the individual risk models. Each sub-target is analyzed separately, and the other sub-targets belong to the environment of the sub-target being analyzed. This means that the other sub-targets can serve as environmental causes of risk that need to be taken into account for the sub-target being analyzed, and that the sub-target in question can be the cause of risks for the sub-targets in its environment.

In the following we introduce our notion of risk model encapsulation by presenting our underlying conceptual model. The concrete modeling support is presented in Section 5 to Section 7.

In the UML [17] class diagram of Figure 1 the term *target* denotes the target of analysis. The goal of the analysis is to build the *risk model* for the target. The target may be decomposed into a number of more fine-grained targets (which we often refer to as sub-targets). There are two crucial features of our approach to risk model encapsulation. First, for each target we need to understand how it relates to its *environment*. Second, we need a precise notion of *interface* which consists of the risk information that is needed in order to compose the risk model in question with other risk models.

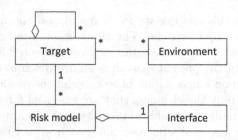

Fig. 1. Risk model

Figure 2 depicts the interface for risk model encapsulation in further detail. The interface consists of three sets of ingredients. The first one is a set of *threat relations* originating *from* the *environment* and impacting the target. These relations represent ways in which the environment may influence the risk model of the target.

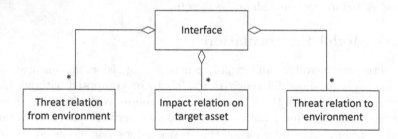

Fig. 2. Interface for risk model encapsulation

The second ingredient is a set of *impact relations* describing potential harm *on target assets*. A target asset is something of value inside the target that must be protected from unacceptable risk. For example, if the target is a database, a target asset could be the integrity of the information on the database. This in contrast with an environment asset that is something of value in the environment. Such an asset could, for example, be the reliability of a web service that uses the database.

The third ingredient is a set of *threat relations* from the target *to* the *environment* that represent ways in which the target may influence the risk model of the environment.

Before demonstrating the application of these concepts we next introduce our example.

3   The Petroleum Work Permit Example

Accidents on oil & gas rigs can have large consequences in terms of loss of life, damage to the environment and economic loss. Non-routine work that takes place on a rig, such as welding or replacement of defect gas detectors, may increase the risk. Therefore, all work except daily routine tasks requires a work permit (WP). This allows decision makers to obtain an overview of all the different types of work that is planned and ongoing on all locations on the rig at all times, to oversee all extra safety measures related to the work, and to reject or stop work if necessary. Every 12th hour, a WP meeting is held on the rig to decide which work permits to release for the next shift. When deciding whether to release (accept) or reject a WP, the decision makers need to take a number of safety considerations into account, including potential conflicts or interference with other work, the current state of safety barriers, and the weather. This is very challenging as the number of applications can be very high, meaning that only a few minutes or even less is available for each decision.

In the following we assume that a petroleum operator has initiated a project in collaboration with a software tool and service provider to update their ICT system for work permit management. In addition to functionality for registering, releasing and rejecting WP applications, the system will provide decision support in the form of an automated smart agent that collects relevant information for each WP application and provides advice to the human decision makers. The advice will be either a warning that the agent has detected something that might indicate that the WP should be rejected or considered extra carefully, accompanied by an explanation, or simply an empty message. Human decision makers will still be fully responsible for the final decision.

The UML collaboration diagram of Figure 3 shows an overall view of the system. The class RigSystem represents all ICT infrastructure related to WPs that are installed on the rig itself. WPAgent represents the automated agent. This will be developed and maintained by the software provider, as represented in Figure 3 by WPAgent maintainer. WeatherService is an Internet-based meteorological

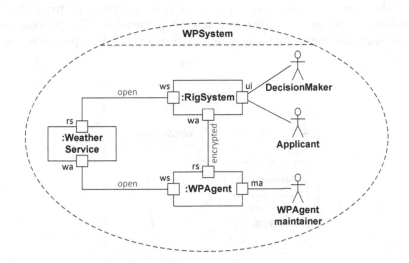

Fig. 3. Overall view of the system

service offering weather forecasts. The small boxes on the borders represent communication ports. The port ui on RigSystem represents the user interface of RigSystem, while the port ma on WPAgent represents the interface through which the WPAgent maintainer performs maintenance. All other ports represent technical interfaces.

The WPAgent will need information from WeatherService. It will also need to interact with the components of RigSystem, which explains the lines that are included between WPAgent and each of these entities. The communication between WPAgent and RigSystem goes via an encrypted Internet connection, while the communication with WeatherService uses an open line.

The internal details of RigSystem are shown in the UML internal structure diagram of Figure 4. Each of the internal components of RigSystem is available to WPAgent through the port wa on RigSystem. We have not assigned names to the internal communication ports. WPManager handles WP applications and release/reject decisions. All communication with users goes through WPManager, which also includes a screen showing weather data and forecasts that are continuously updated from WeatherService. DeviationsDB is a database where deviations related to the state, maintenance, testing etc. of equipment on the rig are recorded. For example, this includes information about any faults that have been detected, as well as tests and maintenance that have not been carried out. WPDB is a database that stores all WPs and related information, such as the location where the work takes place, who does the work, when the work starts and stops, what type of equipment will be used, and so on. WPManager includes a user interface for querying DeviationsDB and WPDB, as the Decision-Maker might want to obtain information from these databases before deciding whether to release or reject a new WP.

The WP application process is shown in the UML sequence diagram of Figure 5. Note that the update of weather data from WeatherService to RigSystem/WPManager is a continuous process that is independent from the WP application process and has therefore not been included. The process starts with the Applicant registering a new application for a WP, represented by the

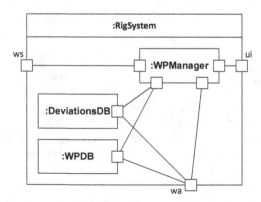

Fig. 4. Internal structure of RigSystem

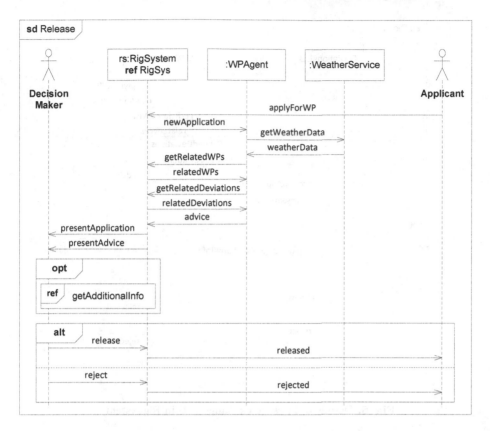

Fig. 5. Message exchange for the WP application process

applyForWP message. This information is forwarded to WPAgent, as represented by the newApplication message. WPAgent then collects the information it needs from the WeatherService and (the internal components of) RigSystem, as represented by the next six messages going from and to WPAgent. After collecting this information, the WPAgent produces its advice (a purely internal process that is not shown) and sends it to RigSystem, which then presents the application and the advice from WPAgent to DecisionMaker. At this point DecisionMaker may optionally decide to retrieve information about other WPs, deviations, and the weather. All this information is stored in WPDB, DeviationsDB and WeatherService, and made available to DecisionMaker through a user interface that is a part of WPManager (and therefore also RigSystem). In Figure 5 this is represented by the reference getAdditionalInfo, which has not been detailed further as its content is of little relevance for our purpose here. Finally, the DecisionMaker may either release or reject the WP, as illustrated by the two operands of the alt operator.

The UML sequence diagram in Figure 6 shows a decomposition of the RigSystem lifeline of Figure 5. All communication with external components go to/from WPManager, except the requests from WPAgent to WPDB and DeviationsDB.

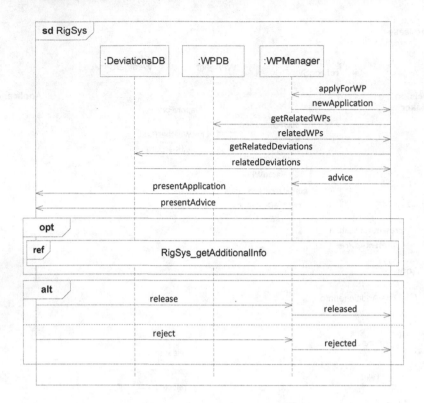

Fig. 6. Details of message exchange within RigSystem

4   Outline of a Method for Compositional Risk Analysis

In this section we outline a method for compositional risk analysis that makes use of target decomposition and risk model encapsulation. The method follows a top-down approach where we start with a high-level view of the target as a whole. The target is then decomposed before a risk analysis is conducted for each sub-target separately.

Our method is closely based on the risk analysis process as defined by the ISO 31000 standard on risk management. The process consists of five consecutive steps described as follows. 1) Establish the context involves defining the external and internal parameters to be accounted for when managing risk, and to set the scope and risk criteria for the risk management policy. 2) Risk identification is to find, recognize and describe risks. 3) Risk estimation is to comprehend the nature of risk and to determine the risk level. 4) Risk evaluation is to compare the risk estimation results with the risk criteria to determine whether each risk and its magnitude are acceptable or tolerable. 5) Risk treatment is the process of modifying the risk. Step 2–4 are referred to as risk assessment.

The main novelties of our compositional method are the target decomposition, the sub-target risk assessment, and the risk model composition. The remaining activities mainly follow the standardized process. The target decomposition happens during the context establishment, whereas the risk model composition happens at the end of the risk assessment. In the following method overview we focus on the steps that are specific for our method, omitting details that are explained in the ISO 31000 standard.

- **Context establishment**
  - Model and document the overall target of analysis
  - Identify the assets of the overall target of analysis
  - For each asset, identify the part of the target to which the asset belongs
  - Decompose the target (and possibly the assets) such that each asset belongs to exactly one sub-target
- **Compositional risk assessment**
  - Conduct risk assessment for each sub-target separately
  - Specify the risk model interface for each sub-target
  - Build the overall risk model by composing the sub-target risk models using their interfaces

A part of the context establishment in any risk analysis consists of describing and documenting the target of analysis at an adequate level of detail. In our top-down approach to compositional risk analysis we start by modeling the whole target of analysis at a level that is suitable for providing a high-level overview and for identifying the system level assets that should be the focus of the overall analysis. For each of the assets we next identify to which part of the target it belongs, i.e. where it is located. This means that the assets must be sufficiently specific. For example, if confidentiality of health records is an asset and the records are stored at different places, we may need to split this asset up and rather specify assets like confidentiality of health data as stored on a specific database. The target is then decomposed according to the location of assets. Note that while an asset can belong to one sub-target only, one sub-target can have several assets.

In addition to taking the asset location into account, the target decomposition should ensure that each sub-target is of a size and complexity that can be handled in one analysis. If the complexity of one sub-target is too high, it must be decomposed further.

Once the target is decomposed into adequate sub-targets separate risk assessments are conducted for each sub-target individually. This basically follows the standard risk assessment process, but we also need to take into account environment threats and environment assets. Once the sub-target risk models are completed, the respective encapsulated risk models are created. This is done by a straightforward mapping from the sub-target risk model that easily can be automated. Finally, the overall risk model is built by composing the sub-target risk models using their interfaces.

We demonstrate and exemplify the method and our techniques for compositional risk analysis over the next three sections using the petroleum work permit system. The examples illustrate essential aspects of our approach, and also serve to elaborate and further explain our notion of risk model encapsulation as introduced in Section 2.

The initial modeling and documentation of the overall target of analysis that is part of the context establishment was presented in Section 3. Before proceeding with the risk assessment, the assets need to be identified, and the target needs to be decomposed.

There are of course a number of critical information and service assets in the WP scenario. For the purpose of the example we select only a few that we focus on. Considering the rig system, it is obvious that availability of the WP data and availability of the WP advice are essential for both WP manager and for the decision maker. The availability of WP data is also essential for the WP agent that needs data for creating the advice. Considering the WP system as a whole, it is also critical to ensure the dependability of the WP agent. Because the WP agent is a software for automated decision support, the integrity of the software—including the implemented algorithms—needs to be protected. In the WP system analysis we are concerned about information security risks with respect to these assets.

Based on the identified assets we have decomposed the target into two sub-targets as indicated in Figure 7. Two of the assets are associated with the rig system, and two of them with the WP agent and its communication line to the rig system. In the remainder of the chapter we refer to the former as *sub-target A* and to the latter as *sub-target B*. Note that in this analysis the Internet weather service is part of the environment of the overall target of analysis.

In Section 5 and Section 6 we do the risk assessment and modeling for sub-target A and sub-target B, respectively. Subsequently we do the composition of the results in Section 7.

5   Risk Modeling for Sub-Target A

In this section we give a stepwise introduction to how we do the risk assessment for sub-target A by describing three different cases. We start with the simple situation where all threats and assets are internal, i.e. Case I is the identification of risks with respect to threats and assets only within sub-target A. Then we also consider external threats, i.e. Case II takes into account also environment threats, namely the external causes that can stem for other sub-targets or from the environment of the overall target. Finally, we address the general situation, i.e. Case III considers also environment assets, namely the assets of other sub-targets for which sub-target A can act as a source of risk. Note, importantly, that this stepwise introduction is only for pedagogical reasons, and does not indicate a specific order of what to consider during the risk assessment.

5.1   Case I: Internal Threats and Assets Only

The main purpose of our compositional approach to risk analysis is to allow individual parts of the target of analysis to be analyzed separately. In our example

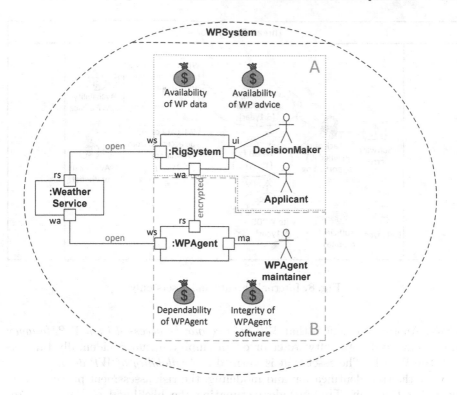

Fig. 7. Target assets and target decomposition

we have used the CORAS approach [15] for the risk assessment and risk modeling. CORAS is based on the ISO 31000 risk analysis process and comes with a language for specifying, assessing and documenting the identified risks by using so-called threat diagrams. However, our principles for risk model encapsulation and composition can be applied using also other notations for risk modeling.

Figure 8 shows our format for compositional risk modeling. It consists of three compartments, where the middle compartments includes all the threats, vulnerabilities, assets, etc. that are internal to the sub-target in question, i.e. to sub-target A in Figure 7. In the compartment to the left we model environment threats, and in the compartment to the right we model environment assets, neither of which are relevant when we restrict our attention to internal threats and assets only. The use of the latter two compartments are exemplified and further explained in the next two sub-sections.

Our example diagrams are rather small as the purpose is only to illustrate the approach. While they are based on a real industrial scenario we do not show here the actual results of a real risk analysis.

The threat diagram in Figure 8 identifies risk with respect to sub-target A. One of the identified unwanted incidents is that *WP advice cannot be accessed from WPManager*, which could be due to a software error that leads to malfunction of the WP manager. This incident harms the asset of *Availability of WP*

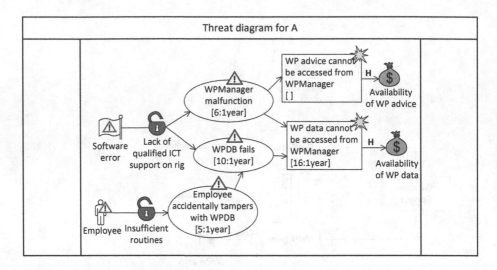

Fig. 8. Internal threats and assets only

advice. Another incident is that *WP data cannot be accessed from WPManager*, which may be due to software error or an employee that accidentally tampers with the WPDB. The asset that is harmed is *Availability of WP data.*

After the risk identification and modeling, the risk assessment proceeds with the risk estimation. This includes estimating the likelihood of the unwanted incidents to occur, as well as their consequences for the assets they harm. In the diagram the consequences are annotated on the impacts relations from unwanted incidents to assets. In our example we have used frequencies for the likelihood estimation, and we have used a scale of the three consequence levels high (H), medium (M) and low (L) for the consequences. The consequence values must be precisely defined for each asset, but this is omitted here as it is not important for the purposes of the chapter.

When estimating the frequencies for incidents to occur, we make use of likelihood estimates also for the threats and threat scenarios that lead to the incidents. The reader is referred to existing literature on CORAS for the calculus to reason about likelihoods and to do consistency checking [15,20]. In Figure 8 we have estimated that *WP data cannot be accessed from WPManager* occurs 16 times per year. The likelihood of the other incident, however, is not estimated at this point. This is because the analysts know that the availability of the WP advice depends also on the WP agent. Hence, we need to take into account also environment threats.

5.2 Case II: Also Considering Environment Threats

For a given sub-target the environment threats are the causes or origins of risks that are external to the sub-target. In Figure 9 we see that one such external threat to sub-target A is that *WPAgent fails to deliver advice.* Importantly,

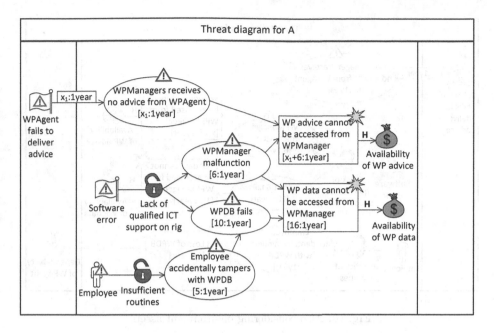

Fig. 9. Also considering environment threats

because this threat occurs outside of A, the estimation of its likelihood is not part of the risk assessment of A. Instead the variable x_1 is used such that we get a parameterized specification of the likelihoods of the scenarios and incidents that this threat may cause.

The environment threat in question may lead to the threat scenario *WPManager receives no advice from WPAgent*. Assuming that the identified threat is the only cause of this scenario, the estimated frequency is x_1 per year as annotated in the diagram. The estimation of the frequency of the resulting incident is done on the basis of the two scenarios that lead to it. As specified in Figure 9 the estimated frequency is the sum $x_1 + 6$ occurrences per year.

As we will see later the estimation of x_1 is done as part of the assessment of sub-target B, and this input is used when composing the threat diagrams to generate the risk picture for the overall target.

5.3   Case III: Also Considering Environment Assets

As we explained in the previous sub-section, compositional risk assessment must take into account also environment threats. In order to understand and analyze how one sub-target can act as an environment threat for another sub-target, we need a way to systematically consider all the other sub-targets.

Our approach to do this is to take into account all assets of the overall target in each individual risk assessment. However, while considering all assets, we still distinguish between the internal assets and the environment assets. This is illustrated in the threat diagram for sub-target A shown in Figure 10. One of the

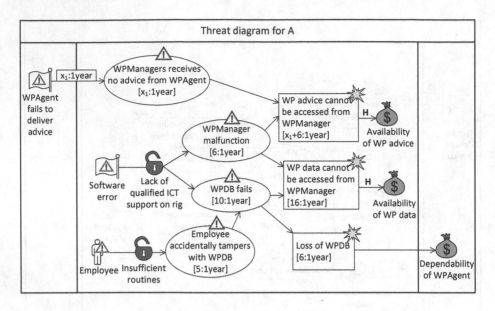

Fig. 10. Also considering environment assets

assets of the analysis that do not belong to A is *Dependability of WPAgent*. In the diagram this asset is placed in the environment compartment to the right. As part of the risk assessment of A we identify all incidents that may have an impact on any of the environment assets. In the example diagram, one such incident is *Loss of WPDB*. We use the environment impacts relation to specify this potential impact from A to the environment asset in question.

Note importantly that the consequence estimation for the environment assets is not done as part of the risk assessment of the sub-target in question. Exactly how incidents of the sub-target in question may impact assets belonging to other sub-targets needs to be analyzed as part of the risk assessment of each of the impacted sub-targets. This includes the estimation of the consequences.

6   Risk Modeling for Sub-Target B

In Figure 11 we exemplify a completed threat diagram for sub-target B. We see here that the incident *WPAgent fails to deliver advice* may impact the external asset *Availability of WP advice*. This asset belongs to A, which is why this incident occurs as an external threat in the threat diagram for A shown in Figure 10. From the diagram in Figure 11 we also see that incidents of one sub-target may impact its own assets as well as environment assets.

In the threat diagram for B there are two environment threats, namely *Cyber threat* and *Loss of WPDB*. The latter stems from A, while the former stems from the environment of the overall target. More specifically, in this case the cyber threat initiates an attack on the weather service that is provided over the Internet. Such a threat could, for example, be denial of service or malware.

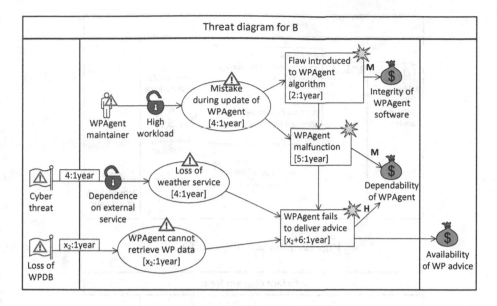

Fig. 11. Threat diagram for sub-target B

For the assessment of B it suffices to take into account the potential loss of the weather service and to estimate the likelihood.

Recall from the previous section that in principle we do not estimate the likelihoods of environment threats. This is why *Loss of WPDB* is assigned the variable x_2 in Figure 11. However, for environment threats that are part of the environment of the overall target, we can choose to make an estimate. This is exemplified for the cyber threat where we have specified the frequency 4 : 1 *year*. Such an estimate can be based, for example, on logs or historical data. Alternatively these estimates can be done during the risk composition. In that case the risk assessment for the sub-target in question gives a parameterized specification of also these kinds of environment threats.

The frequency estimation of the incident *WPAgent fails to deliver advice* is based on the estimates of the two scenarios and the incident that lead to it. Using x_2 as input variable, the estimate for this incident is $x_2 + 6$ occurrences per year.

7 Risk Composition

The threat diagrams introduced in the previous sections give the white-box view of the risk model for each sub-target; their purpose is to support the full risk assessment of the sub-targets, including all the internal threats, vulnerabilities and threat scenarios. To facilitate their composition, however, we create their corresponding interface diagrams.

The interface diagrams for A and B are depicted in Figure 12 and Figure 13, respectively. The interface diagrams contain the information that is needed to

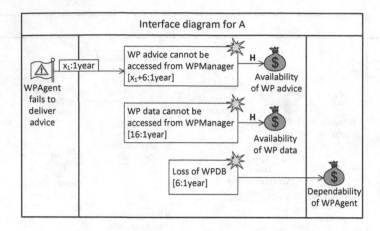

Fig. 12. Interface diagram for A

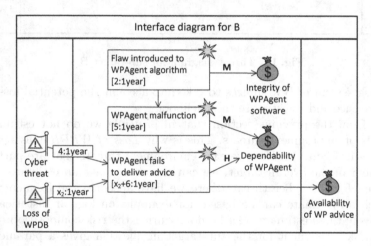

Fig. 13. Interface diagram for B

compose the different diagrams to yield the overall risk picture, and to document all of the risks with their risk levels.

When composing the threat interface diagrams the variable x_2 in Figure 13 is instantiated with the value 6 from the incident *Loss of WPDB* in Figure 12. The likelihood of the unwanted incident *WPAgent fails to deliver advice* is then calculated by $x_2 + 6$, which gives $12 : 1$ *year*.

The resulting threat interface diagram for A and B composed, and hence for our overall target of analysis, is depicted in Figure 14. Since the diagram covers the whole target the set of environment assets is empty. Moreover, the only environment threat is the one that belongs to the environment of the overall target.

The interface diagram for the full target shows all unwanted incidents with respect to the assets we identified during the context establishment. It also shows

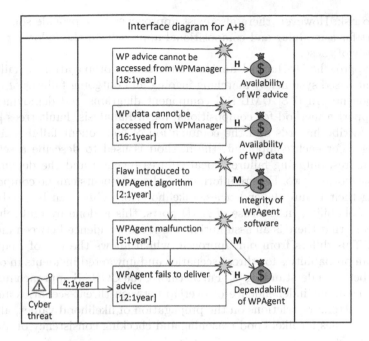

Fig. 14. Interface diagram for the composition of A and B

the likelihood and consequence estimates for each of the incidents. Because a risk is defined as an unwanted incident with its likelihood and consequence, we have in our example identified five risks. The risk levels are calculated by using a risk function such as a risk matrix.

In this paper we have focused on risk model encapsulation and compositional risk assessment. The steps of our outlined method cover the first four steps of the risk analysis process as defined by the ISO 31000 standard. The last step is the risk treatment, which is outside the scope of this chapter. Deciding which risks that need to be considered for possible treatment is done by comparing the resulting risk levels with the risk evaluation criteria that are defined during the context establishment.

8   Related Work

Few approaches to risk management and security assessment provide support for modularity, decomposition and compositionality. Similar to [18], by compositionality we mean that risk models can be composed without considering their internal details.

Traditional risk assessment methods typically do not take into account that the risk level towards component-based systems may change given changes in the environment of the systems [21]. Instead, they rely on analyzing systems as a whole [14], without providing means for deducing the effect of composition with respect to risk. However, there also exist approaches that provide some degree of support for a modular and compositional approach. In the following we give an overview of these.

Some approaches to hazard analysis address the propagation of failures in component-based systems by matching ingoing and outgoing failures of individual components. In [7,8] UML [17] component diagrams and deployment diagrams support a method for compositional hazard analysis. Fault trees [10] are used to describe hazards and the combination of component failures that can cause them. For each component, the method is used to describe a set of incoming failures, outgoing failures, local failures (events) and the dependencies between the former two. Failure information of components can be composed by combining their failure dependencies. Likelihood of failure can be analyzed in terms of probability. In the case of AND ports, this is done by multiplication, which means that there is an assumption about independence between incoming elements. This differs from our approach, which allows the use of frequencies rather than probabilities for threat scenarios and unwanted incidents in order to facilitate better understanding [9]. Furthermore, the CORAS approach makes no assumptions about independence or overlap between threat scenarios and does not impose strong restrictions on the propagation of likelihood values, although a number of rules for likelihood reasoning and checking consistency of diagrams are offered [15].

A technique for compositional fault tree analysis (FTA) is proposed in [13]. Component failures are described by specialized component fault trees that can be combined into system fault trees via input and output ports. Similar to our approach, different component fault trees can be developed by different user groups, composed without considering internal details, and reused. However, as usual for FTA-based approaches, likelihood analysis is performed in terms of probability and makes independence assumptions. Moreover, there is no specific support for risk analysis concepts such as unwanted incidents, threats and vulnerabilities, or links to an overall risk management process.

A denotational model for component-based risk analysis is presented in [4]. Here, a component model is provided that integrates the explicit representation of risks as part of the component behavior. Similar to our notion of encapsulation, a hiding operator is defined which allows partial hiding of internal interactions. However, interactions affecting the component risks are not hidden. Unlike our approach, the intention is to provide a theoretical foundation. Hence, the focus is on formal representation and analysis rather than direct support for practitioners. Component behavior is represented by probability distributions over communication histories, and the use of frequencies is not supported. The model is aimed exclusively at component-based systems.

In [3] dependent risk graphs are introduced as a technique to support modular risk modeling and assessment. Dependent risk graphs provide support for documenting and reasoning about assumptions and dependencies. The approach uses an assumption-guarantee style by dividing a risk graph into an assumption part and a target part. Typically, the assumptions concern the environment of the target. This facilitates modular risk assessment by the support for decomposing the target of analysis and later combining the assessment results. For example, when decomposing a target system into two, the target in one may serve as the assumptions in the other and vice versa. Once the two separate risk assessments are completed, a calculus provides rules for combining the results into one risk graph. However, no notion of risk model encapsulation is provided.

The use of risk graphs as the basis facilitates instantiation in other graph-based risk modeling approaches. In [3] this is demonstrated by the instantiation in CORAS. In [5] this modular and component-based approach to risk assessment using CORAS is integrated into a component-based system development process to support risk assessment in the development process. The instantiation in CORAS is further elaborated in [15], resulting in an extension referred to as Dependent CORAS.

In [22] an extension of CORAS is suggested that explicitly supports components by representing them with reusable threat interfaces. Threat composition diagrams representing more complex systems can then be composed from the threat interfaces, although the approach is not fully compositional. Unlike our approach, threat interfaces have (only) vulnerabilities as input ports and unwanted incidents as output ports. In addition, relations between input ports and output ports show propagation of likelihood. Even if the original CORAS method is asset-driven, assets are not included in the threat interface for a component, and there is no distinction between internal and external assets. Likelihood calculations are done in terms of probability in a similar way as for fault trees, although [22] allows directed acyclic graphs, rather than just trees. To this end, AND/OR gates and dependency sets are introduced. The dependency sets distinguish between different occurrences of an unwanted incident depending on triggering conditions and their dependencies. These additions facilitate detailed analysis of probability at the cost of significantly increasing the complexity of the approach.

While some of the above works share certain characteristics with our approach, we are not aware of existing approaches similar to the one we propose. It is designed to be compositional, simple and general. The approach is simple in the sense that no new constructs are added to the modeling language except from the diagram frames. It is general in the sense of being applicable not only for component-based systems, but also for other settings where a partitioning of risk models is appropriate, for example based on aspects or business concerns. As illustrated above, most methods and techniques focus primarily on failure rate, likelihood or risk level assessment in a component-based setting. While this is an important ingredient of component-based risk analysis, the lack of an encapsulation mechanism for many existing techniques complicates composition and means that composed models may become very large and complex, and thus hard to understand and work with.

9   Conclusion

We have presented a top-down approach to compositional risk analysis where the target of analysis is decomposed in such a way that each identified asset belongs to exactly one sub-target. A separate risk model is then developed for each sub-target, and the individual risk models are eventually combined to arrive at a risk model for the whole target. The approach follows ISO 31000, but provides additional support for the context establishment and risk assessment phases specifically aimed to facilitate decomposition and composition.

At the core of the approach is a novel notion of risk model encapsulation, where only the elements that are essential for composition are exposed through an explicitly defined *risk model interface*, while internal details are hidden. All one needs to know in order to compose risk models is the contents of their interfaces. By hiding the internal details we make it easier for practitioners to compose risk models, while at the same time reducing the size and complexity of the resulting model. An added benefit is that a risk model interface contains the information that would typically be of interest for managers and decision makers who often have little time and have not themselves taken part in the risk assessment.

Encapsulation is a key reason for the success of object-oriented programming. We believe that significant benefits can be achieved by introducing this concept into risk management and analysis. We are not aware of any other approach offering a clear encapsulation concept for risk analysis allowing compositional reasoning.

The work presented here opens up a number of interesting directions for further research that we hope to pursue. In particular, a more complete method with detailed techniques and guidelines for practitioners should be developed. We would also like to explore how our notion of encapsulation could be applied in a bottom-up approach. The added challenge here is that we cannot assume that the environment of a target is known at the time when the corresponding risk model is developed. Finally, we would of course like to validate and refine our results by applying them on a variety of case studies.

Acknowledgments. The research presented in this chapter was partially funded by the European Commission via the FP7 projects NESSoS (256980) and RASEN (316853), by the ARTEMIS Joint Undertaking and the Norwegian Research Council via the CONCERTO project (333053 and 232059), and by the Norwegian Research Council via the Dynamic Risk Assistant project (217213).

References

1. Agence nationale de la sécurité des systèmes d'information: EBIOS 2010 – Expression of Needs and Identification of Security Objectives (2010) (in French)
2. Alberts, C.J., Dorofee, A.J.: OCTAVE Criteria. Tech. Rep. CMU/SEI-2001-TR-016, CERT (December 2001)

3. Brændeland, G., Refsdal, A., Stølen, K.: Modular analysis and modelling of risk scenarios with dependencies. Journal of Systems and Software 83(10), 1995–2013 (2010)
4. Brændeland, G., Refsdal, A., Stølen, K.: A denotational model for component-based risk analysis. In: Arbab, F., Ölveczky, P.C. (eds.) FACS 2011. LNCS, vol. 7253, pp. 12–41. Springer, Heidelberg (2012)
5. Brændeland, G., Stølen, K.: Using model-driven risk analysis in component-based development, pp. 330–380. IGI Global (2011)
6. CRAMM – The total information security toolkit, http://www.cramm.com/ (accessed June 13, 2012)
7. Giese, H., Tichy, M.: Component-based hazard analysis: Optimal designs, product lines, and online-reconfiguration. In: Górski, J. (ed.) SAFECOMP 2006. LNCS, vol. 4166, pp. 156–169. Springer, Heidelberg (2006)
8. Giese, H., Tichy, M., Schilling, D.: Compositional hazard analysis of UML component and deployment models. In: Heisel, M., Liggesmeyer, P., Wittmann, S. (eds.) SAFECOMP 2004. LNCS, vol. 3219, pp. 166–179. Springer, Heidelberg (2004)
9. Gigerenzer, G.: Calculated Risks – How to Know When Numbers Deceive You. Simon & Schuster (2002)
10. International Electrotechnical Commission: IEC 61025 Fault Tree Analysis, FTA (1990)
11. International Organization for Standardization: ISO 31000 Risk management – Principles and guidelines (2009)
12. International Organization for Standardization/International Electrotechnical Commission: ISO/IEC 27001 – Information technology – Security techniques – Information security management systems – Requirements (2005)
13. Kaiser, B., Liggesmeyer, P., Mäckel, O.: A new component concept for fault trees. In: Proc. 8th Australian Workshop on Safety Critical Systems and Software (SCS), vol. 33, pp. 37–46. Australian Computer Society (2003)
14. Lund, M.S., Solhaug, B., Stølen, K.: Evolution in relation to risk and trust management. Computer 43(5), 49–50 (2010)
15. Lund, M.S., Solhaug, B., Stølen, K.: Model-Driven Risk Analysis – The CORAS Approach. Springer (2011)
16. Microsoft Solutions for Security and Compliance and Microsoft Security Center of Excellence: The Security Risk Management Guide (2006)
17. Object Management Group: OMG Unified Modeling Language (OMG UML), Superstructure. Version 2.3, OMG Document: formal/2010-05-03 (2010)
18. de Roever, W.: The quest for compositionality – A survey of assertion-based proof systems for concurrent programs, part 1: Concurrency based on shared variables. In: Proc. IFIP Working Conference on the Role of Abstract Models in Computer Science. North-Holland (1985)
19. Stoneburner, G., Goguen, A., Feringa, A.: Risk management guide for information technology systems. Tech. Rep. 800-30, NIST (2001)
20. Tran, L.M.S., Solhaug, B., Stølen, K.: An approach to select cost-effective risk countermeasures exemplified in CORAS. Tech. Rep. A24343, SINTEF ICT (2013)
21. Verdon, D., McGraw, G.: Risk analysis in software design. IEEE Security & Privacy 2(4), 79–84 (2004)
22. Viehmann, J.: Reusing risk analysis results – An extension for the CORAS risk analysis method. In: Proc. 4th International Conference on Information Privacy, Security, Risk and Trust (PASSAT), pp. 742–751. IEEE (2012)

Preserving Data Privacy in e-Health*

Riccardo Conti, Alessio Lunardelli, Ilaria Matteucci,
Paolo Mori, and Marinella Petrocchi

Istituto di Informatica e Telematica - C.N.R., Pisa, Italy
`name.surname@iit.cnr.it`

Abstract. Privacy of data is a crucial aspect in nowadays life, from economy to leisure, from public administration to healthcare. Specification, authoring, and validation of appropriate policies are the basis for the sound application of such policies during the subsequent enforcement phase. This chapter reviews different components in a framework for privacy policy management and specifically focuses on the e-health scenario. Starting from different existing approaches to policy authoring and policy validation, we then focus on a specific solution aiming at integrating three tools covering the whole phase of policy generation, *i.e.*, a user-friendly authoring tool allowing definition of privacy preferences in natural language, a formal analysis tool to detect conflicts among policies, and a conflict solver implementing a solution strategy that privileges the most specific policy among a set of conflicting ones.

Keywords: Privacy, e-Health, Policy Languages, Policy Authoring, Policy Validation, Conflict Detector and Solver, Analytic Hierarchy Process.

1 Overview

Daily, hospitals, medical labs, and specialized research centers provide benefits and services to their patients, producing, at the same time, a huge amount of electronic documents, such as reservations, diagnosis, prescriptions, and reports. Such a myriad of electronic documents naturally contains sensitive information, whose improvident management can be detrimental to the privacy of patients and people such reports refer to. The legislation of several countries protects sensitive clinical data in compliance with privacy regulations, which ensure the use and sharing of data for the purposes intended by law and according to specific protocols dictated by the healthcare organizations where the data are produced. Also, the European Directive on Data Protection (95/46/EC, and its reform IP/12/46 of January 25, 2012), embraced by the legislation of different European countries, recognizes the right of the individuals to consciously control the use of their personal data.

---

* The research leading to these results has received funding from the European Union Seventh Framework Programme (FP7/2007-2013) under grant no 256980 (NESSoS) and from the Registro.it project MobiCare.

M. Heisel et al. (Eds.): Engineering Secure Future Internet Services, LNCS 8431, pp. 366–392, 2014.

To protect clinical data from abusive access/disclosure/processing, appropriate access rules, known as "privacy policies", have to be defined. In principle, these rules can be defined by multiple individuals, with various roles and from different organizations, guided by the intention to protect data that, directly or not, refer to them. However, there is both a technological and social gap between the need to protect sensitive data from unauthorized online access and the ability of stakeholders to generate consistent machine-readable privacy policies.

First, the specification of the rules is, today, a not simple task. Indeed, common users are not expert of technical languages for privacy policies specification. Policy composition is essentially dark and tedious, with the result that citizens see the way of ensuring privacy to their data more a difficulty than a personal advantage. Furthermore, the lack of familiarity with technical language for writing privacy policies prevents the non-expert both from defining fine-grained access rights to their data, and from frequently renewing their preferences, to possibly meet new privacy requirements. Secondly, since distinct individuals specify their own policies for data processing, and given that the policies written by distinct individuals can refer to the same data, different policies may be applicable to the same access request, with opposite effects (*i.e.*, one policy could allow the access, another one could deny it). In this case, the applicable policies are *in conflict* with each other.

This chapter aims at offering an overview of technical solutions for user-friendly policy authoring and effective policy validation (with an eye to conflict detection and solution), focusing on the e-Health scenario. The remainder of the chapter is organised as follows. In the next section, we recall the notion and structure of privacy policies. In Section 3, we describe a general privacy policy-based infrastructure, whose components are devoted to sustain the lifecycle of a policy, from its generation to its enforcement. Section 4 recalls several existing solutions for policy authoring and analysis, while the remaining sections, from 5 to 8, focus on a specific architecture, whose components are being integrated in a unique framework. Finally, Section 9 summarises and gives conclusions.

2 Examples of Privacy Policies

This section describes the reference structure for the privacy policies considered later on, and depicts a very simple, but plausible, set of policies regulating the controlled exchange of medical information.

Each time a subject tries to access a medical document (*i.e.*, the object), an access request including all the required data is created, and it is subsequently evaluated against the set of privacy policies in order to determine whether this access should be allowed or denied.

Privacy policies are expressed in terms of the following elements: *subject*, *object* (or resource), *action*, and *environment*. Furthermore, policies can be divided into two main classes, according to their effect:

- **Authorizations** express the actions that a subject is *allowed* to perform on an object within an environment.
- **Prohibitions** express the actions that a subject is *not allowed* to perform on an object within an environment.

The above assumptions are not unrealistic: for example, the eXtensible Access Control Markup Language (XACML), the well known, de facto, standard for access control [33], relies on similar assumptions. Hence, we consider a privacy policy as a set of rules that are evaluated, for each access request, to decide whether a given subject is allowed to perform a given action on a given resource, in a given environment. The features of the four policy elements, *i.e.*, subjects, objects, actions, and environment, are expressed through *attributes*. Policy rules evaluate the value of these attributes to determine which rule can be applied to each access request.

For the aim of the chapter, hereafter we consider a restricted set of attributes for each policy element.

Subject. The attributes for subjects are: ID, Role, and Organization.
- ID expresses an unique identifier of the subject, *e.g.*, "*abcde*123".
- Role specifies the functions and the capabilities of a subject. As an example:
  - *general practitioner* has a general view of the medical history of his patients;
  - *psychiatrists, orthopedists* ... identify doctors that are highly specialised;
  - *rescue team member* retrieves the first information at the incident location;
  - *patient* is used when the subject acts as a patient.
- Organization represents the organization the subject belongs to, *e.g.*, the "Red Cross" or "Psychiatric Hospital ABCD".

Object. The attributes for objects are: ID, Patient, Issuer, and Category.
- ID is a code that expresses the identifier of the object, *e.g.*, "*xyz*".
- Patient is the ID of the patient referred by the document;
- Issuer is the ID of the subject who produces that object;
- Category is *medical*, including documents that collect medical information about the patient, and *administrative*, including documents collecting personal information, such as the patient's name, surname, address.

Action. We consider their IDs only, *e.g.*, "Read", "Print", "Create", "Append", "Delete".

Environment. The attributes of the environment are:
- Time, with the obvious meaning;
- Location, which represents a physical position (contextualising, it could be either of the object or of the subject);
- Status, which specifies the exceptionality of a situation, such as an emergency one.

The Reference Healthcare Scenario. Hereafter we provide a very simple example of set of Authorization and Prohibition policies that could have been emitted by the National Healthcare System (NHS) and by a patients, such as Mr. Paul Red. We recall that this is a simple example meant to describe our approach.

National Healthcare System

N1 Subjects having the role *"General Practitioner"* can read documents having category *"medical"* of patients;

N2 Subjects having the role *"General Practitioner"* can read documents having category *"administrative"* of patients;

N3 Subjects having the role *"Rescue Team Member"* and belonging to the organization *"Red Cross"* can read documents having category *"medical"* of patients in an emergency situation;

N4 Subjects having the role *"Emergency Doctor"* can read documents having category *"medical"* of patients in an emergency situation;

N5 Subjects having the role *"Administrative Personnel"* can read/print documents having category *"administrative"*;

N6 Subjects can read documents they have issued;

N7 Patients can read documents that refer to them.

Mr. Paul Red

P1 Subjects not having role *"Psychiatrist"* cannot read/print/append the document with ID *"xyz"* if the current date is before 31/12/2020;

P2 Subject with ID "dr12345" cannot read the document with ID *"xyz"*;

P3 Subjects having role *"General Practitioner"* can read/print/append the document with ID *"abc"* from 16/07/2013 to 24/07/2013;

P4 Subjects having the role *"Administrative Personnel"* cannot read/print documents having category *"administrative"* until 31/12/2020.

Either in case a privacy policy is defined by an organization over data it hosts, or which it has rights on (*e.g.*, the National Healthcare System, the hospital, *etc.*.) or by an individual over data she has rights on, an inclusive support is needed that offers the appropriate technology to enable setting and applications of such policies, over all their lifetime. Considering the above policies in the reference healthcare scenario, we may assume that the prohibition policies P1 and P2 have been set by a patient, say Mr. Paul Red, because the document with ID *xyz*, issued by a Psychiatrist, is a drug prescription and the patient does not want to disclose it to anyone but Psychiatrists. Dr. Jack Brown, whose unique ID is dr12345, is the General Practitioner of Mr. Paul Red, and he is also a Psychiatrist, but the patient does not want to disclose that document to him, for some reason that is immaterial here. Finally, it is worth noticing that, in the above example, the patient has expressed both authorization and prohibitions policies.

In a real scenario, a wider set of attributes can generally be used in order to define more complex policies. For example, the policy N1 could be refined specifying that subjects having the role *"General Practitioner"* can read documents having category *"medical"* related to their patients only.

3   A General Policy-Based Infrastructure

This section describes the architecture of a policy-based privacy infrastructure, general enough to encompass different use cases in the e-Health privacy management scenario, and supporting the two main phases of a policy lifetime: the *i)* policy generation and the *ii)* policy enforcement. In the first phase, the policy administrators at the healthcare organizations set general privacy policies over the data they host, according to National laws and internal organization planning. Patients as well may express privacy preferences over their medical data, and these preferences are translated in privacy policies. In the second phase, instead, each time a request for accessing a medical data is received, the evaluation of the policies governing access to those data is executed to decide whether the access must be granted or denied.

Figure 1 gives the graphical representation of the architecture along with the operation workflow.

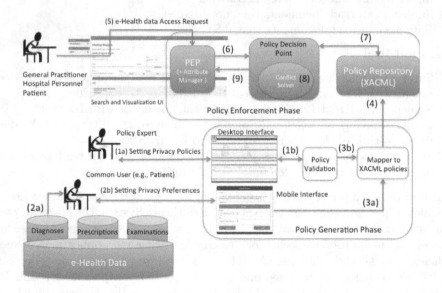

Fig. 1. Policy-based Infrastructure

The policy generation phase consists of the following steps.

1 At system initialisation, the policy experts compose the privacy policies that represent the rules stated by the healthcare organization that produces and stores the data. In some countries, such rules are defined by public agencies and follow requirements for protecting sensitive data of private citizens and organizations. The experts use a desktop interface that requires some specific skills in policy specification (1a). In real environments, policy makers set a not negligible number of policies regulating the management and sharing

of all the data produced and stored at their healthcare organizations. To come up with a consistent set of policies, policy experts are supported by a validation tool, that guide them in composing conflict-free policies (1b). It is worth noticing that it is an offline analysis that guides the policy experts to compose conflict-free policies. The validation tool alerts the user that a conflict occurs between two policies, in such a way that the user is able to come back to the authoring phase and eventually modifies the conflicting policies. Sections 5.1 and 7 describe, respectively, the desktop interface and the policy validation steps.

2 In the healthcare scenario the subject who produced a document, *e.g.*, a General Practitioner who issued an e-prescription, is entitled to define some access restrictions on this document. Moreover, patients should also be able to set privacy preferences on their medical documents (such requirement is defined, for example, by the European Directive for Data Protection 95/46/EC, and its reform IP/12/46 of 25 January 2012). In our model, we assume that, as soon as a new medical document is produced, the patient is notified (2a), and he can set up the privacy preferences on that document through the mobile interface (2b). Each subject can also modify his preferences in a successive step, by querying the medical document repository and choosing which documents will be the object of their privacy preferences. Obviously, patients can express privacy preferences only on their documents and, in general, subjects can only express privacy preferences on the document they have some rights on, *e.g.*, the issuer of a document has the right to express her preferences on the document she issued. The mobile interface is described in Section 5.1.

3 Both the general policies written by experts and the privacy preferences expressed by patients and document issuers are given as input to a mapper that converts them into enforceable policies (3a and 3b). A standard and well supported formalism for enforceable policies is XACML, the well known language for specifying machine-readable access control and data protection rules [33]. It is worth noticing that there is no validation phase of the global set of policies due to the possible huge amount of edited policy. They are evaluated at run-time by for each access rquest considering only the ones applicable to that particular request.

4 The enforceable policies are stored in the Policy Repository (4) and they will be processed in the policy enforcement phase.

The policy enforcement phase consists of the following steps.

5 Different users, such as patients, administrative personnel, doctors, and researchers at the healthcare organizations, try to access some medical documents by formulating an access request through a search and visualization interface (5).

6 The access request is intercepted by a Policy Enforcement Point (PEP) that temporarily suspends the request and invokes a Policy Decision Point (PDP) (6) to evaluate the privacy policies associated to the document whose access

is being requested. In our model, we assume that PEP retrieves the attribute values necessary to evaluate the policy (*e.g.*, the requester's credentials, as her identifier and role, and the date, location, and time at which the request has been sent).

7 The PDP retrieves the privacy policies produced in the policy generation phase (7).

8 The PDP evaluates the privacy policies against the access request. In case more than one policy applies to the access request, their results could be in conflict one of each other. A conflict exists when at least two out of a set of policies return a different result (*e.g.*, one policy would allow the request, the other one would deny it). A policy conflict solver is in charge to detect possible conflicts and eventually solve them (8). Section 8 depicts a possible strategy for resolution of conflicts, based on the degree of specificity of a policy.

9 The PDP returns the evaluation result to the PEP. Finally, according to the evaluation result, the PEP allows, or denies, the access request to the medical data.

4   Related Work on Policy Authoring and Validation

Over the last decades, researchers have investigated several solutions for (platform-independent) policy-based infrastructures, to specify, analyze, and deploy privacy, security, and networking policies. Hereafter we revise some work focused on policy authoring, with an eye to usability issues. Then we discuss some results about policies conflict detection and resolution.

4.1   Authoring Frameworks

Series of work in [20,5,35,6,18] connect policy authoring tools with the capability of common users to use them. In [20], the authors carry out a laboratory evaluation of a variety of user-centered methods for privacy policies authoring, to identify which design decisions should be taken for flexible and usable privacy enabling techniques. Work in [5] continues this line of research, by providing a parser which identifies the privacy policy elements in rules entered in natural languages: identification of such elements is a key step for subsequent translation of natural sentences in enforceable constructs (such as the XACML language [33]). Authors of [35] recall security and privacy policy-authoring tasks in general, and discover further usability challenges that policy authoring presents. In [6] the authors present the Coalition Policy Management Portal for policy authoring, verification, and deployment, with the goal of providing "easy to use mechanisms for refining high-level user-specified goals into low-level controls". Recently, work in [18] advances the notion of templates-based authoring tools, for users with different roles and different skill sets, such as, *e.g.*, patients, doctors, and IT administrators could be in the e-health scenario. The authors propose different templates to edit privacy policies, each of them needing different user skills to compose high-quality policies.

The FP7-EU project *Consequence* (Context Aware Data Centric Information Sharing) designed and developed an integrated framework for the authoring, analysis, and enforcement of Data Sharing Agreements (DSA), that are formal documents regulating data exchange in a controlled manner. The authoring tool developed within the project was intended for users with some knowledge on policy specification, see, *e.g.*, [10,29]. The use of a controlled natural language (*cfr.* CNL4DSA [28]) and the insertion of a help-on-line facility partly mitigate usability issues, whose complete solution need however further investigation.

The FP7-EU project *CoCoCloud* (Confidential and Compliant Clouds) is aimed at designing and developing a framework for the writing, understanding, analysis, management, enforcement and dissolution of DSA, thus allowing users to securely and privately share their data in the Cloud environment. The high level descriptions of DSA (close to natural language) will be translated to system enforceable data usage policies.

From a business perspective, Axiomatics [3] offers an authorization framework based on the XACML standard [33], that covers all the phases of the policy life-cycle, including policy creation, exploiting a graphical user interface for policy authoring, policy test and validation, and policy deployment and enforcing. Moreover, the Axiomatics framework also provide a policy auditor that, through a simple and user-friendly graphical interface, simplifies policy the analysis and validation phase by supporting the execution of several type of queries to analize the policy effects.

From a social networking perspective, work in [41] presents a *collaborative* authoring tool, allowing several individuals to specify policies over data published on social networks, and whose disclosure may affect their privacy. The authors acknowledge some usability issues in their prototype implementation, and future work are foreseen towards a user-friendly authoring interface.

4.2   Policy Conflict Detection and Resolution Frameworks

Data protection policy analysis is essential to detect inconsistencies and conflicts before the actual enforcement. Work in [28,29,27,24] focus on Data Sharing Agreements (DSA), legal contracts regulating data sharing. In [28], the authors propose a controlled natural language for formally specifying DSAs without loosing simplicity of use for end-users. Subsequent work [29] deals with DSA usability, by presenting, besides the above-cited authoring tool, an analysis tool to visualise all the authorisations and prohibitions present in a set of DSA clauses and identify possible conflicts among such clauses. The authors of [27] apply the policy analysis framework in [29] to detect conflicts among medical data protection policies, as presented in Section 7 of this chapter. Finally, work in [24] distinguishes between unilateral and multilateral DSAs (the latter being agreements constituting of data sharing policies coming from multiple actors) and proposes a refined conflict detection technique, with respect to previous papers. In [4], it is shown that the Event-B language (www.event-b.org) can be used to model obliged events. The Rodin platform provides animation and model checking toolset for analyzing specifications written in Event-B, thus leading to capability of obligations analysis [2]. The authors of [32] propose a comprehensive framework for expressing highly complex privacy-related policies, featuring purposes and obligations. Also, a formal definition of conflicting permission assignments is given, together with efficient conflict-checking algorithms. The Policy Design Tool [34] offers a sophisticated way for modeling and analysing high-level security requirements in a business context and create security policy templates in a standard format. To conclude, there exists generic formal approaches that could a priori be exploited for the analysis of some aspects of data protection policies. As an example, the Klaim family of process calculi [13] provides a high-level model for distributed systems, and, in particular, exploits a capability-based type system for programming and controlling access and usage of resources. Also, work in [16] exploits a static analyzer for a variant of Klaim.

Policy conflict detection is generally followed by resolutions of conflicts. Not necessarily tied to data protection, existing work concerns general conflict resolution methods for access control in various areas. The approach adopted by the eXtensible Access Control Markup Language (XACML) [33] is a very general one, defines standard rule-combining algorithms: Deny-Overrides, Permit-Overrides, First-Applicable, and Only-One-Applicable. As an example, the Deny-Overrides algorithm states that the result of the policy is Deny if the evaluation of at least one of the rules returns Deny. A classification of anomalies that may occur among firewall policies is presented in [1]. In the same work, an editing tool allows a user to insert, modify, and remove, policy rules in order to avoid anomalies. Also, work in [15] proposes methods for preventing policy conflicts, more than a strategy for solving them when they occur.

In [17], the authors propose a conflict resolution strategy for medical policies, by presenting a classification of conflicts and suggesting a strategy based on high level features of the policy as a whole (such as the recency of a policy). If such characteristics are not sufficient for deciding which policy should be applied, the *default deny* approach is applied. With respect to that solution, the approach in [26] aims at defining a finer grained strategy, based on a finer definition of the policy specificity. In particular, it firstly evaluates the specificity of the policy in identifying each element, namely: subject, object, action and environment. Then, it combines these values through a weighted sum, that allows the authors to assign more relevance to the specificity of the definition of one the policy element with respect to the others (*e.g.*, we could choose that the specificity in defining the subject is 2 times more relevant than the specificity in defining the object).

In [23,39] the authors deal with both the detection and resolution of conflicts. Work in [23] defines a policy precedence relationship that takes into account the following principles: *a)* Rules that deny the access have the priority on the others; *b)* Priorities could be explicitly assigned to policy rules by the system administrators; *c)* Higher priority is given to the rule whose distance with the object it refers to is the lowest, where a specific function should be defined to measure such distance; and *d)* Higher priority is given to the rule that is more specific according to the domain nesting criteria. In [39], the authors investigate policy conflict resolution in pervasive environments. They discussed different strategies for conflict detection but the part dedicated to the conflict resolution strategy just refers to quite standard strategies, *i.e.*, role hierarchies override and obligation precedence. Also in [14], four different strategies for solving conflicts are considered. They distinguish among solving conflicts at compile-time, at run-time, in a balanced way leaving to run-time only potential conflicts, or in ad-hoc way accordingly to the particular conflicts. In general they take into account the role of the requester for deciding which policy wins the conflict. Also in this case, the strategy is based only on one criterion.

The approach in [23,39] is extended in [25]. Indeed, the authors introduce the definition and employment of the precedence establishment principals in a context-aware-manner, *i.e.*, according to the relation among the specificity of the context. The decision criterion is a unique one that groups a set of contextual conditions.

Work in [7] presents a formal model, based on deontic logic, to detect and, possibly, solve conflicts among security policies. An implementation of the model is left as future work. In [12], the authors present *Or BAC*, a methodology to manage conflicts occurring among permissions and prohibitions. Within this approach, rules are grouped according to the organizations that emit them. The advantage of this proposal is to reduce the problem of redundant policies.

The procedure known as *Break the Glass* [19] may be applied in extraordinary situations, bypassing all the existing applicable rules. As an example, by applying this methodology, rescue team members can access patient medical documents in an emergency situation, whatever the policies related to those documents are. A proper audit support should be used to monitor the accesses.

In the rest of this chapter, we show more in detail three approaches for policy authoring, policy validation, and policy conflict solution. In particular, the authoring tool presented in Section 5 will mix features of the tool developed within the Consequence project (see [10]) with the "user-expertise level" approach of [18]. On the one hand, the former guarantees that the authored policies are amenable for analysis, because the controlled natural language that is at the basis of the authoring tool is CNL4DSA [28] (mappable to executable formal languages in input to automatic analysers, see, *e.g.*, [29]). On the other hand, by following the former approach, users with few, or no, expertise in policy specification (as it is reasonable that the majority of patients will be) will have the opportunity to set their privacy preferences in few clicks. The policy validator that we will describe in Section 7 is a strongly revised version of that proposed in [10]: the validator is able to automatically detect conflicts amongst a set of privacy policies, against all the possible access requests that may happen given a pre-defined set of contextual conditions. This will allow the policy experts responsible for policy validation (at organisation side) to perform the analysis in a "user-friendly fashion". Instead of asking the tools for conflicts between two specific policies, the policy expert will only select the contextual conditions under which the validation will have to be executed. Then, the validator will automatically checks for conflicts amongst all the available policies that has been set at organisation side, against all the possible access requests. The upgraded version of the validator tool has been presented in [24]. Finally, we will present in Section 8 a strategy for dynamic conflict solution that is actuated to solve, at the time an access request takes place, possible conflicts that arise among policies set by different authors. In pus scenario, the different authors are, on the one hand, the patients of an healthcare organisation and, on the other hand, the organisation itself, that have set their policies offline, and have already validated them through the policy validator of [24]. At the time a requestor will actuate a real access request, the policies applicable to such request will be translated into an enforceable format. This is the main reason why the policy strategy we propose is envisaged to be applied to a set of enforceable policies in language *à la* XACML [26,22].

5   Policy Authoring

With reference to Figure 1, this section focuses on design and implementation of an authoring tool specifically tailored for the creation and management of healthcare privacy policies, see [11].

The architecture of the authoring tool is shown in Figure 2. It has been designed according to the three-tier paradigm, where the three levels are: 1) the User Interface (Mobile + Desktop), developed using HTML and Javascript; 2) the internal engine, composed by the Server Modules, the Controller and the Model Module, both implemented using the PHP language; and 3) a Relational Database, developed as a MySQL database server.

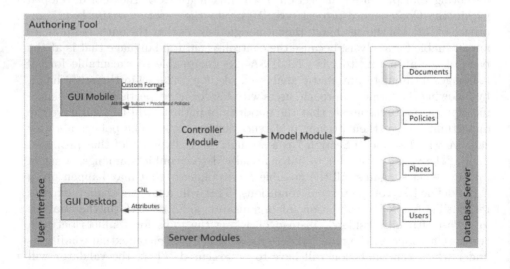

Fig. 2. The authoring tool architecture

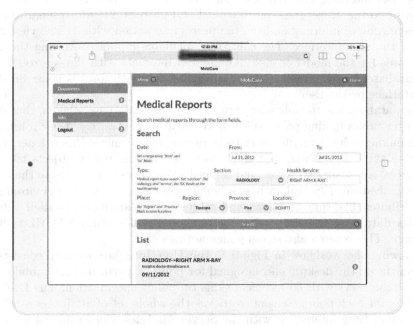

(a) Object selection

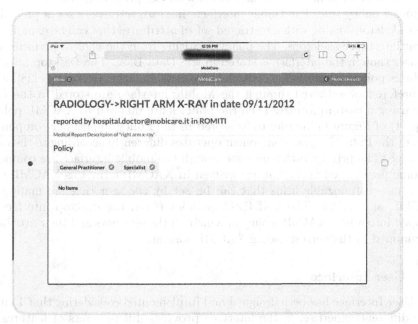

(b) Subject selection

Fig. 3. Object and Subject selection

The user interface, the controller, and the model module have been designed according to the *Model-view-controller* (MVC) pattern [21] which separates the representation of information from the user's interaction with it. The view consists of the user interface. The controller mediates inputs converting them to commands for the model or view. The model interacts with the controller and the database, by querying the latter according to which form is being filled at the interface by the user.

The database has the following structure: *Users* data base schema, that contains user tables linking policy subjects to their attributes, *e.g.*, their roles, and tables linking subject attributes to their values, *e.g.*, General Practitioner; *Documents* data base schema, that contains tables linking policy objects to their attributes, *e.g.*, their categories, and tables linking object attributes to their values, *e.g.*, medical; *Places* data base schema, consisting of tables of environmental attributes, like time and date, and tables linking attributes to their values; *Policies* data base schema, storing the authored policies in a XACML-fashion language. This schema also stores policy actions.

Following the workflow in Figure 1, the User Interface actually consists of two interfaces, the desktop one, designed for policy experts, and the mobile one, for common users with no technical skills on policy specification. The Desktop interface, for each policy element, retrieves the whole set of attributes available in the Data Base interacting with the Server Modules. The graphical interface helps the user to combine these attributes with the proper operation in order to produce a policy rule. The Mobile interface, instead, retrieves a set of predefined policy skeletons, along with a restricted set of attributes that can be exploited to instantiate those skeletons. The policy resulting from the choices performed by the user though the interface is stored in the Data Base. The Desktop interface produces policies expressed in controlled natural language, CNL4DSA [28], while the preferences authored through the Mobile interface are stored in the Data Base using a custom format. Then the policies are mapped to XACML policies (step (4) of Figure 1) in order to be stored in the Policy Repository component. Indeed, the Policy Mapper component operates differently according to the input language. The privacy preferences set trough the mobile interface are composed by some pre-defined fields that are written in XACML format as XACML rules and some customizable fields that can be set by the user that are mapped in XACML at runtime. The CNL4DSA policies (from the desktop interface) is mapped into a new XACML policy in which all the elements and their attributes are mapped in the corresponding XACML format.

5.1   User Interface

The User Interface has been designed and implemented considering that 1) users have different expertise; 2) the interface provides different sets of features according to the user expertise; and, 3) the interface is accessible by mobile phones, tablets, and desktops. As in [18], two user categories are considered:

Common Users, *e.g.*, patients or doctors that produced the medical documents, that are unaware of the constraints they can impose on their data. These authors are driven in the authoring phase through the *Mobile Interface*, that 1) is *document-centric*, *i.e.*, it allows users to compose their privacy preferences over specific documents they own in few clicks; 2) it offers a simple and guided way to compose such preferences; and, 3) is accessible from smart-phones and tablets.

Policy Experts, with a high-level understanding of the policy domain. These authors may be driven in the authoring phase through the *Desktop Interface*. The policy experts are not expected to have in-depth technical knowledge of how the policy will be evaluated and enforced, but they are familiar with high-level policy specification languages. Examples of policy experts are policy makers of national healthcare systems, that assess standard guidelines for access control and usage of sensitive medical data in their countries. The desktop interface has been especially designed for them, since, reasonably, setting the high level privacy policies fixed by national healthcare systems and healthcare organisations is an activity carried out during ordinary workdays. Obviously, a policy expert could act as a common user, in the sense that also policy experts can use the mobile interface to compose policies over specific documents they own.

Mobile Interface. Some screenshots of the mobile interface are shown in Figures 3 and 4. Designed for non expert people, possibly ignoring technical aspects of policy specification, its design is minimalist, to reduce the cognitive load of the user. Commands are grouped in a sliding panel on the left side of the screen, see Figure 3 a). The menu is retractable to leave space to the content that, in this way, appears not to be crushed and it is usable at different resolutions. The bar at the top of the screen allows the user to return to the homepage and to previously visited pages, and to open the panel menu (on which there is the logout button).

The Mobile Interface is *document-centric* because it allows the user to set privacy preferences on documents by firstly selecting such documents. Filling the form in Figure 3 a), the user obtains a list of the documents for which she is allowed to edit access preferences. In particular, patients are allowed to set the access preferences of their medical document, while doctors are allowed to set the access preferences of the document they produced. The visualization of such list can be constrained by requiring to visualize only those documents issued within a certain time interval, or on a certain date, or of a certain category (*e.g.*, only radiological reports). Constraints on how to visualize the document list are enacted by selecting specific values from an autocomplete input.

Pairing users with the list of documents available to be visualized is possible through a two-step phase of authentication and authorization. First, a user logs into the interface by presenting her own credentials. Once logged in, the system automatically retrieves the set of profiles associated to the user. Each profile represents a set of attributes paired with the user. For example, with reference to the attribute set defined in Section 2, a given user could have two profiles: the profile *patient*, which includes the role attribute, whose value is, obviously, *patient*, and the profile *doctor*, which includes the role attribute, with value

Psychiatrist, and the Organization attribute with value *Psychiatric Hospital ABCD*. The profiles are defined by the entities that issue the users attributes. A user with more than one profile, *e.g.*, *patient* and *doctor*, must choose to use the interface selecting one of them. Selecting the profile *patient*, the user will be able to edit preferences only on medical documents regarding herself as a patient. Instead, the same user, which selects the profile *doctor*, will be able to compose preferences over all the medical documents she issued, although these documents refer to different patients.

Upon document selection, the interface shows to the user different buttons associated to commands that encode partly customizable authorizations. Consider a user that has the role *patient*. First, she selects the document over which she may want to compose her privacy preferences. This document becomes the object of the policy. As an example, in Figure 3 a), she searches and selects the medical report "Right Arm X-Ray 09/11/2012". Then, she chooses the subjects of her policy, *i.e.*, the subject to whom this rule will be applicable (see Figure 3 b), in which she can select either subjects with role *General Practitioner* or *Specialist*). Upon subject selection, she can further select 1) the kind of action that the subject is allowed to perform on the object, *e.g.*, "read"; and 2) the temporal validity of the authorisation (Figure 4). In such a way, the user sets policies as the following one: *The General Practitioner with ID "dr12345" can read the medical report with ID "abc" from 16/07/2013 to 24/07/2013*. Such policy is saved when the user presses "Ok". Instead, "Cancel" allows the user to go back to the previous step without saving.

It is worth noticing that the Mobile Interface can be conveniently adapted to support the editing of general attribute-based policies, considering, e.g., the location of the requestor, or the organisation she belongs to, or the purpose of use. As a final remark, we acknowledge that specifying policies on a per-document basis could not provide a scalable management. Indeed, physicians

Fig. 4. Action and Environment selection

may not want to be burdened with managing each document individually, especially not in large organisations. One possible solution could be to define specific groups of documents, and let the physician to set privacy preferences over those groups, instead of over one specific document. Another solution is discussed in the following section: a Desktop interface has been realised in order to define default rules at the healthcare organisations. Such rules deal with categories of documents, rather than single ones.

Desktop Interface. The Desktop Interface is shown in Figure 5. It allows the editing of privacy policies in a more complex way with respect to simple setting of privacy preferences provided by the mobile interface. Its usage is reserved to Policy Experts (see above in this section). This interface presents four tabs,

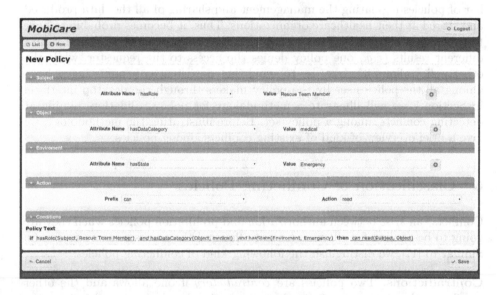

Fig. 5. Desktop Interface

one for each policy element (*subject, action, object,* and *environment*), plus one tab labeled *conditions*. The latter drives the user to set comparisons between attributes. For each element, the users can select from a drop-down menu which attributes to set and the attributes values (from another menu). As an example, let the reader suppose that the user aims at composing the following authorization: *"The rescue team member can read any medical report in emergency situations"*. First, she selects the subject attribute *role* from the drop-down menu. Second, she selects the values for this attributes, *i.e.*, *rescue team member*. Then, she selects the object attributes *category*, plus their values, *medical*. The same procedure is applied for specifying the action and the environment attribute. Finally, to add, or remove, an attribute for the same element, there are the plus and minus buttons, respectively, at the end of value field.

The *conditions* tab allows to refine the policy by adding comparisons between attributes of the elements that constitute the policy. The drop down menus propose only the attributes that have been set in the previous tabs. As an example, a comparison could state that "Location of the subject must be equal to Location of the object", or "ID of the subject must be equal to Issuer of the object".

The resulting policy is shown in a text box located under the tabs, and it is expressed exploiting the controlled natural language CNL4DSA, defined in [28]. The resulting policy for the considered example is

if hasRole(Subject, *Rescue Team Member*)
and hasDataCategory(Object,*medical*)
and hasState(Environment,*Emergency*)
then *can* read(Subject,Object)

In a real environment, policy makers are supposed to set a not negligible number of policies regulating the management and sharing of all the data produced and stored at their healthcare organizations. Thus, it becomes probable to have two, or more, policies that would apply to the same access request and return different results (*e.g.*, one policy denies the access to the requester, while the other policy allows it). In order to avoid the co-existence of conflicting policies among all the policies set by the policy makers through the desktop interface, in Section 7 we will illustrate a methodology for policy validation, aiming at detecting conflicts among a policy set. Before illustrating the methodology, we give a brief overview of kind of existing conflicts among policies.

6   Classification of Conflicting Policies

Conflicts can arise between authorization and prohibition policies when they are going to be applied for allowing (or not allowing) the access to some resources. Similar to [17], we distinguish the following kind of conflicting policies:

Contradictions. Two policies are *contradictory* if one allows and the other denies the right to perform the same action by the same subject on the same object under the same environment. The policies are exactly the same, except for their effect.

Exceptions. One policy is an exception of another one, if they have different effects (allow and deny) on the same action, but one policy is a "subset" of the other one, *i.e.*, the subject (and/or the object, and/or the environment) is specified with more specific attributes than those of the other. Let the reader consider Authorization N1 and Prohibition P2:

N1 Subjects having the role "*General Practitioner*" can read documents having category "*medical*" of patients;
P2 Subject with ID "dr12345" cannot read the document with ID "*xyz*";

P2 is an exception of N1, since the subject with ID dr12345, *i.e.*, Dr. Jack Brown, cannot access the document with ID "*xyz*" even if he is a "*General Practitioner*" and that document has category "*medical*".

Correlations. Two policies are correlated if they have different effects (allow and deny) and the attribute set of a policy intersects the attribute set of the other one.

As an example, the following policies are correlated:

N5 Subjects having the role *"Administrative Personnel"* can read/print documents having category *"administrative"*;

P4 Subjects having the role *"Administrative Personnel"* cannot read/print documents having category *"administrative"* until 31/12/2020;

Both the policies exploit the attribute role of the subject and the attribute category of the object, but the second one also exploits the environmental attribute Time.

In the following, we will present a technique to spot conflicts over the three categories of conflicting policies.

7   Policy Validation

In this section, we describe a policy validator performing a series of static analyses over a set of privacy policies. The analysis process allows to detect conflicts between policies, and, complimentary, to answer questions related to single clauses and visualize the complete table of authorised accesses. As illustrated in Figure 1, Section 3, the validator works in conjunction with the authoring desktop interface and it is reserved to policy experts, supporting them to edit complex policies.

The validation process checks if a set of policies is conflict-free, by performing pairwise analysis over all pairs of authorisation and prohibition clauses. The validator exhaustively simulates all the possible access requests, under a set of contextual conditions defined by the policy expert (*e.g.*, she can set date and time of the access request, role of subject, category of data, etc.). Thus, the validator checks if there exist, at least, one authorisation and one prohibition that, simultaneously, allows and denies the same subject to perform the same action on the same object, under the given set of contextual conditions. Also, the validator answers questions on specific authorisations, like, *e.g.*, "is it true that subject x is authorized to perform action z on object y, under a set of contextual conditions?". Finally, the validator shows, for a given set of contextual conditions, all the authorised actions within a policy set.

The validator consists of two parts:

- a formal engine that actually performs the analysis of the policies;
- a graphical user interface that allows the user to dynamically load contextual conditions and launch the analysis of the set of policies.

The validator has as input the CNL4DSA policies written through the authoring desktop interface.

The Engine. The formal engine performing the analysis of policies is Maude [8]. Maude is an executable programming language that models distributed systems and the actions within those systems [8]. The validator input language, CNL4DSA [28], has been designed with precise formal semantics rules, regulating states and transitions between these states. This allows for a precise translation of CNL4DSA in Maude, as shown in [30].

The choice of using Maude for policy validation is driven by the fact that rewrite rules (which Maude build upon) are a natural way to model the behaviour of distributed systems, and we see a policy exactly as a process where different subjects may interact with each other, possibly on the same set of objects. Maude is executable and comes with built-in commands allowing to search for allowed traces, *i.e.*, sequence of actions, of a policy specified in CNL4DSA. These traces represent the sequences of actions that are authorized, or denied, by the policy. Also, exploiting the implementation of modal logic over the CNL4DSA semantics, as done in [40,9] for process algebras such as CCS [31], it is possible to prove that a modal formula, representing a certain query, is satisfied by the Maude specification of the policy.

The Validator User Interface. The validator user interface is deployed as a Web Application and it allows the user to query Maude and visualize human-readable results. The user interface is in charge of retrieving the set of policies that the policy expert wants to analyze and the associated vocabulary (the set of specific terms associated with those policies). The vocabulary is that in the database of the authoring tool (see Figure 2, Section 5). The inner logic of the validator user interface exploits the vocabulary to create and show the interface menus.

The interface helps the policy expert to define the contextual conditions under which the analysis will be performed (Figure 6).

It is possible to compose different types of queries, related to authorisations and prohibitions (Figure 7). Once the policy expert has selected contextual conditions and queries, the interface sends all the inputs, *i.e.*, the vocabulary, the high level description of the policies, the context defining the conditions on which the policies have to be evaluated, and the set of queries, to Maude. When the analysis has been performed, the results are sent back and shown by the user interface. As an example, Figure 8 shows a pop-up window, alerting that a conflict occurs between an authorization and a prohibition.

It is worth noticing that the validator is enhanced with an help on line facility suggesting the operators the right way to set contextual conditions and queries for performing the analysis. A further improvement could be to set up a wizard that automatically proposes specific conditions and queries. Finally, as usual for automated tools operating an exhaustive search on the system state, the internal engine of the validator may suffer from the problem of state explosion. Appropriate test should be set up in order to evaluate its performance, and we leave this as a further step in future work.

Context:

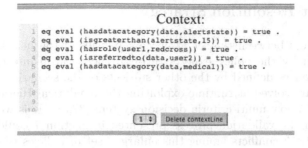

```
1  eq eval (hasdatacategory(data,alertstate)) = true .
2  eq eval (isgreaterthan(alertstate,15)) = true .
3  eq eval (hasrole(user1,redcross)) = true .
4  eq eval (isreferredto(data,user2)) = true .
5  eq eval (hasdatacategory(data,medical)) = true .
6
7
8
9
10
```

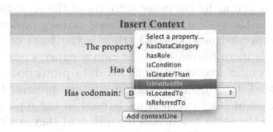

Fig. 6. Screenshot of the context insertion box

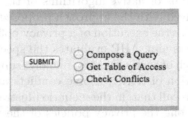

Fig. 7. Alternative analyses

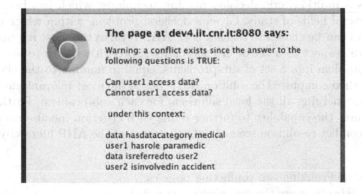

Fig. 8. Conflict detection

8   Conflict Resolution Strategy

Possible conflicts between the set of privacy policies of the healthcare organization, defined by the policy experts through the desktop interface, and the privacy preferences defined by the other subjects of the scenario, *e.g.*, patients and doctors, are solved at runtime exploiting the Analytical Hierarchy Process (AHP), a well know multi-criteria decision system [37,38]. It is worth noticing that, although the validation process presented in Section 7 could a priori be exploited to check conflicts among this enlarged set of policies (defined by the policy experts as well as by the other subjects of the scenario), this would act as a bottleneck in the system, mainly because privacy preferences by common users are not expressed in CNL4DSA, that is the basis of the validator tool in [24]. Thus, it is more convenient to let policy experts use the validator tool, to guarantee a conflict-free set of standard data protection policies at the organisation. Instead, the conflict resolution strategy presented in this section is actuated whenever at least two policies (stored in the repository in Figure 1) are applicable to the same real access request, and they conflict one with each other. Since this occurs within the enforcement process, policies have been already translated into an enforceable language. We will thus assume that conflicts are first detected by means of native algorithms of the XACML authorisation framework, and then solved with the approach proposed hereafter.

AHP allows to prioritize the execution of a privacy policy with respect to a set of conflicting ones. To this aim, AHP evaluates the specificity of the conflicting policies in identifying each of their elements, namely: subject, object, action, and environment. The adoption of AHP to solve conflicts among policies has been described in [26,22]. We recall that, in the scenario illustrated within this chapter, the internal conflicts among the privacy policies of the healthcare organization have been already statically solved after the policy authoring, as described in Section 7.

AHP is a multi-criteria decision making technique, which has been largely used in several fields of study. Given a decision problem, within which different *alternatives* can be chosen to reach a *goal*, AHP returns the *most relevant* alternative with respect to a set of *criteria*. This approach requires to subdivide a complex problem into a set of sub-problems, equal in number to the chosen criteria, and then computes the solution (*i.e.*, choose the most relevant alternative) by properly merging all the local solutions for each sub-problem. Furthermore, AHP features the capability to further refine each criterion in sub-criteria.

In the conflict resolution scenario, the elements of the AHP hierarchy are the following:

- The *goal* is ranking two conflicting policies.
- The *alternatives* are the two conflicting policies.
- The *criteria* are the following:
  Specificity of the subject. This criterion evaluates the attributes exploited in the two policies to identify the subject, to determine which of the policies define a more specific set of subjects.

Specificity of the object. This criterion evaluates the attributes exploited in the two policies to identify the object.

Specificity of the environment. This criterion evaluates the attributes to identify the environment.

- Each criterion has a set of *subcriteria* that are the attributes of the criterion:

Subcriteria for subject: ID, role, and organization.

Subcriteria for object: ID, category, and issuer.

Subcriteria for environment: status, time, and location.

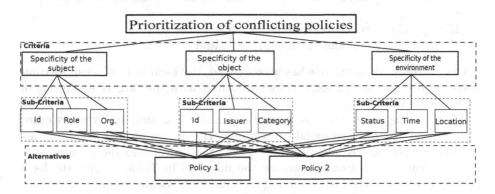

Fig. 9. AHP Hierarchy for Policy Conflict Resolution

Figure 9 represents the hierarchy previously described. However, the methodology allows the insertion of further criteria and subcriteria that may be helpful to evaluate the alternatives.

Once the hierarchy is built, the method performs pairwise comparison, from the bottom to the top, in order to compute the relevance, hereafter called *local priority*: i) of each alternatives with respect to each sub-criteria, ii) of each sub-criterion with respect to the relative criterion, and finally, iii) of each criterion with respect to the goal. Note that, in case of a criterion without sub-criteria, the local priority of each alternative is computed with respect to the criterion.

Comparisons are made through a scale of numbers typical to AHP (see Table 1) that indicates how many times an alternative is *more relevant* than another.

Computation of Local Priorities. Let the reader suppose that Policy1 and Policy2 are two conflicting policies. They become the two alternatives in the hierarchy and they are evaluated with respect to subcriteria. To this aim, k 2x2 pairwise comparison matrices, where k is the number of subcriteria (in our case, $k=9$), are built according to a very simple approach, based on the presence of the attributes in the policies. Given that a_{ij} is the generic element of one of these matrices:

Table 1. Fundamental Scale for AHP

Intensity	Definition	Explanation
1	Equal	Two elements contribute equally to the objective
3	Moderate	One element is slightly more relevant than another
5	Strong	One element is strongly more relevant over another
7	Very strong	One element is very strongly more relevant over another
9	Extreme	One element is extremely more relevant over another

- Policy1 and Policy2 contain (or do not contain) attribute A: then $a_{12} = a_{21} = 1$.
- If only Policy1 contains A, than $a_{12} = 9$, and $a_{21} = \frac{1}{9}$.
- If only Policy2 contains A, than $a_{12} = \frac{1}{9}$, and $a_{12} = 9$.

Once a comparison matrice has been defined, the local priorities can be computed as the normalized eigenvector associated with the largest eigenvalue of such matrice [36].

Then, moving up in the hierarchy, we quantify how subcriteria are relevant with respect to the correspondent criterion. Hence, we evaluate how the attributes are relevant to identify the subject, the object and the environment. In particular, in our example we use the matrices in Table 2, with the local priorities shown in the last column of each matrice. As an example, in the matrice that compares the subject's attributes (the left-most one in Table 2), we write $a_{12} = 9$ since we think that the subject ID allows to identify the subject *extremely* better than the subject role. Indeed, the subject ID exactly identifies one subject. For the same reason, we put $a_{13} = 9$ (ID *vs* the organization the subject belongs to). More details are in [26].

We remark that the values in these matrices simply represent the perception of the authors on the relative relevance of the attributes. Other values could have been chosen as well.

Finally, we quantify how the three criteria are relevant for achieving the goal of solving conflicts. Without loss of generality, we hypothesize that all the criteria equally contribute to meet the goal. In this straightforward case, the pairwise comparison matrice is a 3x3 matrix with all the elements equal to 1, and the

Table 2. Comparison matrices and local priorities for subcriteria w.r.t. criteria

SUBJ	ID	role	organiz.	$\bar{p}_{Subj}$
ID	1	9	9	0.818182
role	$\frac{1}{9}$	1	1	0.0909091
org	$\frac{1}{9}$	1	1	0.0909091

OBJ	ID	issuer	category	$\bar{p}_{Obj}$
ID	1	5	7	0.7454
issuer	$\frac{1}{5}$	1	$\frac{4}{3}$	0.1454
category	$\frac{1}{7}$	$\frac{3}{4}$	1	0.1091

ENV	status	time	location	$\bar{p}_{Env}$
status	1	7	7	0.777778
time	$\frac{1}{7}$	1	1	0.111111
location	$\frac{1}{7}$	1	1	0.111111

local priorities of the criteria with respect to the goal are simply 0.33 each. Hence, for the computation of the global priorities, $p_g^{c_j} = 0.33$, $j = 1,\ldots,3$ (see below).

Computation of Global Priorities. Once all local priorities are computed, the following formula computes the global priorities. For the sake of simplicity, we have in mind a hierarchy tree where the leftmost $n1$ criteria have a set of sub-criteria each, while the rightmost $n2$ criteria have no sub-criteria below them, and $n1 + n2 = n$ is the number of total criteria.

$$P_g^{a_i} = \sum_{w=1}^{n1} \sum_{k=1}^{q(w)} p_g^{c_w} \cdot p_{c_w}^{sc_k^w} \cdot p_{sc_k^w}^{a_i} + \sum_{j=1}^{n2} p_g^{c_j} \cdot p_{c_j}^{a_i} \tag{1}$$

$q(w)$ is the number of sub-criteria for criterion c_w, $p_g^{c_w}$ is the local priority of criterion c_w with respect to the goal g, $p_{c_w}^{sc_k^w}$ is the local priority of sub-criterion k with respect to criterion c_w, and $p_{sc_k^w}^{a_i}$ is the local priority of alternative a_i with respect to sub-criterion k of criterion c_w. $p_{c_w}^{sc_k^w}$ and $p_{sc_k^w}^{a_i}$ are computed by following the same procedure of the pairwise comparisons matrices illustrated above.

It is worth noticing that, in our approach, we do not consider as a decisional criterion the specificity of the action. This is because we evaluate the action only according to its ID, always present in a policy. So the evaluation of the alternative policies with respect to the criterion *action* is constant, and it does not add any meaningful information for taking the final decision.

In [22], we developed a prototype implementation of the conflict solver, highlighting a twofold advantage. First, the prototype is specifically based on the XACML engine and it extends the native XACML combining algorithms for conflict resolution, aiming at a finer granularity in the evaluation of conflicting rules. Secondly, we experienced good results in terms of execution time, negligible to human beings up to a quite large amount of conflicting rules (for example, execution time is 275 milliseconds with 64 conflicting rules composed by three attributes each).

9 Conclusions

Protecting personal data from abuses is an issue regulated by the legislation of different European countries, with the support of common European directives. Technically, data access, processing, and sharing can be regulated defining (and enacting) appropriate privacy policies. Technologically enabling data protection means simple but powerful tools guiding both expert personnel and common people to compose consistent policies. This chapter offered an overview of technical solutions for user-friendly policy authoring and effective policy validation (with an eye to conflict detection and solution), focusing on the e-Health scenario. In particular, starting from a general policy-based infrastructure and its operative workflow, we focused on three techniques for authoring, validation, and conflict resolution, that operate in an integrated framework for medical data protection. The effectiveness of the approach has been shown by the prototype implementation of the described tools, based on the XACML standard. As future work, we will focus on usability issues and we will validate our approach on a real scenario, testing the authoring tool with real users, defining with doctors and patients of a healthcare organization which is the set of privacy preferences they would be interested in, and verifying whether those preferences can be easily expressed and managed.

References

1. Al-Shaer, E.S., Hamed, H.H.: Firewall policy advisor for anomaly discovery and rule editing. In: Goldszmidt, G., Schönwälder, J. (eds.) Integrated Network Management VII. IFIP, vol. 118, pp. 17–30. Springer, Boston (2003)
2. Arenas, A.E., Aziz, B., Bicarregui, J., Wilson, M.D.: An Event-B Approach to Data Sharing Agreements. In: Méry, D., Merz, S. (eds.) IFM 2010. LNCS, vol. 6396, pp. 28–42. Springer, Heidelberg (2010)
3. Axiomatics.com. Policy Administrator Point, http://goo.gl/A5OEHW (last checked July 24, 2013)
4. Bicarregui, J., Arenas, A., Aziz, B., Massonet, P., Ponsard, C.: Towards Modelling Obligations in Event-B. In: Börger, E., Butler, M., Bowen, J.P., Boca, P. (eds.) ABZ 2008. LNCS, vol. 5238, pp. 181–194. Springer, Heidelberg (2008)
5. Brodie, C., et al.: An Empirical Study of Natural Language Parsing of Privacy Policy Rules using the SPARCLE Policy Workbench. In: SOUPS. ACM (2006)
6. Brodie, C., et al.: The Coalition Policy Management Portal for Policy Authoring, Verification, and Deployment. In: POLICY, pp. 247–249 (2008)
7. Cholvy, L., Cuppens, F.: Analyzing consistency of security policies. In: IEEE Symposium on Security and Privacy, pp. 103–112 (1997)
8. Clavel, M., Durán, F., Eker, S., Lincoln, P., Martí-Oliet, N., Meseguer, J., Talcott, C. (eds.): All About Maude - A High-Performance Logical Framework. LNCS, vol. 4350. Springer, Heidelberg (2007)
9. Colombo, M., Martinelli, F., Matteucci, I., Petrocchi, M.: Context-aware analysis of data sharing agreements. In: Advances in Human-Oriented and Personalized Mechanisms, Technologies and Services (2010)
10. Consequence Project. Infrastructure for data sharing agreements (December 2010), http://goo.gl/is7cpR
11. Conti, R., Matteucci, I., Mori, P., Petrocchi, M.: Expertise-driven Authoring Tool of Privacy Policies for e-Health. In: Computer-Based Medical Systems, Tech. Rep. IIT-CNR TR-02-2014 (2014)
12. Cuppens, F., Cuppens-Boulahia, N., Ghorbel, M.B.: High level conflict management strategies in advanced access control models. ENTCS 186, 3–26 (2007)
13. De Nicola, R., Ferrari, G.-L., Pugliese, R.: Programming Access Control: The KLAIM Experience. In: Palamidessi, C. (ed.) CONCUR 2000. LNCS, vol. 1877, pp. 48–65. Springer, Heidelberg (2000)
14. Dunlop, N., Indulska, J., Raymond, K.: Methods for conflict resolution in policy-based management systems. In: Enterprise Distributed Object Computing, pp. 98–109. IEEE (2003)

15. Hall-May, M., Kelly, T.: Towards conflict detection and resolution of safety policies. In: Intl. System Safety Conf. (2006)
16. Hansen, R.R., Nielson, F., Nielson, H.R., Probst, C.W.: Static Validation of Licence Conformance Policies. In: ARES, pp. 1104–1111 (2008)
17. Jin, J., Ahn, G.-J., Hu, H., Covington, M.J., Zhang, X.: Patient-centric authorization framework for electronic healthcare services. Computers & Security 30(2-3), 116–127 (2011)
18. Johnson, M., Karat, J., Karat, C.-M., Grueneberg, K.: Optimizing a policy authoring framework for security and privacy policies. In: SOUPS, pp. 8:1–8:9. ACM (2010)
19. Joint NEMA/COCIR/JIRA Security and Privacy Committee (SPC). Break-glass: An approach to granting emergency access to healthcare systems (2004)
20. Karat, J., Karat, C.-M., Brodie, C., Feng, J.: Designing Natural Language and Structured Entry Methods for Privacy Policy Authoring. In: Costabile, M.F., Paternó, F. (eds.) INTERACT 2005. LNCS, vol. 3585, pp. 671–684. Springer, Heidelberg (2005)
21. Kransner, G.E., Pope, S.: Cookbook for using the Model-View-Controller User Interface paradigm. Object Oriented Programming, 26–49 (1988)
22. Lunardelli, A., Matteucci, I., Mori, P., Petrocchi, M.: A Prototype for Solving Conflicts in XACML-based e-Health Policies. In: Computer-Based Medical Systems, pp. 449–452. IEEE (2013)
23. Lupu, E.C., Sloman, M.: Conflicts in policy-based distributed systems management. IEEE Trans. Softw. Eng. 25(6), 852–869 (1999)
24. Martinelli, F., Matteucci, I., Petrocchi, M., Wiegand, L.: A formal support for collaborative data sharing. In: Quirchmayr, G., Basl, J., You, I., Xu, L., Weippl, E. (eds.) CD-ARES 2012. LNCS, vol. 7465, pp. 547–561. Springer, Heidelberg (2012)
25. Masoumzadeh, A., Amini, M., Jalili, R.: Conflict detection and resolution in context-aware authorization. In: Security in Networks and Distributed Systems, pp. 505–511. IEEE (2007)
26. Matteucci, I., Mori, P., Petrocchi, M.: Prioritized Execution of Privacy Policies. In: Di Pietro, R., Herranz, J., Damiani, E., State, R. (eds.) DPM 2012 and SETOP 2012. LNCS, vol. 7731, pp. 133–145. Springer, Heidelberg (2013)
27. Matteucci, I., Mori, P., Petrocchi, M., Wiegand, L.: Controlled data sharing in e-health. In: STAST, pp. 17–23 (2011)
28. Matteucci, I., Petrocchi, M., Sbodio, M.L.: CNL4DSA: A Controlled Natural Language for Data Sharing Agreements. In: SAC: Privacy on the Web Track. ACM (2010)
29. Matteucci, I., Petrocchi, M., Sbodio, M.L., Wiegand, L.: A design phase for data sharing agreements. In: Garcia-Alfaro, J., Navarro-Arribas, G., Cuppens-Boulahia, N., de Capitani di Vimercati, S. (eds.) DPM 2011 and SETOP 2011. LNCS, vol. 7122, pp. 25–41. Springer, Heidelberg (2012)
30. Matteucci, I., Petrocchi, M., Sbodio, M.L., Wiegand, L.: A design phase for data sharing agreements. In: Garcia-Alfaro, J., Navarro-Arribas, G., Cuppens-Boulahia, N., de Capitani di Vimercati, S. (eds.) DPM 2011 and SETOP 2011. LNCS, vol. 7122, pp. 25–41. Springer, Heidelberg (2012)
31. Milner, R.: A Calculus of Communicating Systems. Springer-Verlag New York, Inc., Secaucus (1982)
32. Ni, Q., et al.: Privacy-aware Role-based Access Control. ACM Transactions on Information and System Security 13 (2010)
33. OASIS. eXtensible Access Control Markup Language (XACML) Version 3.0 (January 2013)

34. Policy Design Tool (2009),
    http://goo.gl/20wesa
35. Reeder, R.W., Karat, C.-M., Karat, J., Brodie, C.: Usability challenges in security
    and privacy policy-authoring interfaces. In: Baranauskas, C., Abascal, J., Barbosa,
    S.D.J. (eds.) INTERACT 2007. LNCS, vol. 4663, pp. 141–155. Springer, Heidelberg
    (2007)
36. Saaty, T.L.: A scaling method for priorities in hierarchical structures. Journal of
    Mathematical Psychology 15(3), 234–281 (1977)
37. Saaty, T.L.: Decision-making with the AHP: Why is the principal eigenvector nec-
    essary. European Journal of Operational Research 145(1), 85–91 (2003)
38. Saaty, T.L.: Decision making with the Analytic Hierarchy Process. International
    Journal of Services Sciences 1(1), 83–98 (2008)
39. Syukur, E.: Methods for policy conflict detection and resolution in pervasive com-
    puting environments. In: Policy Management for Web (WWW 2005), pp. 10–14.
    ACM (2005)
40. Verdejo, A., Martí-Oliet, N.: Implementing CCS in Maude 2. ENTCS 71 (2002)
41. Wishart, R., Corapi, D., Marinovic, S., Sloman, M.: Collaborative Privacy Policy
    Authoring in a Social Networking Context. In: POLICY, pp. 1–8. IEEE (2010)

Author Index